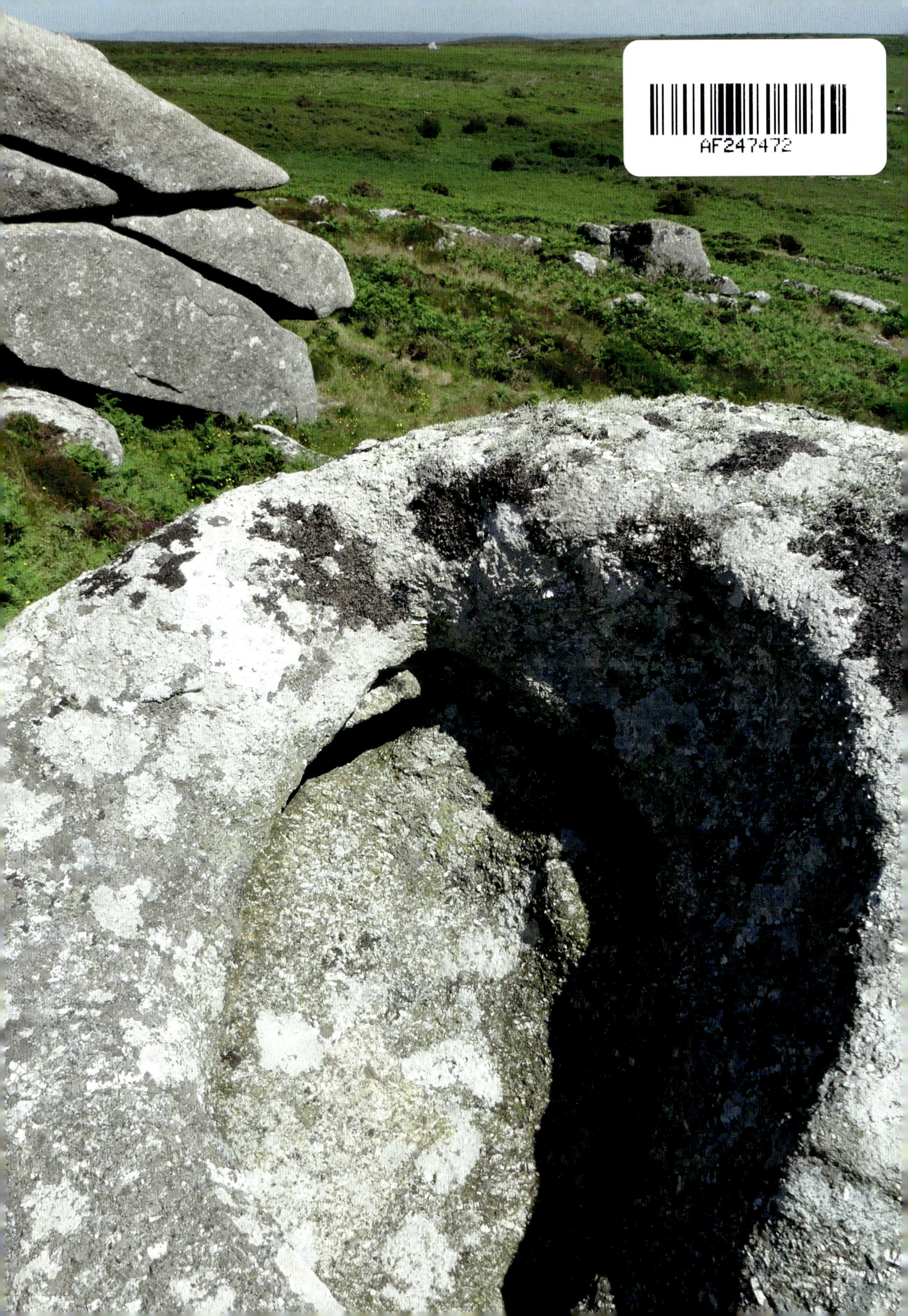
AF247472

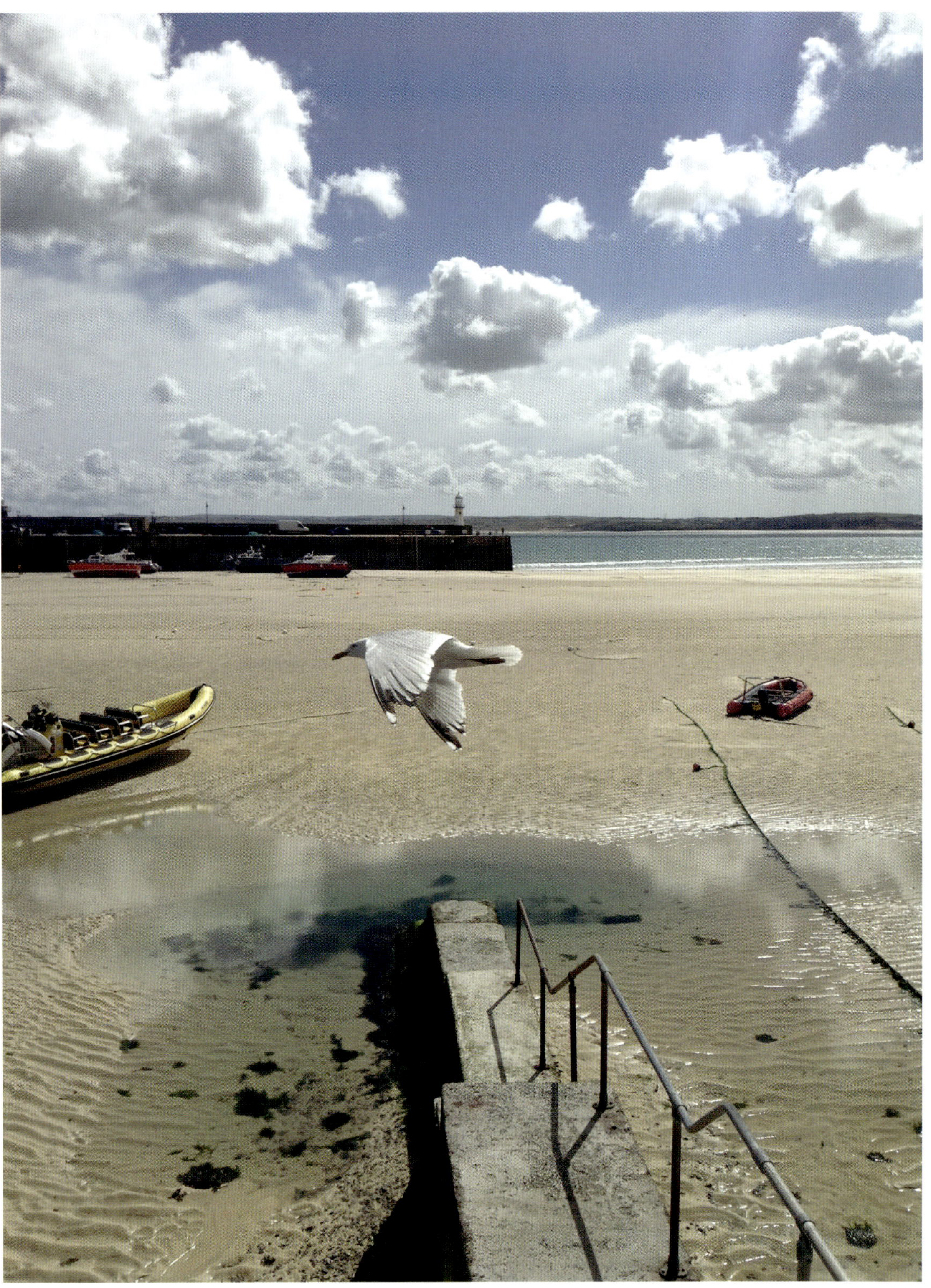

St Ives Allure

engagements with
art & place
in west cornwall

David Whittaker

wavestone press

Table of

Contents

St Ives Allure: Engagements with Art & Place in West Cornwall

ISBN: 9780954519490

Wavestone Press
6 Rochester Place, Charlbury, Oxon OX7 3SF

01608-811435/07772769363

Email: wavestone@btinternet.com
Web: www. wavestonepress.co.uk

I have been deeply touched by countless acts of generosity & thoughtfulness by so many people keen to assist in making this project a success. A heartfelt thanks to all of the following:

Rob Airey of the Wilhelmina Barns-Graham Trust; Michael Gaca, Richard Blackborow & Dominica Williamson of Belgrave Gallery, St Ives; Ylenia Haase & James Barry of New Craftsman Gallery, St Ives; Phil Jackson of Minack Theatre; Simon Canney for allowing me the free run of the excellent website devoted to his father www.michaelcanney.co.uk Also Janet Axten, Sophie Bowness, Toby Cornish, Ursula Cornish, Florette Dijkstra, Bridget Fallon, Gail Featherston, Martin Hammer, Rose Hilton, Andrew Hopwood, Lyn Le Grice, Andrew Lanyon, Martin Lanyon, Jane O'Malley, Elisabeth Price, Helen Scott, Chris Stephens, Pippa Stillwell, Sarah Stoten, Sylvia Thompson , Toby Treves, Brian Wall, Luke Weschke, Brian Whitton, Billy Wynter.

I am especially grateful to those subscribers whose faith in me, by way of pecuniary contribution, proved enormously helpful: Jane & Neil Armstrong, Anthony Astbury, Felicity Blair, Ursula & James Cornish, Ronnie Duncan, Scott Grant, Rose Hilton, Dave Jacobs, Joy & Ray Kell, John Sims, Mary & Luís de Sousa, Bryan & Sarah Stoten, Lucinda & Mike Watts, Simon Whitehead. As well as those whose modesty forbad exposure.

My everlasting love and appreciation to my wife Penny & daughter Alice – for constancy of care, patience, reassurance & jollity of stimulation.

Book design & layout: David Whittaker & Keith Rigley. Thanks, as ever, to Keith for transforming my vision into a desirable object (we hope).

Main text set in Brioso, accompanied by Zapfino & Optima.

Printed by Henry Ling Ltd, Dorchester, Dorset.

Preamble

*One should always apologise for talking
about painting*

                            Paul Valery

THIS BOOK IS an assemblage of writings, both old and new, that have grown out of my seemingly endless fascination with the Land's End peninsula, which now extends over four decades. The approach is a personal engagement with art and place and, with a few exceptions, it is therefore unashamedly subjective in tone and its selective criteria. Perhaps it should be seen as a sharing of experiences and enthusiasms for anyone who can be bothered to take the time. (See *Appendix C* for a development of some of these themes.)

Some older pieces that have appeared before, in various guises, have all been substantially revised and expanded for this publication.

There is inevitably some awkward overlap of motifs here and there and perhaps even repetition of phrases, provoking a feeling of *déjà vu* in the persistent reader. For this I beg forgiveness, as the pieces in question occasioned a particular response at the time that I feel should still stand within the context of being issued between the same covers (a few have an obituary style while others have a dictionary style). Some degree of duplication and redundancy is also unavoidable when dealing with a distinct group of people, at a particular time, in a relatively small location.

I had the great pleasure of meeting several of the characters featured, including Wilhelmina Barns-Graham, Rowena Cade, Conor Fallon, Jeremy Le Grice, Breon O'Casey, Tony O'Malley, Roger Slack, Michael Snow and Nancy Wynne-Jones. In addition I got to know various members of the Lanyon, Wynter and Canney families, as well as many of Sydney Graham's close friends. This also contributes to the personal accent of the book.

Into the bargain, the design of the book is largely my own, *ergo*, it looks exactly the way I want it to look (with many of my own photographs). For me a book is far more than a vehicle for information or entertainment. It should also nourish the eye as an aesthetic object.

The obituaries were all contributed to the *Guardian*, while the dictionary entries include Moss, Colquhoun and Tunnard. They were written for inclusion in a rather demanding and unfulfilled project, a *Who's Who of St Ives*.

I offer a brief note on the genesis and provenance of each piece.

Bryan Wynter & the Carn first appeared in *Zawn Lens* (2003). I owe so much of my initial awareness of post-war Cornish art to the almost miraculous appearance of Tate St Ives, out of an old and insignificant gas works, in 1993. This is where I first encountered Wynter's work in the flesh, as it were (I had already frequented the area around his derelict cottage from my explorations of nearby Zennor Quoit). I was instantly captivated by what I saw and was further intrigued on learning about Wynter's 'romantic' location. The overgrown cottage soon became a regular site of pilgrimage for me on every visit to Cornwall.

Tea with Miss Barns-Graham speaks for itself. I gave this as a talk at the St Ives September Festival (2007), and it appeared in print in *Stonelight* the same year.

W. S. Graham & the Artists is a summary version of the treatment I gave to Graham's significantly important friendships with visual artists in my book *Give Me Your Painting Hand*.

Tony O'Malley: The Watching Windhover is the latest in a line of writings on the man and his work that started when I wrote his obituary for the *Guardian*, followed by a short book-length study of his Cornish years, followed by a talk given at the St Ives September Festival 'Senses of Place in the Art of Tony O'Malley' (which subsequently appeared in *Stonelight*). This piece mainly focuses on the Trevaylor years during the early 1960s.

The Healing Art of Dr Roger Slack can be traced to an obituary I wrote for the *Guardian* that was further expanded into a commission from Bonham's auctioneers in Bond Street, as an introduction of sorts to a catalogue when part of his collection of art came up for sale in 2008. This forms the first part of the essay followed by a more personal account of a treasured friendship.

Seize the Day: Jeremy Le Grice I was contacted by Jeremy in 2005. He liked my study of Tony O'Malley and suggested I write the text of a catalogue for a major retrospective of his work at the Royal Cornwall Museum in Truro, planned for 2006. I accompanied Jeremy, with a small tape recorder in hand, over several days wandering around Penwith, while he talked endlessly about his experiences in one place or another. In due course the RCM decided they didn't want a text for the catalogue. When he died I wrote an obituary for the *Guardian* that forms the basis of this piece, with the addition of quotes from the tapes.

Michael Canney & Newlyn Art Gallery Over the years I have always enjoyed visiting the Newlyn Gallery – a place of pleasant surprises (or at least it used to be). Canney is now a sadly overlooked figure, a very talented painter and erudite writer, who was also responsible for boosting the reputation of the gallery during his decade in charge.

Lamorna Trio A handful of years ago I had the rather dotty idea to assemble a *Who's Who of St Ives*. Constraining myself, for various reasons of economy, to the years when Hepworth and Nicholson arrived in the town (1939), to the death of Peter Lanyon (1964). My initial list amounted to 100 fairly significant artists and writers all worthy of inclusion. I planned a dictionary entry accompanied by their photographs and, in the case of the artists, several examples of their works. Alas, for too many frustrating reasons, the project was not realised (but remains on hold). However, I did make a start and Moss, Colquhoun and Tunnard were, conveniently for present purposes, completed. I have always enjoyed walking the cliffs around Lamorna. This unusually lush area of Penwith has exerted a pull on artists for over a hundred years (including Lamorna Birch and Dame Laura Knight). But it struck me as an extraordinary coincidence that in the 1940s and '50s these three eccentric and reclusive characters, each with an international connection with Surrealism or Constructivism, should be neighbours in such an intimate location. They must have passed each other almost on a daily basis, but there is no evidence that I have been able to find of contact between them. It's also worth mentioning the painter John Armstrong. He settled at Lamorna in 1945, staying for ten years. Another unique outsider and painter of the strange, whose work has a strong surrealist feel, I briefly considered including him, therefore turning the trio into a quartet, but in the end decided against, as most of his achievements, over a long life, happened outside of Cornwall.

Timeless Art: Breon O'Casey started life as an obituary offered to the *Guardian*. However, it was rejected and I was politely informed that they already had one on file. So here it is, waste not …

A Celtic Item: Nancy Wynne-Jones & Conor Fallon Two obituaries for the *Guardian*, sadly separated by only eleven months. As I have kept them as distinct pieces, there is a degree of overlap of information.

Michael Snow: But is it Finished? Another obituary for the *Guardian*.

Rowena Cade & the Minack Theatre I had a memorable meeting with Miss Cade in 1976. This is a short account of her monumental achievement.

Selected Place-Names of West Penwith Having published two books about the place-names around my home, it made sense to have a modest go at where I love to visit.

Rust, Rocks, Ruins & Wrecks (a photo essay) See *Appendix C* for musings on this assortment of holiday snaps.

Peter Lanyon's Articulations of Place Peter Lanyon (1918-1964) was a force of nature to be reckoned with. A weatherman who could, literally, conjure images from thin air. Bard of the Cornish Gorsedd, he had much of interest to say about the artistic process and its rootedness in Cornwall. Here is only a fraction of the large body of written work he left behind. A highly complex man of robust fragility, he once explained:

> *I try to give back a sense of happening in a moment of time and in a definite place …*

> *My preference is for lonely places where physical danger and challenge are met. For high places and for edges. Painting as adventure.*

Sadly, his personal exhilarating adventure came to a sudden premature halt. But more than half a century on, as I write, his works are very much alive and well and continue to stimulate the perceptive viewer into the endlessly fresh adventure of their appreciation.

(It's worth noting that the lecture he provided for the British Council, in 1963, contained 38 illustrations – impossible to reproduce here. I have made a small selection where the words are of interest in their own right without a pictorial referent.)

Artists on Artists & a Writer A selection of mainly hard to find articles relevant to some of the essays in this book.

Setting the Seen (& the Unseen) A self-interview. Less a self-indulgence than a means of answering frequently asked questions about my infatuation with Cornwall (and its art), as well as clarifying to myself an underlying philosophical and aesthetic outlook that might also prove of interest to fellow seekers of the elusive spirit of place.

I leave the final word here to the Spanish poet, Antonio Machado:

> *Walker, your footsteps*
> *are the road, and nothing more.*
> *Walker, there is no road,*
> *the road is made by walking.*
> *Walking you make the road,*
> *and turning to look behind*
> *you see the path you never*
> *again will step upon.*
> *Walker, there is no road,*
> *only foam trails on the sea.*

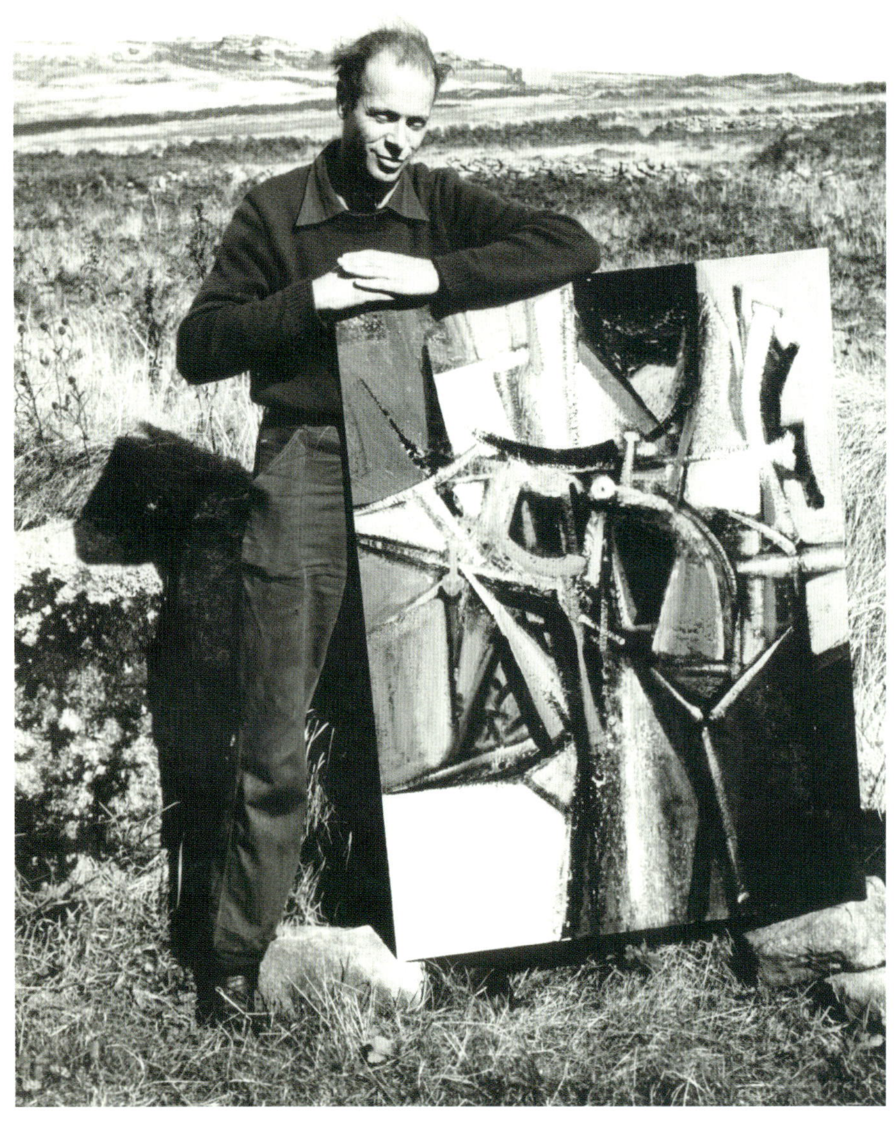

1

Bryan Wynter & The Carn

YOU CAN JUST about see it from the road near Eagles Nest. It can also be spotted from the high Trewey Hill road between Zennor and Lady Downs. If the day is clear enough, and binoculars will certainly help, it can be seen from the midpoint of the St Ives to Zennor coastal path. But you have to know what it is to pick it out.

'It' is the chimney of Carn Cottage (*carn* being Cornish for 'rock-pile'). In this instance the name implies its excellent camouflage, the chimney acting as a kind of turret or periscope emerging from the surrounding litter of massive boulders. The deeds for Carn Cottage go back to 1804 but it is probably older and will surely have been an abode linked to mining and quarrying. It is located 237m above sea level, with the Logan Stone just to the west and Zennor Quoit to the south-east, and is most conveniently reached by foot on a half-mile track that leads off from the main road.

To this day it has a sinister reputation amongst the locals. The fact alone that it is rather hidden and isolated from the community has prompted stories of hauntings and witchcraft. These stories had been partially endorsed by the presence, in the 1930s, of the self-styled 'Great Beast', Aleister Crowley. He is supposed to have summoned up the very Devil himself in the cottage and performed a black mass down the hill in Zennor's church. There was also an unfortunate episode at the Carn when Ka Arnold-Foster (the wife of Will Arnold-Foster, founder member of The League of Nations, who then lived at Eagles Nest)

went up there to comfort the sick wife of the writer Gerald Vaughan. The following morning Mrs Vaughan was found quite mad while Mrs Arnold-Foster was quite dead.

Sydney Graham, who stayed there for three months in 1950, referred, in a letter, to the possible druidical history of the moor and said: 'Christ knows what has been done in the name of magic and worship'.

However, it is worth noting that this mythology of the Carn, that still fuels our imaginations today, did not deter families from settling in the vicinity and living undisturbed lives. In fact it is very difficult for us to conceive that this austere environment was once well inhabited with large communities of people involved in mining, quarrying, farming and fishing. And the latter two activities were still essential to the local economy when Bryan Wynter, on his motorbike, arrived in the St Ives area sometime in June 1945 (he already knew the place from happy childhood holidays).

Wynter, a Londoner, was a pacifist who had spent the war years as a registered Conscientious Objector. His duties entailed working with ditching gangs in Oxfordshire on land drainage, as well as the disheartening task of looking after animals used in laboratory experiments at the University of Oxford (in a department run by Solly Zuckerman). The war had disrupted his studies at the Slade, which he intended to resume in the very near future (in fact he was to live in Cornwall for the remaining thirty years of his life). He now turned to an accessible but nevertheless outlying fringe of what felt to be a dissipated civilization. Yearning for a revitalization to his artistic life, Carn Cottage appeared to meet Wynter's criteria for an alternative, simple life style.

The ambience of these harsh moors clearly had a deep resonance for Wynter. There is often a forlorn orchestration of sound as the wind plays its way through the cracks and crevices in the rocks. The geological formations, with their shifting theatre of shadows, elicit strong reactions from the subconscious of the human observer, particularly at dusk. These rocks definitely have varied character and there is a heavy sense of brooding as if they are giants petrified and slumbering, patiently biding their time until the final trumpet broadcasts the hour of waking. Over the centuries many of these rocks even acquired names, such as 'the polar bear' (sadly this was all part of local oral lore, now forgotten and never registered on any map). There are also many days when visibility is almost zero due to the heavy mist. (While visiting the Carn area I have sometimes seen this 'mizzle' rapidly approaching, like an incoming tide, and it can be a startling and disorienting experience to be suddenly engulfed in a thick cloud and lose your bearings completely.)

Carn Cottage was semi-derelict and without plumbing or electricity, but this was of little consequence to a man of Wynter's inventive and industrious temperament. Rainwater was collected in a tank from the roof and fed through pipes into the cottage, while a wind generator supplied 12 volts (later replaced by a diesel generator). It was not unusual at this time to use paraffin-fuelled lamps, irons and cookers. A small vegetable plot was tended and if visitors were lucky they could expect a 'gourmet' treat of Algerian wine (a cheap tipple at the time) with the additional luxury of gulls' eggs, secured by Wynter, with much risk, from fairly inaccessible nesting places. They could also expect a spoken greeting from the tamed raven, Doom.

Life at the Carn was not all solitude and silence however, as Wynter married Susan Lethbridge (who had a toy-making shop in St Ives), with whom he had a son and a daughter. He also remained sociable and enjoyed the local pubs as well as occasional sorties to London (where he kept a studio). People enjoyed his wit, intellect and wicked sense of humour (he was a compulsive punster as well as a prankster, especially when in tandem with Sydney Graham). But these remote, untamed surroundings continued to provide some kind of essential anchor for a more elemental, primordial level of Wynter's being as an artist. His enthusiasm for this new environment is conveyed in a letter to a friend:

> My solo expeditions onto the moors or to the coast are almost feverishly exciting … It is like an enthralling book which I cannot lay down.

And in another letter from this period Wynter communicates a credo that would remain a guiding principle throughout his career:

> I mentioned as a theory of art the linking up of the inner and outer worlds, as though it were a question of breaking down an artificial barrier and experiencing the two on the same plane at once, seeing it not in terms of inner and outer, of observer and the thing observed, but as one thing – the 'experience', probably the only humanly possible approach to reality. Well here, in this landscape, even when you are not drawing or painting, it happens quite of its own accord. The real landscape overflows into the unconscious and the unconscious

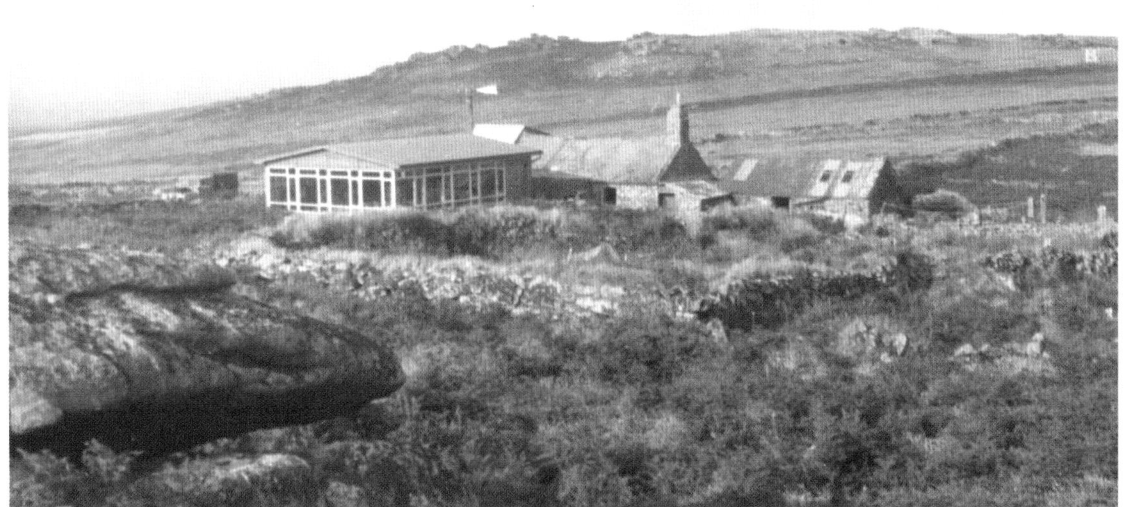

Towards the end of the war Wynter had
undergone several months of Jungian analysis,
throughout which he kept a dream diary.
He also made a close reading of whatever
volumes he could then find of Jung's books in
translation. On the moors he now drew from
this psychoanalytic reservoir to create many
disturbing images of nature 'red in tooth and
claw'. These related to the dark gothic, spiky
works of other Neo-Romantic painters of the
time (Sutherland, Ayrton, Vaughan, even John
Piper) who had lived through the recent war
years having witnessed the world turned into
a surrealist nightmare. Wynter's landscapes
(usually gouaches on paper) of ruined cottages,
chapels and tin mines also owed something to
Braque's late Cubism in their flat composition.

Sometime in 1954 Wynter responded
to a newspaper article looking for artists as
volunteers to take mescalin, in controlled
experiments, to observe how this might affect
their painting and drawing. The article was
by Rosalind Heywood, a leading light in the
Society for Psychical Research. Around this
time he read Aldus Huxley's book, *The Doors
of Perception*, which takes its title from a line of
Blake: 'If the doors of perception were cleansed
everything would appear to man as it is,
Infinite'. In fact Wynter would continue to take
mescalin throughout the decade, not as part of
a lifestyle, but as a means of gaining insight into
the activities of human consciousness in pursuit
of the workings of nature. The resultant change
in his art was quite dramatic. He turned,
with increasing confidence, to using oils in a
tachiste manner on larger canvasses, to unleash
an elegant chaos of lush shimmering colours,
the effect being simultaneously disturbing
and invigorating. Wynter was subconsciously
mapping the lively dance activated between the
workings of his enhanced nervous system with
the enriched dimensions of his environment,
embodying his own wiry, lithe physique in the

calligraphic brushstrokes, as in a distinctive signature. You can get lost in the deep space of these paintings, as they bewitch the curious eye into an exploration of the mysterious flora and fauna of an exotic, psychic jungle. Patrick Heron said it feels you could shoot an arrow into them (an apt metaphor as, around this period, Wynter was also reading Eugen Herrigel's book, *Zen in the Art of Archery*). These pictures included *The Indias, Seedtime, Elemental, Firestreak, The Interior* and *Riverbed*. He provided some clues to their understanding in various catalogue statements (taken from Bowness, 1976):

> *I think of my paintings as a source of imagery, something that generates imagery rather than contains it. Obviously it is I who have put into them what they contain but I have done so with as little conscious interference as possible, allowing them at every stage in their growth to dictate their own necessities.*

> *Discipline is usually associated with conscious method, something learned, mastered, perfected by use. The discipline I cultivate aims in the opposite direction and so has to be constantly renewed at every moment to fox the intention, the conscious ordering; a discipline that will put the eye in a position where it can confront the canvas as it stands at any one moment and act freely without preconception upon it. I think of the eye as standing at the extreme perimeter of its experience to date and letting the painting dictate its own development.*

> *I find it helpful to think of that moment at which the eye looks out at the world it has not yet recognized, in which true seeing has not yet been translated into the useful concepts with which the mind immediately*

swamps it. This moment of seeing is in fact a fragment of a continuous process which underlies and precedes recognition, a kind of 'substance' from which we construct our world of human experience. I think of myself as embodying this 'substance' in paint.

> *One should be able, ideally, to make paintings which throw off imagery of different kinds at different times to different people, continually unfolding different aspects of themselves, ambiguous and paradoxical paintings with no main 'theme', from which the spectator may, by participation, extract his own images (1957).*

> *My paintings are non-representational but linked to the products of nature in as much as they are developed according to laws within themselves and are a static record of the processes that have brought them about.*

> *A stream finds its way over rocks. The force of the stream & the quality of the rocks determine the stream's bed. This in turn modifies the course of the stream, channelling out new sluices and hollows. The stream erodes the rock, the rock deflects the stream, until, at some high point, the stream bursts its banks and falls into the ravine. The dry stream bed, carved and hollowed, remains. Its form contains its history.*

> *There are no rocks and streams in my paintings but a comparable process of dynamic versus static elements has attended their development and brought about their final form (1960).*

> *About 1956 I was trying to create a kind of visual flux, a surface on which the eye found it difficult to rest so that, if it were not rebuffed, it would be compelled to push deeper and come to terms with the forces*

underlying the painting. This demanded an act of imagination from the spectator.

Although, in a sense, this still holds good for my present painting, less demands are made on the spectator in his choice of interpretation. People tend to say: 'You are using larger forms.' There is a confusion here. 'Form', as usually understood, is not at issue. The small brush marks function as units of energy rather than as separate formal entities. A stream of such marks may enter and leave the canvas as from outside it. It may encounter another similar stream. The turbulence thus set up engenders new forces which in turn hinder or deflect the original paths. So the painting generates its own laws of development. But painting is an imaginative activity. Each development reflects the predilection of the artist and the life that surrounds him.

These paintings, then, are not pure abstractions. Nor do I abstract from 'nature'. I approach 'nature' from the other side.

I used to be a landscape painter. Am I still influenced by landscape? The landscape I live among is bare of houses, trees, people; is dominated by winds, by swift changes of weather, by the moods of the sea; sometimes it is devastated and blackened by fire. These elemental forces enter the paintings and lend their qualities without becoming motifs (1962).

April 1956 brought some welcome new neighbours down the hill, within sight, at Eagles Nest. Patrick Heron, a friend from the Slade years, arrived with his wife and two young daughters. Heron bought this impressive Victorian pile from the son of Will Arnold-Foster. The house boasted one of the most significant gardens in England with a huge range of rare plants from around the world, the colours and patterns of which soon fed into Heron's work. (The house also had an interesting history of visitors, including a holidaying Virginia Woolf, and in the late 1930s, while in exile from Ethiopia, the Emperor Haile Salassie.) Heron would prove to be a very loyal, life-long champion of Wynter's art. It's curious to think that over the years the two artists, separated by a half-mile of dirt track, must often have practised, unknowingly, a form of synchronised painting (though with very different results).

In the summer of 1957 Wynter built a wooden studio extension to the cottage, which provided a bright airy space with windows on three sides looking out at the moors, the rocks and the sea. Wynter's marriage to Lethbridge had by now ended and he had a new partner, Monica Harman, a pupil from the Bath Academy of Arts (Corsham) where he did some teaching. They married in 1959 and a resilient Monica gave birth to two boys there, Tom and Billy.

Isolated though the Carn was, Wynter did not always have to venture out into the broader art world as the art world sometimes came to him. As well as the many artists and writers in Penwith who frequently stopped by, there were some very illustrious visitors indeed. In 1959, Mark Rothko and his wife, in chic cosmopolitan attire, trudged their way up the dirt track guided by Peter Lanyon, while the influential New York based critics Lawrence Alloway and Clement Greenberg also made the pilgrimage.

It was the St Ives artist, Bill Redgrave, who gave Wynter an old wartime searchlight (a large concave parabolic mirror). The potential to somehow incorporate this object into his art nagged away at his fertile imagination

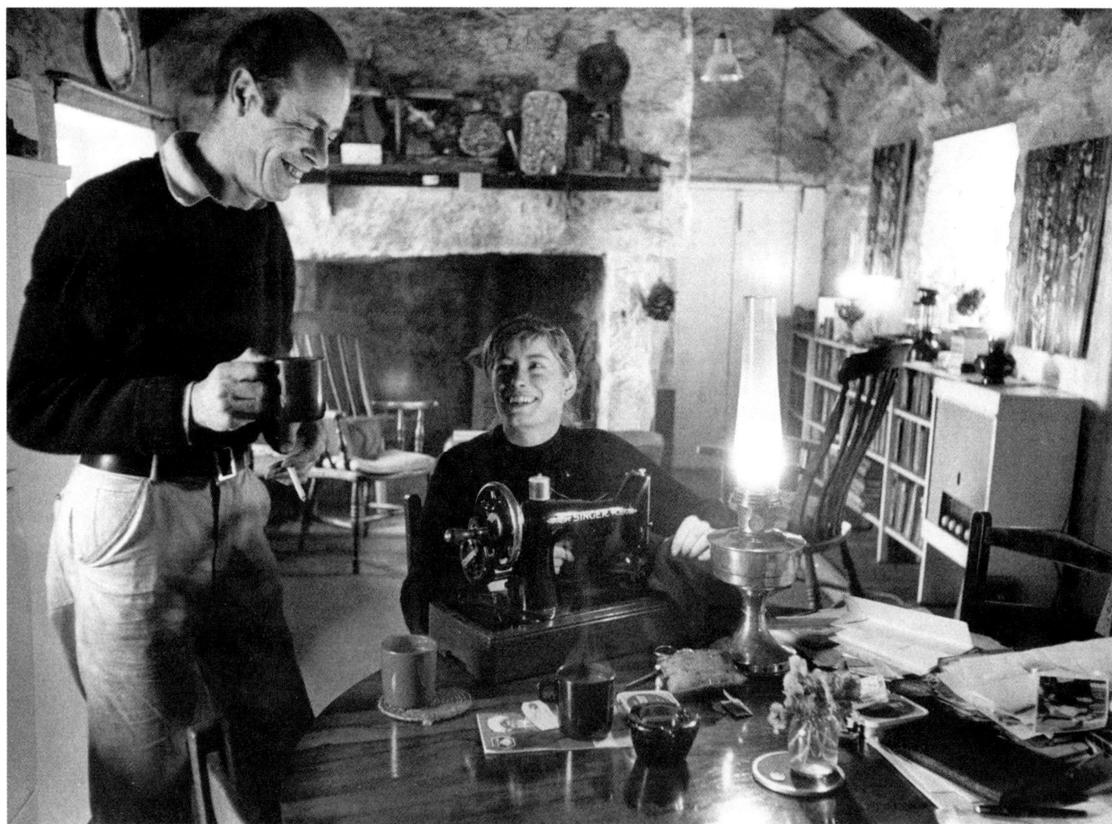

Bryan & Monica, late 1950s

and over a period of time the *IMOOS* (*Images Moving Out Onto Space*) were born. These consisted of different shapes of coloured card suspended on threads in front of the mirror and their reflections gave the impression of ever shifting, strange and elegant patterns floating, with cloud-like elegance, in the space ahead of the viewer (it was the necessity of exhibiting in a gallery context that dictated the later box format). About a dozen of these were constructed over the next few years, each of them supplying a unique combination of illusions. This kinetic art was a sensible extension of his attempts to represent flux in his paintings; Sven Berlin called them 'timeless clocks'. (There was an occasion when the Wynters, going away on a trip, stored a mattress in the new studio where it was less damp than in the cottage. On their return they were horrified to see the mattress resemble a huge charcoal biscuit. One of the mirrors, acting as a large magnifying glass, had each day been focussing the early morning sun on the mattress, leaving it totally charred. It could well have led to a disastrous conflagration in their absence.)

Fire, indeed, was a feature of life at the Carn. Annually, between January and March, farmers would burn areas of gorse in a controlled way to allow new grass to grow for rough grazing. This was always an exciting and sometimes intimidating event. There were some worrying occurrences when the fires got threateningly close to the cottages on the moors and twenty-four hour vigilance was called for.

Intimations of mortality first came

knocking on Wynter's door in May 1961 when, one night, he had a serious heart attack. A heavily pregnant Monica ran down the track to Eagles Nest to phone for help and Dr Roger Slack soon arrived in a Land Rover that could negotiate the track and managed to ferry the ailing artist to an ambulance waiting on the road.

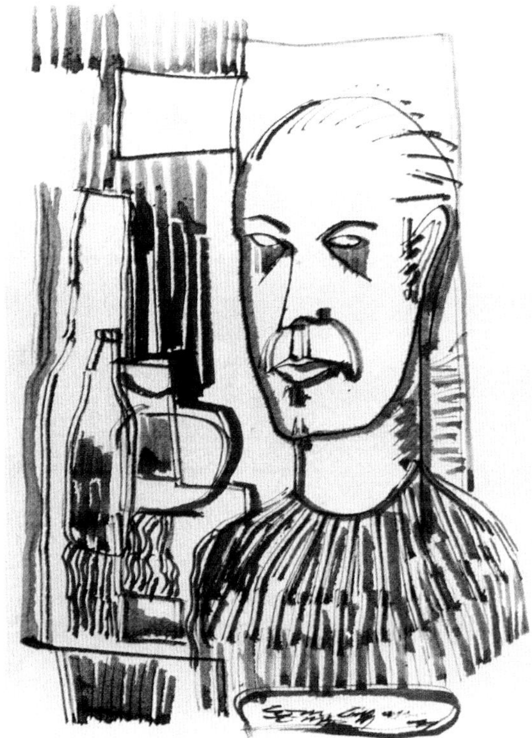

Tony O'Malley – *Bryan Wynter – Edward Hain Hospital, St Ives* 1961, coloured ink on paper, 35.5 x 25.4 cm

Wynter spent nearly three months of prescribed rest in the Edward Hain Hospital in St Ives. It just so happened that another artist, recently arrived from Ireland, also had a heart attack at the same time and ended up in the next bed – this was Tony O'Malley. The Irish artist regaled Wynter with an endless stream of delightful blarney, apparently never once repeating himself. They were to remain close friends (even touring Ireland together in 1967).

There was another patient who fascinated Wynter for different reasons. He was a young man who had been badly burned while making his own fireworks, and he provided Wynter with the potent recipe for their concoction. Not long after release from hospital this information was applied to characteristically mischievous practice.

For some time the peace of the moors was regularly shattered by low flying helicopters on exercise drills from RNAS Culdrose. Heron even reported that they flew so low they disturbed the gravel on his drive. Wynter saw a tactical opportunity to experiment with the 'fireworks'. The mixture included weed killer and sugar, the home-made rockets completed with bamboo sticks. Very soon this low-tech, but very effective arsenal was seeing off the noisy invaders. It wasn't long before the RNAS (coincidentally?) diverted their routines elsewhere.

Swimming, snorkelling and kayaking had always been regular pursuits, and having been impressed by a Jacques Cousteau film, Wynter now made his own aqualung. A glass-bottomed boat was also constructed allowing him to study the flowing forms of underwater flora and fauna, with attendant eddies, vortices and currents (another kind of deep space). These were much featured in the later paintings and drawings.

It was 1964 that the Wynters at last moved from Carn Cottage to a larger, more comfortable, conventional home at Treverven House on the south-facing coast near Porthcurno. And it was here, on February 9, 1975 that Wynter, while repairing a puncture on his Mini, had another heart attack. The fourteen years since the first attack had been very busy and creative, and Wynter seemed to have survived again, but he died two days later, aged 59, in hospital in Penzance.

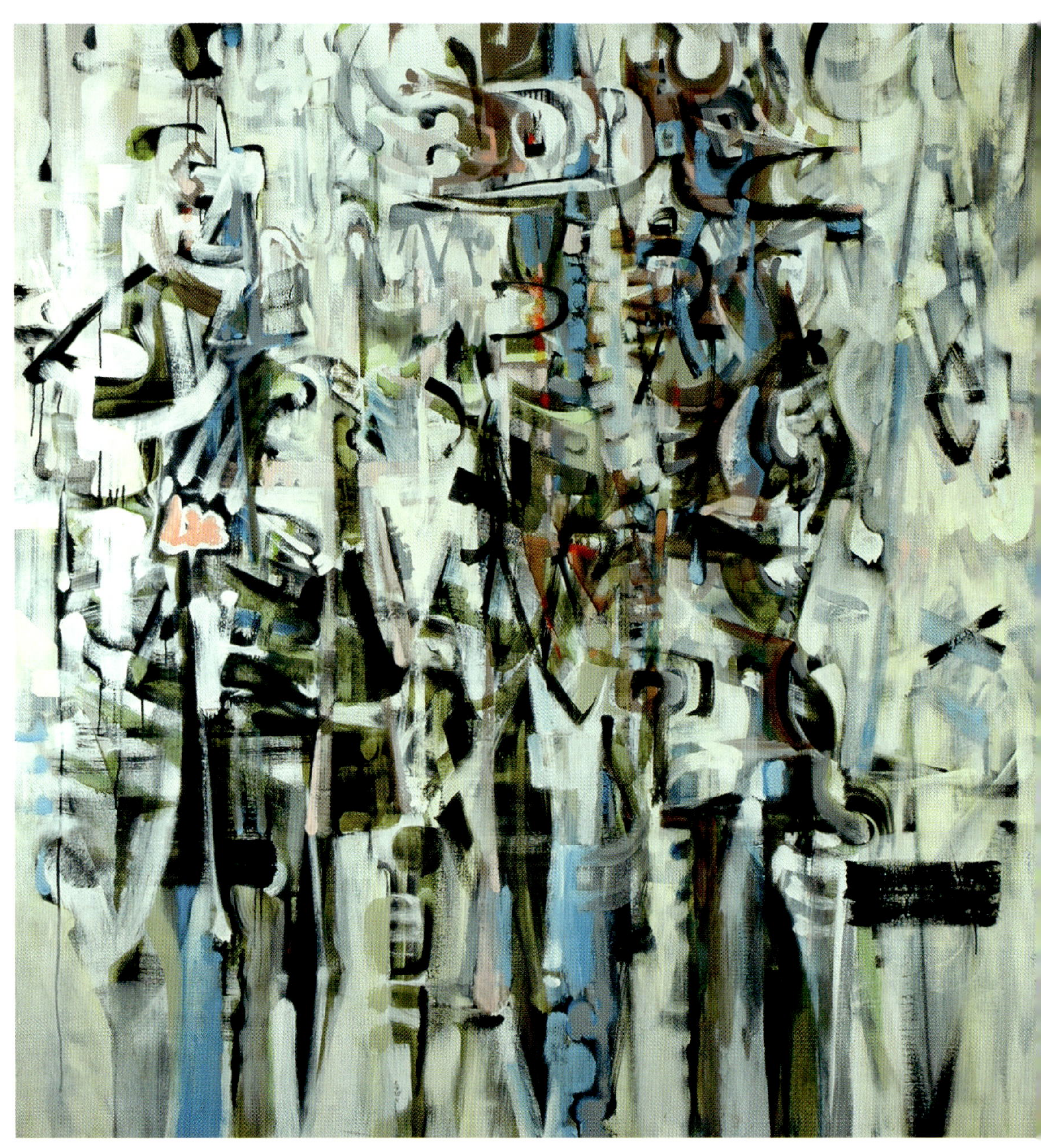

Atavistic Group 1959, oil on canvas, 143.5 x 139 cm

Bryan Wynter was a non-partisan man in the sometimes combative and jealous world of art politics. He was extremely popular, and in speaking to people who knew him the same word recurs – *gentle*. Peter Lanyon said: 'He was a very generous human being but remained anonymous with it'. He was a romantic who could incorporate the sciences into his art; a literary man widely read in poetry and philosophy. His death elicited some fine elegies, especially from his dear friend Sydney Graham, as well as from David Wright, Sven Berlin and Arthur Caddick. Patrick Heron, in his obituary for *Studio International*, said that Wynter's art 'was characterised by the brilliant, searching, restless, inventive intelligence of one of the loneliest and most individual talents of our time'.

A simple stone marks Bryan Wynter's grave in Zennor churchyard. The stone was taken from the old count house on his beloved moors just next to Carn Cottage where, for 19 years, he had lived, loved, and worked, producing art of enduring vigour and beauty.

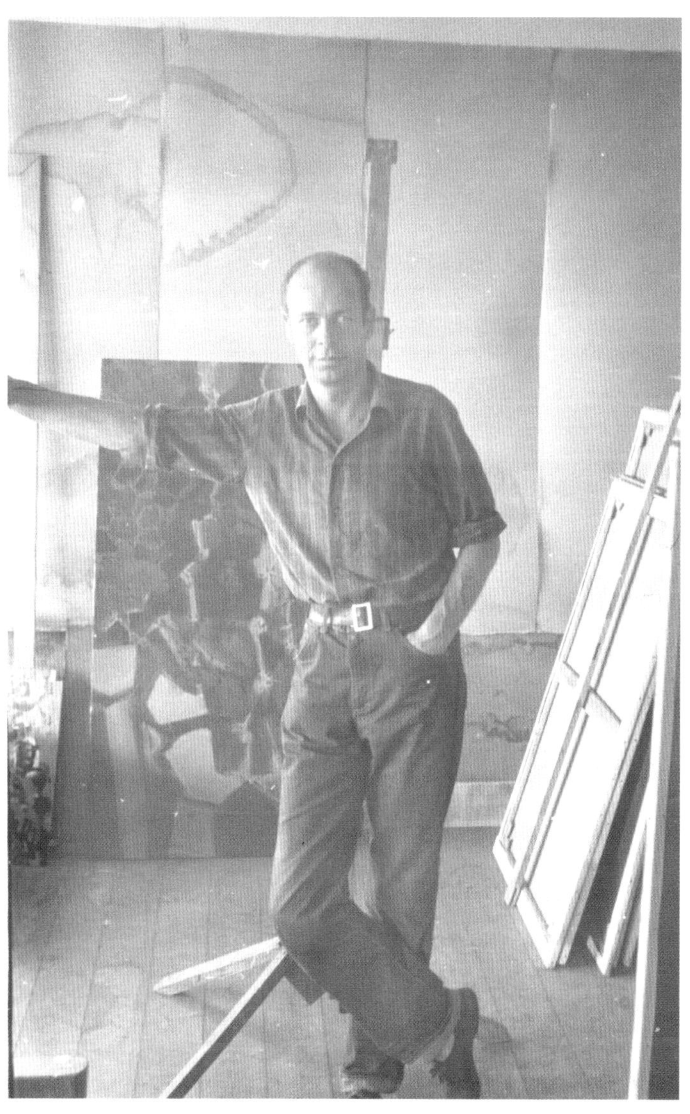

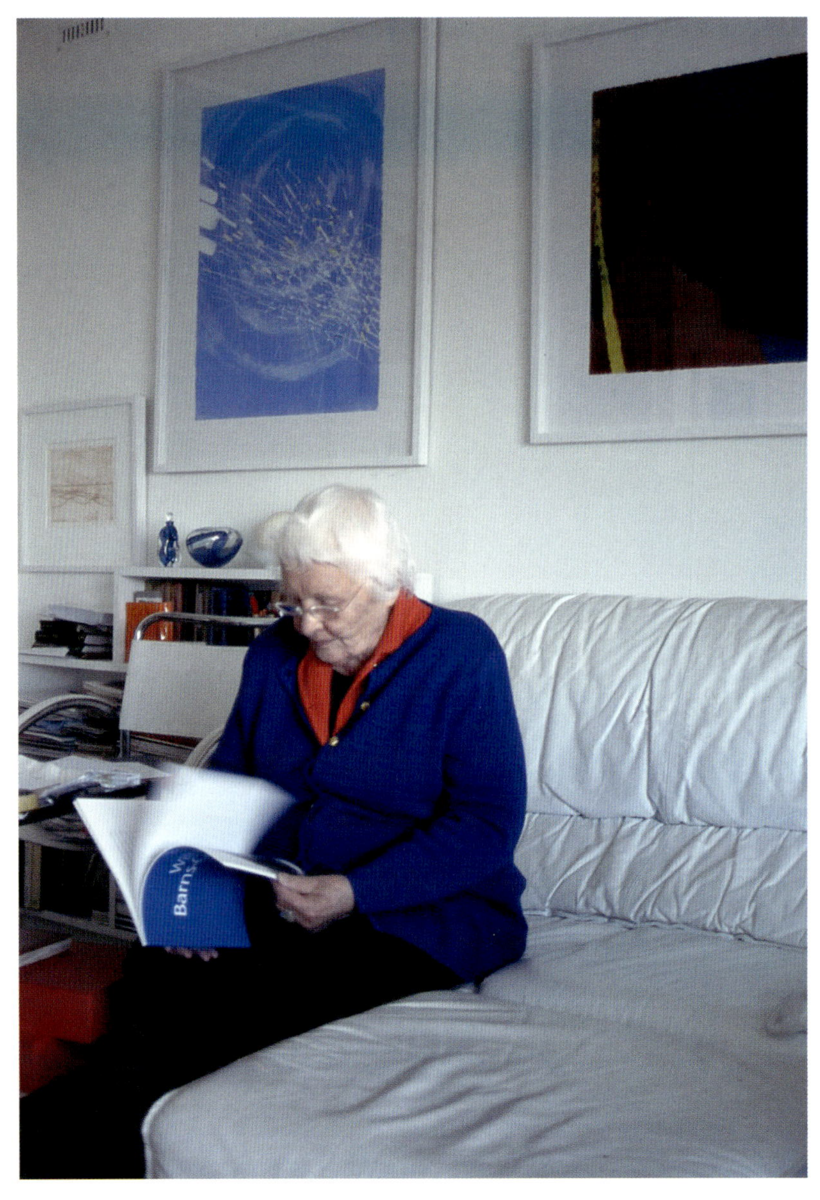

2

Tea with Miss Barns-Graham

FORMIDABLE – THE WORD recurred
when I told people of my planned visit to
see the painter Wilhelmina Barns-Graham
(henceforth known as Willie). And one person
who knew her well enough said: 'Good luck
mate!'

She was born in 1912 at St Andrews in
Scotland and moved to St Ives for health
reasons in March 1940. This was just six
months after Barbara Hepworth, Ben
Nicholson and Naum Gabo had moved there
from London at the outbreak of war. The latter
two men exerted a strong influence on Willie,
but her work would gradually evolve into an
incomparable style (or variety of styles) always
changing and developing as her keen eye led
her to experiment with colour, form, space and
texture. Her later work gave way to a dynamic
freedom and energy, indicating a youthful zest
remarkable for her age. As early as 1956 she was
described as 'Britain's foremost woman abstract
painter'. She received a CBE in 2001.

Her life had fallen into a pattern of dividing
the year between the Cornish resort and
her native home (in 1960 she inherited the
Balmungo estate in Fife from her aunt), escaping
the hordes of tourists over the summer months.

It was a Sunday afternoon in late January
2003 when I arrived in the town to meet
Willie for an informal interview; she was in
her 91st year. Most of the shops were shut but
I found one corner shop open where I bought a
chocolate cake from the fridge: my token gift in
the face of the formidable challenge to come.

Willie lived in a stylish block of flats along

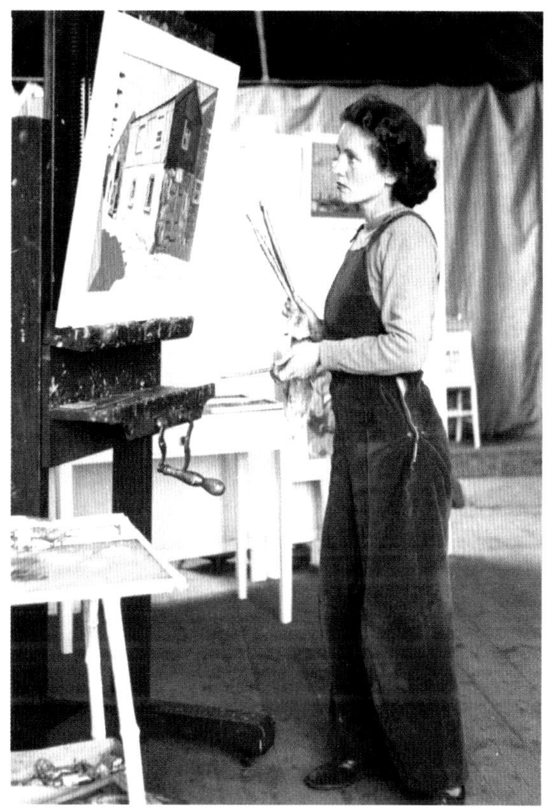

WBG, 1947

Back Road West, not far from Alfred Wallis's
humble abode (indeed she had met Wallis soon
after her arrival). I rang the doorbell and braced
myself. A petite figure in blue approached
through the frosted glass and opened the
door. Softly spoken with only a hint of accent,
she had a slightly formal manner and led me
through to her sumptuous living room, which
commanded outstanding views over Porthmeor
Beach. It had an elegant modernist feel to it.
Cream leather sofa and chairs, augmented with
steel and glass. There were many books and her

own striking paintings graced the walls. It was comfortable, once again in a slightly formal way, but not cold, and all the while there was the panoramic sea and sky to captivate the eye.

Willie called down the stairs: 'Prepare tea for Mr Whittaker.' A woman's strong Cornish accent called back: 'Miss Barns-Graham, will Mr Whittaker be 'avin' milk?' Willie looked to me and I nodded: 'Mr Whittaker takes milk.' The voice from the deep called up again: 'Miss Barns-Graham, will Mr Whittaker be 'avin' sugar?' Another glance from Willie and I shook my head, 'No, Mr Whittaker doesn't require sugar. Please bring up some plates for the cake that Mr Whittaker has kindly brought.'

We got ourselves settled while I explained who I was, where I came from and what I hoped to achieve. My Irishness interested her and this Celtic link had a sudden thawing affect, manifesting in a warm, attractive and beguilingly youthful smile. She noticed my interest in the bookcase next to me full of poetry books: 'I used to read a great deal of poetry when I was younger', she explained.

The tea was now provided along with my tasteful peace offering. The most obvious topic of conversation was the view: an ever shifting and dramatic Cinerama of sea, sand and sky. I noticed Willie's replies were becoming more and more laboured and with horror I realised that the cake I'd brought had not yet defrosted and was proving to be dentally challenging for her. I hastily suggested she might enjoy it better later. 'Perhaps you're right', she mumbled.

We spoke about the arts in general and she revealed that Cezanne, Miro and Klee made up her pantheon of greats. She was amazed to have read recently that Marcel Duchamp was voted the most influential artist of the twentieth century.

I was keen to get first-hand impressions of some of her illustrious peers and asked her about Peter Lanyon: 'I personally believe he's now overrated. He was paranoid about "foreigners" taking over his territory. He was a proud Cornishman and could be vituperative. But I can understand and have sympathy for this. He was born and raised here and suddenly there's an onslaught of other artists turning the place into a colony. I would have felt the same in my native corner of Scotland.' At the same time she believed Roger Hilton to be the most underrated painter of that period. She also talked of the many arty-parties that were always going on somewhere in the peninsula back in the '50s and '60s, but she rarely attended them as her work always came first (here I sensed a hint of regret). I mentioned I had stopped off to have lunch with Michael and Margaret Snow, who were good friends of Willie, and told her about his lengthy procrastinations over finishing a painting. There was no sympathy in her sharp response: 'It's an excuse for laziness.' I thought this slightly harsh and imagined that Michael would be shocked to hear such criticism.

I was interested to discover that she clearly had some gift for dealing with people suffering distress. She was close to Sydney and Nessie Graham and said that Nessie had come to her for comfort when their marriage was going through a difficult period, while they lived at the lodge opposite Trevaylor in the early 1960s. Alan Lowndes was another example of someone struggling with depression and alcoholism, who also came to her for her calming effect. 'Artists have their faults, they're very vulnerable people.' She was an integral part of the Hepworth and Nicholson group and emphasised the tremendous kindness that Nicholson had shown her (she also pointed out that a recent biography of him was 'complete rubbish').

Speaking of places, I told her of my love for Zennor and this led her to speak of her psychic

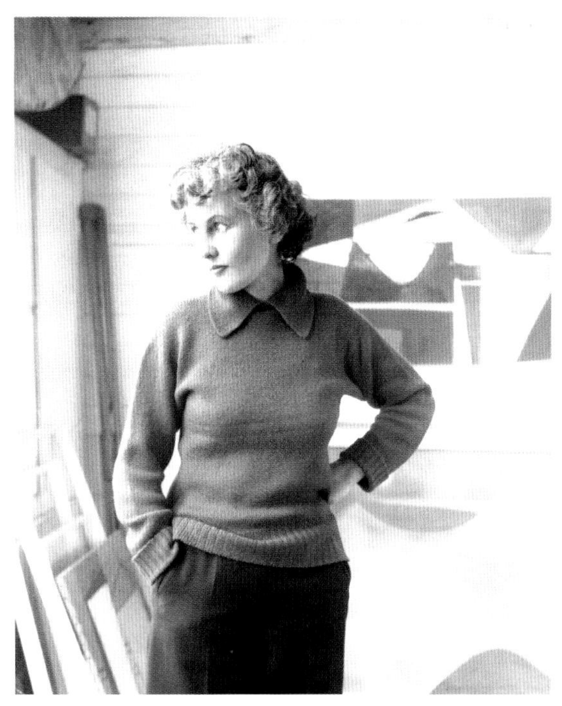

WBG, mid-1950s

experiences. Once, when staying in a cottage there on her own, while in bed, she heard footsteps coming up the stairs: 'Soft thuds, as if someone was wearing gumboots', and they proceeded towards her door. A terrified Willie cowered under the sheets awaiting the phantom guest to appear, but no one ever materialised. This occurred on several evenings; she'd had similarly inexplicable experiences throughout her long life. (There is a Scottish word 'fey' that could be applied to her. It refers to someone with second-sight, particularly regarding premonitions of death.)

I now spoke of my enthusiasm for the painter Tony O'Malley. I had visited Tony and Jane only two months earlier. He had been very frail and I showed her a photograph of him with me beside his bed, his firm grip on my hand. The picture had an alarming affect on her. Looking startled she handed it back to me saying: 'That man has death in his face.' At the time of my visit to the O'Malleys there was still a degree of optimism that Tony would rally, as he had done often enough before. Looking into the distance she spoke very affectionately of their friendship: 'He would often call around in the evenings for a tot of whisky, after a day in the studio, and show me some of his sketchbooks, saying: "Here's a good one, and here's another good one", but of course they weren't all good, he did far too much work, he just never stopped. I believe it's important for an artist to stop and take stock.' (She did a good impression of an Irish accent, in fact she was something of a mimic, also doing impressions of the local Cornish folk.)

She went on: 'He was an enormously loved man. You would nearly fall off your chair laughing at his stories! He knew so much about everything he was so well read. Tony was uncomplicated but he certainly wasn't simple'.

It was now time to call a halt and she suggested I look in again before heading home in three days time. As I was leaving she said: 'Thank you for bringing Tony back into my mind.'

She had kept me on my toes throughout and corrected me on various dates and details. I was impressed by her incisive and well thought out replies to my probing and left feeling stimulated.

I duly returned with the intention of taking a couple of photographs of Willie before driving back to Oxfordshire. But as she opened the door and ushered me into her living room there was an anxious, concerned look about her: 'Have you heard the news?' I shook my head. 'Tony died two nights ago.' This was certainly a bombshell following on so quickly from our previous conversation. She offered me whisky but I thought better of it with the long drive ahead. We both sat in silence while staring out solemnly at the gentle ebb and flow of the waves, which took on a special poignancy. The interplay of sea, sand, rocks and clouds carrying

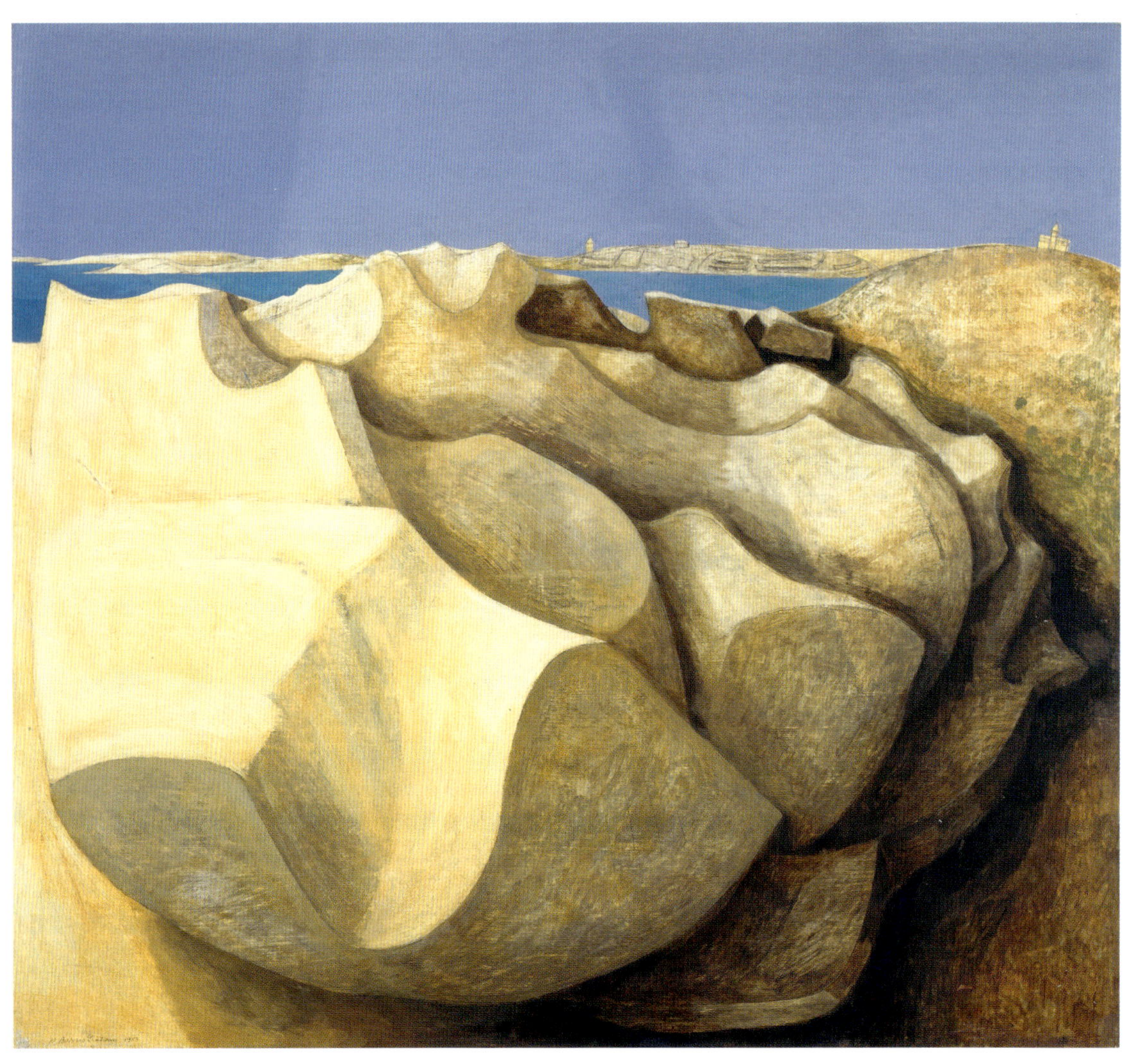

Rocks, St Mary's, Scilly Isles 1953, oil on board, 102.8 x 114.3 cm

on as normal (a view Tony would have known well from his Porthmeor Studio), punctuated by the plaintive cry of the gulls contributing to the melancholic gloom.

Only eight months earlier I had been at my mother's side when she died, and I felt a sudden need to speak to Willie in detail about this. I spoke about watching her final breaths coming and going and how gently the concluding breath left her body, instantly leaving her looking like an empty husk. Somehow, dying seemed the easiest and most natural thing in the world. Willie appeared intrigued and appreciative of this sharing of grief. She revealed a spiritual side, expressing a belief that the best qualities of people somehow get recycled by life: 'It can't all be meaningless'. She said she had been very close to her late brother, and dearly wanted to believe they might meet again in some afterlife, but honestly felt it to be unlikely.

We concluded with her saying we must emphasise the positive in everybody: 'There is so much gossip and back stabbing in art communities, I find one has less ego as one gets older'. I took several photos (in not the most relaxed of atmospheres) and left.

A couple of weeks later Willie phoned. She wanted to thank me; apparently she had been depressed herself for some time and hadn't been working, which increased the vicious circle she felt trapped in. But she had a strong feeling from the moment I started talking of Tony, with the photograph, that this was somehow auspicious. His death, linked closely in time with my visit, confirmed this and she took it as a sign to get painting again; in fact from the moment she closed the door behind me she hadn't stopped! She was working on a painting for Tony and would let me see it on a future visit. In the meantime she had received copies of the photos I'd taken of her, but said she didn't like them much as they made her look old.

The following month I was back (this time I decided it was safer to take flowers). Willie's good friend and neighbour Dell Casdagli was on hand to make the tea and we settled down to this before a tour of the studio. Willie complained that her doctor had warned about her high blood pressure and was finding it a bore that she wasn't allowed her evening whisky. I then made the mistake of taking from my bag a handsome new book about Nancy Wynne-Jones (who had lived in the area in the '50s and '60s). This produced a look of horror quickly followed by rage. 'That woman's name has never been mentioned under this roof for years', she snapped. I was really worried that the aforementioned blood pressure would go through this same roof. It made me wonder if there was still some latent resentment, after all these years, about competing with another local female artist. But before long the mood changed again when the doorbell rang and two old friends of Willie arrived unannounced. I sensed that it was a bit much for her and soon left (disappointed to have missed the studio tour). Back at home a few days later Willie phoned. She apologised for the interruption during my visit and said she had attempted, unsuccessfully, to locate the guest house where I was staying in Morrab Road in Penzance, as she was keen that I see her work-in-progress on the O'Malley painting. Oh well, next time for sure …

Meanwhile, on the world's stage the invasion of Iraq had just happened and I had several phone calls from Willie venting her Celtic spleen at the madness she perceived: 'George Bush is a recovering alcoholic and he has obviously suffered serious brain damage.' She also expressed concern at the terror that the bombing would induce in domestic pets in Baghdad. I was always pleased to hear her and felt privileged to have built such a comradely

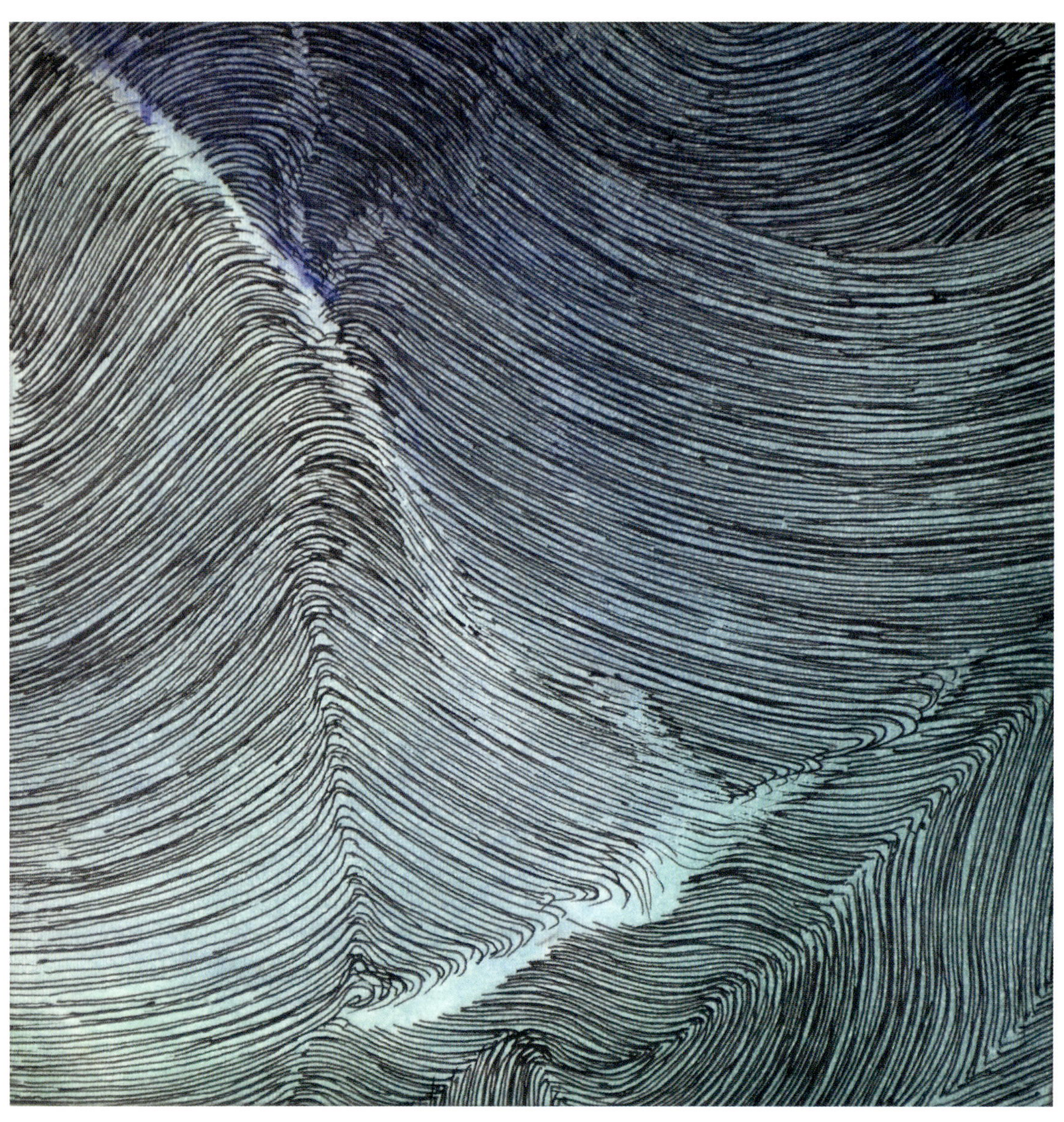

Music of the Sea 1976, pen, ink, oil on card, 15.2 x 15.2 cm

rapport so quickly (I also received some nice letters from her). I now sent her a list of questions regarding the nature of the artistic process and how it impacts on one's life (in the philosophical sense). I politely suggested that it would be interesting to pursue this line of thought on my next visit in a few weeks time.

The last time I saw Willie was in late April when I bumped into her having tea at Tate St Ives with the Cornish painter Margo Maeckelberghe, and she invited me to stop by the next day when we could go through the questions. On arrival I was surprised by a different, much taller figure approaching through the frosted glass door. This was Rowan James, Willie's long-time friend and amanuensis. The atmosphere was now quite different, Willie explained that a film crew was due shortly to interview her for a TV programme about Barbara Hepworth. However, she had taken some care to write out replies to my questions (she said she'd been up since 6 am working on them), and she would now read them to me. Needless to say they were all insightful comments. She went on to explain that they would be typed out and sent to me soon (but sadly, they never materialised). Out of luck again with seeing her studio I beat another hasty retreat, but remained optimistic that there would be a next time.

Shortly after this Willie left for Scotland, not realising that this was the last time she would close her front door in St Ives behind her. She would never again see the little fishing harbour where she had worked so happily with great energy and creativity for over sixty years. And so it came to pass, that exactly a year to the week from my first tentative encounter with Wilhelmina Barns-Graham, it was now time for her own considerable qualities to be recycled. Formidable to the end, she remains an inspiration to us all.

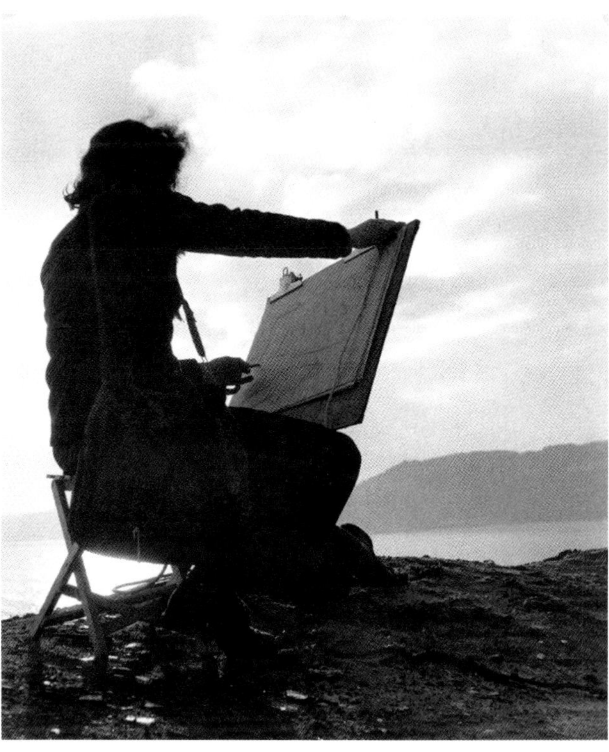

WBG sketching above Porthgwidden, 1947

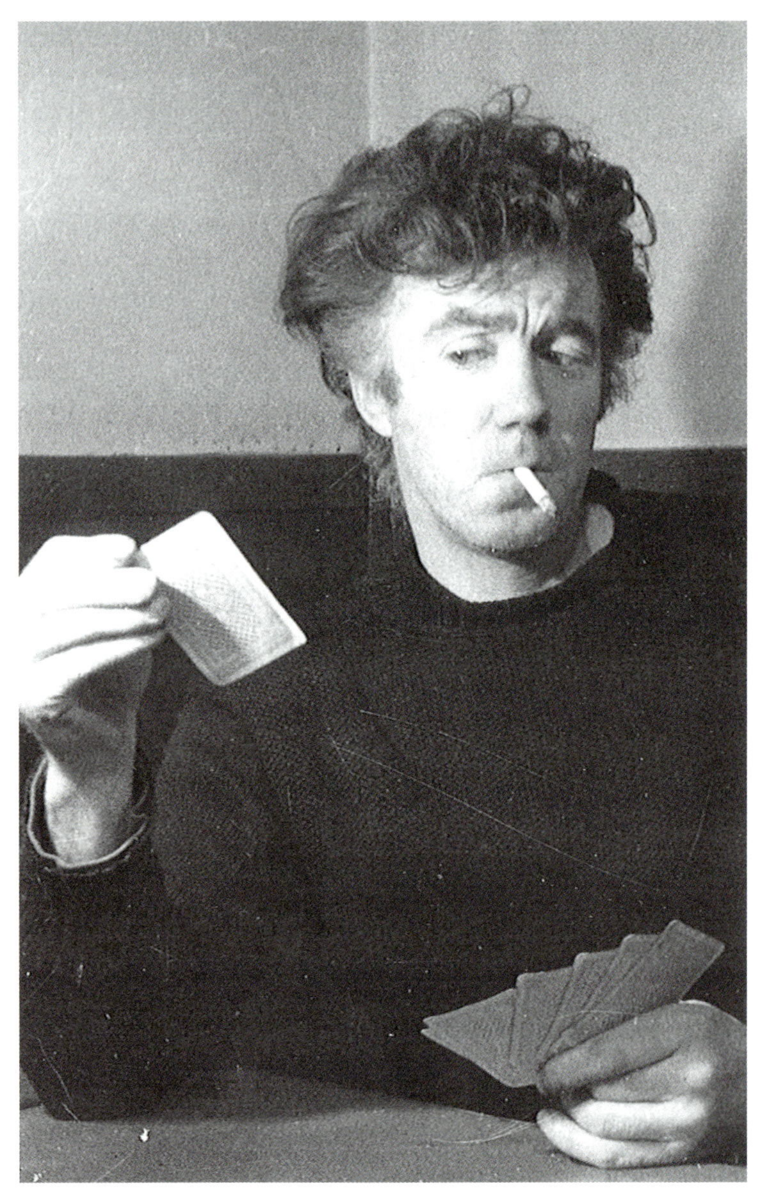

3

W. S. Graham & the Artists

WILLIAM SYDNEY GRAHAM'S first encounter with visual artists was in Glasgow during the war in the early 1940s. The city was a fairly safe destination for anyone fleeing the London Blitz, as well as for refugees desperately escaping the fascist terror across Europe. Graham had failed an army medical due to an ulcer and was given work, as an engineer, in a torpedo factory at Fort Matilda near Greenock. It was in 1941 he encountered David Archer, bookseller, publisher and generous patron of the arts. Archer, newly arrived from London, had already published poetry by David Gascoyne, Dylan Thomas and George Barker. He now set up the Scott Street Art Centre as a stimulating meeting place for budding writers and artists. His strong philanthropic streak also saw him offer accommodation and hospitality to anyone he approved of, particularly if they were impecunious, at his flat in Sandyford Place. This is where Graham would hang out in any spare time he had from the factory work and it would prove crucial for his development as a poet.

Two refugees he quickly got to know were the Polish Jewish artists Joseph Herman and Jankel Adler. Herman was a social realist painter while Adler had been friendly with Picasso and Paul Klee. Adler made quite an impact on everyone who met him for his professionalism and dedication to his calling as a painter. In 1942 he published an influential article about Paul Klee in *Horizon* magazine and Graham helped him with the translation. Adler proved to be a significant exemplar for Graham's own pursuit of perfection. In addition Adler's regular use of stylised faces would crop up in Graham's manuscripts and letters and decorative art works throughout his life, almost as his own unique signature or mark.

Other painters here Graham became very friendly with were Benjamin Creme and Robert Frame, as well as Robert Colquhoun and Robert MacBryde ('the two Roberts'). When Archer published Graham's *Cage Without Grievance* in 1942, Creme and Frame provided illustrations.

In 1942 Graham got work teaching at Kilquhanity, a progressive school in Galloway. He developed a relationship with a fellow teacher, Mary Harris. It just so happened that her family owned two gypsy caravans in Germoe in Cornwall and the couple decided to make a break with convention and try to live a self-sufficient simple life there. However, after a few months a pregnant Harris returned to Scotland where she gave birth to their daughter, Rosalind. Graham was now in the county where he would spend most of the rest of his life and before long he was keen to make contact with the art community. He wrote to Ben Nicholson, then living at Carbis Bay with Barbara Hepworth, asking if he could come over on his bicycle. They appear to have had several meetings but there is no record of what they spoke about, we only have a tantalising reference in a letter Nicholson wrote to Herbert Read in 1944, saying of Graham 'his method of working at his writing seems like my method of working at my painting'. Graham also mentioned to a friend that Nicholson was like Adler.

Nessie Dunsmuir now joined Graham in the caravans. He had met her in 1938 at Newbattle Abbey College. She was also a poet and would be his future wife, but there were a few hurdles to cross before that day came.

Graham sometimes hitchhiked to London during the war. There he would meet up in Soho with yet more painters, including the Neo-Romantics Keith Vaughan and John Minton. The latter in particular became close to Graham for a while. He also got to know Dylan Thomas quite well and the two displayed a healthy mutual respect. Minton, Vaughan, Colquhoun and MacBryde all came to stay at various times in Cornwall.

Around this time he met the charismatic sculptor, painter, writer and self-conscious bohemian, Sven Berlin. Berlin was working on the first book length study of the 'primitive' artist Alfred Wallis (who had died in the Madron Poorhouse in 1942), and commissioned Graham to write a poem for inclusion in the book. The result was 'The Voyages of Alfred Wallis', a poem showing the strong influence of Anglo-Saxon poetry, with its alliteration and knotty compound words, which Graham was reading at this time. Wallis would remain very much in Graham's mind particularly twenty years later when he moved to Madron. Berlin became a good drinking pal and also shared with Graham Benzedrine tablets that he got on prescription, which Graham felt gave him a necessary boost to work through the night at his poetry.

In 1947 the couple moved to a cottage in the fishing harbour of Mevagissey, courtesy of the writer Frank Baker. The Ship Inn was a regular port of call, and before long Graham was invited to join a local fishing crew on several outings, an invaluable experience for the poet now embarked on writing his long poem 'The Nightfishing'. Later in the year the couple agreed

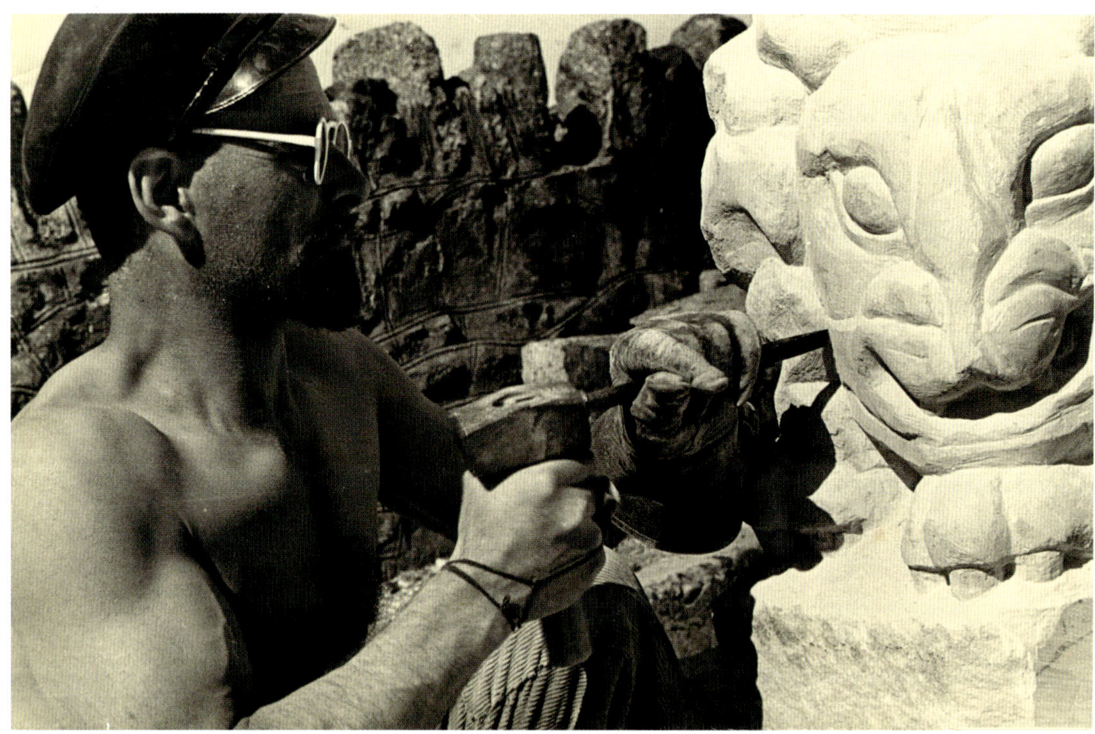

Sven Berlin working on a St Austell Brewery commission, *c. 1948*

to a temporary separation and Nessie went to Paris to teach English at the Berlitz school.

This was an odd peripatetic period for Graham when, over the course of five years he visited the US on two occasions as well as Italy and lived in London. Also during this time he had his book *The White Threshold* selected by T. S. Eliot to be published by Faber & Faber in 1949. On one of the American trips he visited Ezra Pound, then incarcerated in a psychiatric hospital in Washington DC.

Bryan Wynter became another important painter friend and in 1950 lent Graham his remote Carn Cottage on the moors above Zennor for a few months.

1953 saw Graham in pursuit of Nessie in Paris. He was just in time as she was close to marrying a wealthy businessman, but chose to hitch her wagon with the impecunious poet instead. They were married in 1954. 1955 saw the publication of *The Nightfishing*, now considered to be one of the most important sea poems in the English language. He would not publish another book for fifteen years.

Early in 1956 the couple were back in Cornwall looking for somewhere to live and Berlin came to the rescue again. He temporarily provided his cottage at Penderleath not far from St Ives until they found the Old Coastguard cottage out at the wild and windswept Gurnard's Head. The cottage was basic in the extreme and Sylvia Skelton gives this account:

> *It had a leaking roof, no cooking stove, no electricity, an outside toilet and no bathroom. I remember visiting them and taking food with me – but there was nothing to cook it on. On my next visit I took them a primus stove – before this they were cooking on an open fire, when they could find fuel. They used an oil lamp for light and a paraffin stove for heat.*

Crucially, there was the Gurnard's Head Hotel nearby. It was then run by Jimmy and Daphne Goodman, a slightly eccentric couple, who always made artists very welcome and the place acquired a reputation for fun and games and late night singalongs. As it happened, this was a remarkable time to be an artist in West Cornwall. Of course Hepworth, Nicholson and Leach were well established major figures in St Ives, but the whole area was teeming with talent, including Peter Lanyon, Patrick Heron, Bernard Leach, Bryan Wynter,

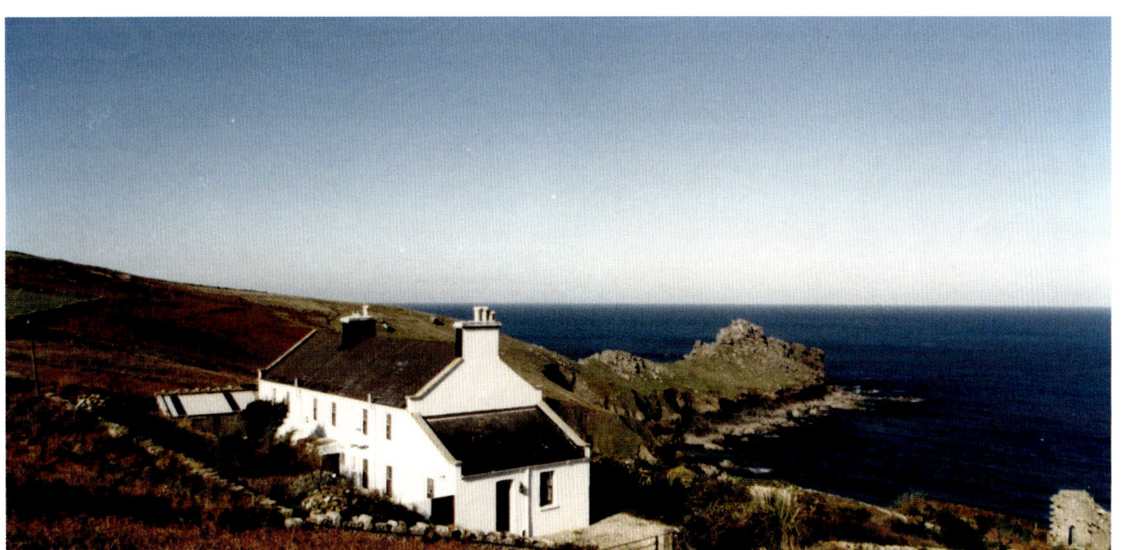

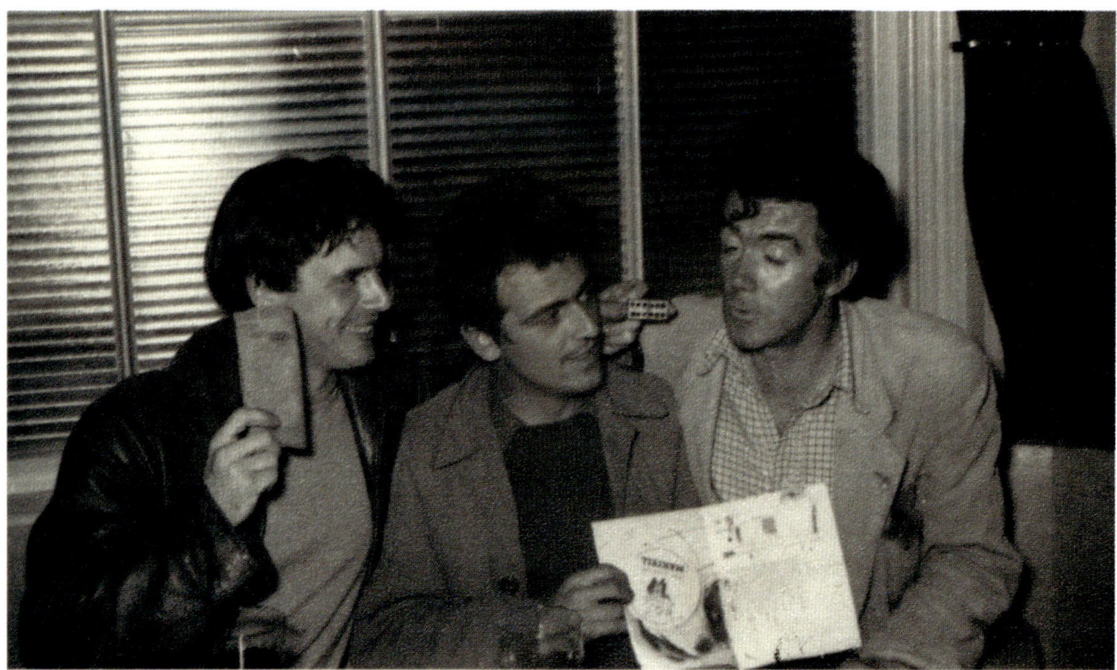

Trevor Bell, Brian Wall & WSG, *c.* 1958

Wilhelmina Barns-Graham, John Wells, Terry Frost, Karl Weschke, Brian Wall, Trevor Bell, Alan Lowndes and many more. Graham was in the thick of it with all these people and the exchange of ideas within this diverse community certainly helped shape his poetry. Many of these characters were extremely generous to the Grahams. This was just as well, as Nessie caught the bus into St Ives for seasonal work in the hotels, and this was their main meagre income.

Around this time the sculptor Brian Wall befriended him and has made these illuminating observations:

I first met Sydney Graham as I was walking down Fore Street shortly after I arrived in St Ives in the mid-fifties. He had just published The Nightfishing *and he had a copy in his hand. When I was introduced to him he said, 'Here's a copy of my poems and you owe me three shillings and sixpence'. I was slightly taken aback, but I gave him*

the money and we went for a drink in The Sloop. That was the beginning of a long and very fruitful friendship. He asked me what kind of an artist I was and when I told him that I was a sculptor he seemed less interested. As I got to know him over the years, I realized that he really liked being among painters and the reason for that becomes clear in the way that he spoke about his poetry. The layering and movement of words was very akin to the way that painters use paint. He was always looking for the structure in painting, similar to the structure in his poems. As painters shift paint from one side of the canvas to the other, he could move the focus of a poem. The forcefulness and integrity of his character was a strong influence, which stays with me to this day. The journeys that I made out to Gurnard's Head with supplies to see Sydney and Nessie were great moments of joy and intellectual rigor. At other times, when he was in St Ives, he crashed in my studio at Wheal Dream. Looking back to that time when we all gathered together – painters, sculptors, writers, poets, filmmakers, ceramicists – Sydney was the spark that ignited our conversation. We would be working away in our studios and then one by one everyone would drift into the Sloop Inn or the Castle Inn. We would talk about nothing and everything, and we learned that one couldn't be sloppy in an argument. We held Sydney in very high esteem as a poet, and he made one cognizant of what it takes to be an artist. (Personal correspondence)

It was at Patrick Heron's imposing residence, Eagles Nest, that the Grahams were introduced to Roger and Ruth Hilton. The latter was a musician and her technical knowledge was to prove very useful to Graham, for whom music was an essential part of life (see *Appendix B*). Though it would be 1965 before Hilton moved from London to Botallack, with his second wife Rose and their sons. There was an immediate rapport, as Graham's letters testify, followed by an intense relationship sparking a collision of egos, lovingly antagonistic, whisky-fuelled and painful for those in attendance. But the two men somehow fulfilled a provocative need in each other for a creative conflict that spurred on their art. Graham wrote some of his most inventive and lively letters to Hilton, but it's worth noting that, regrettably, Hilton's lengthy replies have not survived, leaving us incapable of fully understanding this unique, volatile liaison (the fact that Graham had an affair with Ruth can only have added further spice to the tortuous dynamic). The friendship resulted in two poems from Graham: 'Hilton Abstract' and the elegy 'Lines on Roger Hilton's Watch' – 'Which I was given because/I loved him and we had/Terrible times together'.

Nancy Wynne-Jones arrived in St Ives in 1957 and attended Lanyon's art classes at St

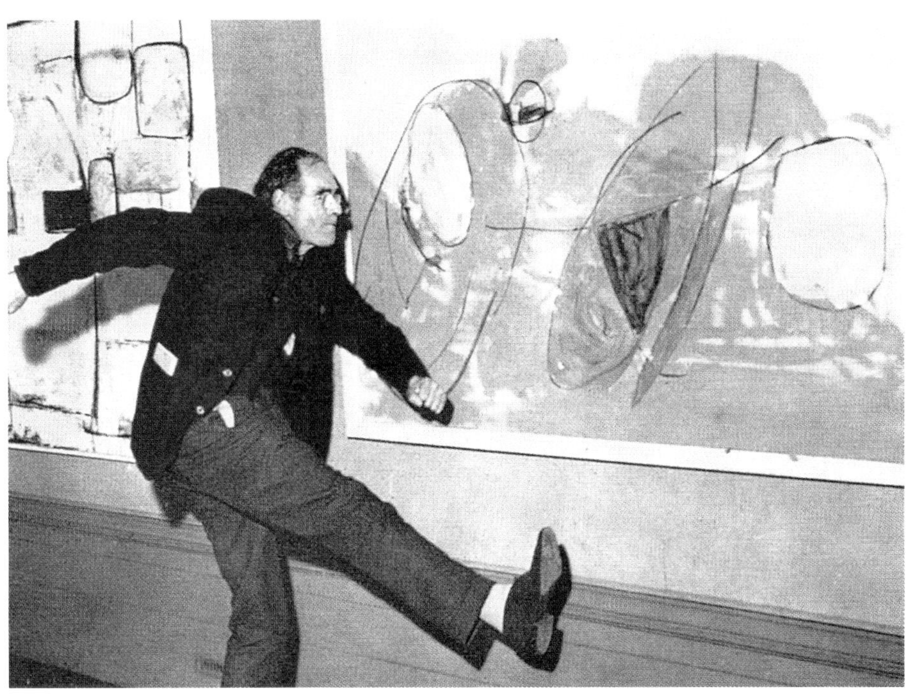

Roger Hilton attacking his own painting, 1963

Peter's Loft. She gives an account of first getting to know Graham:

Sydney (some called him Jock – he didn't mind) a gregarious but shy man, was unable to face people without the support of a drink. The artists' pubs in St Ives were The Castle, The Queen's, and especially The Sloop, a small old fashioned pub on the harbour front, frequented also by the local fishermen, who got on very well with the artists. Sydney would play darts, or table skittles, with Tommy the harbour pilot, before sitting down on one of the long polished benches, which would fill up with friends. He liked to hold the stage, was witty and brilliant.

He would often call in at St Peter's Loft, as he fancied himself as an understander of painting, would give us all an impromptu lecture on abstract art and how to do it. Peter Lanyon would say, 'Sydney has a great understanding of the creative process, but no plastic sense', and this was true – Sydney's drawings derive whole-heartedly from Picasso, were full of invention and charm, but strictly one-dimensional.

I believe this to be a fair assessment of Graham's visual work, except I would emphasise the Adler influence alongside Picasso. She goes on to describe the interior of the Coastguard's cottage:

Inside the house was a large room filled to the roof with jumble. Old clothes, old bottles, tattered books, thousands of yellowing newspapers and magazines, mouldering shoes, strange objects of all kinds. One day Sydney rummaged around in a heap for a while and emerged with an eighteenth-century snuffbox, which he gave to me. I have it still.

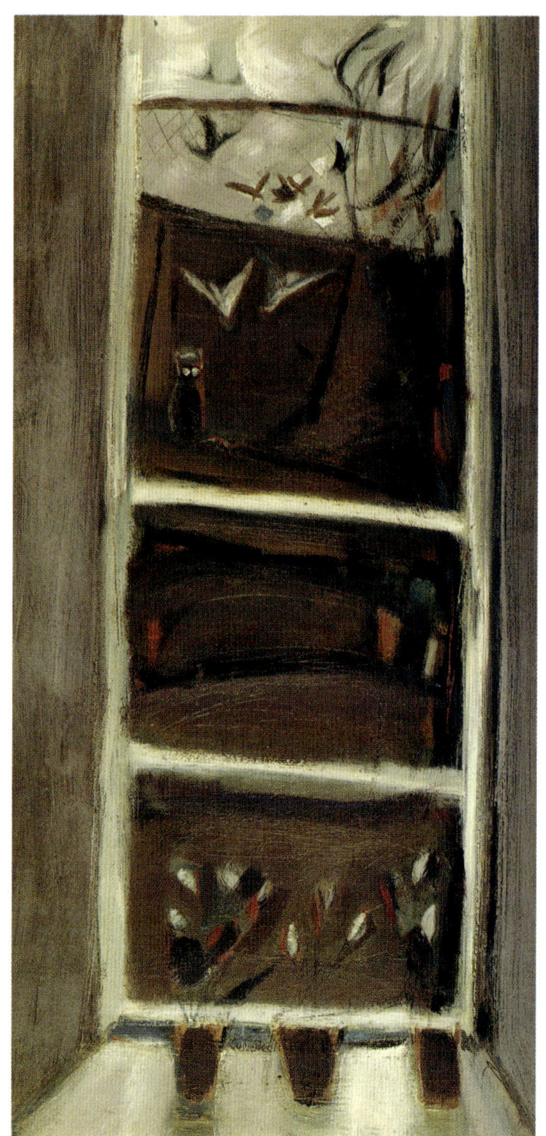

Tony O'Malley, *Sydney & Nessie Graham's Window, Trevaylor* 1963, oil on board, 122 x 61 cm

Beyond this room was another, equally large, where Sydney and Nessie lived. It had two large windows overlooking the sea, and between the windows was a kitchen chair, and a table with Sydney's typewriter on it. Other chairs were around, and there was a bed in the corner. Books, and pieces of paper with writing on them, were everywhere – on shelves, on chairs, on the floor. Sydney would

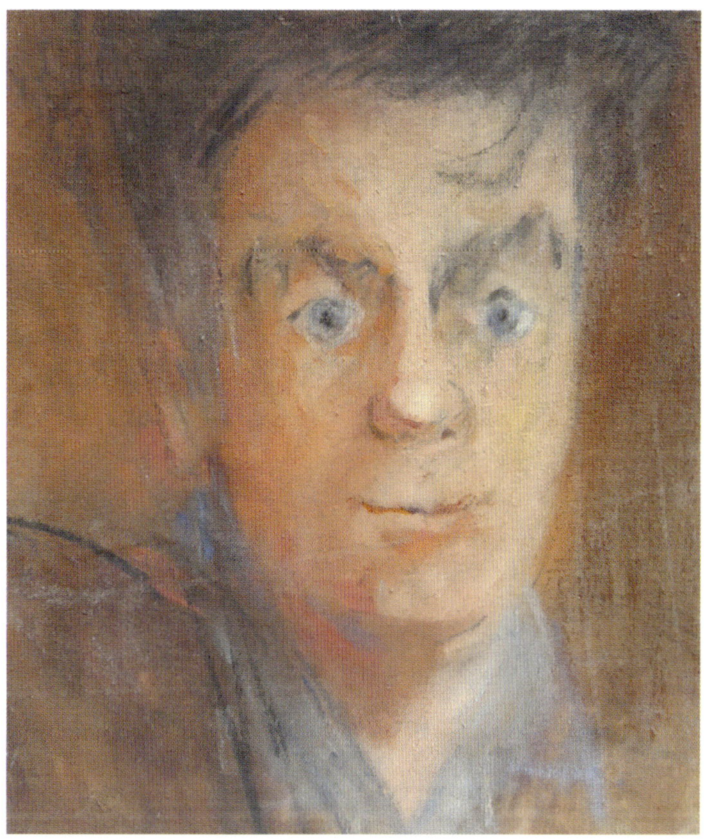

WSG by Rose Hilton, 1968, oil on canvas, 30.5 x 25.4

have decorated the room with odd grasses, or pieces of wood or stone which he had painted with Picasso-like heads or with geometric designs. At one time he cobwebbed the whole room with a huge three-dimensional design of string – and this some years before artists began to make similar things. There was no electricity in the house, and at night the room was lit by oil-lamps.

Wynne-Jones proceeded to play a significant role in the lives of the Grahams (in one way or another). In 1962 she bought Trevaylor House near Gulval. There was a small lodge on the other side of the road that she offered to the couple. They were only too pleased to move from the more remote and perishing poverty of the Gurnard's Head and apparently simply walked out of the Coastguard's cottage abandoning everything, ready to make a fresh start. They named the lodge Woodfield. For neighbours in the big house they had Tony O'Malley, Bill Featherston and the potter Boots Redgrave, amongst others.

O'Malley had arrived from Ireland in 1960 and quickly became a particularly close friend with Graham – two Celts in self-imposed exile. O'Malley had a richly poetic, lyrical turn of mind and was an avid reader of poetry. Highly musical, he played the squeezebox and harmonica, he also liked to break into song, further endearing him to Graham. O'Malley did many portraits of Graham and they collaborated on a piece *Owls Ruling a Wood at Night*. Graham dedicated the poem 'Master Cat and Master Me' to him.

Featherston, a Canadian, was a sculptor.

Some years later, in 1973, after he had returned to his homeland, Graham would stay with him on a reading tour he did of the country.

The tight-knit artistic community of St Ives was devastated when Peter Lanyon died suddenly, aged 47, in August 1964 as a consequence of a gliding accident. Graham clearly had informed conversations with him about the arts as evinced in his outstanding elegy 'The Thermal Stair': 'You said once in the Engine/House below Morvah/That words make their world/In the same way as a painter's/Mark surprises him/Into seeing new.'

Meanwhile, back at Trevaylor a difficult and complicated situation had developed when Graham became rather too involved with an enamoured Wynne-Jones, putting some strain on Nessie's fortitude. The situation improved later in 1964 when Nancy met the Irish sculptor Conor Fallon and they married shortly after.

But Wynne-Jones was always exceptionally generous to the Grahams. In 1961 she paid for Sydney to travel to Iceland, and in 1964 she took them both to Greece. Finally in 1967 she bought a cottage in nearby Madron for the Grahams to live in rent free for the rest of their lives.

Alan Lowndes was a self-taught artist from Stockport who lived, with his family, in St Ives and then Halsetown. In his art he was a sensitive observer of working class people going about their daily lives, in a figurative slightly 'primitive' style. He could be intellectually combative and Graham found him great company when trawling around the pubs in the area.

Michael Snow, along with his wife Margaret, were always supportive and encouraging to Graham (see *Appendix B*). A close reader of Graham's writings, Snow was strongly influenced by the aesthetic ideas they generated. Many decades later the Snows edited an invaluable edition of Graham's letters.

Karl Weschke had been a German PoW who stayed on in England after the war. He settled initially near Zennor in the 1950s, living in D. H. Lawrence's old cottage at Tregerthen before settling high above Cape Cornwall. Another self-exile, he remained an outsider to the so-called St Ives school with his sometimes savage figurative art. He has recognised a correspondence with his work and Graham's.

Artist and mountaineer Don Brown had been camping at Gurnard's Head in 1962 when he met Graham who was intrigued enough by Brown's rock climbing activities to write the poem 'The Don Brown Route'. Many years later Brown constructed a memorial cairn for Graham, containing a copy of the poem, on the edge of a glacier in the Himalayas.

Anthony Benjamin, an ex-pugilist, was living near St Ives, and had been friendly with Graham, when he enrolled at the teaching

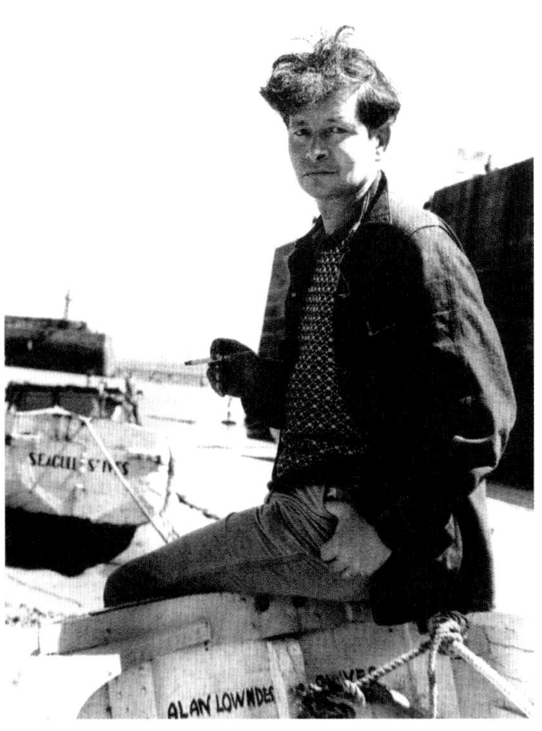

Alan Lowndes, St Ives harbour

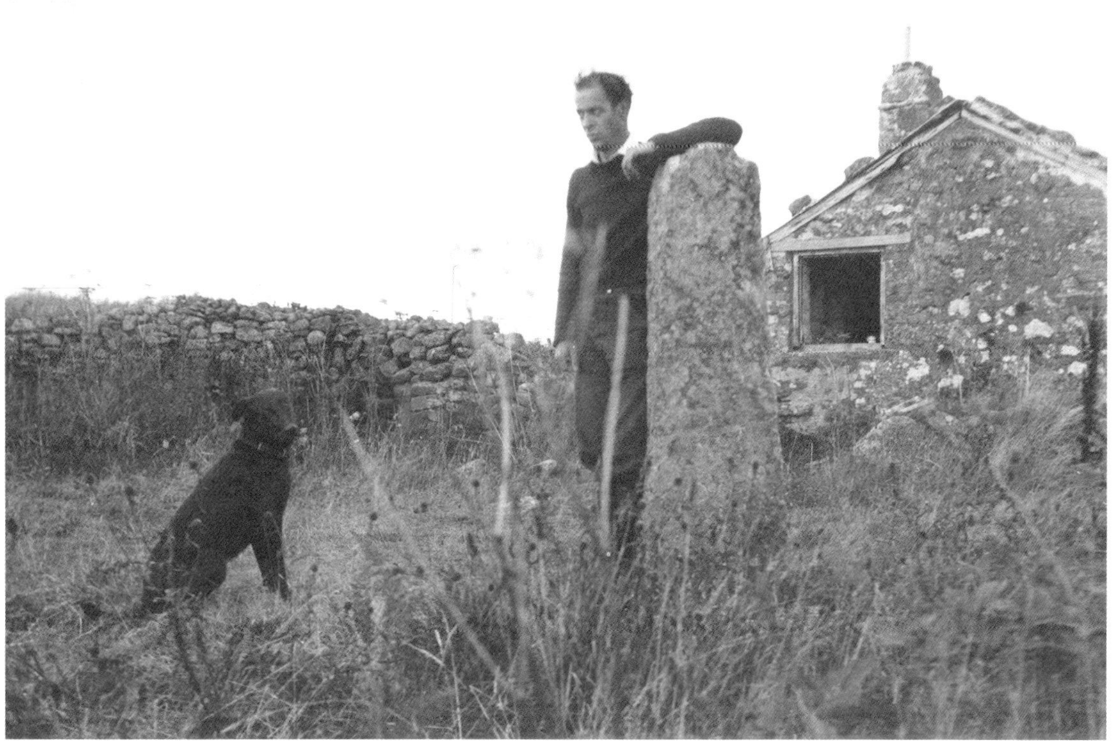

Bryan Wynter at Carn Cottage, early 1950s

studios, Atelier 17 in Paris, of the innovative printmaker S. W. Hayter. Benjamin happened to have with him a copy of *The Nightfishing* and he responded to 'The Seven Letters' section by producing seven etchings using automatist, aleatory techniques resulting in fluid, aqueous and highly abstract images. Proofs of the etchings were sent to a London gallery, from Paris, in 1959 but were lost, while the original plates were forgotten until their rediscovery in 1993 (still wrapped in French newspapers) and a limited edition followed in 1999.

Bryan Wynter remained a staunch supporter of Graham. They also shared an outrageous sense of humour, delighting in practical jokes and a love of puns. 'Wynter and the Grammarsow' is full of this sense of fun. Graham's letters to Wynter demonstrate a huge

affection as well as gratitude and after Wynter's death in 1975, Graham produced perhaps his most touching elegy 'Dear Bryan Wynter', lamenting: 'And nobody will laugh/At my jokes like you.'

This is an incomplete catalogue of the extraordinary number of visual artists who Graham engaged with throughout his mature life. There were many more, including Terry Frost, Trevor Bell (who designed posters for Graham's readings at Newlyn), Robert Brennan, Pat Dolan, Jeremy Le Grice (for whose children Graham knitted hats), Michael Canney and Tony 'Doc' Shiels, but we don't have much on record to draw on regarding their relationships.

Immersed as he was in a community of mainly experimental artists, there can be no doubt that their efforts at undermining the

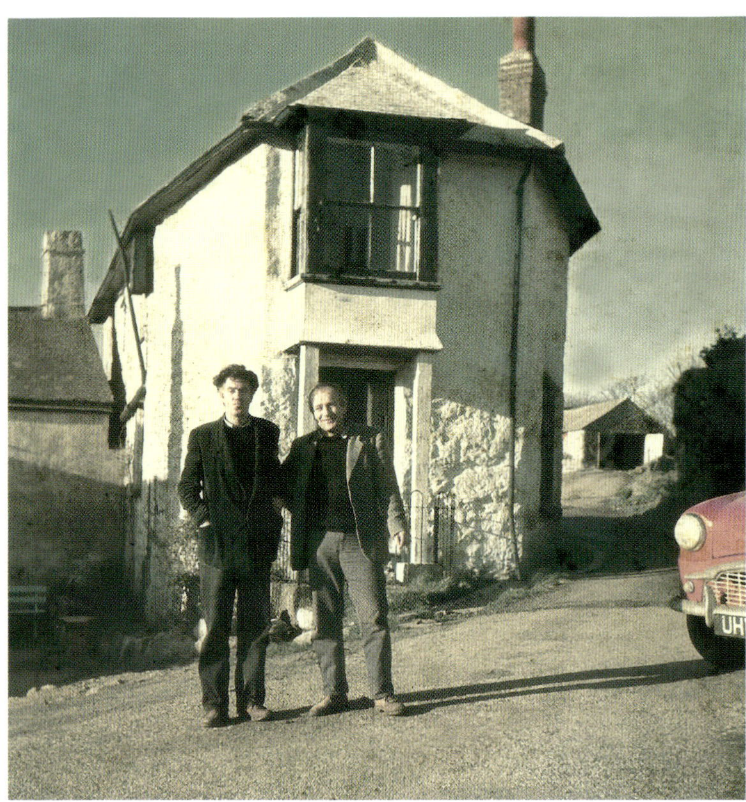

WSG & Karl Weschke, Zennor, *c.* 1958

habits of visual perception entered his own struggles to 'disturb the language' of the written word. There was much talk of space amongst these artists and Graham too was interested in the space the page offered him in constructing his poems. There are various accounts of how he surrounded himself with words and phrases written on large pieces of card, and something of the engineering skills he acquired as a young man came into play here. But it wasn't only a matter of syntax, a shuffling of the words to create a kind of mosaic. Graham's real exertions had to do with semantics, how to impress an abstract meaning into the poem that was capable of spanning the space between him and the reader. There was one more essential ingredient for Graham in how to achieve this: *the sound of the poem*. He frequently asked friends to read aloud his work before showing them how it should be done. (It's worth seeking out any opportunities to hear recordings of Graham doing this.) And here *time* comes into play. He often spoke of the shape of the poem and we're inclined to look at the pattern of words on the page. But when heard, the poem comes alive in a very different way as it unfolds, the pauses or silences (difficult to detect on the page) gradually acquire a potency that assist in conveying a significance to the attentive listener or reader, and this is perhaps where his concern with music also comes into play.

As a poet, Graham had rather a lonely existence in Cornwall. It's a curious fact that his friendships with fellow poets during these three decades were conducted largely through correspondence. There exist fascinating letters regarding his craft to Edwin Morgan (in Glasgow), Robin Skelton (in Canada), Michael

Hamburger (in Suffolk), Norman Macleod (in the US) and C. H. Sisson (in Kent). There had always been a strong competitive streak in Graham, and it may well have suited him that the Land's End peninsula was reserved all to himself as the leading wordsmith.

After Graham settled in Cornwall in 1956 he stayed put for the remaining thirty years of his life. Though the area was packed with painters, sculptors and potters of a remarkably high calibre it lacked writers, and particularly poets, of equal distinction. Arthur Caddick was a formidable writer in his way but was chiefly a satirist and writer of comic verse; Norman Levine also wrote some excellent short stories, but Graham was very much *the* writer of the 'group' and most of the artists looked to him as at least an equal if not a paragon in how a 'poet or painter steers his life to maim/Himself somehow for the job'.

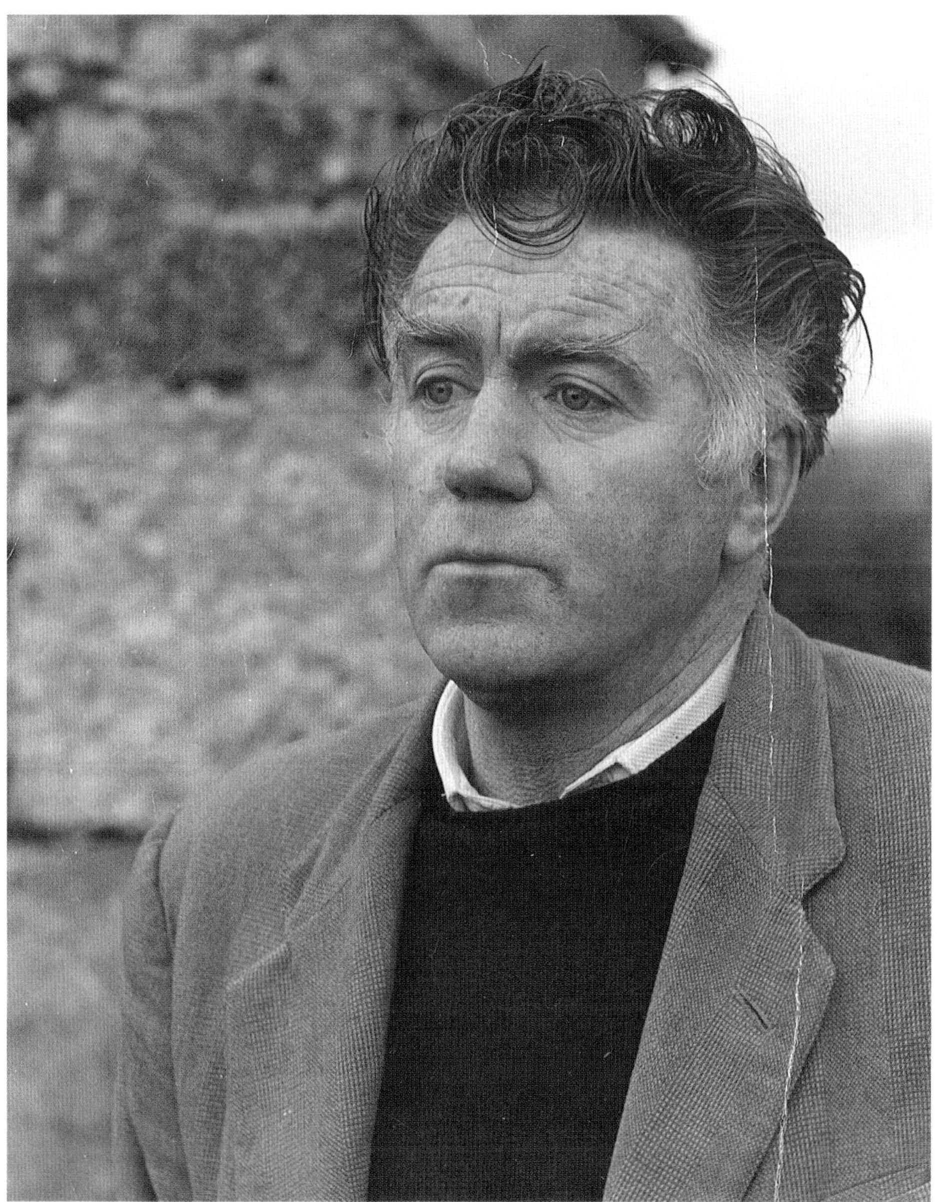

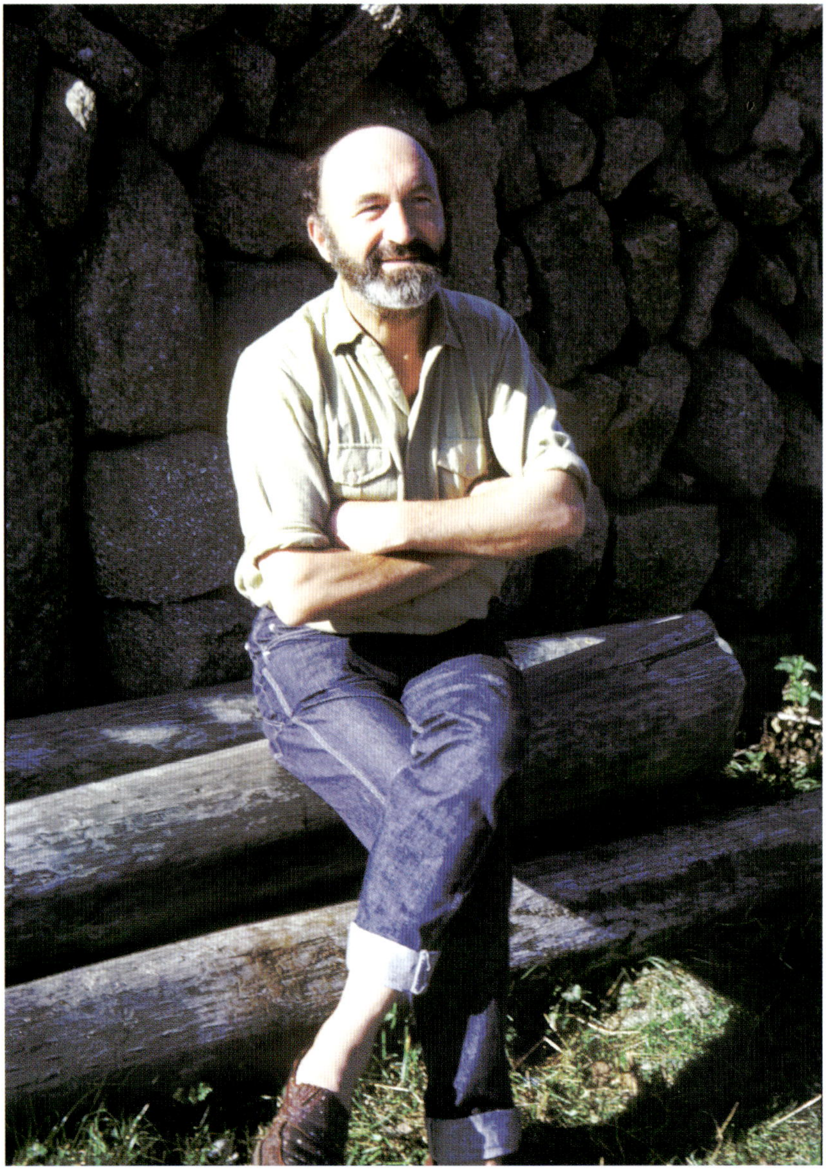

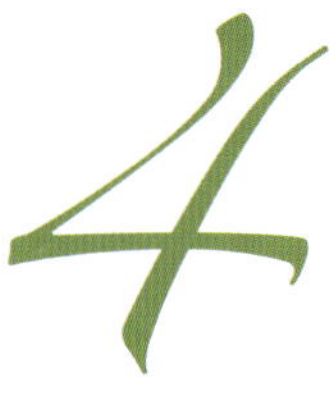

4

Tony O'Malley:
The Watching Windhover

GERARD MANLEY HOPKINS was a priest and a poet, two conflicting roles, as it turned out, during his short, troubled life (he died in 1889 in Dublin aged 44). It is, of course, in the role of poet that he will be remembered, leaving some of the most original poems in the English language including 'The Wreck of the Deutschland' and 'The Windhover', developed from his own preoccupations with an inimitable technical virtuosity. But another important side to Hopkins is often overlooked, and that is his prose writings, particularly his journals (not written for publication). Perhaps no writer has ever matched his acute powers of observation of natural phenomena, including descriptions of clouds, trees, flowers, rain, wind, shifting shades of light, the movement of waves and the flowing of streams, geological formations, and constellations. As a further aid to his graphic acumen he developed his own vocabulary, including the terms 'inscape' and 'instress', of which he made no formal definitions. But they can be roughly summarised in saying that 'inscape' is a principle of dynamic pattern formation, immanent in the natural world, that gives each thing its unique essence, while 'instress' is the ability of the human mind to detect 'inscape'.

Tony O'Malley was an avid reader of Hopkins, as indeed he was of many poets. He also loved windhovers, a dialect name for the kestrel (and occasionally falcons), and their significance is apparent in the titles of important paintings, including *The Windhover – He searches Winter* (a series), *The Grave of the*

Windhovers, The Watching Windhover. In fact there are countless paintings and drawings throughout his entire oeuvre featuring nearly every type of bird (but birds of prey, including owls, take prominence during the early 1960s). 'Inscape' also features in titles and O'Malley eagerly seized on the word as a potent and meaningful concept for what he was attempting to achieve in his art and it regularly cropped up in his conversations:

> Although I have lived in Cornwall for thirty years, my home place and its landscape is still in my psyche. I call it inscape – inner revelations of the outer psyche.

O'Malley was born in the small town of Callan, near Kilkenny, in 1913. Growing up, he received no encouragement whatsoever in the arts. The only visual art he was exposed to was religious, especially the sculptural carvings in churches and ruined abbeys in the area. He spent his spare time exploring the countryside (mainly fishing), but he did start sketching in his mid-teens. Soon after finishing school he secured a position with the Munster & Leinster Bank that required travelling around the various branches and this remained his job for the best part of the next twenty-five years. Along the way, serious health issues intervened, including pleurisy, pneumonia and full blown TB (the latter requiring the collapsing of a lung as part of the cure). Regular periods of treatment and recuperation were called for in various hospitals and sanitoria, and it was under these somewhat uncomfortable and depressing circumstances that O'Malley, for assuagement, turned to drawing, and in 1945 produced his first oil painting (a still life) – the course of his life as an artist was now set.

Unfortunately Ireland in the 1950s couldn't have been less congenial for someone seriously wanting to pursue the arts as a career. It was a highly conservative, reactionary society and any kind of cultural innovation was frowned upon and even mocked as the Catholic Church maintained a suffocating stranglehold on what people were allowed to think and do. It was a remarkable stroke of luck for O'Malley when he spotted an advert in *The New Statesman* for a painting course in St Ives in Cornwall and he duly turned up there in May 1955 (in rather formal tweed jacket and tie, looking every inch a bank official). It was held in St Peter's Loft, above the present location of the Penwith Gallery, and was run by Bill Redgrave and Peter Lanyon. It was the latter in particular who acted as exemplar for an excited O'Malley:

> *I did realise that Peter had broken – it's the equivalent to say, breaking the sound barrier – the appearance barrier, to break through the outer skin into the underneath. That this man had done it – that was why I regarded him as an innovator.*

> *One thing I felt from him was sympathy; he was sympathetic to people, he would detect their aims. He had his own landscape and he had reached it – 'inscape', I suppose. I was more interested in 'inscape' than 'outscape', the subjective side of painting, and subjectivity itself, it was a thing that tormented me. Yet it was outside, to be dealt with and knotted together in some way by just me for my own sake, and for nobody else's.*

> *Peter was generous because he had immense vitality and enthusiasm; he was really enthusiastic for paintings and for others' paintings, he made you feel everything was possible – that was really one of his great facets.*

On this visit, lasting three weeks, O'Malley met most of the key artists working in the area and the whole experience proved a revelation for him: he would never look at the world in the same way again and his return to Ireland was to prove a dispiriting experience after this taste of artistic and social liberation. He returned to St Ives for more of the same in 1957. After the death of his close brother Matty, and with much encouragement from his good friend the poet Padraic Fallon, he finally departed the Irish shores, by cattle boat, early in 1960.

O'Malley soon settled in at the welcoming guesthouse run by Boots Redgrave (wife of Bill), and acquired the Old Piazza Studio (he had a modest pension from the bank to help him along). In Ireland he had developed his own style of Expressionist figurative painting and drawing. Inevitably, considering his new milieu, there was a gradual shift to non-objective work (his own preferred term over 'abstract').

O'Malley's new life almost ended before it had begun when, in May 1961, he suffered

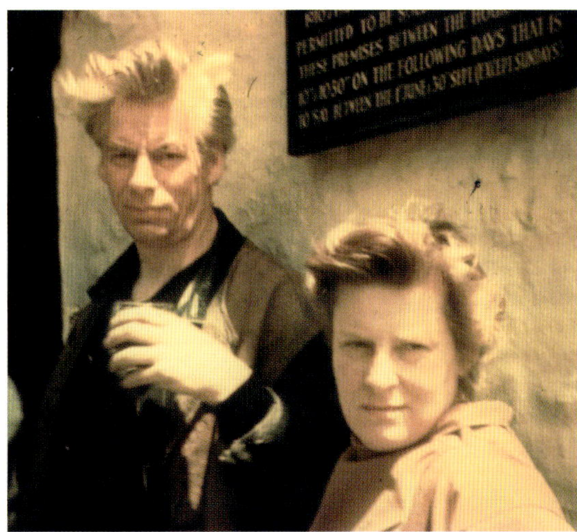

Bill & Boots Redgrave, St Ives, mid-1950s

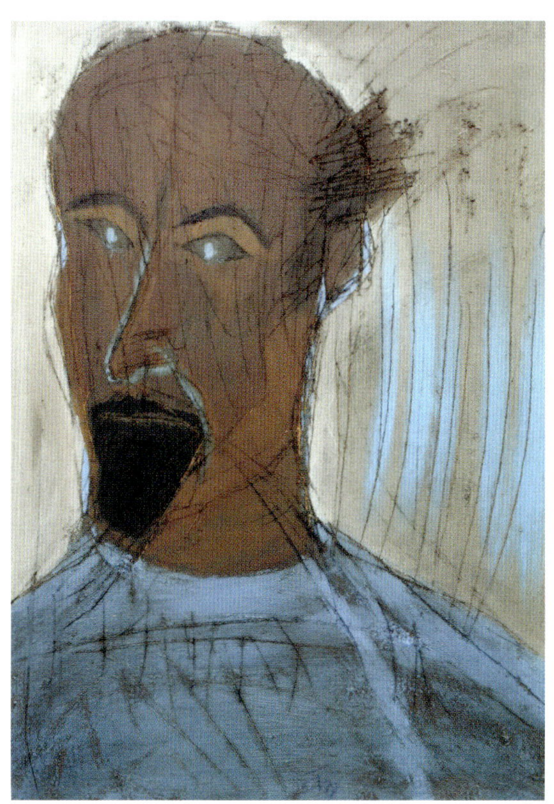

Self-Portrait 1963, oil on board, 91.5 x 61 cm

a severe heart attack. Thanks to some speedy work by Dr Roger Slack his life was saved and he spent some time in Edward Hain Hospital, sharing a room with Bryan Wynter, who also suffered a heart attack the same week, and they developed a close friendship. Nevertheless, his continuing ill health kept him forever wary that the Grim Reaper may well be lurking in the vicinity, impelling him to keep working and not waste time.

O'Malley said that, 'Nature was there for me before art' and in 1962 he moved further into the countryside at Trevaylor House, near Gulval, as part of a small artists' colony set up by Nancy Wynne-Jones and Boots. (He shared the facilities there with Nessie and Sydney Graham, and Bill Featherston, amongst others.) The rural feel of the place, including nearby Trevaylor Woods, fed his particular brand of

nature-based abstraction. At night he often lurked in the grounds listening and responding in kind to the hooting of the owls. By day he took his inspiration from the surrounding antiquities (quoits), Ding Dong mine, one of the oldest mine workings in Cornwall, and a local quarry, all enhanced by his great knowledge of the flora and fauna.

Despite this seemingly idyllic set up O'Malley now showed signs of being depressed. His condition can be detected in the many self-portraits he frequently produced, they were like a visual diary of his daily moods. He still painted, from memory, scenes from his area of Ireland, as well as images prompted from Irish mythology and literature. This suggests a longing or homesickness. He was, as an acutely sensitive artist, forced into self-exile for the sake of psychological survival. It's difficult to convey to anyone who didn't live through these decades

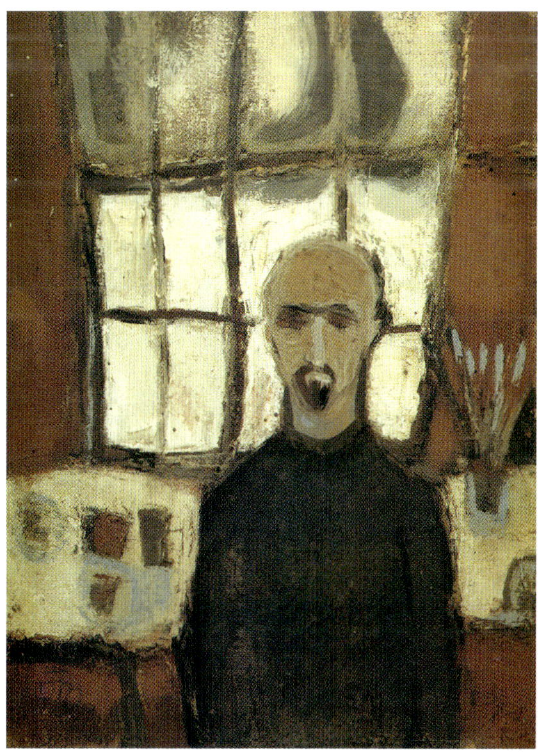

Self-Portrait, Winter, Heavy Snowfall at Trevaylor 1962-63, oil on canvas, 46 x 36 cm

in Ireland the stifling tyranny of the Church hierarchy, the incessant cruelty, harshness and abuse of power meted out to innocent citizens by the clergy. Cornwall was O'Malley's salvation, but it came at a price, he had been a man very much rooted in Ireland, with a rich family lineage going back hundreds of years. He now felt adrift from his element. Nevertheless, Cornwall (and especially the Land's End peninsula) chimed with O'Malley's spirit, and its rich multi-faceted inscape lifted him to paint some of his finest work. Memory is inextricably entwined with a sense of identity, and Irish ghosts haunt the landscape from this period as he detected psychic echoes of a shared Celtic ancestry. The Cornish people had also suffered immense exploitation by those in power intent on reaping the rewards of the copper and tin mining industries. He explained:

> In Ireland I was attached to all the old historic places, which were loaded with history … They weren't just landscapes, they were powerscapes if you like; they were invested with a certain type of power for me. I continued painting them even after coming here. It was an invisible force, but I had to recognise it as a certain kind of force inside myself.

Of course O'Malley could be wonderfully gregarious and entertaining company, but he was essentially intensely private. He needed solitude to focus on his work, and this was much respected by his fellow artists at Trevaylor. Music was an important ingredient for creating certain moods. For example, Schubert's *Winterreise* ('Winter Journey') could be heard playing in his room, repeatedly, while he worked on certain bleak chilly pictures. Many paintings have the seasons feature in the titles, but during these early years in Cornwall winter predominates, including *Winter Morning,*

Winter Silence, Winter Lamp, Winter Landscape, He Searches Winter - The Windhover. It was a season in tune with his overall mood, but the winter twilight, uniquely, has the capacity to activate something mysterious, normally undetected in the harsh, silent landscape. O'Malley also played Messiaen's *Le Reveil des Oiseaux* while working on the intricate *Bird Song Circle* series. The latter, in particular, suggests a synaesthetic sensibility where song is visualised in colour and pattern.

At this time his preferred medium was oil on board. These boards were heavily scored, in keeping with the carving effects of his Kilkenny forebears (particularly the O'Tunney family of sculptors from the fifteenth and sixteenth century). He then applied layer upon layer of paint. (It's a sad fact that this textural intricacy cannot be adequately conveyed in book reproductions.) Curiously, this proved to be a form of inverse excavation, the more the layers built up the deeper O'Malley descended into his psyche to explore his personal 'inscape'. There is an ancient Greek term *katabasis*, meaning a descent into the underworld as part of a mythic quest. It was explored in literature by Homer and later by Ovid and Virgil (the myth of Orpheus is a classic example). This may well throw some light on O'Malley's plight as a man in psychological crisis. He also drew, literally, inspiration from his lucid dreams. Growing up in rural Ireland O'Malley was always exposed to the world of the supernatural by way of folklore. It nourished his imagination and kept him alert to the possibility that just below the surface of the natural world there were other, sometimes darker, forces for the human subconscious to contend with. This is not to say that O'Malley was a man enthralled to the Kingdom of Faerie, far from it. He had, after all, held down a serious bank job for a quarter of a century. But there is no doubt he was a lyrical, mythopoeic

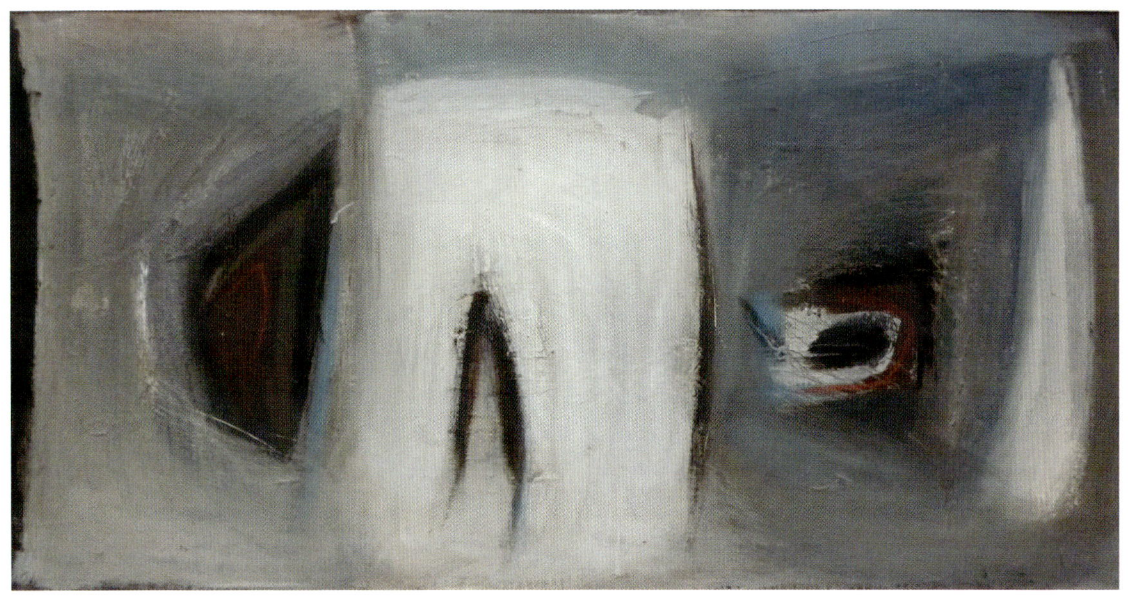

Reflections of an Old Landscape 1964, oil on board, 61 x 122 cm (detail below)

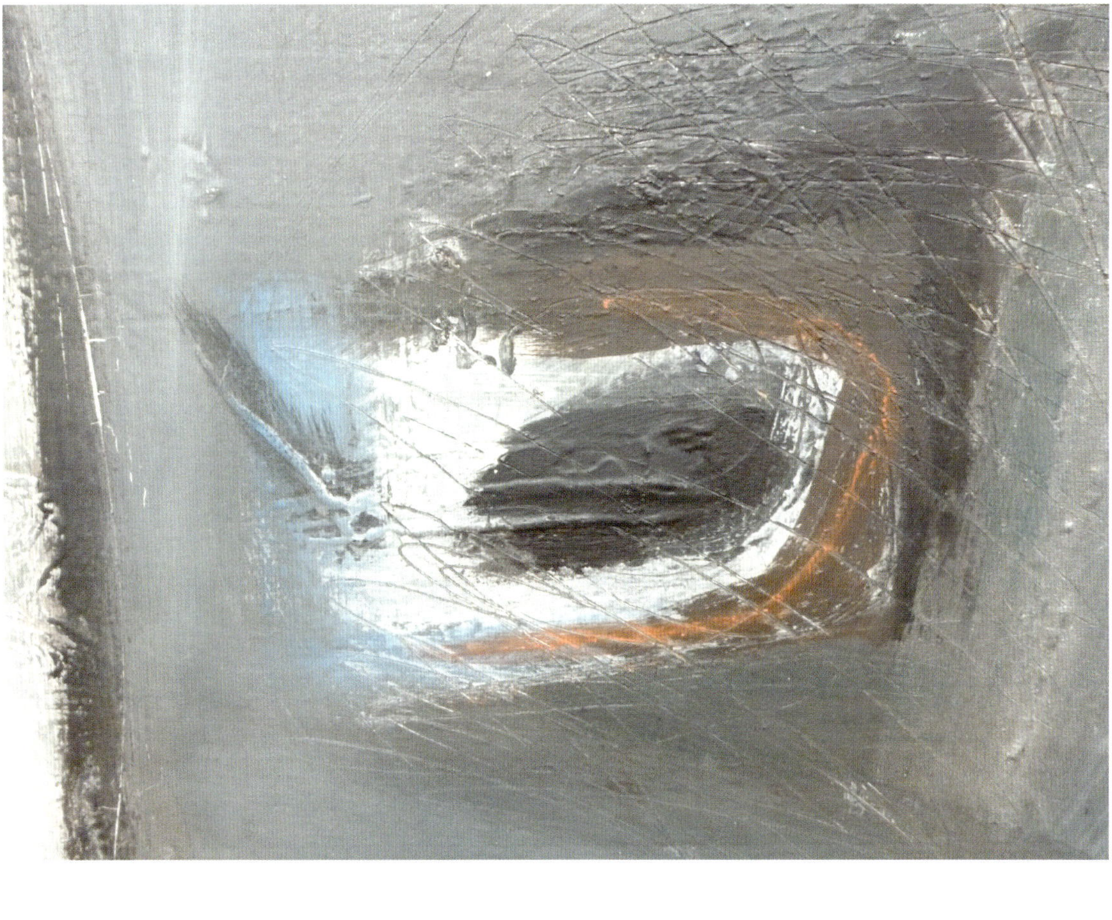

artist, diving into a pool of unconscious, archetypal imagery to explore a bountiful inner life, evinced in a highly personal visual language. The results have a chamber music melancholy, with a primitive, elemental aura radiating a luminous absence. This subtle quality was noted by Patrick Heron, when he pointed out: 'Despite its low key, chromatically speaking, and despite its almost granular textures, the surface of an oil painting or a gouache by O'Malley *invariably* glows.'

I am not suggesting that O'Malley was self-consciously applying ancient myth to dealing with an existential predicament as some form of therapy. Though he was no longer a practising Catholic, there were still aspects of his religious upbringing that remained essential for his dealing with the enigmas of life. For example, annually he produced a Good Friday painting (some of his most powerful work), implying an ongoing concern with the moving story of the Easter Passion. He was also hugely influenced by the Buddhist aesthetics of China and Japan, and knowledge of the latter, in particular, came from Bernard Leach, who proved to be a significant mentor. In addition, he regularly expressed an affinity with pantheism, seeing the whole of nature as an expression of immanent divinity. In other words, for the artist O'Malley, life was a spiritual odyssey.

He was only too painfully aware of the difficulties his profoundly incomparable work presented to the viewer, but the act of creation proved just as formidable for himself:

I think the word 'hermetic' would apply to it. The subjectivity of the painting itself, of the relationship, the dialogue between me, and that piece of board or surface, is very mysterious to me … I am linked up in one extraordinary way with it to the point that I accept something after a long, long, almost interminable time working at it.

There is no immediacy in it at all – slowness actually. That I accept it then – it's what I've done but it somehow speaks back to me, and yet I like to think that it might speak to somebody else as well, that it might have communication in it.

Under the weight of despondency O'Malley looked to the skies for redemption. The abundance of bird life where he was living gave him immense pleasure (in fact wherever he was, birds enter into his art), in particular the raptors, creatures of solitude. They are revealed in the many titles of work from the '60s, including (we've already mentioned windhovers): *Hawk and Quarry in Winter, The Hawk Owl, Hawk's Landscape, Owls Ruling a Wood at Night, The Falcon's Gyre* and *Winter Owl.* These creatures have fascinated humans the world over and play a potent role in folklore and myth, often acting as omens and harbingers. With intense observation, through his painting (and following the mode of Hopkins), O'Malley gradually entered into the inscape of these creatures. He allowed his ego to dissolve as he took flight and underwent a metamorphosis of perception of the landscape. Not just an imagined bird's eye view, but their invisible flight paths became scored and traced as lines of force into his painting, to define and embellish an otherwise 'empty' space. O'Malley's identification with this soaring freedom took him out of himself and uplifted his spirits.

Katabasis is complemented by *anabasis*, meaning 'an ascent.' In Greek myth it refers to the return of the hero from the underworld, often stronger and wiser after the endurance experienced. O'Malley had some additional help in achieving this when, in 1970, he met the Canadian artist Jane Harris, more than 30 years his junior. They married in 1973 and had a fulfilled loving relationship until O'Malley's death in 2003, aged 89.

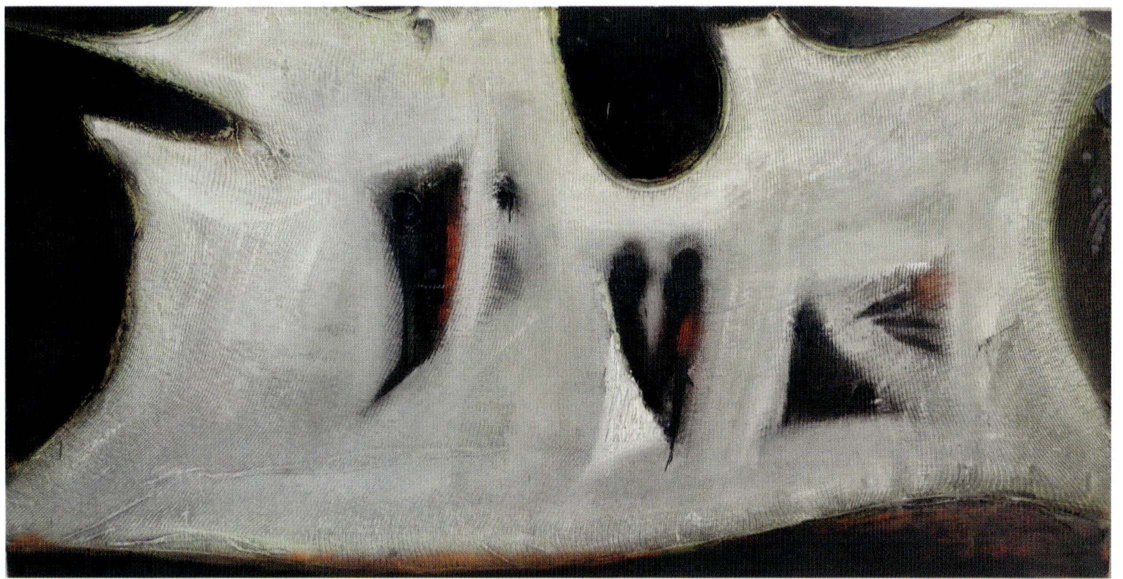

The Grave of the Windhovers 1965, oil & mixed media on board, 61 x 122 cm (detail below)

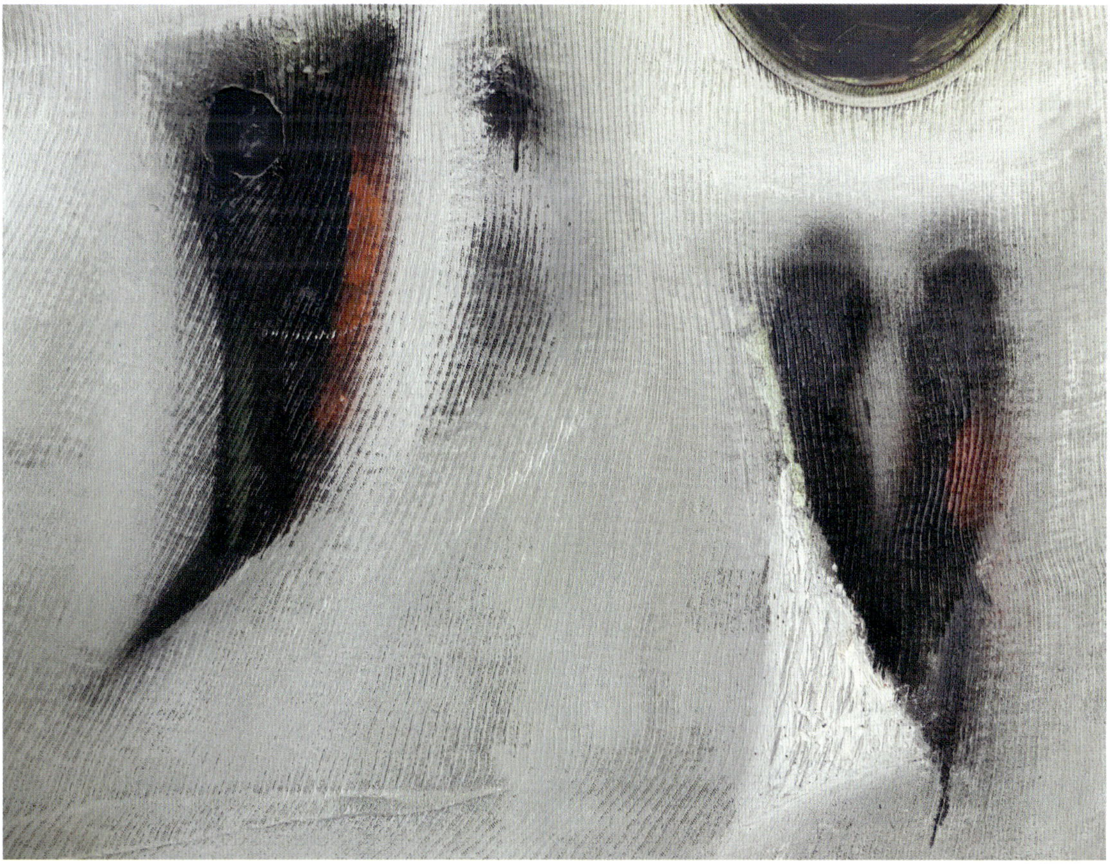

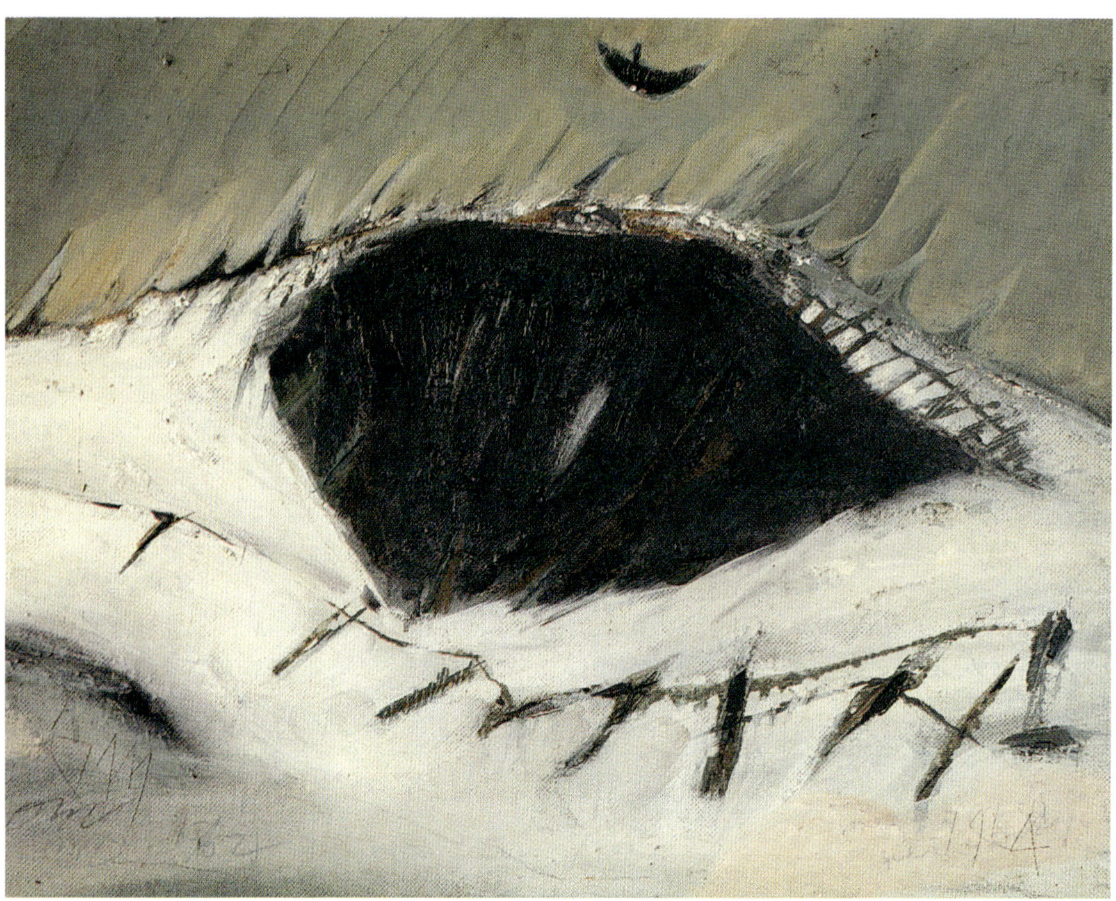

Hawk and Quarry in Winter, in Memory of Peter Lanyon 1964, oil on board, 53 x 72.5 cm

They travelled to the Bahamas regularly where O'Malley's artistic palette underwent a totally unexpected transformation, resulting in an exotic chromatic explosion, in response to the brilliant light and flora. In fact it's difficult to reconcile the art that developed from the 1970s onwards to what went before. O'Malley emerged from the saturnine '60s as a new man with a spring in his step and a revitalized vision of the world. But that's another story altogether.

He remained a modest, gentle man of integrity (and is recalled by many with touching affection). He also maintained an almost childlike amazement that his private daily mark making somehow resulted in art that enchanted many people. Speaking with typical, cultivated naivety he said:

I paint over paint all the time, because I like to feel that there's a lot of paint building up to something. So the unconscious side of painting is very important to me – an image appears and I hold onto it and maybe a minute later I dismiss it and go on to something else. I always think of a good painting as something that really slumbers on the wall and has a certain power emanating from it; and I'd presume to say you give it that power by not thinking about it. I think painting is only what I call an emanation of all these feelings and poetries and sensations and is unspeakable,

*if you like, is the word. It's like singing a
song or playing a tune on the mouth organ
or something like that – a force from inside
and the painting is only an evidence of these
forces. The kernel of the painting is the part
you cannot speak.*

Finally, at O'Malley's funeral the presence
of Gerard Manley Hopkins was manifest when
'The Windhover' was read, with feeling and
understanding, by Seamus Heaney. A fitting
farewell for a poet of the brush, who shared
an acute creaturely kinship with that soaring
master of poise and grace.

> *I caught this morning morning's minion, king-*
> > *dom of daylight's dauphin, dapple-dawn-drawn Falcon, in his riding*
> > *Of the rolling level underneath him steady air, and striding*
> *High there, how he rung upon the rein of a wimpling wing*
> *In his ecstacy!*

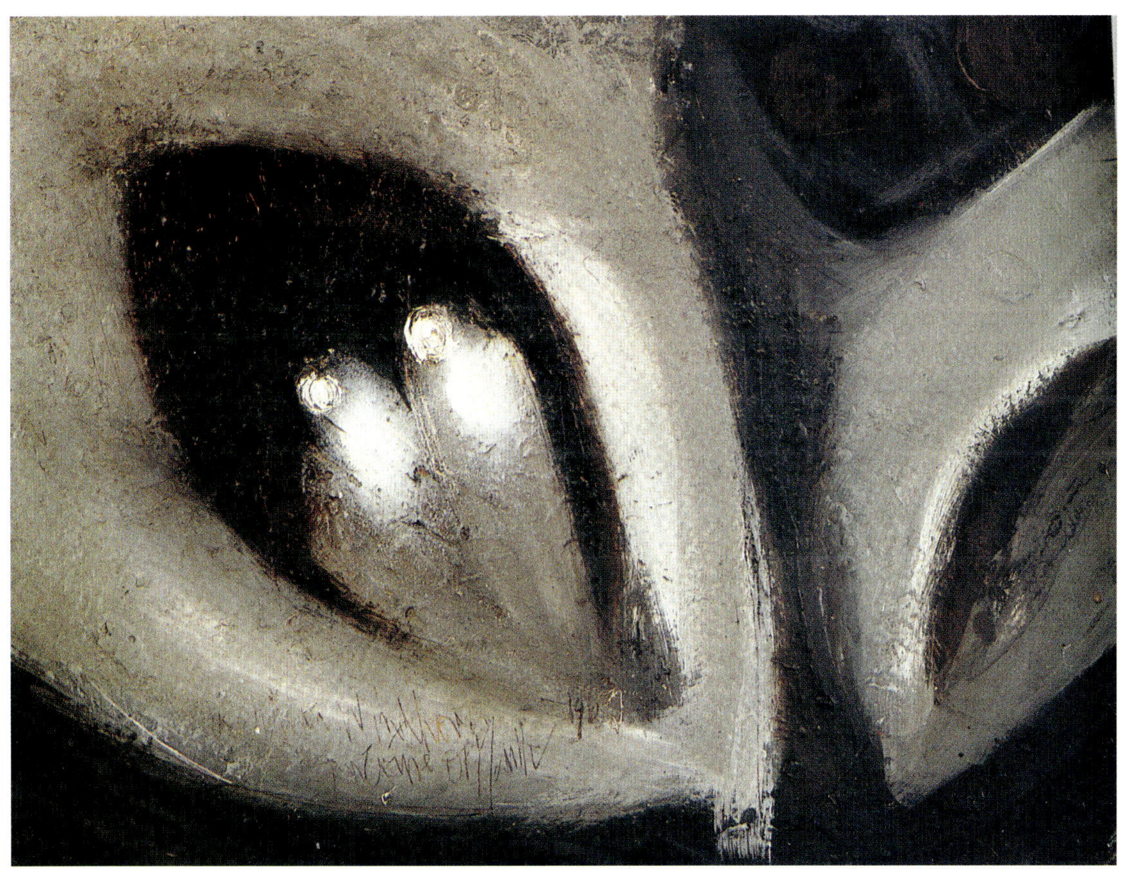

The Windhover – He Searches Winter, No. 2 1963, oil on board, 41.9 x 54.6 cm

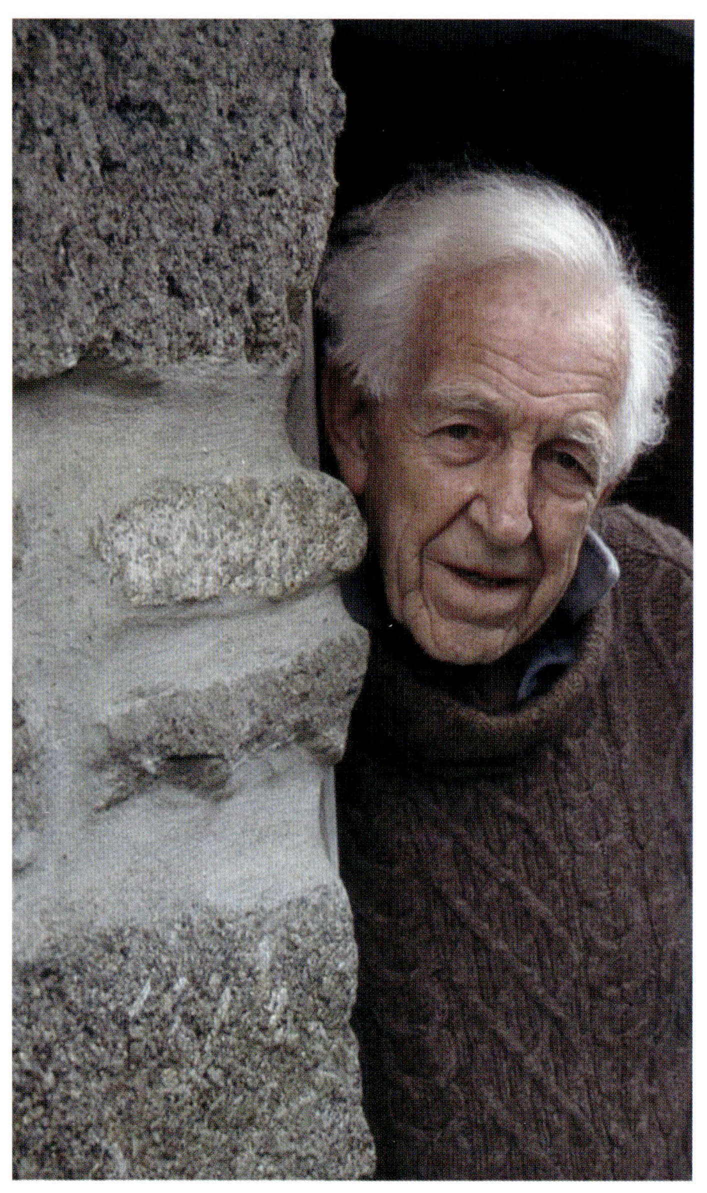

5

The Healing Art of
Dr Roger Slack

COURTESY, CIVILITY AND old-world-charm combined with a deep sense of empathy are virtues rather neglected in the modern age. But Dr Roger Slack, who was the GP for St Ives between 1947 and 1984, oozed such qualities in a reassuring manner to everyone who met him.

Born in Warrington in 1919, Roger went to Shrewsbury School before pursuing the study of medicine in 1937 at St John's College Cambridge (though he might well have become an engineer). His newly acquired skills were called on in the most harrowing way during the war, dealing with U-boat casualties, when he served as a naval lieutenant on destroyers in the North Atlantic.

On a brief leave from this horror show, while in playful combat on the rugby pitch, Roger was concussed. As it turned out, this fortuitous incident gained him the caring attention of an attractive young nurse called Janet, and they married in 1944 (going on to have three children: Elisabeth, Pippa and Jonathan).

In searching for a practice in post-war austerity, St Ives came to light purely as somewhere affordable and they soon settled into Sycamore Cottage just over the road from the Leach Pottery. It just so happened, at this time, that the small harbour town was becoming a magnet for artists and writers, partly drawn there by the presence of Ben Nicholson and Barbara Hepworth, as well as the famous Cornish light and the economy of living. Most of them fell under the care of Roger.

Rarely, if ever, in the annals of medical history can there have been a physician with such an illustrious clientele of artistic patients. Not only Hepworth and Nicholson (the latter, despite being a Christian Scientist still sought out Roger's ministration) but also Peter Lanyon, Patrick Heron, Bryan Wynter, Terry Frost, Breon O'Casey, Sven Berlin, Alan Lowndes, Wilhelmina Barns-Graham, Tony O'Malley, Bernard Leach, Denis Mitchell and the poet Sydney Graham. These are just a few of the better-known names, but over the course of nearly forty years there was hardly an artist in the area of west Cornwall who escaped Roger's attention, if not examination. The Slacks soon became a part of the social artistic scene and Sycamore Cottage gradually filled up with art works donated by various artists, testifying to their affection and appreciation for Roger's therapeutic abilities. This resulted in an impressive collection, which included a Hepworth sculpture, *Sphere with Inner Form*, given to them in 1965 and placed, slightly incongruously, in their small back garden. Roger even found time to be a fine sculptor himself, demonstrating sleek modernist lines, and Hepworth was impressed enough to share some of her precious marble with him.

During the 1950s Roger began to tape-record reminiscences of elderly local people, which included memories of the 'primitive' painter Alfred Wallis. This was the start of his archival instincts and over the coming decades Roger was a regular figure with his camera at the private viewings of the many art shows in and around St Ives, leaving us a unique record of the town's art scene. These photographs are now housed at the St Ives Archive Study Centre.

Roger was amused when, in his mid-sixties, he told the poet Sydney Graham how much he was looking forward to retiring. The impecunious bard replied, in a slightly startled and superior tone, 'But we poets *never* retire'.

His retirement saw him playing another archival role recording, also on tape, concerts and talks for the International Music Seminars based at Prussia Cove. Indeed, music was an important part of home life, as Janet played piano (in addition to being a highly regarded jewellery designer).

'YOU MUST SPEAK to Dr Slack', urged Jane O'Malley on more than one occasion, while I was working on my study of Tony. And so it was, on a January morning in 2003 that I found myself at the door of tucked away Sycamore Cottage. I rang the bell (an *actual* bell) and was welcomed by a tall dignified figure and a man who liked to wear his collar protruding up from under his jumper. Roger introduced me to Janet, now rather frail and in poor health. His gentle, caring manner with her was immediately apparent and touched me deeply. It was an old rambling cottage with low beams and everywhere I looked there were books, piles of magazines and journals, paintings and pottery. There was also a Samick baby grand piano with a portrait of Chopin placed on it. Janet played regularly, particularly Chopin as well as Beethoven. Roger took me on a little tour pointing out work by various artists including John Wells, Patrick Heron, Bryan Pearce, Roger Hilton, Peter Lanyon, Bryan Wynter, Alfred Wallis and several by Tony O'Malley. Many items of Leach pot were

also dotted about the place, not so much as art but for everyday utilitarian use. He explained that he had, regrettably, sold the Hepworth sculpture as they found it very difficult to insure during a period when her public work was regularly being stolen. As a long-time bookdealer and bibliophile I was very impressed by his collection of books. He showed me a presentation copy of Sven Berlin's infamous fictionalized autobiography *The Dark Monarch*. (Which was promptly banned and withdrawn soon after publication in 1962). Roger was a member of the Folio Society and I was pleased to browse through an elegant edition of Joyce's *Ulysses*. I mentioned I had read it three times and it turned out to be one of Roger's favourites as well. We concurred that we couldn't understand the fuss some people made about it being unreadable. He also showed me a huge limited edition of Lorca's poetry with Terry Frost etchings.

It was now time to turn to Roger's large collection of photographs amassed over several decades. Many of them were taken at various Private Views of art shows around Penwith. Nearly every picture told a story and Roger clearly enjoyed recounting some amusing anecdotes about the individuals involved. From now on every trip to Cornwall would include a visit to Sycamore Cottage (when we sometimes had tea in the garden shaded by the eponymous tree). We also started a lively little correspondence.

Later in the year I sat down and recorded a chat with Roger. The conversation ranged around people and places from his many decades working in St Ives and environs.

He spoke about a time, very soon after arriving in Cornwall, he stopped his car to give a hitchhiker a lift and this was how he met Bryan Wynter (who was temporarily living in a pantechnicon in a lay-by opposite Eagles Nest).

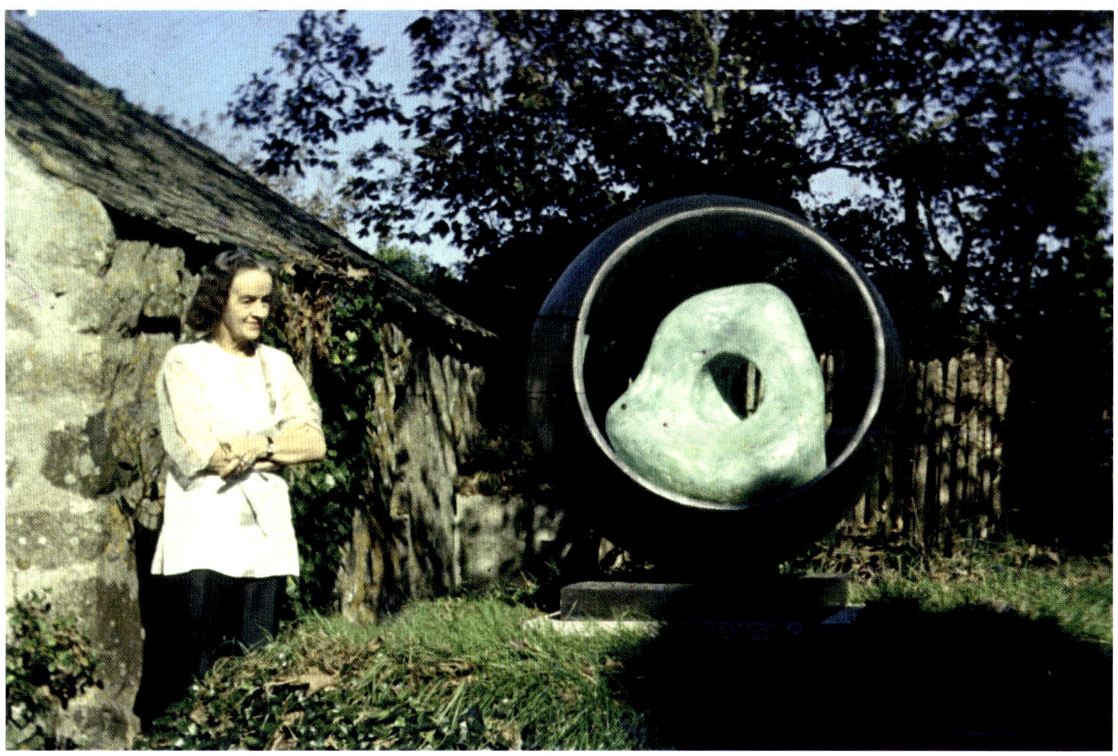

Barbara Hepworth in the garden of Sycamore Cottage, 1965

His first encounter with O'Malley was rather more dramatic and especially fortunate. While passing Boots Redgrave's guest house she ran out to say Tony was in a bad way inside and the good doctor quickly diagnosed a coronary (not for the last time) and had the patient rushed to the Edward Hain hospital. Roger grew especially fond of Tony and said what a very popular and much loved figure he had been, adding that many people still spoke of him with great affection. Before meeting Jane, in 1970, Tony had led rather an unstructured batchelor existence. Roger said that every time he visited Tony in his studio he seemed to be living on nothing other than whiskey and anchovies on toast! Tony would often show him some of the day's work in his sketchbooks saying, 'Sure isn't that a lovely one' and whenever Roger showed any enthusiasm for a piece Tony would tear it out and hand it to him (leading to an embarrassing tussle), hence Roger's accumulation of some of these works. They also had several holidays together on the Scillies. When O'Malley moved to nearby Trevaylor, in 1962, Roger carried on visiting him and ended up ministering to everyone else there, including Nancy Wynne-Jones, Sydney Graham and the Canadian sculptor Bill Featherston. In fact the latter fell out of the upstairs window (don't ask how) onto a bed of red-hot pokers requiring some patching up from Roger. Trevaylor was a place with a reputation for lively parties and Roger explained how a safety net had been installed on a landing by the steep stairwell in order to catch any wayward artist who, as a result of being mildly inebriated, lost their footing. What fun and games!

He mentioned how Roger Hilton was usually smartly dressed in a suit (a rare thing for an artist) and how charming he could be,

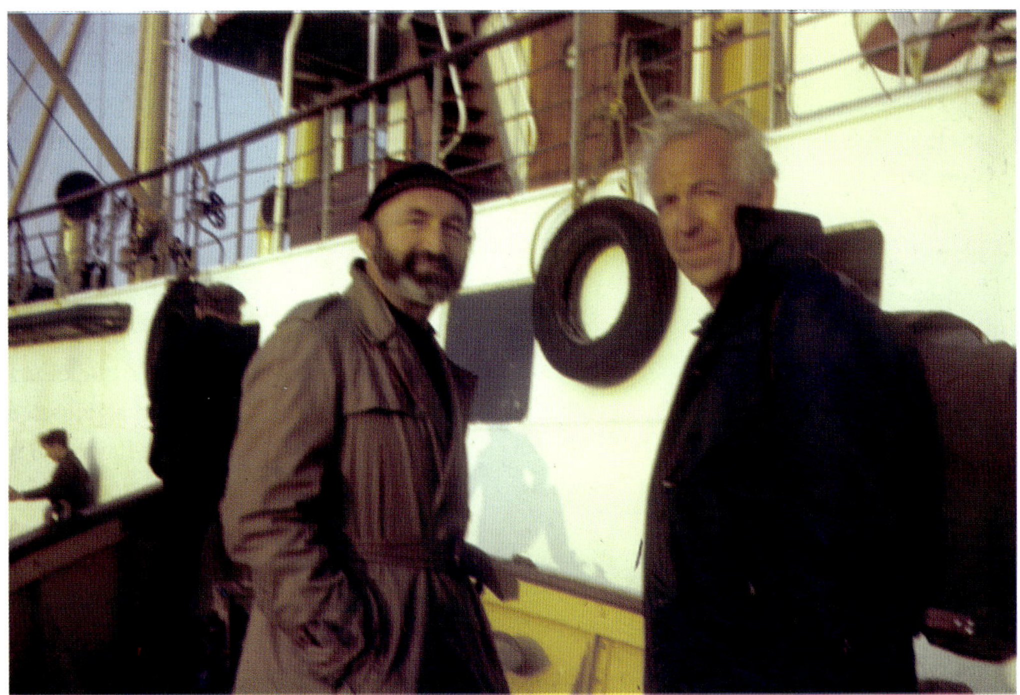

Roger with O'Malley on the *Scillonian*, 1964

but was more often than not deeply disruptive and offensive once the drink kicked in.

Roger had looked after the Lanyon family, which included six children. He said how Peter could be quite truculent when riled (and even when not). Once, when visiting him in his Attic Studio Lanyon pointed out that he could just about hurl a hand grenade from there into Hepworth's garden! (This was soon after he had resigned from the Penwith Society of Arts following a row with Hepworth and Nicholson.)

Roger was also good friends with Patrick Heron's family. He kept a diary throughout his life and he was, of course, extremely discreet, but he did send me some fascinating portions of it that he felt might be of interest for my researches into the lives of some of the artists. The following is an excerpt from May 1965:

I called on Patrick in his studio a day or two ago, finding him not painting, but about six unfinished works on the walls. He is getting worried about lack of progress, as he has an

exhibition in July I think. These were almost all of the 'mixed vermilion' type paintings producing remarkable colour degradation by proximity, and brilliant after images enhanced by the areas of untouched white canvas.

One particularly strong after image was produced by two yellow areas which lay at the periphery of my field of vision; I was concentrating on a Chinese vermilion area, and when I attempted to project the after image of this onto the white studio wall the result was very feeble, but the peripheral after image of the yellow area was quite startling , even though I had not been looking in that position.

Last week when I visited him, he made a remark that he thought that the future of painting lay in experiments with colour, and I asked him about this and he agreed that such was the case. He showed me a

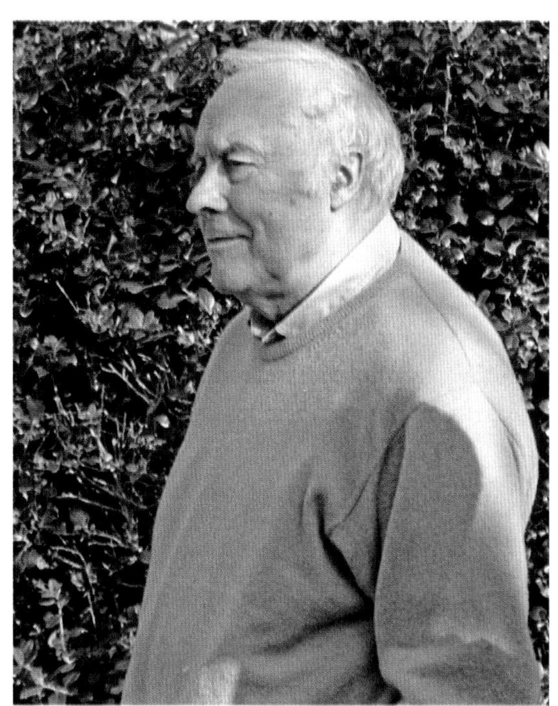

Patrick Heron, 1998

catalogue of his Zurich exhibition in which he expressed similar ideas.

In one of my letters I asked Roger if it was true about John Wells' reputation for passing out at parties, and he replied:

He wasn't always drunk and certainly not in his latter years. Most of the time that Janet and I were with him he was charming, a good conversationalist and extremely knowledgeable not only about painting but also natural history and Baroque music. He used to go to the Catholic church in Newlyn and I always supposed him to be a Catholic but such was not the case: he just enjoyed the service in Latin and when it was changed to the vernacular he stopped going.

Further to this, Roger sent another extract from his diary, dated November 11, 1965 regarding an early meeting with Wells at a party. It demonstrates some of the insight that Roger had into people's psychology:

About quarter of an hour later he came up to me rather diffidently and asked if I would care to see a photo, and for this I was drawn out into the hall. He produced a faded sepia print in a battered frame, a picture of an old fashioned laboratory with four men in it who were named as Leonard Colebrook, his father, Sir Almroth Wright and Sir Alexander Fleming (the discoverer of penicillin). Returning to the party he told me his life story starting with 'I'm riddled with guilt, the hero's child.' His father died when John was two, from glanders which he contracted whilst doing research into the disease. John's youth and education were supervised and helped by Colebrook and Wright and by his mother who earned £18 per annum from some unspecified job. He went of course to Epsom, then to St Mary's Hospital and then as a houseman to Norwich, doing first surgery and then ENT. Finally went to Nottingham as a houseman before buying the practice in Scilly. The only reference to private life he made was that he thought that it was a mistake, young and unmarried, to take a practice in Scilly. When he first arrived there were no facilities and all maternity work was domiciliary, a great hazard on the off-islands. He was instrumental in obtaining a hospital in conjunction with some Midland industrialist who provided £6,000, a man named Birkenshaw if I remember correctly, but the design of the building and determination of facilities was left to Wells. When the war came in 1939 and with it many servicemen to Scilly, he was able to obtain good equipment for the hospital at government expense. After the war he gave up medicine, and the flow of conversation did not allow me to ask the question for which I most of all wanted the answer. Why? What my instinct told me was required was not satisfaction of my own curiosity but some effort to lighten the burden of guilt that he bears for abandoning the profession into which he was placed and in which he was supported by outsiders, in what John supposes was the hope that he would fulfill the promise of his heroic father. The line I took was that by the end of the war he had behind him the respect and affection of the Scillonians and a considerable achievement: that he had long since discharged his obligation towards his benefactors whose motive was probably no more than to see the son of a deceased colleague adequately educated. I thought that his change to the arts, which he had hankered after all his life, was totally justified … John Wells is a man of sensibility brought up with a sense of dedication to his profession, from his conversation obviously deeply concerned with the more humanitarian principles and with the example of his father's literally total involvement before him, knowing for certain that he was a good and useful doctor, but no doubt seldom certain that he is a great painter. Soothing words from strangers will never bridge that psychological chasm.

As for Barbara Hepworth, Roger had nothing but praise for her friendship and generosity. She had given gifts of her work to various members of his family including a grandchild and had commissioned jewellery from Janet. Of her ghastly death in a fire at her studio he said: 'I was away on holiday thank God, or I'd have to have been involved'.

Regarding Roger's own impressive sculpture,

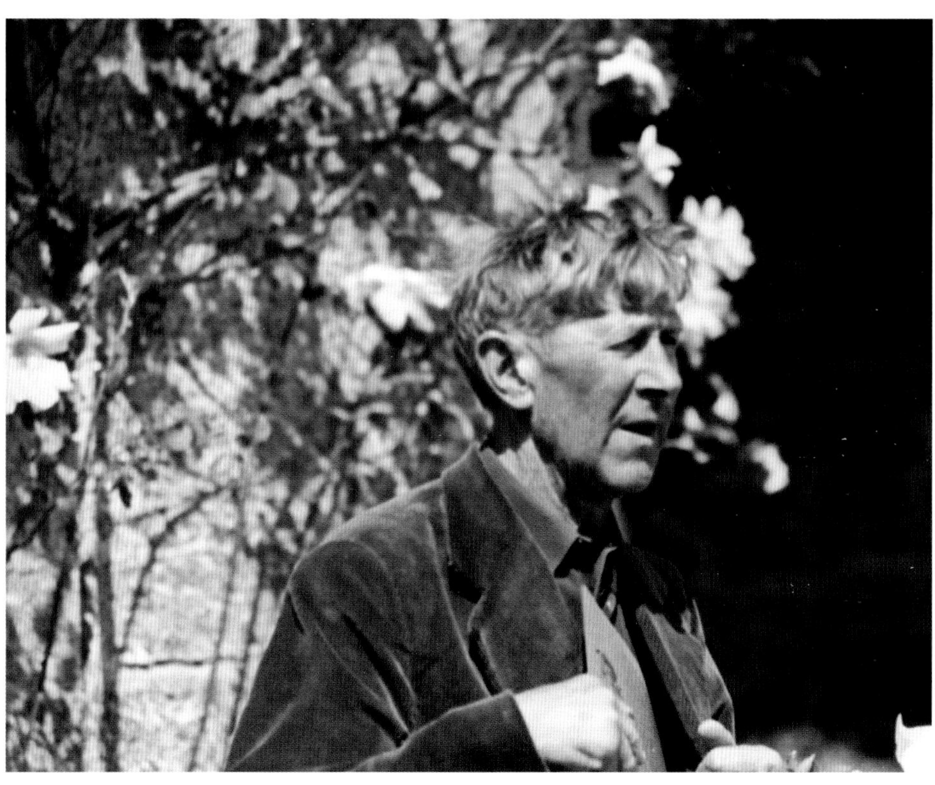

John Wells, 1980

I mentioned that on entering the house I immediately thought this work dotted about was by Denis Mitchell. He sighed and said his aim in life was *not* to be Denis.

His letters continued to come my way, often including copies of photos of one artist or another. Though I always looked forward to a letter from Roger, the one that arrived in December of 2004 was certainly not welcome. In it he told of the recent death, peacefully in her sleep, of Janet, concluding: 'We would have been married for 61 years in January and I could not have been luckier.'

It was two months later that I met with Roger, along with my wife and daughter, in Tate St Ives for tea and cake. We then went back to the cottage. The place now had that peculiar sense of absence often felt soon after someone dies. He was coping admirably well, pragmatic as ever, he had just returned his driving licence to DVLA saying it was the most sensible thing to do when you reached a certain age. He would now have his daily routine of walking down to town for his shopping and returning up the steep hill by taxi.

I now had to knuckle down to getting on with my O'Malley study and a book launch was organized for the St Ives September Festival. Roger couldn't have been more helpful with going through his archive and sending me photographs and information. In early summer we had lunch in Zennor and a little nostalgic tour around the area with Roger giving a running commentary on various patients he'd treated as we passed their houses. He seems to have known everyone in Penwith. There were some funny stories, including the phone call he got in the middle of the night from a distraught woman gasping, 'Come quickly doctor, my husband has dropped dead!' Roger hastily dressed and sped to some remote corner of Penwith, to be greeted at the door of the house by a beaming wife who said, 'Don't worry doctor, he's better now'.

I later sent some photographs I'd taken of him that day, but he wasn't impressed and quoted Richard Ingrams: 'I don't trust photographers. I am now a relaxed, contented 60-year old, but look at my pictures and you will see a crazy bug-eyed serial killer'.

Having cared for Janet over the last few years he now enjoyed a degree of independence and had a busy social life. Though sometimes, on a relaxing evening out, he got more than he bargained for:

> *I came to life a bit last night by going to a midsummer party … very enjoyable, good food and good company and many clearly surprised to see me, supposed that I was dead I think. A slightly difficult moment, when I was asked to see one of the guests who had fainted. This was a situation that our Medical Protection Society warns all retired doctors about. Guess wrong and you will be sued and the case will be indefensible. The only thing to do is look wise and concerned and send for someone with a stethoscope. Kernowdoc was summoned and arrived promptly (they wear a uniform, yellow and green diagonal stripes no less), by which time of course the lady was fine and wondering what all the fuss was about. However, as I have no doubt told you before it is nice to be still wanted in one's dotage.*

The O'Malley book duly arrived in time for the book launch and the day before I called on Roger to present him with a copy. The book had a dedication that took him by surprise and momentarily left him speechless: 'Dedicated to Dr Roger Slack & the memory of Janet Slack – *gentleness personified, kindness exemplified*'.

A few months later I stopped by for coffee. Roger had been rereading *Ulysses* but was interrupted that morning by the arrival of another Folio Society publication, this time it was *The Anatomy of Melancholy* by Robert Burton. First published in the 1620s, this encyclopaedic rambling tome speculates on the many causes of what was then known as melancholia. Roger first encountered it as a medical student and was delighted with this handsome three-volume edition in a slipcase. I also expressed admiration and he was interested to know that I had read some of it a few years before. He wanted to take me out to dinner in St Ives that evening and later when I called around to pick him up he pointed to a large carrier bag on the table. 'That's for you' he said and I was flabbergasted to find the Burton set therein! Incredibly kind, as poor Roger had hardly a chance to look through it never mind enjoy it. It's a set I continue to treasure.

In 2007 Roger was perceptibly growing more frail and was spending a lot of time with his daughters Pippa who lived nearby and Elizabeth in Devon. There were also many grandchildren to keep him occupied. I last saw him in May and came away with an ominous feeling that we wouldn't meet again. As indeed was the case, he died on July 11, 2007. I managed to get down to his funeral by train, not without some difficulty as most of Oxfordshire was submerged in floodwaters. But there was no way I was going to miss it. There was a moving service in St John's Church very close to Sycamore Cottage. A fellow doctor told some wonderful stories of Roger's selfless dedication to his patients. While two of the grandsons read a diary extract, revealing a lyrical and poetic side to Roger's observations:

February 25, 1963

Last night was telephoned by Denis Leslie from Penzance asking me to see to the Captain of a small Dutch Coaster, who gave a story over the radio suggestive of pneumonia: he was not anxious to go into Penzance because of heavy seas from a southeaster, and so was coming round to St Ives, with an E.T.A about 9 pm. This proved an unsatisfactory hour, as the pilot boat was high and dry in Hayle basin, and no prospect of refloating until at least 2 pm. I received the news with mixed feelings, an excuse for reading late and the suspicion of not very much bed.

Made my way down to the Power Station quay at Hayle, hurrying as I feared that I might be late, a precaution which caused a few extra minutes on the hour I had to spend pacing up and down the freezing quayside. Underway about 3.15, and quite quickly out to the ship. As we went out over the bar, the whole sky seemed to be a-twitter, the sound of many curlews quite invisible in the dark. The area of disturbance was quite circumscribed, lasting for about five minutes of the boat's progress, but sounding like many scores of birds during that period. Further out to sea we disturbed several gulls roosting on the water. The whiteness of their plumage showed great luminosity in the semi-dark; and the rapid flutter of their wings as they took to flight on the edge of the circle of glooming light cast by the masthead lamp was a blur to the eye. This is a strange contrast to the effect in daylight, when the wings, however rapid, remain in focus. Perhaps the alteration is concerned with a slowing down of the eyes' ability to detect interrupted movement in the dark.

A very calm, cold night, so no difficulty in getting aboard the coaster. The Captain sick, feverish, restless and coughing, so it seemed sensible to take the ship alongside in Hayle. Much too cold to risk taking him ashore in the open pilot boat.

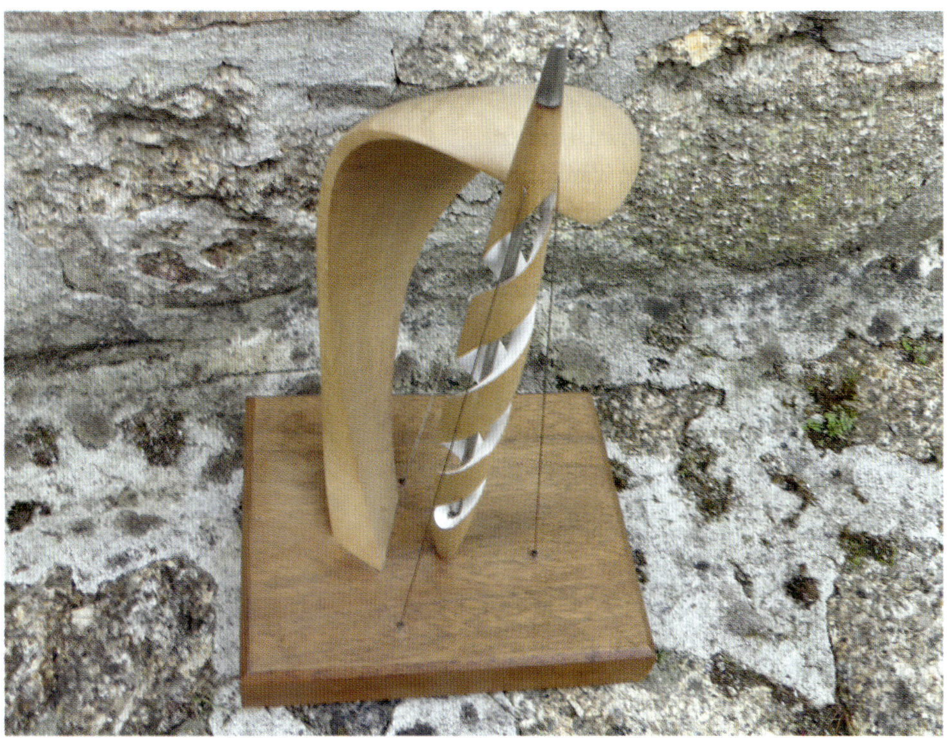

Roger Slack – *Corndhu* 1993, pearwood & stainless steel, 30.48 cm high

The entrance to Hayle is extremely narrow, and shallow over the bar so that we had to wait until 5.15 am before going in. I was most impressed by the work of the Pilot, Dan Paynter, both in handling the ship in such narrow waters, and the amount of work involved in handling the wheel. Apparently without mechanical assistance, it was heavy to turn, and required about thirty turns from lock to lock, the full manoeuvre being frequently required. Dan was quite breathless at the end.

Home to bed at 6.45 am.

We all adjourned to the cottage in perfect Cornish weather and I enjoyed hearing so many expressions of gratitude from a lovely group of people, including Sir Alan and Lady Bowness, Andrew Lanyon, Paul Feiler and Monica Wynter, while Jane O'Malley had flown over from Ireland.

Roger really felt he had a wonderful fulfilled life and was genuinely amazed that he had, by pure chance, played a respected and essential part in the community of St Ives for four decades, particularly during a golden era of creativity in British art. But we must look to his premier calling in a multi-faceted life to see how he utilized his innate skill as a brilliant diagnostician and healer, with a sympathetic touch that had him in great demand. Of course I regret not having known him earlier, our relationship was curtailed all too soon. Nevertheless I count his friendship as one of the most important of my life and still look to him as an exemplar in the delicate and difficult art of being humane.

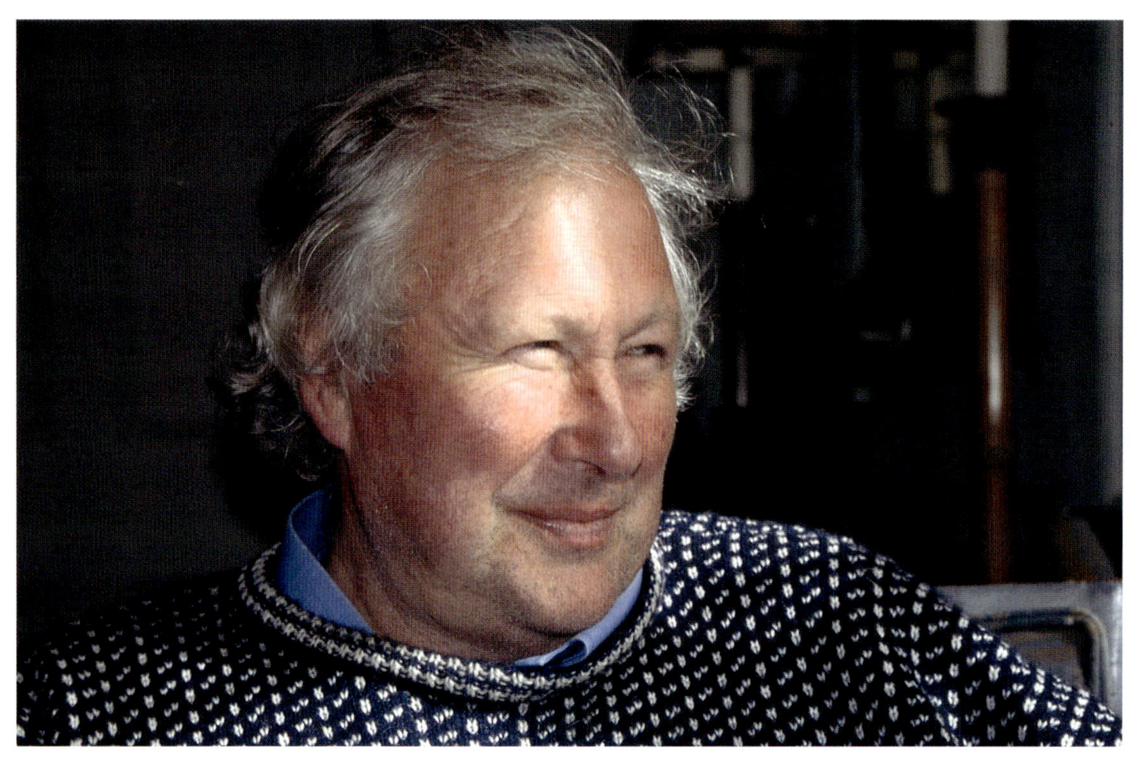

6

Seize the Day: Jeremy Le Grice

Meandering around the busy working
harbour of Newlyn in the company of Jeremy
Le Grice was a lively instruction concerning
all things maritime. From when he was pushed
along the quay in his pram until his death he
was totally infatuated with the daily hubbub
and commotion of the fishing trade. He
always spoke of the place with a compelling
fascination:

> *I feel committed here as a painter for the
> rest of my life, I find the activities endlessly
> exciting and can't have enough of it. One
> has to discover new ways of painting it in
> order to see it fresh.*

Jeremy aspired to catching the essence of
Newlyn, its basic unkempt griminess, as befits
a utilitarian anchorage, including rotting old
hulls (which he developed an affection for), and
abhorred the tendency of too many painters to
prettify the place with 'saccharine trash – art
merely as merchandise'. Of course he painted
further afield, including India, Germany, France
and Italy, but Newlyn remained the still point
of his sometimes shambolic, turning world.

In any conversation with Jeremy it never
took long before he referenced one of his
forebears. He had an amazingly detailed
knowledge of his whole genealogy, both
patriarchal and matriarchal, and he clearly drew
from this long lineage as a means of defining his
identity. The Le Grices went all the way back to
the Norman invasion when they acquired land
around the Norfolk/Suffolk border. They served
as vicars of Bury St Edmunds Church for 700
years from about 1200 to 1870. As a footnote to
English literature, Charles Valentine Le Grice
was a part of the Romantic literary circle of
Coleridge, Charles Lamb and Wordsworth. In
1796 he came to west Cornwall to act as tutor
to the son of a widow, Mrs Nicholls, who lived
at Trereife House. She owned a great deal of
land in the area, and before long the young Le
Grice married her and they had a son, Charles
Day Perry, Jeremy's great, great grandfather.
This is how the Cornish connection came about
for the Le Grice family. However, fate would
intervene to prevent Jeremy from being a true
Cornishman:

> *I was born, a twin, in September 1936. We
> were due to be born in Cornwall and were
> being driven there when my father had to
> rather swiftly put on the brakes at Walton-
> on-Thames, because my mother went into
> labour early and my sister Jen and I were
> born, weighing about two pounds … So
> we weren't born in Cornwall, much to my
> fury. My father was working for Lloyd's
> Insurance as an underwriter, and he bought
> a little cottage in Dachet, just outside of
> Windsor, on the river.*

Their childhood was tragically interrupted
three years later with the outbreak of war, when
Jeremy's father served in the Duke of Cornwall's
light infantry. At Dunkirk, while leading his
platoon up a farm track, he was killed by a burst
of machine gun fire when he inadvertently
triggered a booby trap (his body was never
recovered). This woeful loss for the three-year

old Jeremy continued to haunt him for the rest of his life, indeed Jeremy believes this emotional upheaval led to his developing a stammer. Throughout these difficult early years the family had regular visits to Cornwall, providing Jeremy with some solace:

Cornwall was my salvation during the holidays. I used to despise the suburbia of Surrey, much to my mother's extreme distress, and I can now see how much it hurt her. But Cornwall was part of the Le Grice legacy. My great grandfather, Charles Day Nicholls, gave the land for the Newlyn Gallery to be built on, as well as land between Penzance and Newlyn, which my grandfather sold so my father and uncle could go to Eton.

He went to Amesbury School, near Hazlemere, were he excelled in art and in fact won a competition with his painting of a sailor which appeared in the national newspapers (his first taste of fame):

That was the single event that precipitated me to dedicate myself to art. Art was my retreat and my salvation and arguably has remained so ever since, my buffer with the world.

His next school would offer even more unique and valuable experiences:

I started at Eton on January 1, aged 13. The fees then were about £300 a term, which we couldn't afford. But Eton, in a very enlightened way, gave free places to the sons of those who'd been killed in the war. In the cloisters they had a bronze war memorial of the hundreds of Etonians who'd been killed in both wars, and walking past this, with my father's name, meant a lot to me the whole time I was there. It gave me a sort of semi-detached feeling. Although I didn't feel like a charity boy, I knew I had a sort of birthright to be there. Eton was an amazingly good school, but one thing I despised about it was its snobbery. I felt an outsider and a nonconformist and retreated into the drawing school.

Wilfrid Blunt had a few protégés who he encouraged furiously, and I was lucky to be one of them. He was a very large man who smoked a big herbal pipe. He published books about the Middle East and a history

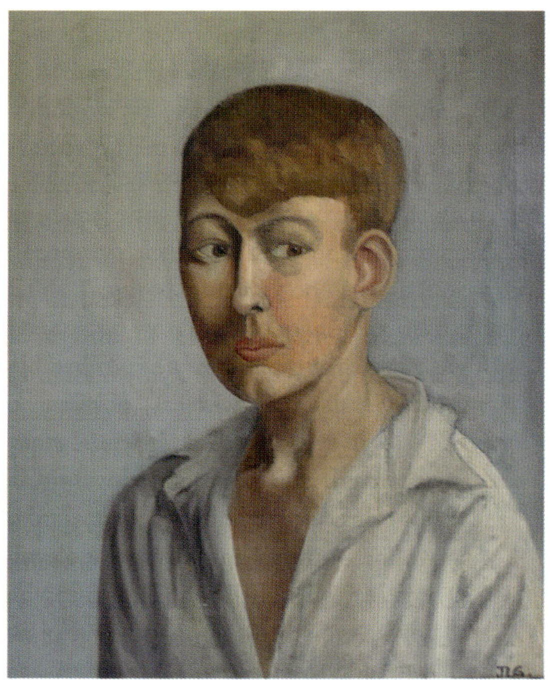

Self-portrait 1952, oil on canvas, 58 x 48 cm

of botanical illustration, a very scholarly man. It was a sort of sinecure then at Eton, and he had a study where he wrote his books and puffed his pipe. He revered his much more urbane brother Anthony, who was lithe, tall and handsome. (Anthony also cropped up later at the Slade.) We had to copy from the Old Masters and Blunt set us to do transcriptions. I was given Vermeer's

Artist in his Studio and I took enormous pains copying it, which turned out pretty good for a fifteen-year old. We were learning draughtsmanship with a philosophy and idealism. When I look around me now there're certain painters who have an attitude of producing commerce, but for us the last thing art was for was producing goods for trade – you were above trade, you were doing it for distinctly idealistic reasons and distinctly uncommercial. I can't bear this approach where one makes commodities just to sell and it all too easily degenerates into decorative rubbish because it sells most handily, I find that deeply disturbing.

Jeremy left Eton in 1954, and started at the Guldford School of Art:

There I found some very radical teachers who'd come out of the army, having fought their way through the war, supporting furiously the Socialist government, with very left wing views. This Etonian was a freak of nature who appeared among the student population, but this politically radical thing appealed to me. One of the first things we did was visit London and see the first production of Waiting for Godot, and another crucial event was John Osborne's Look Back in Anger, and this is the political mast I nailed my colours to. We were taught drawing very seriously, but after a period of time I became very restless and told my uncle I didn't want to be a teacher, I needed to be an artist and wanted to go to the Slade.

But before that a decisive new friendship was to develop (as well as other important relationships):

In the Easter holidays of 1955 I was staying down here and went to Newlyn Gallery, and on the end wall there was this painting Harvest Festival, and I just thought this is what painting is. I raved to my aunt about it and she said that one of her closest friends was Mary Scofield at Godolphin House, whose brother was Peter Lanyon (who did the painting). She rang Mary up and I was taken over to St Ives to meet him. I entered this fairly small house and there were a lot of children, and the first thing to hit me was a wonderful big Alfred Wallis painting. The whole visit was a revelation to me about an artist living as an artist in a family context. Lanyon was struggling at this time and was very hard up. It surprised me that his studio was immediately adjoining their kitchen and there was a strong smell of oil paint. It was when he was painting those rather heavy, dark green and very physical works. He was very ambitious and was quite pleased to have some acolytes in tow.

My aunt treated me to a course at the summer school that Lanyon was running with Bill Redgrave in St Peter's Loft. I stayed at Boots Redgrave's boarding house. Her husband, Bill, was very jealous of Lanyon, who was very much a high-flyer and a high profile extrovert. Boots was a very kind hearted woman and she loved having me there. Tony O'Malley was there as well. He looked very conventional in a tweed jacket and tie. But Peter recognised in both Tony and myself that we were at least potentially serious artists, and he treated us as such. He was always there when you arrived, however early, getting things tidied and prepared. I feel he was at the height of his powers. He took us out to Godolphin one day with great pride in his sister's grand house and we spent the day painting there. He was always encouraging and delighted in what one had achieved from that day's work. However, he never allowed one to rest on one's laurels,

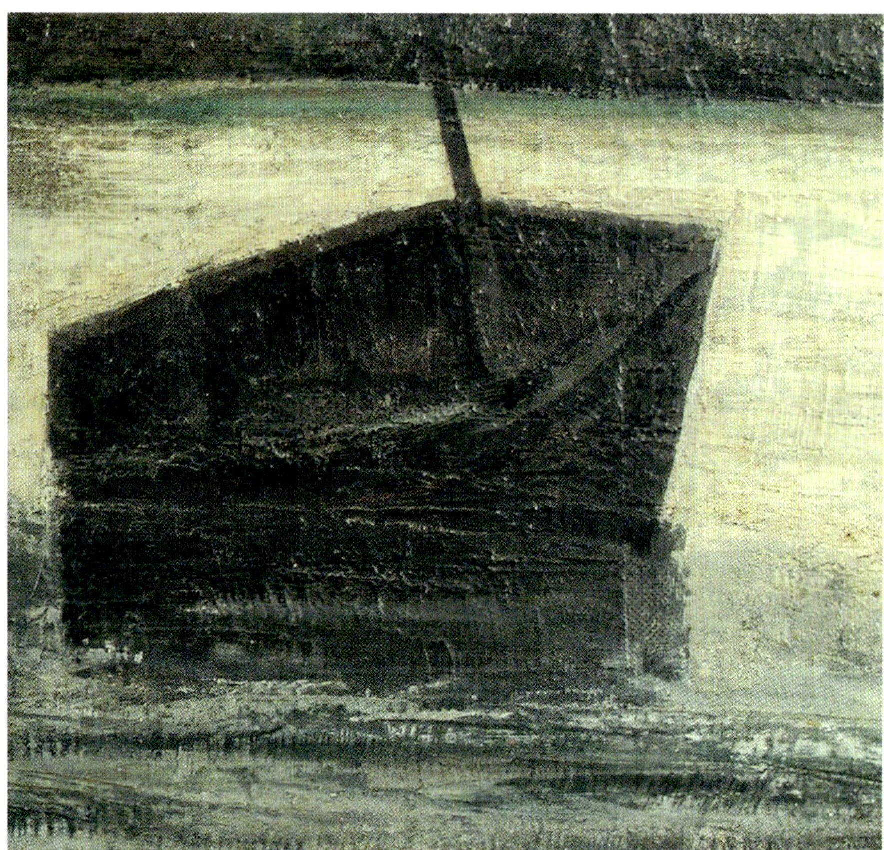

Hull 1956, oil on canvas, 37 x 47 cm

he was pushing one constantly into another attitude. He also encouraged me not to be academic in my approach. Patrick Heron did a critique of the paintings at the end of the course.

I also came across Terry Frost who was very gregarious, as was Denis Mitchell. But Johnny Wells was very ungregarious, he was a very shy, agonized soul. Bryan Wynter was the life and soul of the party, he was very charming and easy to talk to. Heron had a rivalry with Lanyon and Lanyon dismissed Heron's work as 'angel paintings'. They had grown up together and visited Paris where they met Picasso, and he'd said to them: 'Don't people in England know how to paint?'

Hilton turned up for holidays from London, even then he had a reputation for being rude and abrasive and causing a disturbance. There was a party up at Wynter's cottage, and Lanyon had Hilton on the ground, saying: 'Tell me I'm a good painter' and Hilton replied: 'Never, you're a shit-awful painter!'

The Leach Pottery was a landmark on the hill coming out of St Ives. Leach was always working there and I did get to know him. Ten years later when I had a show at Plymouth Museum, Leach opened it with great grace and gave a kind speech and I sold lots of paintings.

I met Francis Bacon, on one of his jaunts down here, at Karl Weschke's place. I first

*met Karl at a mixed show at the Penwith.
He said he liked the picture I had there
and asked to see more of my work. The next
day I drove over to Zennor, where he was
then living, and showed him more of my
paintings and from then on we were lifelong
friends. Karl saw himself as a different
class of painter to the St Ives gang. He could
seem arrogant, but he was in fact a deeply
modest, sincere man. He regarded Heron as
a nonsense painter, and Hilton as belonging
to some School of Paris spinoff. He saw
Lanyon as trying to do something which,
in Karl's terms, doesn't belong in painting.
Though they actually got on as both shared
a certain physicality.*

In preparation for the Slade entrance,
Jeremy worked in a basement room of the
Newlyn Art Gallery, courtesy of Michael
Canney. (As part of his portfolio he included a
most striking portrait of his mother.):

*I took the work up on the night train and
half the paintings were still wet on the
luggage racks. I had an interview with
William Coldstream, and Lanyon wrote
a letter of recommendation for me and
said it will either get me in or will bitch
up completely my chances (as they'd had a
falling out). Anyhow, Coldstream was very
nice about my portfolio and I did get in.
It was a four year course. Keith Vaughan
helped me enormously, and Claude Rogers
was another important man there. Frank
Auerbach was a part-time teacher, as
was Lucian Freud. He had wild romantic
Byronic good looks and would regularly
hypnotise some of the girls into following
him. Bomberg was around too and I
admired him greatly. Ernst Gombrich was
another occasional lecturer on art. He had
a very thick Viennese accent; he was very*

*good on anything up to the 1800s, but he got
bogged down in the German Romantics,
like Caspar David Friedrich, and whenever
he tried to propagate him you could hear
the groans from the students. I lived in
Maida Vale and had a grant to get by on.*

*At the beginning of the second year I saw
this new girl called Mary Stork, who'd
won various art prizes. I took her out on
my Lambretta scooter and we had a crash.
I was badly concussed and Mary broke
her hip. I had to go to Coldstream's office
and say: 'I'm afraid your prize student is
hospitalized.' Then at the beginning of the
next term I had to go to his office and say:
'I'm afraid you're prize student is pregnant'.
He said: 'I'm so delighted, I love students
having babies, and when you have your baby
you can leave it in a pram in the courtyard
outside my office and I'll look after it.' And
he did just that!*

*The moment Mary found out she was
pregnant she stopped painting and didn't
pick up a brush again for seven years, and
she'd been a flamboyantly talented high
profile student. We went on to have three
children: Anna, Thomas and Harriet. In
1961 we settled into a terraced house in
Chapel Street in St Just. The marriage
lasted exactly ten years from 1959 to 1969,
and I'd say that for nine of those years we
were positively happy. But Mary did suffer
from a crisis as she saw her painting life cut
short. I see her a lot now and we get on very
well. But there was a destructive rivalry in
the relationship, which meant it couldn't
last.*

*Lanyon continued to point people in my
direction, which was really helpful for
selling my work. He also got me my first
teaching job at Porthleven Summer School.*

Though there's no denying the significance
of Lanyon's mentoring of the younger
artist, Jeremy remained resolutely wary of
becoming yet another acolyte surrendering
to the charismatic St Ives man. His art was
an attempt to find emotional solutions to his
varying preoccupations, a search to reconcile
contradictions, by utilising the tensions between
abstract and figurative painting. The events
of his early childhood may account for his
partiality to the monochromatic, muted register
of colours. Far from being gloomy the effect is of
an iridescent interplay between dark and light
that evokes mystery and hints at hidden secrets
that intrigue the viewer. In this his work was
close to that of his old friend Tony O'Malley.

The business side of art and the meeting
of deadlines for shows could be slightly
problematic and a challenge to Jeremy's ideals
and high standards: 'You take them as far as

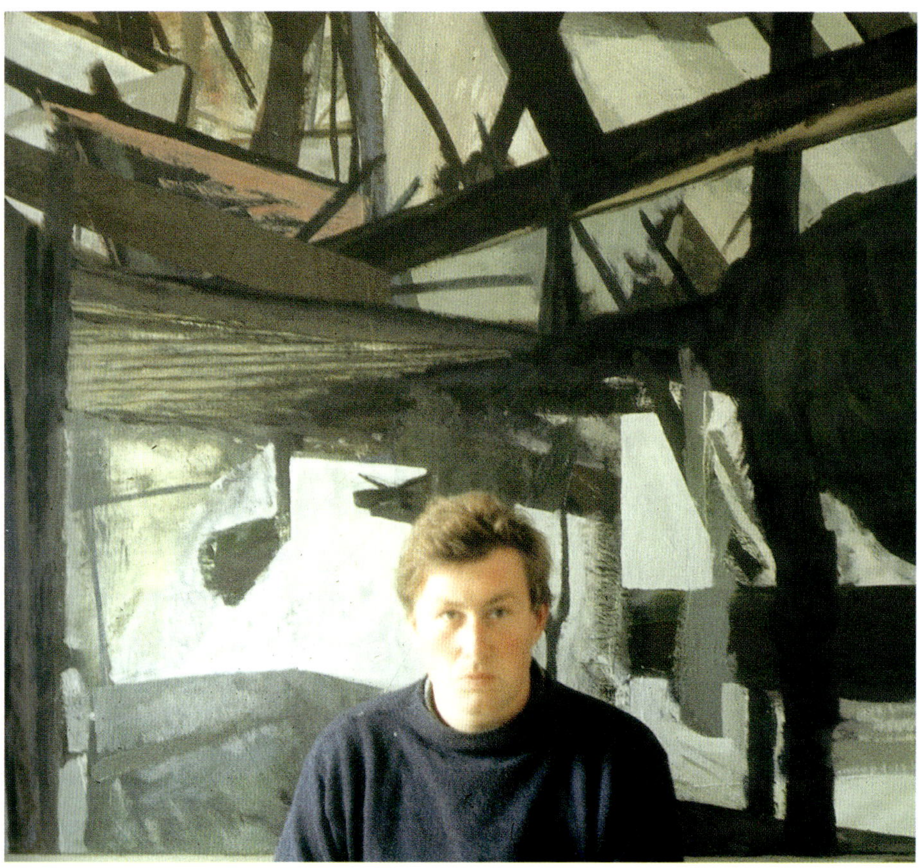

Jeremy with *Barn Interior*, 1964

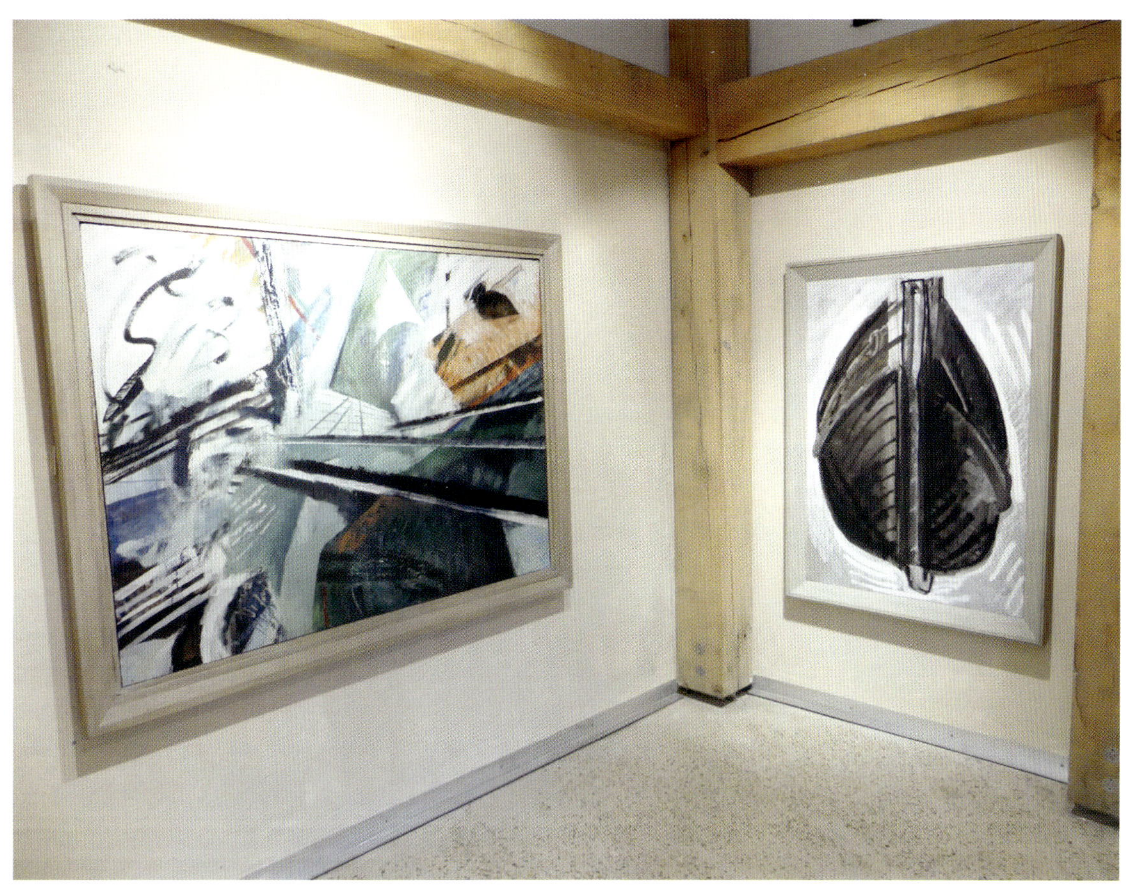

Gagarin's First Space Flight (1965) & Bow (Ripple) (2007)

you can for an exhibition, but it doesn't mean that they're finished.' From time to time he returned to certain works, stored away, and was frequently surprised anew at what he found:

> *It's good to not sell more than you can get by on, and every painting has an invisible story, which has accumulated mysteriously over time in its making, a subliminal emotional message. The best paintings go on after you've come away from the subject, they have their own momentum, and you find the patina of age gives them some gravitas.*

For Jeremy, Cezanne and Picasso were the giants of modern art and he was pleased to find this quote from the latter, regarding his discovery of African art:

> *And then I understood what painting really meant. It's not an aesthetic process; it's a form of magic that interposes itself between us and the hostile universe, a means of seizing power, by imposing a form on our terrors as well as on our desires. The day I understood that, I had found my path.*

On New Year's Eve 1969, in the Gurnard's Head Hotel, Jeremy met his second wife Lyn, an art college lecturer (and subsequent interior designer). This proved to be the beginning of a whole new unexpected chapter for Jeremy and his art. In 1971, very soon after the birth of their son Jude, the family happened to visit Mylor harbour, near Falmouth. Jeremy saw a notice, nailed to the mast of a large Baltic

67

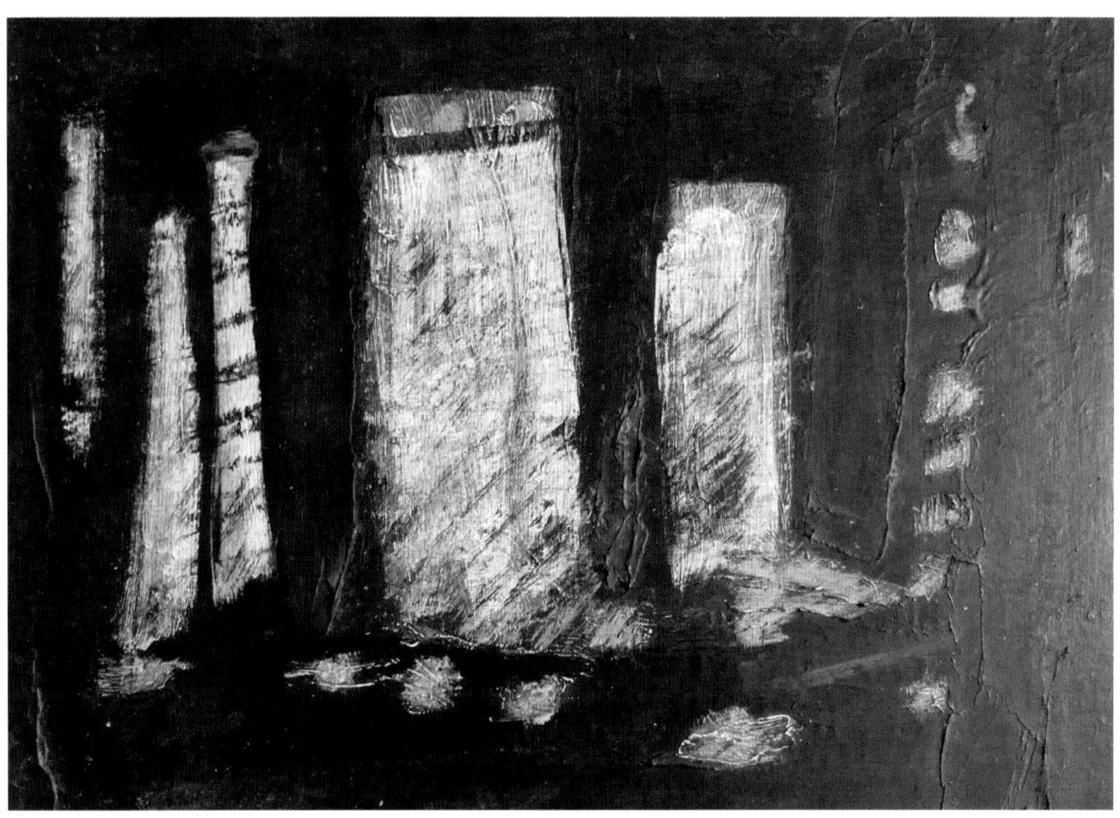

The Supporters II (Newlyn Quay) 2005, oil on board, 27 x 38 cm

Trader, calling for crew members to volunteer in exchange for a return trip to Los Angeles. Intrigued, Jeremy enquired when she was due to set sail and the answer was, 'Tonight'! Very much with Lyn's encouragement Jeremy chose to 'Seize the day' (a recurring motto in his life), and the family hurried back to St Just to pack his bags for the voyage (however, it would be a few more days before wind conditions were favourable.)

As a youngster Jeremy had always loved reading about maritime adventures and here he was in his mid-thirties (with a very new family) embarking on an unpredictable and, as it turned out, rather risky escapade. Not far into the voyage the ship got caught up in a Force 8 Gale, suffering serious damage, requiring some lengthy repairs at Madeira. Jeremy kept a daily log of this exciting journey. They travelled on through the Panama Canal before reaching LA. Jeremy immediately phoned Lyn, who soon joined him there and they went on to explore San Francisco, Mexico City, New Orleans and New York.

Jeremy returned to the UK replenished and really in need of a fresh start and a new challenge, and the couple, with all of the children, moved to the Cotswolds, with Jeremy teaching art at Cheltenham and Hereford colleges.

Much of their time was now taken up with restoring a farm with a large barn conversion. This was so successful and impressive that it was featured in *Vogue*. Though Jeremy also had an exhibition of his Cotswold paintings at the Cheltenham Art Gallery & Museum, the overall feeling was that his prolonged absence from Cornwall left him dissatisfied with this work. The family duly returned in 1984 after 12 years away.

A return from the landlocked Cotswolds, nearer to his maritime background, saw Jeremy's painting block evaporate and henceforth in his art he embraced the quality of creative recklessness in defiance of what he described as 'the tight-arsed school of merchandise production' – though they also had another barn conversion on their hands. They made a good team at this, with Lyn's skills in interior design proving fruitful and profitable, each time they moved on. The new home was in Alsia (pronounced 'Ale-eeya'), near St Buryan During this period Jeremy travelled to Worpswede, in Germany, on a scholarship, where he spent a year painting horses. Some years later they moved into a wing of the family home, owned by Jeremy's cousin, in Trereife, not far from Newlyn.

He also went to India, then to Italy exploring more family roots on his mother's side. He combined his own artistic activities with teaching, which kept him in demand, his pupils being inspired by his infectious enthusiasm (an annual art course in the South of France proved hugely oversubscribed). Jeremy even had a show at Eton for the opening of a new drawing school building, a rewarding experience for him, many decades after being a hesitant, stammering schoolboy. Of course, he was moved to inspect his father's name again on the memorial.

Indeed, the loss of his father continued to haunt Jeremy all of his life. This event may account for his partiality to the lower, muted register of colours. Far from being gloomy the effect is of an iridescent interplay between dark and light, through the mass and bulk of old ships and the shapes of harbours, which evoke mystery and hint at hidden secrets of their history that intrigue the viewer. Having said that, his colour palette also brightened latterly to explore the subtle varieties of vivid blues.

Jeremy died at home of cancer in August 2012, aged 75, and is buried at St Levan. An artist of uncompromising integrity and lyrical vision, he was always very popular as an effusive and ebullient presence. Any future histories of Newlyn must surely include Jeremy as quintessential to the very fabric of the place.

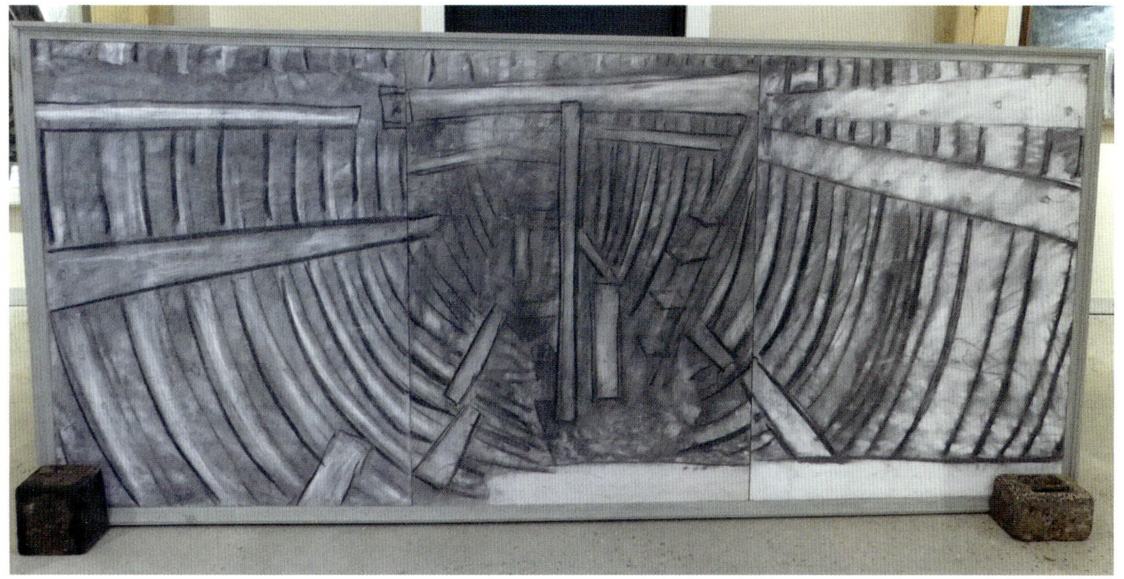

The Ripple II 2004, charcoal drawing

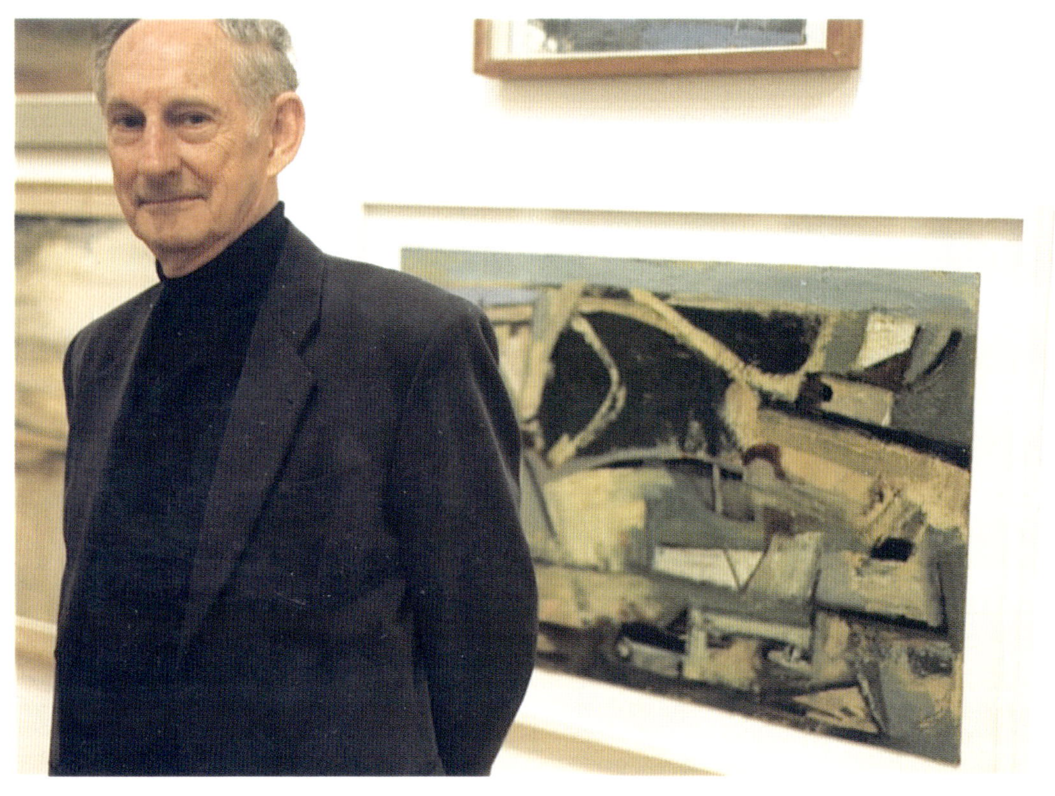

7

Michael Canney & Newlyn Art
Gallery

SON OF A VICAR, Michael Canney was born in Falmouth on July 16, 1923. In 1925 the Reverend Canney was appointed rector of Redruth, which is where Michael grew up. His mother was an amateur painter and her son was exposed to art from an early age with annual visits to the St Ives art show days, when various artists' studios were open to the public. The Reverend Canney, influenced by the writings of Ruskin, believed in the moral necessity of art, particularly architecture and he took the family on a tour of the great cathedrals all over Britain.

At King's College, Taunton, Canney was lucky to have, as art tutor, Lyons Wilson, a fringe member of the Surrealists and friend of Herbert Read. From 1940-42, Canney enrolled at Penzance and Redruth Schools of Art as well as the St Ives School of Painting, the latter run by Leonard Fuller. Here he met some of the distinguished older members, including John Park, Borlase Smart and Misomé Peile. In 1942 he held a small exhibition of his work in one of the Piazza Studios. He saw Alfred Wallis at work in his cottage. He also met Graham Sutherland, then an official War Artist working at Geevor Mine, as well as Ben Nicholson, Bernard Leach, Naum Gabo and Sven Berlin (it would be some time later before he met Hepworth).

The war now interrupted Canney's art career, though it carried on to an extent, and he served in the Royal Engineers as draughtsman, being posted to North Africa, Italy and Austria where he was required to do a lot of drawing. Canney was even lucky enough to do an art course in Florence, where Giorgio de Chirico visited and gave him some words of encouragement. This was also the start of Canney's great passion for Italy.

Canney went to Goldsmith's College of Art between 1947 and 1951. Fellow students were Mary Quant, Bridget Riley and Molly Parkin. Here he met the Constructivist Kenneth Martin, whose ideas would prove to be highly influential to Canney many years later; but for now his own work was inclined towards Neo-Cubism.

Serious health issues intervened, around 1950, in the form of TB, and Canney spent some time convalescing in Cornwall, followed by six months at the Patrick Allan-Fraser Art College in Arbroath. He also managed to lend a hand on Festival of Britain projects on London's South Bank, as well as doing some teaching as art master at a tough secondary school in Essex.

In 1952 Canney worked with the sculptor Denis Mitchell on a variety of large mobiles in sheet aluminium for the St Ives Festival. He then spent the next few years teaching in London. Along the way he married Madeleine in 1954 and they had a son, Simon, the following year. He still visited Cornwall when he could and kept in contact with the artists there. His work now developed an abstract expressionist style, sharing an affinity with Peter Lanyon's approach, by applying gestural swathes of earthy colours.

He first became fully aware of Newlyn Art Gallery while he was a TB patient in the early '50s at the nearby Bolitho Convalescent Home.

On my daily convalescent walks I visited the gallery, which in those days was more like a museum than a showplace for contemporary art. The walls were literally covered with pictures of the sunshine and seagull variety, with too many anonymous portraits, cows, and bluebell woods. It did not appear that the gallery was much visited.

In 1956 an advertisement appeared in the New Statesman and Nation for a new Curator and Secretary of the Society. The salary was £100 a year, with a rent-free flat beneath the gallery, a small commission from art sales, and a free bag of coal. However the main attraction was that the gallery was only open for six months of the year, leaving the curator half of the year free to pursue personal interests, which in my case was painting. I applied for the post and was appointed. When my wife, together with our infant son, joined me a few weeks later, the Society got two curators for the price of one. We had no private means of support, apart from a very small War Disability Pension, and such money as I could make from occasional sales of my own pictures. Times were hard, but we were determined to make a success of the gallery and to instil some life into it.

I cannot claim to be the sole catalyst that sparked Newlyn on a livelier phase, as Mrs Eileen Hunt, my predecessor, had done much to revive the Society after its wartime hibernation. By hard work and much charm she managed to enlist the support of a significant group of modern artists, who included Peter Lanyon, Paul Feiler, John Armstrong, John Tunnard, Ithell Colquhoun, Jack Pender, Alexander Mackenzie and others. The work of these artists was, of course, hardly viewed with

enthusiasm by the older members of the Society, and I discovered that undercover approaches were being made by some members to the St Ives Society of Artists, to see if the amalgamation of the two societies was possible.

The first thing Canney discovered was the poor state of the Society's finances; in fact, initially, they didn't have enough funds to pay his salary. He realised the importance of acquiring an annual grant from some philanthropic body, possibly the Arts Council. But the latter were not interested until the Society improved its standing beyond its current moribund reputation.

I was convinced that we must first find a way of engaging the support of younger and more progressive artists, not an easy task when the existing members enjoyed life membership and were far from anxious to encourage the 'moderns', by whom they felt threatened. Stories of the upheavals in St Ives, because of the 'A' and 'B' rulings (of the Penwith Society), of resignations and stormy committee meetings had reached Newlyn. It was obvious that we must proceed with caution, but proceed we must if the Society was to survive.

It therefore seemed that the only immediate change that was possible, without giving offence to the older members at Newlyn, was to modernise the interior of the building, rather than the Society. That could come later.

By making use of the front downstairs room and initiating new activities such as a film society, this gave the possibility of one-man shows and social occasions. I thought that this would give the gallery a role approaching that of an arts centre, and

I suspected might interest the Arts Council. In fact it was at this time that the latter gave us screens and stands, that not only extended the hanging space but allowed us to show pottery more effectively.

Whilst our public relations were developing, we embarked on a refurbishment of the gallery interior, and the placing of new signboards and notice boards outside. The interior had always been reminiscent of a swimming pool, with rows of wooden battens on which the pictures were hung, stretching around the walls. This system was reasonably effective, but not very attractive. Removing these battens, filling holes, and painting the gallery walls was a lengthy task. In the past such work, and the hanging of exhibitions, was carried out by local artisans, paid for by the Society. This seemed to me to be excessively extravagant in view of the critical financial position of the Society. The 'gentleman's art club' attitude was therefore abandoned, for a more practical approach in which the Curator and members of the Society turned-to with paint-brushes, screwdrivers and hammers, and carried out the work themselves.

Canney had always wanted to run a film club and proposed to the Society that the venue would be an ideal space during the closed months of October to March. They readily accepted. Over the winter this project proved a great success, showing old and rare avant-garde films. When they hosted the Arts Council's touring art-film show, this directly led to the Society at last acquiring an annual grant from them. Here we see the new Curator's canny skills at procuring funding come into play.

The lower room at the front of the gallery was not, strictly speaking, part of the curator's flat, and although it had been used intermittently over the years, in general it seemed to be a wasted area. It is true that John Armstrong had worked there for a time on a vast mural for the ceiling of Bristol Council House, and that the painter Jeremy Le Grice had also used the room as a studio, but the Society had not really made use of it and this seemed regrettable. It was largely a matter of access as the only entry was through the Curator's flat. When the Penzance Public Library indicated that they were prepared to sell a spiral staircase that they no longer needed for ten pounds, this seemed an ideal opportunity to install it in the gallery, by opening up the floor, which we promptly did.

This simple operation provided us with an additional gallery, suitable for one-man shows, for extensions of the gallery's exhibitions, and other activities. A charge was made for the use of this gallery so that the Society benefited in more ways than one. It was indeed in this room that the poet Sydney Graham held poetry readings, that life-classes took place, that slide-shows were held, and a number of artists had their first one-man shows there.

Whilst the gallery was extending its hanging space, the Society was enhancing its reputation in the matter of exhibitions, with the prestigious Early Newlyn Exhibition of 1958, with exhibitions of Newlyn Painters at Falmouth Polytechnic Gallery in 1958, and again at Plymouth City Art Gallery, with the African and Oceanic Sculpture Exhibition of 1960, and a Newlyn Exhibition at Ostend in 1963. The Early Newlyn Exhibition was of particular importance as a homage to the painters who established Newlyn as an art colony in the first place. It also attracted the attention

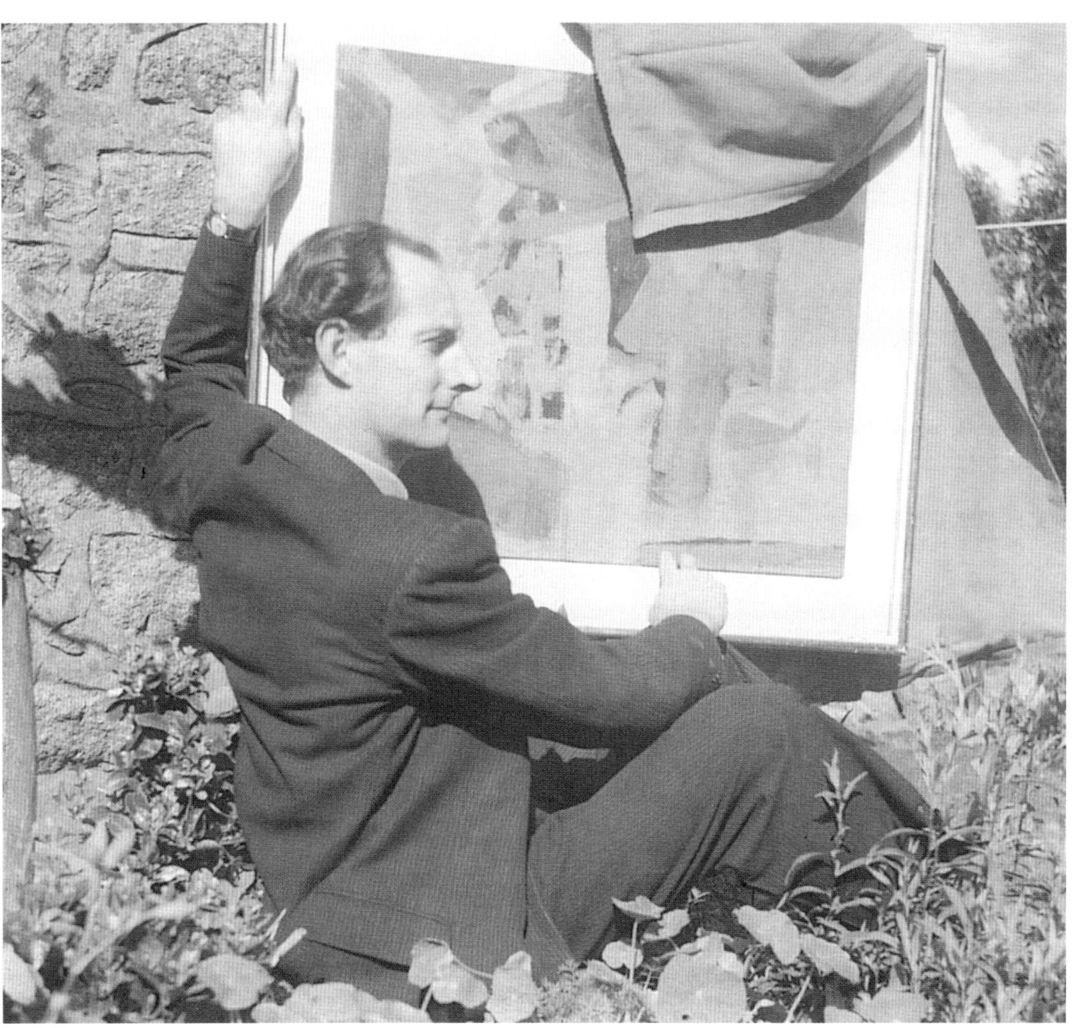

Canney outside Newlyn Gallery, *c.* 1960

Canney was judicious in his mixing of
'traditional' artists with the 'moderns', keeping
the public curious enough to want to visit
the gallery on a regular basis. The former
included Dod Procter, Stuart Armfield,
Alethea Garstin and Charles Simpson. While
the latter regulars included Peter Lanyon,
John Tunnard, Jack Pender, John Miller, Tony

O'Malley, Alexander Mackenzie, Jeremy Le
Grice, Denis Mitchell and Wilhelmina Barns-
Graham. In 1957 Canney also co-organised with
Barbara Hepworth an open-air exhibition of
contemporary sculpture, which included Henry
Moore, at Penlee Park in Penzance.

Canney's energy and imagination, along
with his media skills, using the BBC radio and
television, brought visitors from far and wide:

*Much has been made of the visit of Mark
Rothko to the Gallery in 1959 and he is
probably the most important visitor, but
there were other distinguished artists who*

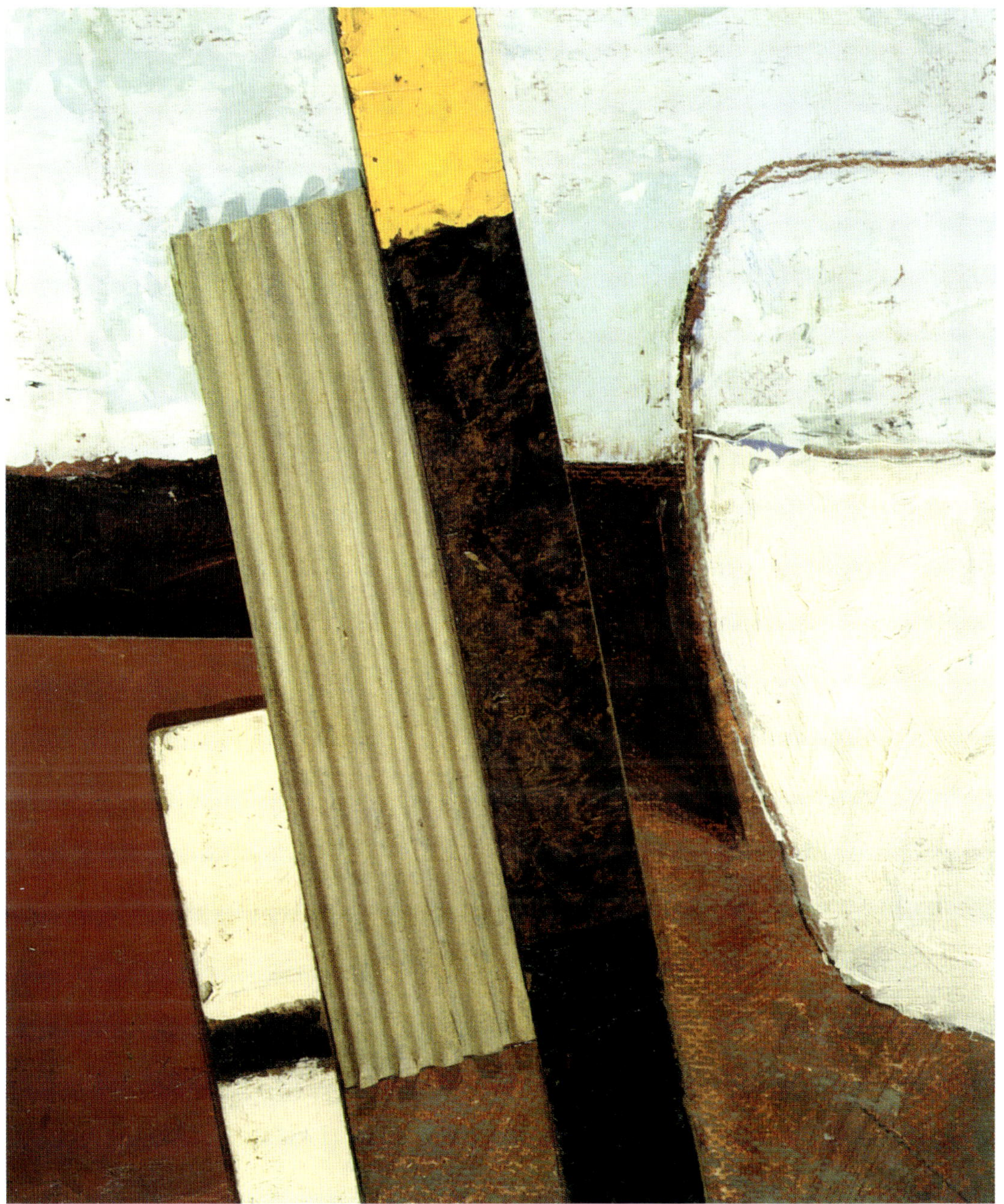

From the Quay, Newlyn 1957, oil on collage on board, 25.4 x 22.9 cm

came from the USA and included Newlyn
on their itinerary, well known dealers and
collectors too. Important figures from the
theatre, from the literary and musical
worlds also came, indicating that Newlyn
was becoming increasingly well known.

Rothko had been staying with Lanyon in St
Ives and the local artist was proudly showing
him around Penwith. Canney later recalled his
impressions of the celebrated visitor:

*A man of great presence and charm, he
was very generous about my work and*

spent some time looking at it. This was very encouraging, as I regarded Rothko as the most important painter on the international scene at that time. In conversation I referred to the majestic calm of one of his large canvasses, but he rejected this interpretation: 'There's actually a latent violence in my work. I am, in fact, the most violent of all the American painters.'

In addition to his daily Newlyn duties, Canney collaborated with the sculptor Brian Wall in the design and construction of a steel and perspex display for a touring exhibition of African and Oceanic sculpture in 1961; with the architect and painter John Miller, he reorganised and redesigned the Fore Street Gallery in St Ives; and, in order to supplement his meagre income, he acted as a part-time coastguard (with his own boat), did freelance broadcasts for the BBC on a variety of topics and, in 1964, taught at Plymouth College of Art.

As a man he was much respected and liked. Jeremy Le Grice, for one, praised Canney's appointment at Newlyn:

The pleasure he took in the company of artists, his powers of observation, mimicry and anecdote, together with a reckless sense of humour and excitement in the earlier days of his job, sharpened the atmosphere considerably.

I was fortunate to be able to observe this at close quarters when, during the winter of 1956/57 I used the lower front gallery as a studio (whilst preparing for Slade entrance). In those days access from the main gallery was via a tortuous metal winding staircase and the ground floor presented a domestic scene of nappies drying in front of a one-bar electric fire, news of the Suez crisis over a crackling radio and Madeleine juggling baby-food, cups of coffee for complaining,

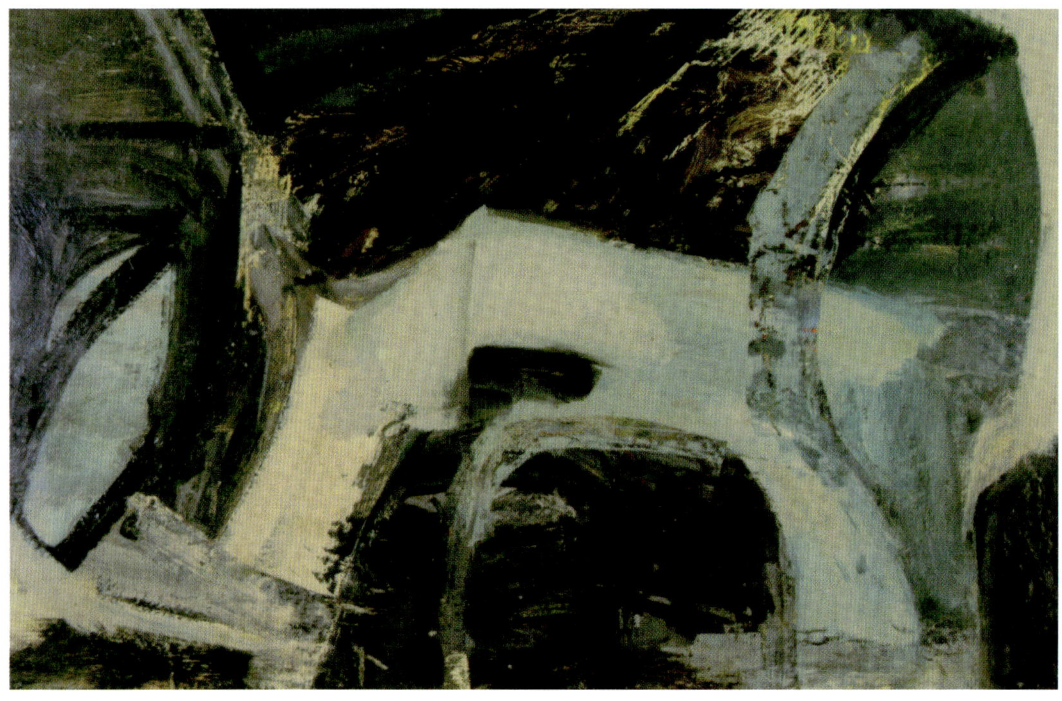

The Night-Fishing 1962, oil on board, 61 x 94 cm

disorientated artists or quietening vociferous poets … Sydney Graham and Arthur Caddick appeared to take the place on as a retreat from the pubs.

It's an indication of his affability and benevolence that he could be on very friendly terms with both Peter Lanyon and Roger Hilton. In fact, the latter stayed with the Canneys in the gallery while he searched for a studio in the area, in 1958 (and in fact found one over the old harbour). As Canney recalls:

Contrary to general opinion, Roger was a perfect guest when he was with us. He was interesting, entertaining, and when not outrageously drunk, very humorous. He gave me good advice with my own work …

Both Karl Weschke and Sydney Graham used to come to our flat under the gallery, to converse with Roger, but these meetings usually disintegrated before the evening was out. On one occasion Hilton accused Weschke of having 'hands stained by the blood of a thousand Jews' – but both then fell about laughing, and Roger exclaimed in his characteristic way – 'But that's ridiculous!' However, this was the only occasion on which I recall Roger hinting at his Jewish ancestry.

Sydney and Roger were much given to drawing on the table on odd scraps of paper, embellishing each other's work – valuable now I suppose, but they were just thrown away. Sydney was also prone to compose on the spur of the moment, and I still have a short poem he wrote about us and our young son which was quite haunting.

Canney has also left us a compelling account of Lanyon's *modus operandi*:

Very few people ever saw Peter at work in his studio. The studio was very much bespattered with paint because he worked with great frenzy at times. People seemed to imagine that some of the pictures more recently – because of the fluid way in which they were painted – were rather knocked off. But this could never have been the case because Peter was always a slow worker and after a long bout of painting of possibly two or three weeks, or two or three months, he would emerge as a public figure again but looking pale and really ill. I think painting took a tremendous amount out of him.

There was a strong exhibitionist element but one was never quite certain whether this was exhibition or whether this was just him. I remember on one occasion we went for a walk into the countryside and he would insist on standing on his head and looking through a gate at the landscape. But this did give him a new view of the landscape by doing this sort of thing.

I think it was partially exhibitionistic at that particular moment but there was no doubt that at some time he had looked upside down at the landscape and then seen the landscape in a new way. And on this particular occasion it was … it was rather interesting because we had visited a Bronze Age village and afterwards I painted a picture of this and called it something like 'Celtic Twilight' but my picture was really very literal – a kind of cross section through the ground with graves – but Peter's picture was called 'High Country' and showed a long meandering shape that went up the picture and which expressed much more the kind of high country that we'd been in, and it derived in part at any rate from a long road – a long meandering road that we'd gone up and afterwards I was surprised and astounded that I hadn't been able to see that this was the thing that would really produce a picture which would give much more a feeling of the place.

After nearly ten years in this far corner of Cornwall Canney was in need of a new challenge and, in 1965, he gratefully accepted an invitation to become Gallery Director and Lecturer at the University of California, Santa Barbara. He moved there for about a year while Madeleine and Simon temporarily lodged at John Miller's big house at Sancreed. He was surprised to find some moving reminders of home:

Seeing Cornwall and Cornish art from California was a valuable experience, and it put events and personalities there in perspective. However, Cornwall was not far away, as I found when I visited the old gold-mining communities in Northern California, and saw the graves of Cornish exiles from such places as Redruth and St Just who never managed to return home.

In 1966, with encouragement from Paul Feiler, Canney returned to the UK to teach at the Royal West of England College of Art in Bristol.

Meanwhile, Canney had made a fairly radical shift from his earlier landscape derived abstraction, admitting:

Lanyon's intensely individual approach was too personal, the pursuit of the genius loci too elusive, and the informed automatism of the painting process too exhausting for me. (Davies, 1994)

His art now moved firmly into Constructivism, playing on the geometric permutations achieved from elementary shapes. As he explained, in 1983:

For a number of years now my work has been broadly related to the Constructivist tradition. However, since 1979 it has relied upon a simple principle, in which the work constructs itself from itself. Based upon a systematic re-orientation of parts of the square, this process suggests an infinite range of possibilities.

The imposition of these limits comes as a reaction against an earlier hedonistic period of improvisatory abstraction. The discipline of these new procedures is a practical aid rather than a moral corrective. Constraints are, paradoxically, imposed to assist invention and as a means towards greater certainty in the structuring of plane surfaces. Such constraints should not be confused with reductivism, for the intention here has been to travel in precisely the opposite direction, namely to master the simple in order to proceed to the complex. For example, the whiteness of the reliefs is not a search for purity or even for a simplicity of statement. White permits the element of relief to show most readily, whereas the addition of colour to relief surfaces tends to obscure the three-dimensionality of the separate planes. It is for this reason alone that I have used white almost exclusively during the last four years.

Despite these later works appearing to be 'placeless' in their purity of abstraction, it's nevertheless interesting that Canney found it necessary to add this footnote, for an exhibition in Chicago in 1987:

Although the principal preoccupation of the artist is of a constructivist nature, and concerned with the layering and overlapping of portions of the square, unconscious figurative references inevitably emerge, related to the artist's life in West Cornwall.

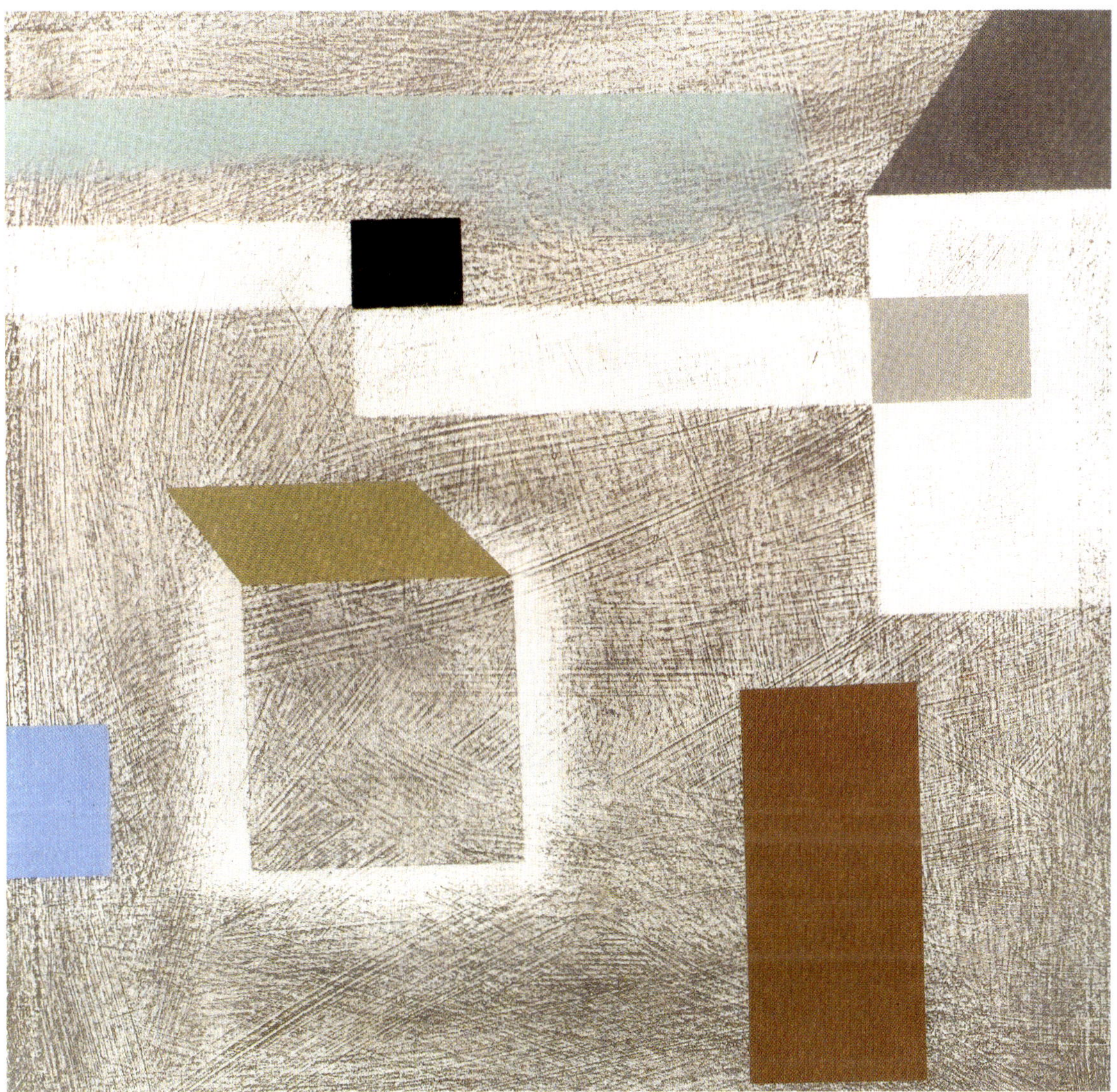

Granite Village by the Sea 1986, alkyd on panel, 35 x 35 cm

After he retired from teaching in 1983, the Canneys relocating to his cherished Italy, where they acquired a fourteenth-century palazzo in the mediaeval hilltop village of Casole d'Elsa (between San Gimignano and Siena). In his bright studio he created a whole new body of work using alkyds, a fast drying paint, as well as hard-edged reliefs.

Canney continued to have successful exhibitions; he also won numerous awards for his TV documentaries.

Restless as ever, they moved to France (the south-west edge of Provence) in 1992, and a year later finally settled in Devizes, Wiltshire, where Canney died on December 29, 1999.

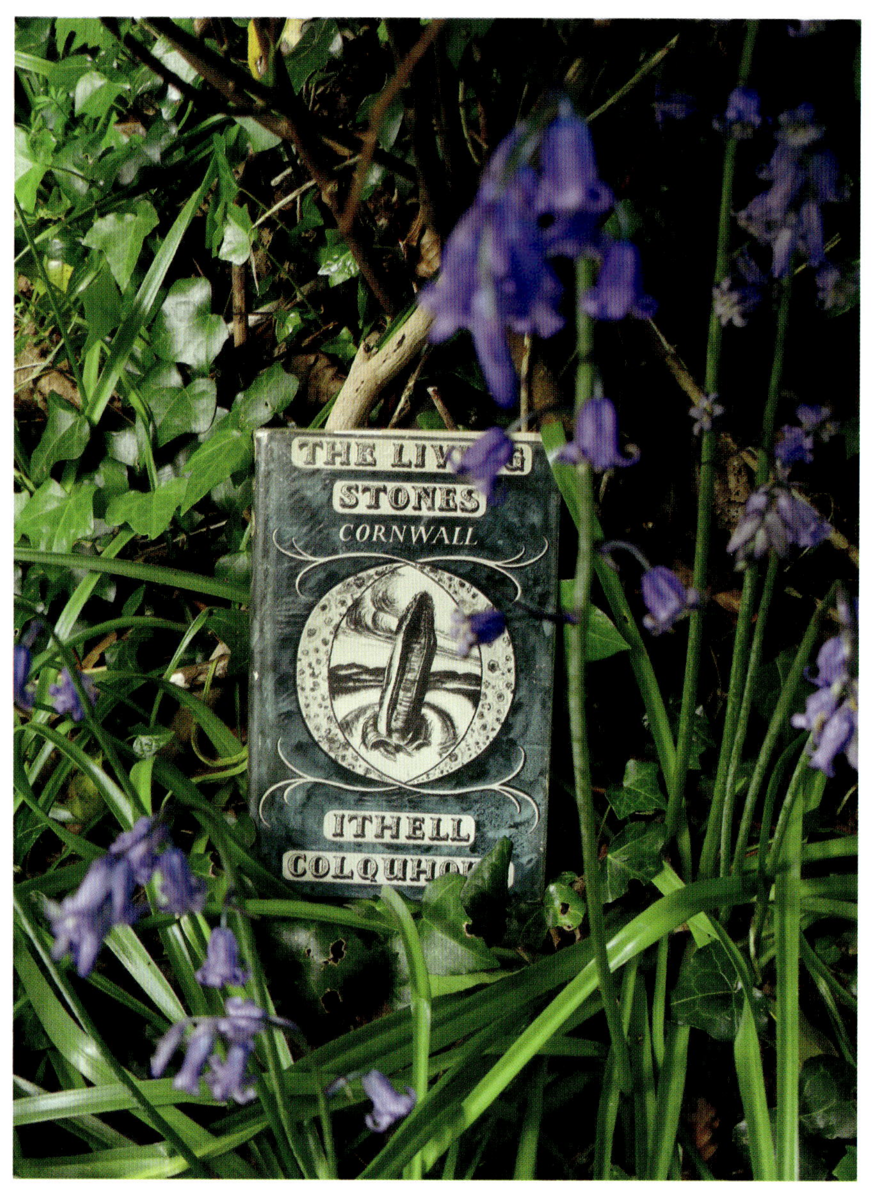

8

Lamorna Trio: Marlow Moss, Ithell Colquhoun, John Tunnard

BORN (MARJORIE JEWELL MOSS) on May 29, 1889 into a Jewish family in Kilburn, London. Her father, Lionel Moss, was a master hosier and clothier. As a girl she studied music and ballet until TB intervened in 1916. She turned to painting and, much against her conservative family's wishes, entered the St John's Wood School of Art and the following year attended the Slade. Uninspired, in 1919 she discovered Cornwall where she stayed for four years and appears to have suffered a psychological breakdown. Despite the family disapproval of her artistic pursuits, she benefited from her father's inheritance, giving her financial independence for the rest of her life.

On returning to London in 1923, she underwent a total reinvention of herself.

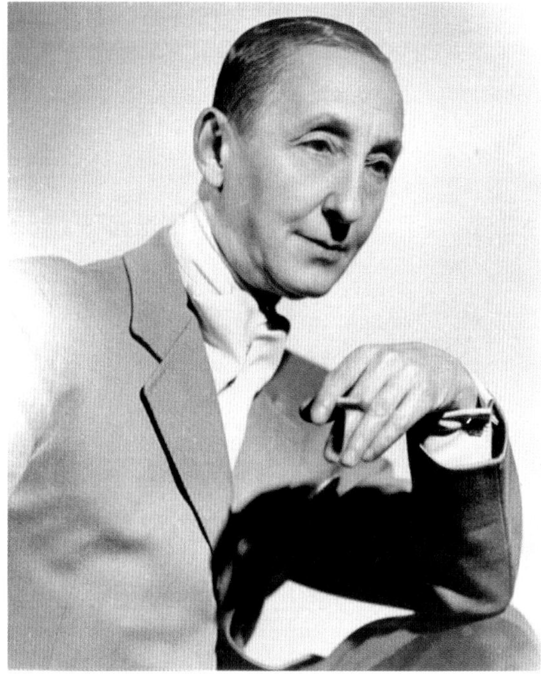

Changing her name to Marlow, she adopted a masculine appearance, and spent most of her time in the British Museum Reading Room, furthering her education in art and mathematics. The ideas of the Romanian mathematician, Matila Ghyka, were particularly influential, with an emphasis on Pythagorean principles, the golden section and Fibonnaci series. (She later listed Marie Curie, Arthur Rimbaud and Friedrich Nietzsche as inspirational figures.) She returned to Cornwall in 1924 and attended sculpture classes at Penzance School of Art. Back in London in 1926 she resumed painting.

In 1928 she travelled to Paris to exhibit her work and here at last she felt at home among the intellectual milieu. This included her great mentor Piet Mondrian, as well as studying with Léger and Ozenfant at the Académie Moderne. The Neo-Plastic movement, with its emphasis on pure primary colours in rectangular arrangements, gave her art a precise focus. She set up house with Netty Nijhoff (wife of the poet Martinus Nijhoff). Frank Elgar, in his study of Mondrian, makes a brief reference to the couple at this time:

> One of his own pupils, a young English woman, was a colourful figure among the dubious clientele of the Montparnasse cabarets. Flanked by an excessively corpulent Dutch woman, she went about, summer and winter, dressed like a jockey.

Throughout the 1930s she was involved in many exhibitions, including the Salon

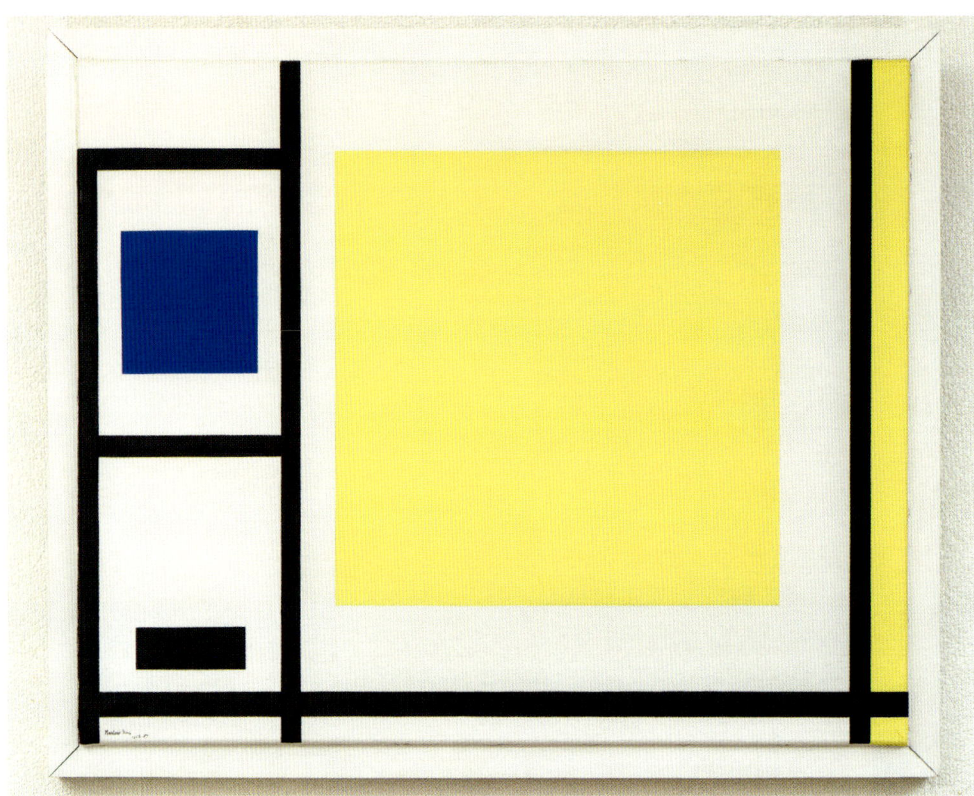

White, Black, Yellow & Blue 1956/57, oil on canvas, 76 x 61 cm

Surindépendents, Association 1940, Parc des Expositions, Salon des Réalités Nouvelles, Groupe Anglo-Americain and Abstract Création (which she co-founded). Outside of France she participated in the Konstructivisten exhibition at the Kunsthalle, Basle (1937) and Abstracte Kunst at the Stedelijk Museum, Amsterdam (1938). In 1937 Moss purchased the Château d'Evreux at Gauciel in Normandy. War was declared while she was on holiday in the Netherlands and her home was occupied by the French Air Force.

Fearful because of her Jewish background, Moss fled, onboard a cargo ship with many refugees, back to England and settled in Lamorna, in a bungalow, for the rest of her life (despite Mondrian, now in London, asking her to accompany him to New York). Back at Penzance she attended architecture classes, which led to her spatial experiments with three-dimensional metal constructions. In 1944 the Château d'Evreux was bombed by the Germans, with the loss of virtually her entire oeuvre up to 1940, as well as all her belongings. Apart from the devastating loss, this episode would prove to be catastrophic for her subsequent career. We only know her late works and this lack of access to the development and context of her painting and sculpture has certainly handicapped her reputation.

Moss was reunited with Nijhoff in 1947 and now spent part of each year visiting the Netherlands and Paris where she was part of the Groupe Espace.

It's a curious fact that she never socialised with Hepworth and Nicholson at nearby St Ives. Not for want of trying by her. She wrote to Nicholson in July 1941:

*I am taking the liberty of writing to you as
advised by Piet Mondrian, who I know is a
good friend of yours …*

*I had the pleasure in Paris of having tea
with your wife and would be very pleased
to see her again, couldn't you both come
over one day? There is a bus service from
St Ives to Penzance then from Penzance to
St Buryan which stops at Lamorna Turn
where I could meet you, if you do not know
Lamorna. If you both feel disposed to accept
my invitation I shall be glad if you will let
me know which day and time to expect you?*

*Mondrian mentions in his letter that your
wife had thought of taking the children over
to America. I also had thought of trying to
go, but there are so many difficulties, that I
do not think it possible.*

*I haven't had the pleasure of meeting you, it
would be very nice to talk to someone whose
work is in the same direction as my own and
so get away a moment from this ghastly war.*

No reply is on record from Nicholson, as
far as I know, and it has been assumed she was
totally ignored. However, Moss wrote again in
May 1943, reiterating the invitation and the bus
details, but adding this:

*Would it be possible for Barbara to lend me
"The Circle" I will take great care of it?*

*Unfortunately I cannot get any of the
publications you noted down for me.*

This hints at some level of contact and some
degree of intimacy (using Hepworth's first
name).

She cut an unusual figure, even by bohemian
Cornish standards, with her cropped hair,
cravat, white blouse, braces, jodhpurs and
riding crop and usually travelled by pony and
trap. Michael Canney, who was in charge of

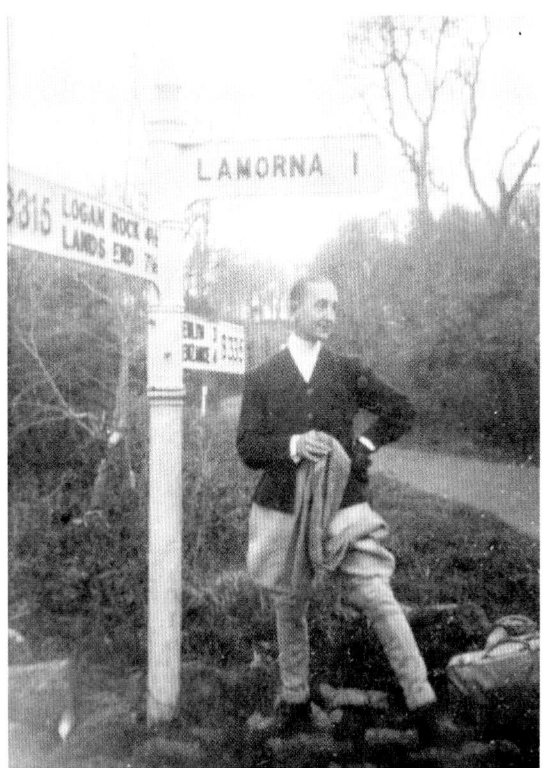

Newlyn Art Gallery, tried in vain to get her
to show there. Financially, she had no need to
sell her artworks. He was one of the few local
artists to appreciate her importance and later
commented, with his characteristic perception:

*In retrospect I find it difficult to credit that
Marlow Moss, perhaps the closest follower
of Mondrian, could have lived and worked
in the midst of a colony of artists in west
Cornwall for so many years, and have still
remained a private figure. It is true that she
was frequently absent on the continent, and
that she deliberately led a secluded life at
Lamorna, where she had a small studio like
a mission chapel. But I do recall one fleeting
image of her on a pony and trap, riding in
style on her way to Penzance market, with
Nettie beside her. On another occasion she
appeared in Newlyn Art Gallery, striding
from picture to picture, small, alert, and
attired it seemed as a kind of jockey. I did*

*not know then, and indeed nobody was
aware, that her work was respected by Léger
and Ozenfant, by Max Bill (a particularly
close friend), by Jean Gorin, Herbin,
Vantongerloo, and a host of other European
artists, of note. She had even been sponsored
by Mondrian himself as a founder-member
of the Abstraction-Création group.*

*As an artist, Moss has been dismissed as
'Too close to Mondrian for comfort', an
indication that her critics are prepared to
ignore the favourable opinions of Max Bill
and Mondrian regarding her contributions
to Neo-Plasticism. Her introduction of the
double line into orthogonal compositions was
sufficiently important to provoke Mondrian
into writing and asking why she had done
it. Moss, the rational artist, justified her
innovation as a rhythmic and dynamic
device, and summoned mathematics to
support her case. Mondrian replied …
'Figures don't mean much to me', but he
nevertheless introduced the same double line
into his own work.* (Davies, 1994)

The Hanover Gallery gave her shows in
1953 and 1958 and she came in for some harsh
criticism by those who saw her as merely a
Mondrian copyist. In more recent years a
debate has opened on whether it was actually
Mondrian who was influenced by Moss,
particularly in his use of the double-line. From
contemporary accounts there's no doubt that
Mondrian took her very seriously indeed.

She died, of cancer, aged 69, in hospital in
Penzance on August 23, 1958 and her ashes were
scattered, following her wishes, over the sea at
Lamorna.

MARGARET ITHELL COLQUHOUN was born
October 9, 1906 in Shillong, Assam, India. Her
father worked for the Indian Civil Service. On
returning to England she attended Thornlow
School, Rodwell, near Weymouth, followed
by Cheltenham Ladies College (1919-25), then
Cheltenham College of Art and Crafts.

In 1928 Colquhoun enrolled at the Slade
School of Art where she studied drawing under
its Principal, the formidable Henry Tonks.
She impressed him enough to be named joint
winner (using a Biblical subject) of the eminent
Summer Composition Prize (1929). In a letter,
Tonks praised her 'remarkable gifts', but went
on to warn her, with some foresight: 'the only
danger in your development is that with your
active and curious mind you may be led to run
after all strange objects.' In 1930 she published
her first article 'The Prose of Alchemy' in
The Quest, revealing what became a lifelong
involvement with the occult. On graduation she
travelled around the Mediterranean where she
did paintings of various archaeological sites.

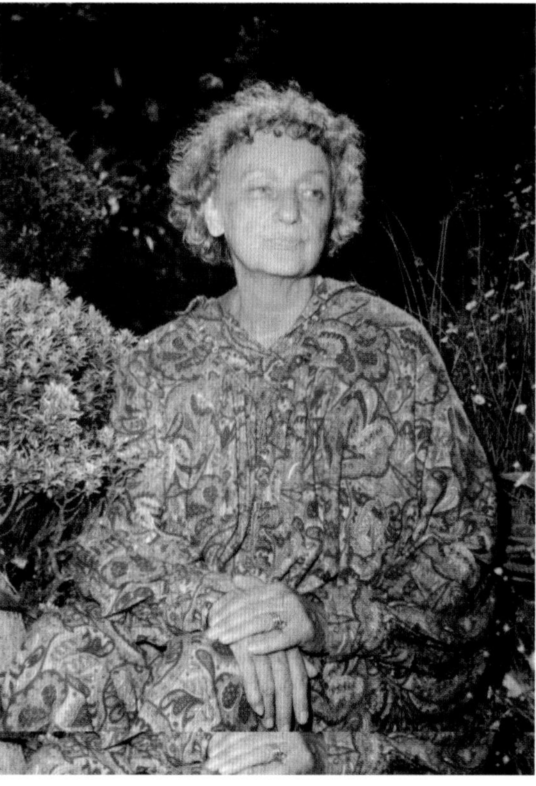

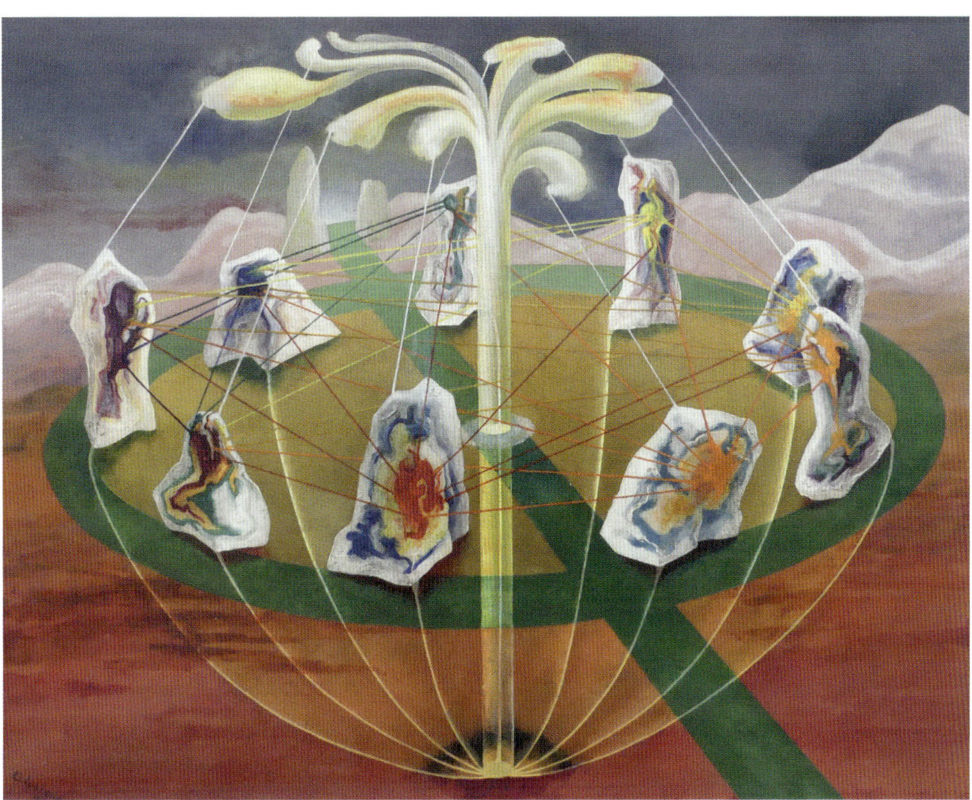

Dance of the Nine Opals 1942, oil on canvas, 51 x 69 cm

Living in Paris in 1931 Colquhoun encountered Surrealism, in particular the work of Dalí, which proved to be a turning point for her. At this time she produced mainly flower and plant paintings, usually with an emphasis on their correspondence to sexual organs (the phallus/vulva conjunction was a constant motif throughout her life's work). She visited the highly influential International Surrealist Exhibition at the New Burlington Galleries in 1936, where she witnessed the extrovert Dalí, flanked by two wolfhounds, almost suffocate in a deep sea diving suit. The Surrealist emphasis on allowing images to manifest from the unconscious, subverting and bypassing the rational mind, had an obvious appeal to someone interested in magic and the supernatural. Colquhoun met the poet W.B. Yeats in 1937 and a brief friendship developed

before his death. The same year she provided mural decorations for Moreton-in-Marsh hospital. In 1939 she had a joint show with Roland Penrose at the Mayor Gallery (where they hired a tramp to sit in the window, thus gaining some useful publicity). She also visited Paris again and met André Breton with the Chilean Roberto Matta (the latter's complex theory of psychomorphology was also added to her working methods).

1940 saw Colquhoun ostracized from the London Surrealist Group when she refused to give unconditional support to its leader E.L.T. Mesens, who disapproved of her occult researches. She now incorporated various exotic techniques of Surrealism into her own *modus operandi*, including automatism, collage, decalcomania, entoptic graphomania, parsemage, fumage and stillomancy. Colquhoun

married Toni del Renzio, an Italian poet
and painter, in 1943 (having saved him from
bankruptcy by paying off debts he'd run
up with the printer of his magazine, *Arson*).
However, the marriage ended in acrimonious
divorce after only four years. She published
the first account of automatism to appear in
English, 'The Mantic Stain', in *Enquiry* (1949).

In 1949 Colquhoun acquired a corrugated
iron studio hut, Vow Cave, in Lamorna Valley
(while keeping a home in Hampstead). This
area of Cornwall is abundant enough in ancient
stone circles, burial chambers, holy wells,
Iron-Age forts, Celtic crosses, inland caves, or
fogues, spooky folklore and legend to have kept
her otherworldly pursuits well nourished. The
valley is also particularly dense in woodland,
rare for Penwith, accompanied by exotic flora.
This enchanting environment soon manifested
in Colquhoun's painting, but perhaps more
importantly for her posterity it led to her
writing a noteworthy travel book: *The Living
Stones: Cornwall* (1957). This was a follow up to
her Irish travel book *The Crying of the Wind:
Ireland* (1955). Colquhoun explores less the
highways than the byways of Cornwall. With
a lyrical eloquence and attuned sensitivity,
Colquhoun delves under the skin of her adopted
county attracted by the 'animist's trinity' of
rocks, wells and trees. Displaying an impressive
knowledge of botany and geology, as well as
forgotten folk traditions and legends of saints,
revealing her animism and pantheism, she
evokes the *genius loci* reposing just below the
surface of an elemental terrain. She goes on to
explain:

*The life of a region depends ultimately on
its geologic substratum, for this sets up a
chain-reaction which passes, determining
their character, in turn through its streams
and wells, its vegetation and the animal-life*

*that feeds on this, and finally through the
type of human being attracted to live there.
In a profound sense also the structure of
its rocks gives rise to the psychic life of the
land: granite, serpentine, slate, sandstone,
limestone, chalk, and the rest have each
their special personality dependent on the
age in which they were laid down, each
being co-existent with a special phase of the
earth-spirit's manifestation.*

Colquhoun also reveals how seriously she
takes the folklore associated with the ancient
sites:

*Stones that whisper, stones that dance, that
play on pipe or fiddle, that tremble at cock-
crow, that eat and drink, stones that march
as an army – these unhewn slabs of granite
hold the secret of the country's inner life.*

Press comments for her travel books
included: 'An attractive writer … a jeweller's
eye for detail' (*Observer*); 'some passages recall
a talent similar to Blake or Walter de la Mare'
(*Times Literary Supplement*); while Elizabeth
Bowen said she had 'a painter's eye, writing
particularly beautifully about skies, twilights
and the intensive atmosphere of the remote
places'.

Unfortunately, the acoustic harmony of
the valley became more and more disrupted
by hordes of holidaymakers and, reluctantly,
she gave up Vow Cave and, in 1959, moved to
Stone Cross Cottage in neighbouring Paul, still
experimenting:

*In the early 1960s, I became intrigued
with the visual and tactile qualities of the
'ready made', first exploited by Marcel
Duchamp. But in my case it was the 'ready
throw-away' which inspired me. I saw a
valid, if silent, statement in what is usually
discarded.*

Thus began her experiments with Merz-reliefs, pioneered by Kurt Schwitters (who she met during the war in Hampstead). She also used 'enamel paint, more or less diluted, in a semi-automatic way to bring about the emergence of what Breton called the Convulsive Landscape.'

In 1961 she published her novel (probably written many years earlier), *Goose of Hermogenes*, a Gothic novel of initiation based on alchemical ideas of transformation. Later in that decade, she had a trip to Egypt and wrote a series of travel articles for the *Times Educational Supplement*.

Considering her reclusive inclinations it is surprising to find that, all through her life, she was a compulsive joiner of esoteric groups. These included the Ordo Templi Orientis, New Isis Lodge, Order of the Keltic Cross (conferred Lady of Honour), Order of the Pyramid and Sphinx, Fellowship of Isis (ordained as a Priestess), Ancient Celtic Church (conferred as Deaconess), Order of the Free and Accepted Masonry for Men and Women (initiated as Master Mason). Much of her art, either explicitly or tacitly, assimilated the wide-ranging symbolism from these movements, particularly the Tree of Life from the Qabalah.

Colquhoun had a large exhibition at Exeter Museum & Art Gallery in 1972. Earlier her work was to be seen in group shows at the Penwith Society of Arts, but she had been a regular exhibitor at Newlyn Art Gallery for years and had a major retrospective there in 1976. The following year, at the same venue, Colquhoun exhibited her designs for a pack of Taro cards (her preferred spelling). She also published a highly regarded biography of MacGregor Mathers, founder of the Hermetic Order of the Golden Dawn, *The Sword of Wisdom* (1975).

A decline in her health in the 1980s saw Colquhoun sell up at Paul and move to a care home back at her cherished Lamorna. She died there of heart failure, aged 81, on April 11, 1988 and, in accordance with her will, her ashes were scattered to the elements along the nearby cliffs. Most of her works were bequeathed to the National Trust.

JOHN SAMUEL TUNNARD was born May 7, 1900 in Caesar's Camp, Sandys, Bedfordshire. His father was a talented amateur painter of country scenes with a zeal for hunting, while his mother was a wealthy heiress. (In time, the younger Tunnard would develop an equal zeal against hunting, leading to a complete breakdown in relations with his father.) He was sent to school at Horton, Ickwellbury, Bedfordshire before progressing to Charterhouse (1914-18), where he won the Strum Robertson prize for drawing two years running. On finishing school he briefly trained

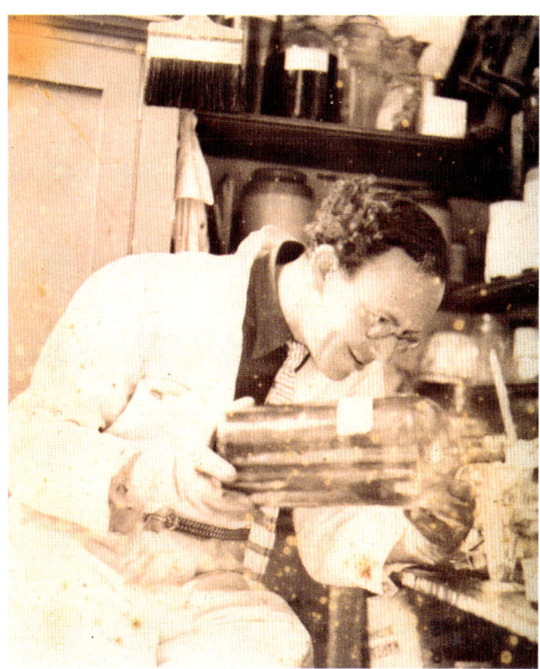

as a stockbroker (he missed a call up for the war by one day), but soon enrolled at the Royal College of Art (1919-21) to study textiles, graduating with a Diploma in Design. (While a student, he performed as a drummer in a dance band and both music and dance would remain a lifelong delight.)

Tunnard started working in Manchester with the textile manufacturers Tootal, Broadhurst, Lee (1921-26), followed by the carpet makers H. & M. Southwell in Shropshire. He married Mary 'Bob' Robertson, a fellow pupil at the RCA, in 1926. In 1928 he became fabric selector for John Lewis in Oxford Street, London. His involvement with textile design exerted a significant influence on the compositional balance and strong formal structure of his later paintings. He rounded off the decade as a part-time teacher at the Central School of Arts and Crafts.

The Royal Academy accepted three of Tunnard's landscape paintings for their summer show in 1931; the same year he exhibited with the London Group (and would do so for the next seven years). 1933 saw the Tunnards settling at Cadgwith, Cornwall, as well as John having his first major show at the Redfern Gallery. At first they lived in a caravan before moving into a fisherman's loft. From here they both ran a hand-blocked silk business (including scarves, handkerchiefs and table cloths). Bob's gift of Herbert Read's book, *Surrealism*, for Christmas 1936, proved to be a revelation for Tunnard, particularly the amoebic forms of Miró and the perambulatory line of Klee. He soon formed part of the Surrealist section at the Artists International Exhibiton in 1937; he was also corresponding with Ben Nicholson, Henry Moore and Ivon Hitchens. At the end of 1938 he was confident enough to approach Peggy Guggenheim at her London gallery, Guggenheim Jeune.

She recorded his colourful character in her autobiography, *Confessions of an Art Addict*:

> *One day a marvelous man in a highly elaborate tweed coat walked into the gallery. He looked like Groucho Marx. He was animated as a jazz-band leader; which he turned out to be. He showed us his gouaches, which were as musical as Kandinsky's, as delicate as Klee's, and as gay as Miró's. His colour was exquisite and his construction magnificent. His name was John Tunnard. He asked me very modestly if I thought I could give him a show, and then and there I fixed the date. (Later, he told me he couldn't believe his luck, he was so used to being turned down.) During this exhibition, which was a great success from every point of view, a woman came into the gallery and asked, 'Who is John Tunnard?' Turning three somersaults, Tunnard, who was in the gallery, landed at this lady's feet, saying, 'I am John Tunnard'.*

The outbreak of war saw Tunnard register as a conscientious objector. He was assigned duty as an auxiliary coastguard on the Lizard peninsula, also doing some paid work on local fishing boats. The long hours spent staring out at the sea's horizon possibly influenced his work through the 1940s, which acquired a deep perspectival depth displaying the skillful deceptions of *trompe l'oeil*. The pictures exuded a strange dreamlike ambiance, depicting the topography of some mysterious uninhabited terrain, proffering a disorienting familiarity, while hinting at an inconceivable dimension. All overlaid with Constructivist patterns, immersed in translucent colours of rich subtlety and maintaining strong architectural, engineering qualities (given a surrealist slant). In achieving these effects Tunnard, ever the boffin, experimented with a complex

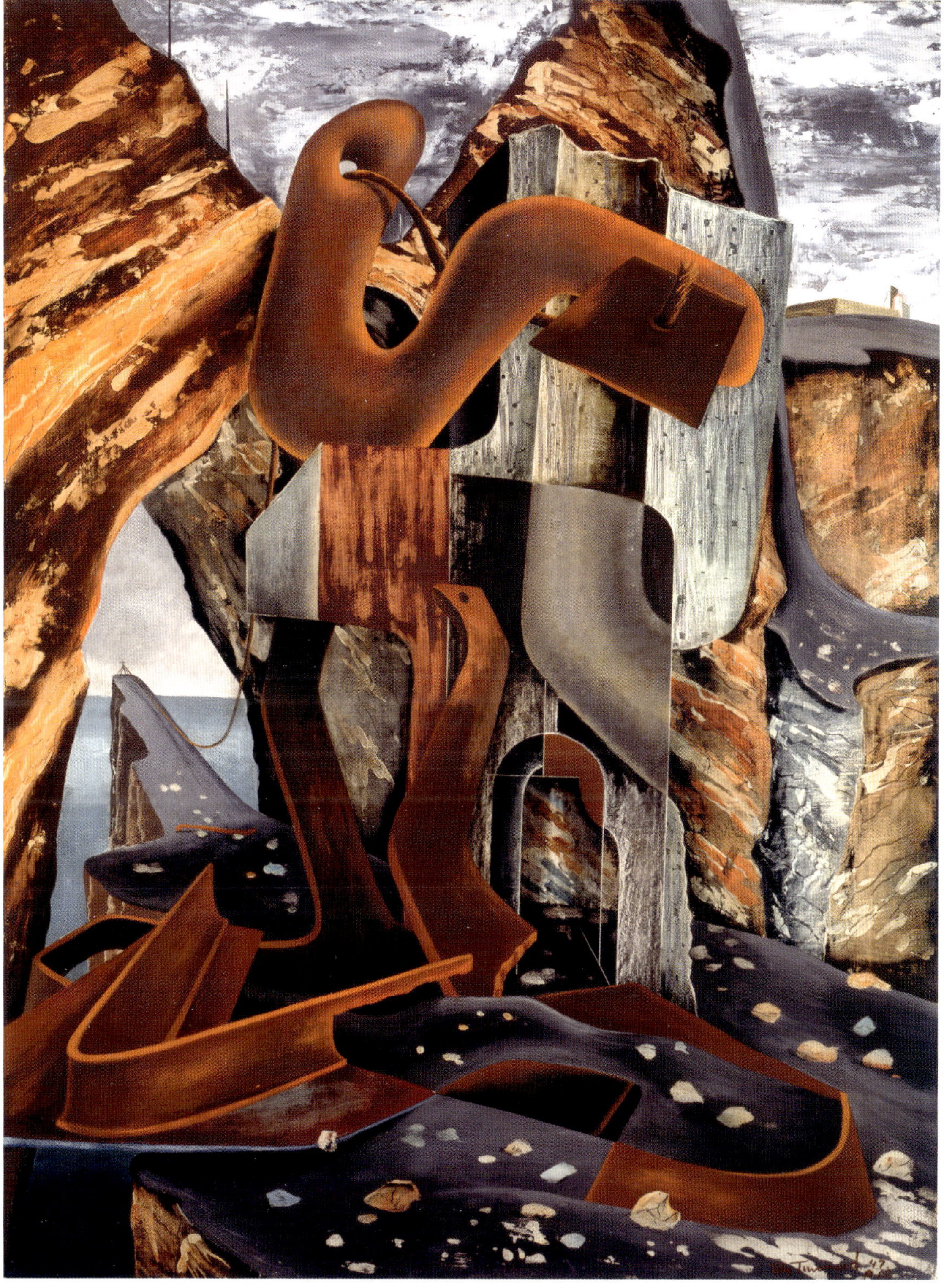

Levant Zawn 1947, oil & gesso-prepared fibre board, 103 x 78 cm

combination of media (including unusual chemicals), on gesso prepared board, resulting in what appeared to be a textured fresco finish. Friends recorded their amazement, when allowed to touch the paintings, that these 'textures' were in fact a perfectly smooth surface.

Immediately after the war Tunnard acquired a job as art master at Wellington College, Berkshire, but this didn't last more than a couple of terms. Drawn back to Cornwall, the couple moved, in 1947, into Garden Mine Cottage, near Morvah, just below Carn Watch, the highest point in west Cornwall. It was so exposed to the elements that Tunnard had to anchor his studio building to the ground with cables. Flora and fauna, as well as inscrutable aquatic life forms, now start to inhabit his pictures. (He was also a keen entomologist and botanist, collecting specimens for the British Museum of Natural History.) He started a job teaching design and etching at Penzance School of Art (1948-65) (one of his etching students happened to be Wilhelmina Barns-Graham). Never a joiner of groups, Tunnard was one of the few artists to decline an invitation to join the recently formed Penwith

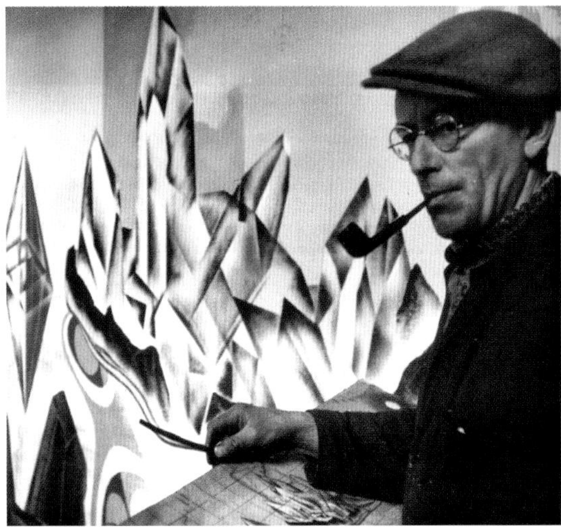
Tunnard working on his Festival of Britain mural

Society of Artists in 1949. Though a few years later he did join the Newlyn Society of Artists.

In 1950 Tunnard's reputation was such that he was commissioned to provide a large painting and a mural for the following year's Festival of Britain. Sir Hugh Casson specified that the mural's theme should be crystallography and extend along the length of the Regatta Restaurant (facing a commission from Victor Pasmore). The death of Tunnard's mother provided the couple with an inheritance allowing them to purchase a large house at Lamorna, in 1952. This was the painter Dame Laura Knight's former house, Trethinnick. It came with six acres of impenetrable jungle, which would take up much of the couple's time and energy, revealing a hitherto shared hidden talent for landscape gardening. From here the Tunnards threw their legendary all-night parties, with John performing his Fred Astaire act, an improvised soft shoe shuffle, to jazz records. He also formed the exploratory Grumbla Club (named from a nearby iron-age village), consisting of a group of archaeological enthusiasts. The couple were avid readers and they especially admired the poetry of Emily Dickinson and E. E. Cummings. When, in 1959, Mark Rothko visited the Newlyn Art Gallery he was impressed to see Tunnard's work on display (as American artists had been aware of him for many years). He was even more surprised to hear that he was still alive and working up the road. Rudolph Glossop, a friend of long standing, leaves us this account of Tunnard at work:

> No one saw John when he painted, for then solitude was essential to him. The studio was quite apart, at Cadgwith in a fishloft on the edge of the cove, at Garden Mine Cottage in a hut on the moor, and at Lamorna in a small corrugated iron

shack, hidden in woodland beside the stream. When painting he entered a state of concentration and absolute absorption such as one associates with philosophers and creative mathematicians. He once told me how, standing before a meticulously prepared gesso ground, he would hesitate in fear before making the first brushstroke which might influence the whole composition. Once started, he worked with extraordinary energy and intensity. Then he would relax and go back to the cliffs and the moors, where he found the natural shapes which inspired and inform even the more abstract and geometrical of his later pictures.

Entering the space age in the 1960s, there was a feeling that Tunnard had anticipated the new vision of interplanetary exploration gripping the public imagination. He achieved a rare successful synthesis of art and science, maintaining an organic balance between his acute observations of nature with developments in technology (revealing intimations of a post-apocalytic world). He was fascinated by the Apollo space mission, and aspects of this ambitious project now informed his paintings. Though for Tunnard his depictions of outer space still implied an inner psychological space, intertwined through a subtle Möbius twist of perception. In 1960 he had a new studio built at Trethinnick, as well as having a major show at the Durlacher Gallery, New York. Remarkably, for a man with an apparent extra-terrestrial viewpoint, Tunnard remained earthbound all of his life and travelled to the US by ship, dancing every night with the band.

He continued to exhibit at the R A, becoming an Associate Member in 1967.

As a painter of chimera-like fabrications, Tunnard was very much *sui generis*, the word 'visionary' may well apply to him more than any of his contemporaries. He possessed a paradoxical character trait of being gregariously entertaining *and* semi-reclusive, mixing little with other artists around the St Ives 'group'. This possibly led to him being often overlooked in the written accounts. Herbert Read was one of the few admiring critics to write with insight about his work:

> *Tunnard is an artist who has acquired by observation a profound intuition of the workings of nature, and this enables him to imagine forms that represent the morphology of nature in its ceaseless flux. That intuition prevents the artist from becoming a mere manipulator of a lifeless geometry. His forms are the inventions of his imagination but that imagination is a complete world, in some sense a prophetic world. He himself has said that after he has painted a picture he will sometimes come across a form he has used without knowing that it existed in nature. This is credible because he works with a visual imagination that is familiar with archetypal forms – those universal patterns from which all particular forms evolve …*

In 1967 Tunnard suffered a stroke, and when Bob died in 1970 he moved into a small flat in Penzance. He died there, aged 71, on December 18, 1971. The Tunnards are buried in Zennor churchyard, next to Bryan Wynter.

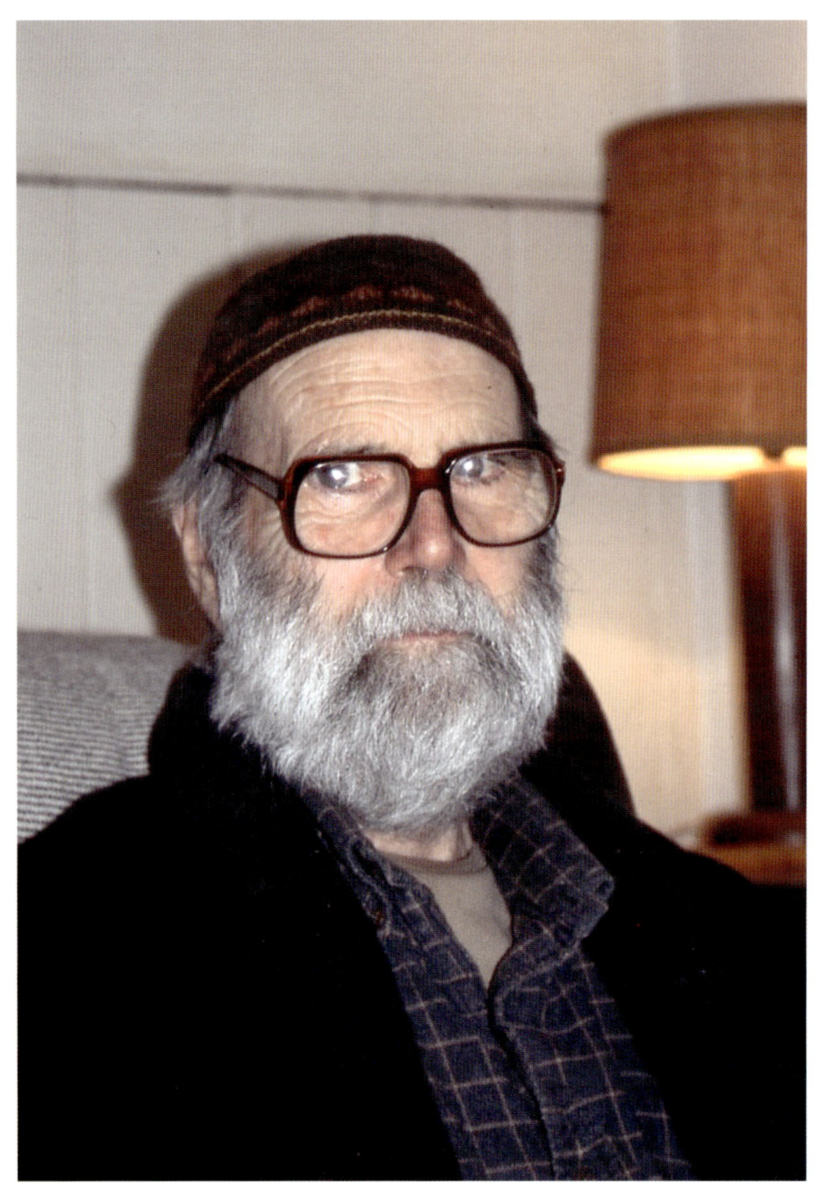

9

Timeless Art: Breon O'Casey

Artists have flocked to St Ives in Cornwall, over many decades, for the remarkable light. But according to Breon O'Casey: 'That's all balls: it was the sense of camaraderie against an, at best, indifferent, and at worst, hostile, world that drew them.' He should know, having spent more than fifty busy years there, displaying great versatility in the roles of painter, jeweller, etcher, sculptor and weaver.

O'Casey was born in Battersea, London on April 30 1928, the eldest child of the great playwright Sean O'Casey and Eileen Reynolds, a chorus girl, model and actress from Mayo. Since the rejection of his play *The Silver Tassie* by Yeats and the Abbey Theatre in 1926, the elder O'Casey had turned his back on Ireland – thus adding his name to the long list of disillusioned Irish writers in exile. (The O'Caseys had two more children: Shivaun, who has become a respected theatre director and actor, and Niall who died tragically of leukaemia aged twenty-one.)

In 1937, following advice from Bernard Shaw, the family moved to Devon to be near the progressive school, Dartington Hall. Breon had a happy time here, where emphasis on physical activities and skills was given equal sway with more academic pursuits and he later claimed to have learned to think with his hands as well as his head. Teachers included Michael Chekov, cousin to Anton, in charge of drama and, more crucially for the young O'Casey, Naum Slutzky, formerly of the Bauhaus, teaching metalwork.

Following National Service, he went to the Anglo-French Art Centre in St John's Wood where he found a stimulating, informal and relaxed atmosphere. Tutors and speakers included Fernand Léger, André Lhote, Oskar Kokoshka, Jacob Epstein, John Minton and Patrick Heron. A class trip to the caves of Lascaux created a lasting impression on O'Casey. (Later he attended sculpture lessons at St Martin's given by Anthony Caro and Elisabeth Frink.) There followed a lethargic and depressing decade full of self-doubt, until this epiphanic moment:

> One day, watching television, some time in the late fifties, I saw a film about Alfred Wallis, a primitive painter who had lived at St Ives in Cornwall. The film incidentally showed St Ives and the studios of artists living there. I realized it was the place for me. I owned a small orange Ford van. I packed the van and went … Coming from Torquay, where I had felt like a rhinoceros walking along the streets, the relief of mingling with other crazy artists was enormous …

The timing was perfect as the little harbour town was at its heyday as a place for inventive and exciting visual art. One of the first people O'Casey met was the sculptor Denis Mitchell and he was lucky enough to become his assistant. This experience taught him about the slow, painstaking attention needed to perfect a three-dimensional work of art (without power tools):

> I learned to accept the tedium of work; the practical way to Heaven, using hammers

*and saws, ropes and pulleys, chisels and files,
among the dust, filings and shavings of the
cold, dark, damp workshops, that now I love
so much.*

In the meantime O'Casey had met and
married Doreen Corscadden (originally from
Northern Ireland). With a growing family –
Oona, Duibhne and Brendan – he desperately
needed to earn more money. Mitchell kindly
recommended him to Barbara Hepworth and
he began with a trial period of three weeks;
he stayed three years. During this time he
worked on her monumental *Single Form* that
would be installed outside the United Nations
building in New York in 1964. Assisting both
these great sculptors turned out to be O'Casey's
apprenticeship, he claimed there was 'no
nonsense about expressing yourself – you did
what you were told.' It also gave him insight
into how to combine the practical world of the
market place with the ideal world of the artist.

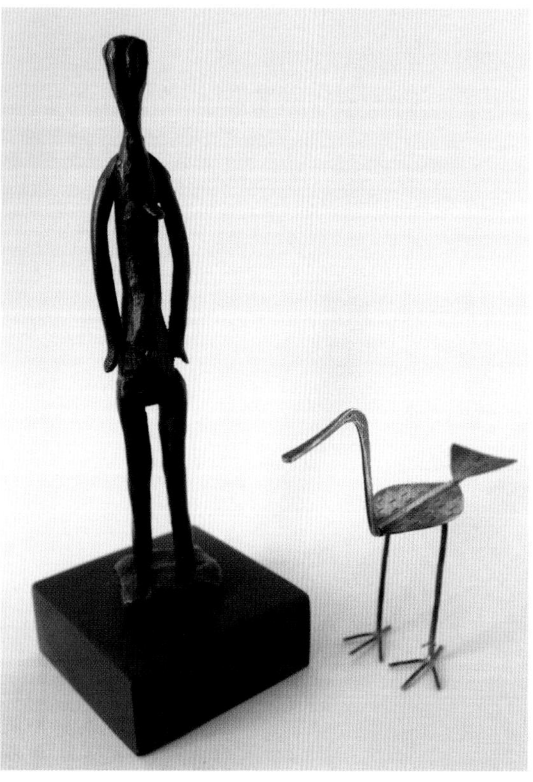

Though he respected Hepworth, he didn't feel
much sympathy for her work, unlike the high
regard in which he held Mitchell's.

O'Casey was now steadily honing his own
craft as a jeweller and as demand for this
intricate work increased he felt confident
enough to go it alone (combined with a part-
time job on the St Ives Telephone Exchange).
His exquisite designs had a primitive feel with a
few basic shapes – including triangle, diamond,
chevron, circle and square – fused with stylized
images of birds, animals, fish and insects. In
1959 he exhibited at the Penwith Society of
Arts (later serving as its vice-chairman)
and obtained one of the Piazza Studios, later
settling into one of the famous Porthmeor
Studios overlooking St Ives bay. In addition
to his painting (which remained somewhat
decorative), he soon branched out into new
fields. Inspired by a book on Navaho tapestries,
he took up weaving and made a loom from an
old bed frame and found this to be a delightful
occupation. (It was with much regret, a few
years later, that he had to give up this activity
as his legs began to give out; the first signs
of muscular dystrophy.) It was also a logical
development to start sculpting. Following
advice from Conor Fallon, he preferred to use
wax, over clay or plaster, before having them
cast in bronze. It was a case of his jewellery
expanding in scale and on his seventieth
birthday he gave himself the gift of 'No More
Jewellery'. In addition he said he enjoyed the
slow rhythm of working on sculpture.

In 1975 the O'Caseys moved across the
Land's End peninsula to Paul, just a stroll along
from the fishing village of Mousehole. In four
new studios Breon managed his gradually
debilitating condition with stoicism and quiet
determination. Latterly he joked that he now
moved like the Tin Man from *The Wizard of
Oz*.

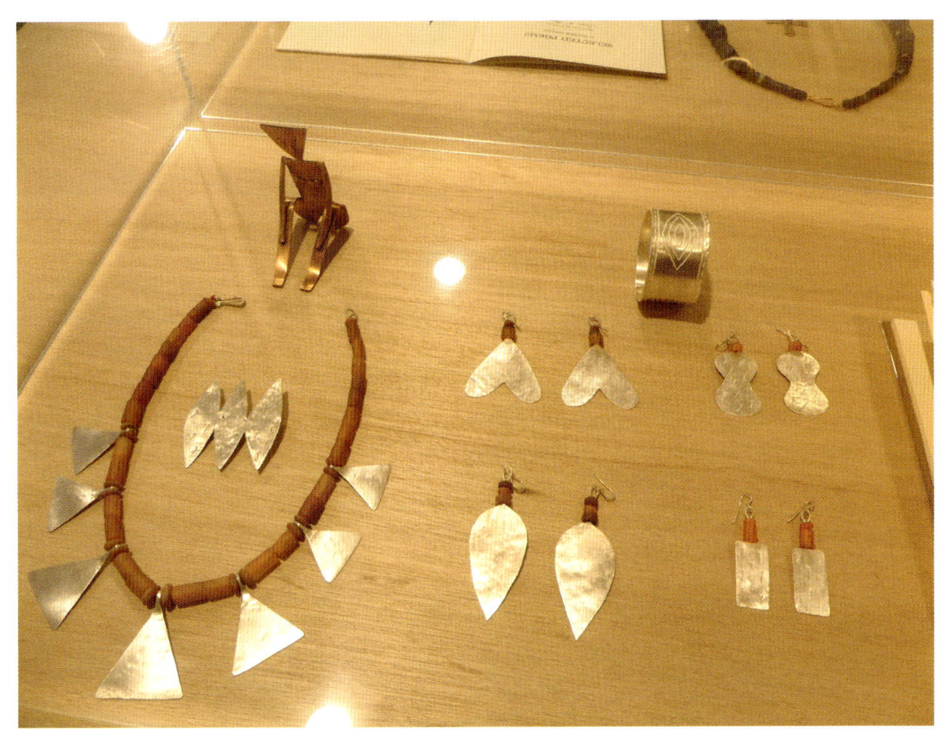

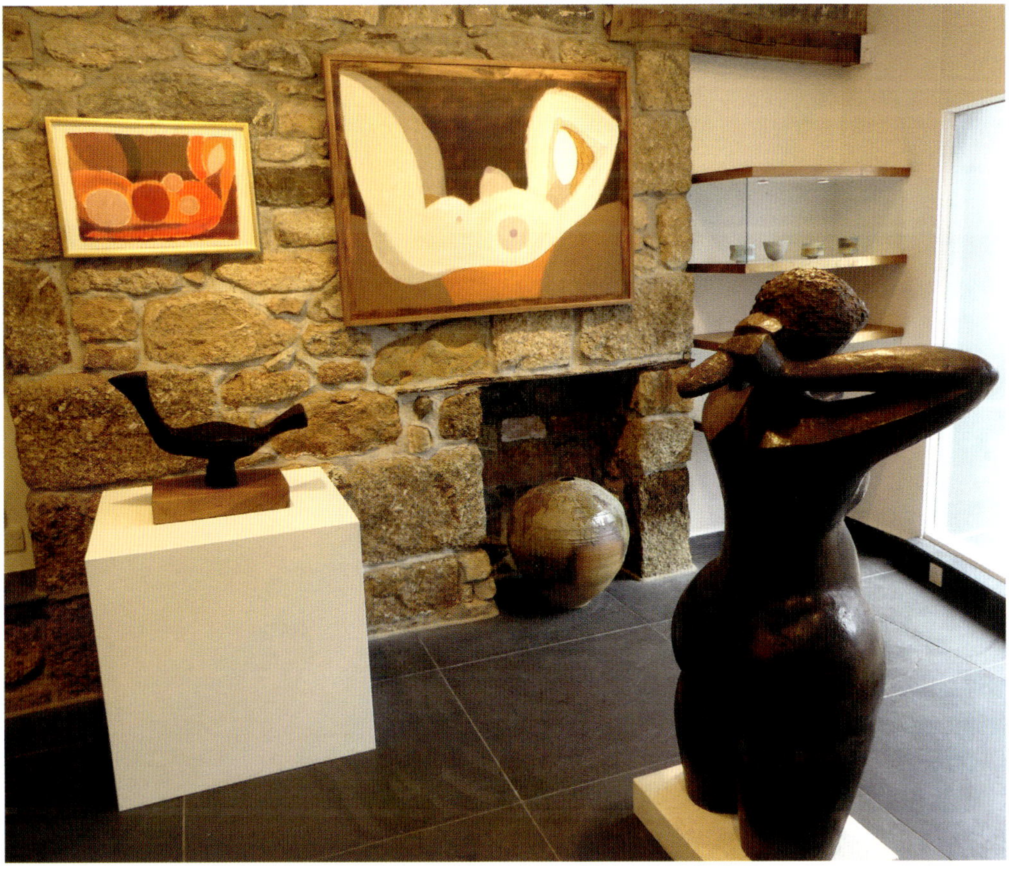

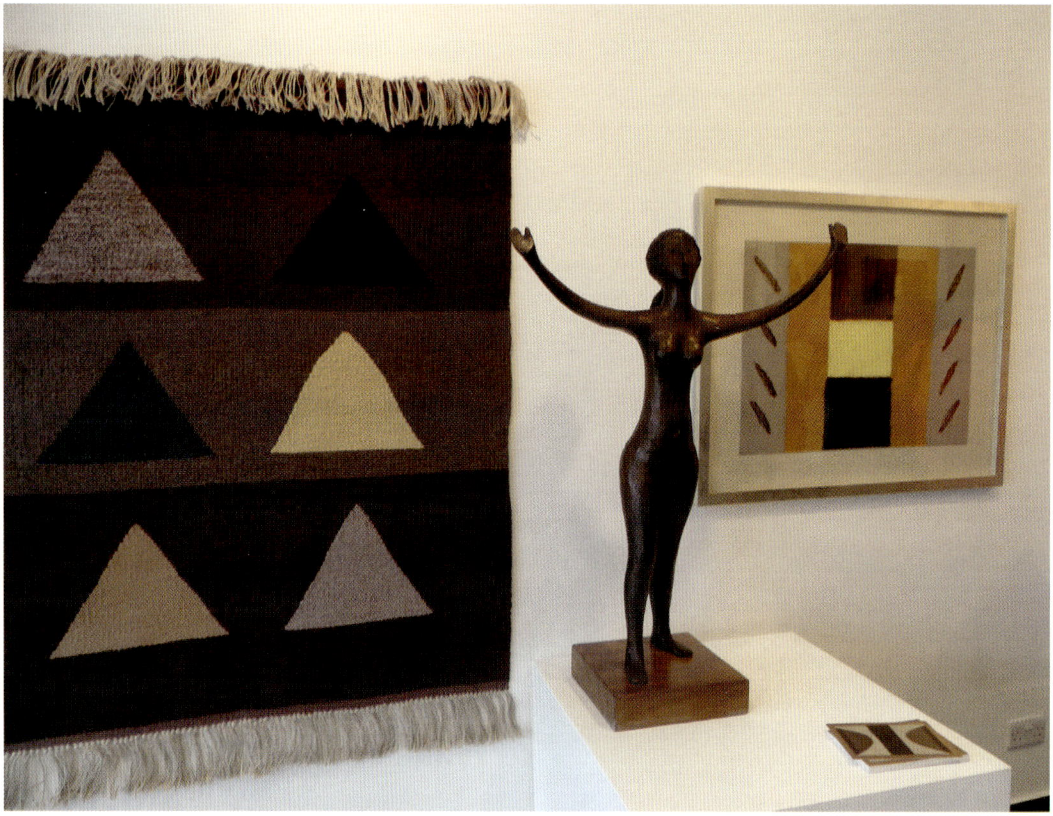

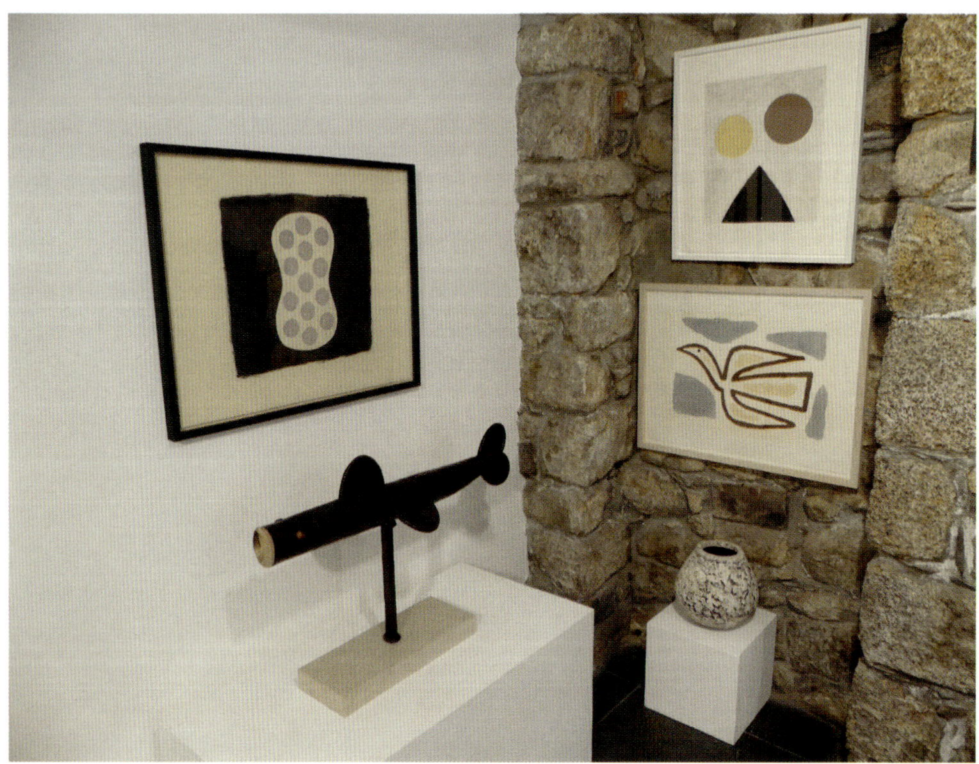

Here his printmaking also blossomed:

A print is a print, and I like to keep them simple. Picasso loved experimenting with different combinations of methods for his linocuts; whereas Matisse's linocuts are white lines on black, his etchings black lines on white: the simplest possible method. I side with Matisse …

Most of my prints are either linocuts or carborundum prints. Carborundum prints are a kind of poor man's etching process …

At least as much effort goes into a print as a painting. The only difference is they can be sold for less money.

O'Casey continued to maintain that, for him, the most inspirational art thrived in a kind of timeless zone:

I have never been interested in theories of art. A group of us visited the Lascaux caves shortly after the war. A thin film of rock had grown over the paintings in the 20,000 years since they had been painted, giving them the fresh look of having been painted yesterday. And the contents were as fresh as the surfaces. Nothing since has improved on those outlines of the horses and cattle of 20,000 years ago. It can certainly be argued that science builds on what has already been discovered and enters new territory, but I doubt if art does. Vasari could show the progress from the ancient Greek world, through to the discovery of perspective and other tricks to a new realism: the Renaissance. But since then one could argue that the journey of discovery went downhill again: a revolt against the 'beefsteak' of

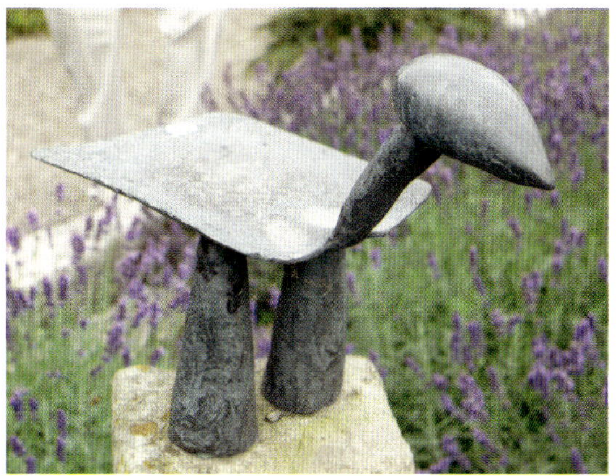

Michelangelo to an art much closer to the early Greeks. How can one improve on a Cycladic figure? All an artist can do, it seems to me, is add to the pile.

If there is no progressive development, only change, then one can, like Picasso, pick at will … This view of the history of art, or non-view, enables one to call the Lascaux cavemen friends; to think of them as contemporaries of Matisse and to think, certainly of Cycladic figures as contemporary with Brancusi. It also allows one to wander at will through the whole of art history, not bothering to be original in any way, since you can no more help being original than having an original nose, or help being contemporary if you're not a ghost. No two peas in a pod are exactly alike.

A guiding maxim for him was: 'The more simply you can do something the better.'

Breon O'Casey, a master craftsman whose trustworthy hands accomplished a high degree of ingenuous sophistication, died on May 22, 2011.

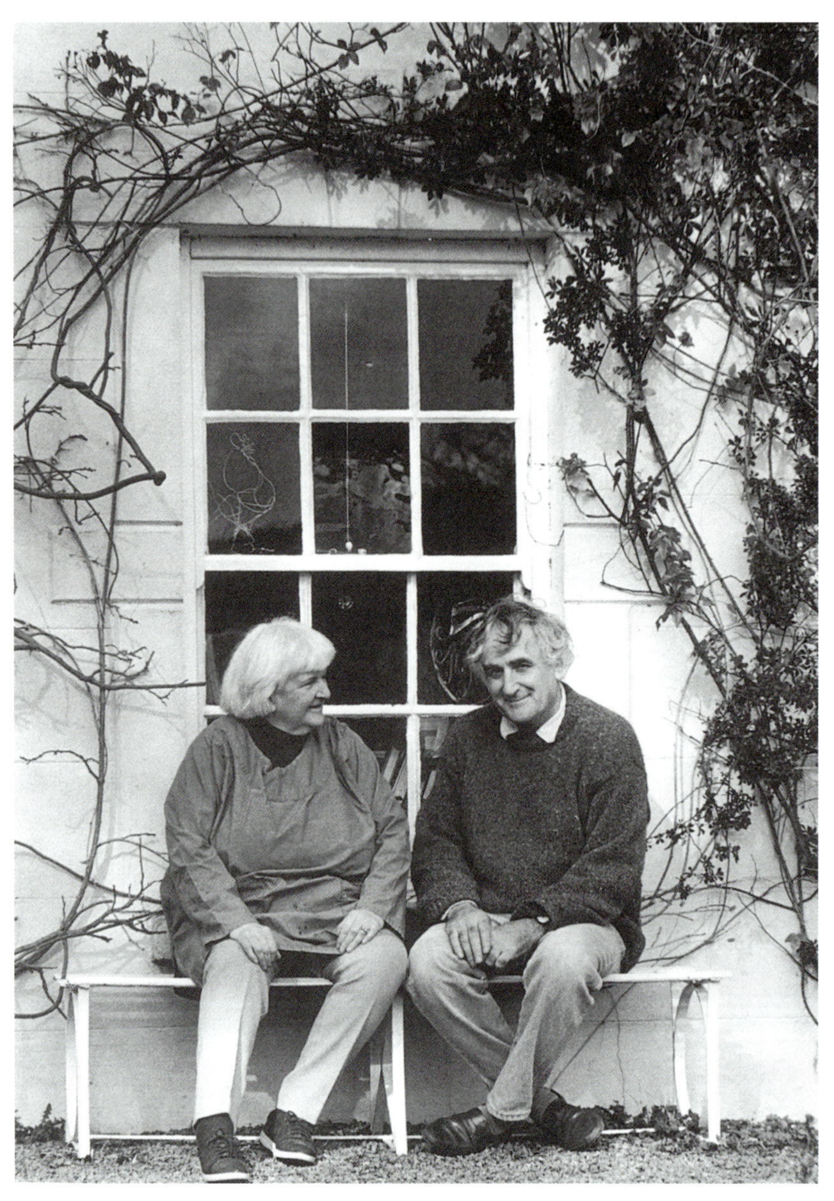

10

A Celtic Item: Nancy Wynne-Jones & Conor Fallon

IT WAS THE wilder regions of Wales, Cornwall and Ireland that bestowed an inimitable calibre of space and colour to the art of Nancy Wynne-Jones.

She was born at Dolgellau, North Wales on December 10, 1922 – the youngest of three children – to Charles Llewellyn Wynne-Jones and Sybil Mary Gella (née Scott), and her paternal pedigree went back through ancient Welsh stock of landed gentry. A delicate child, she was educated at home and her love of animals in particular started her drawing and painting while she received instruction from Ruth Gervis a children's book illustrator. Herbert Read's book *Art Now* was her introduction to abstract painting. As a teenager she was encouraged by a local doctor to take up the violin and compose which led to her entering the Royal Academy of Music in 1940. The war brought great personal tragedy to her family when both of her brothers were killed in action, within a year of each other, serving in North Africa. She volunteered for war work at the Ordnance Survey and left the RAM in 1943.

From 1946 to 1950 Nancy ran the Forum Bookshop in Fulham. This was an extension of her own bibliophilia and never proved much of a financial success (she gradually built up a huge personal library of art books). In 1952 she enrolled in the Chelsea School of Art as a non-degree student and now turned her attention full time to painting.

In 1957 Nancy moved to St Ives, settling in to the Battery on the high point of the Island. She soon fell under the charismatic spell of Peter Lanyon. From him she learned a great deal about the spatial depth and movement of Abstract Expressionism and enjoyed his unconventional teaching methods, encouraging students to engage with the rugged landscape in a more visceral manner:

He was enormously stimulating, even more as a talker than as a teacher in the usual sense. He said he thought painting was terribly difficult and that anybody who did anything was tremendous. He used to take us out in his big car and show us things or details in the local landscape. Once he picked up a handful of sea sand, showed it to me, and said, 'Look, a handful of jewels!' Lanyon was very alive to everything around him. He made us lie on our backs and look up at the sky, and he used to make – as a kind of sketch for his paintings – models out of glass which he would paint. He encouraged us to collect bits of glass from the beach as well, and to stick them together with Bostick as a kind of sculpture. He could get some remarkable results from that; it was a very good way to study space, which was his main interest.

For instance we'd go to where there was an old tin mine called Botallack, and at Botallack the land came out in a little headland. The way out to it was about half the width of this room and it terrified me. I had to have my eyes shut to be taken across. Anyway, this was to get a feeling of space and what happened. He would

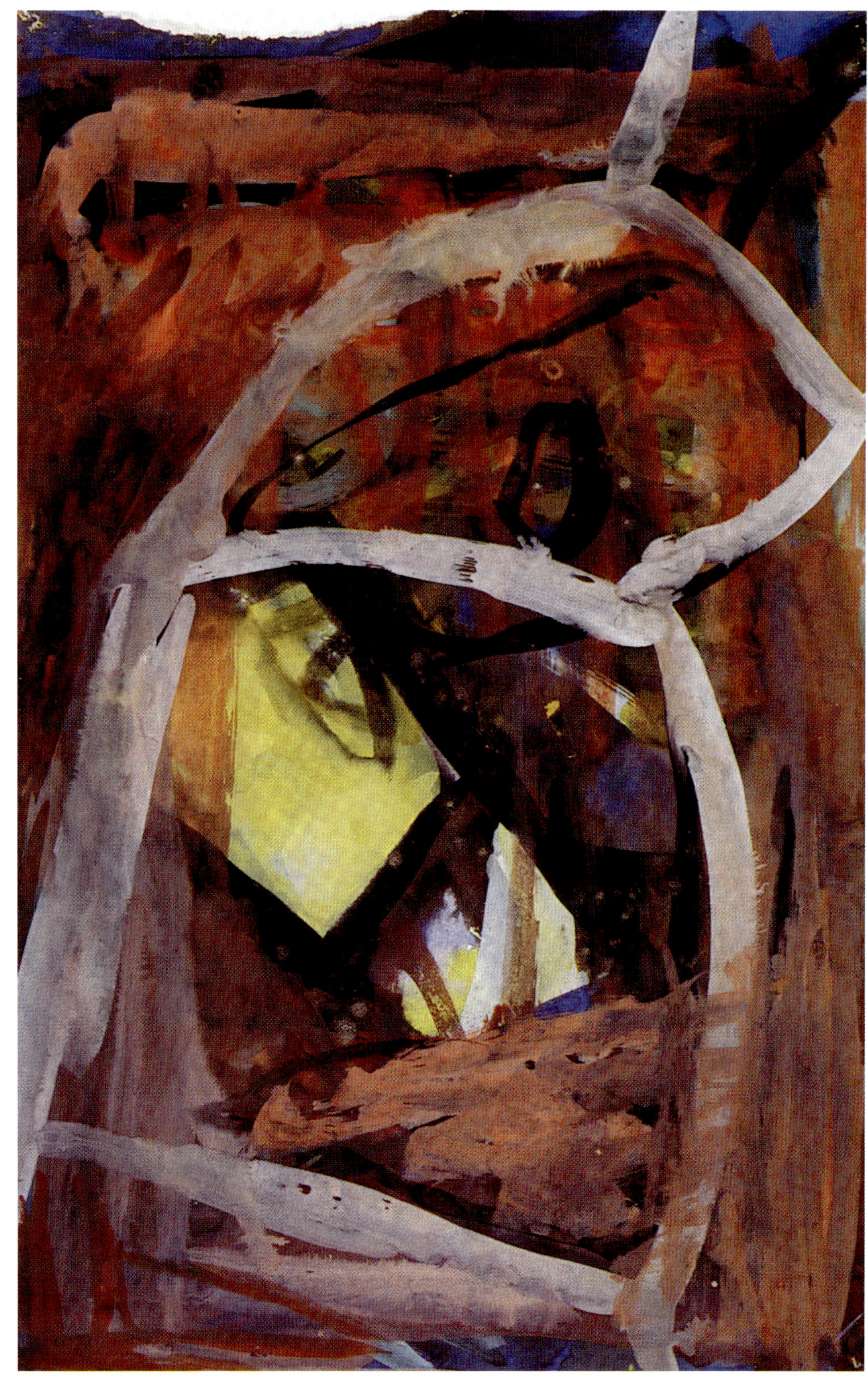

Levant Mine 1956, egg tempera on paper, 38 x 22.5 cm

say, for instance, 'Look at that seagull. See it is crossing the space in between. That articulates the space for you; otherwise you wouldn't know how far off it was.'

Her painting became bright and breezy, in keeping with the spirit of the place, and was meticulously crafted. She was highly gregarious keeping an open house:

> Nearly every Saturday night there was a party somewhere. It was the easiest thing to organise one: you just went into The Sloop, said 'Party in the Battery tonight', and everyone there would turn up, bottle in hand. In St Ives everybody knew everybody; that was what I found so charming. That included the local fishermen and farmers.

Late in 1959 Francis Bacon arrived, for a period, in St Ives and Nancy was soon called on for assistance:

> Francis was down for some months, and I got to be very friendly with him. Boots and Peter and the others all knew him from Soho, though I didn't. He was very much a big city person, but he had taken one of those large studios over Porthmeor Beach to get away from London for awhile and have a part-time place to work in for an exhibition. Francis stayed originally with John Milne, and then afterwards he had a flat of his own right on the harbour in St Ives. I first met him, I think, because Milne came to ask me if I would take him and Francis and his boyfriend into Falmouth. John didn't have a car, and he thought I might like to meet Bacon anyway.

> Francis was marvellous company, and very witty. He used to come up to the Battery and sit around and have a cup of tea. He was a splendid talker, very interesting on art, and very forthright about it too. He thought, for instance, that a tremendous lot of art that was being done was insufficiently personal, and that people were making art out of art, rather than trying to express their own sensations and experiences. He usually had his boyfriend with him. Ron was his name, and he was generally quiet and inoffensive when he wasn't high on amphetamines.

> I remember once in The Sloop, Roger Hilton had been drinking and called out to Francis: 'If you come up to my studio one of these days, I can give you lessons in how to paint.' Bacon replied like a flash: 'How kind of you, darling, I only wish I could give you some of my genius.'

Nancy became good friends with most of the artists in the community, including a lively Bernard Leach:

> I remember dancing with him at parties, and though he must have been in his seventies then, he was very sprightly. He was a very gentle polite man. Pottery, on the whole – though not Bernard's – rather tended to be looked down on, perhaps because it carried a certain image of beards and sandals … But we all used Leach pottery on an everyday basis.

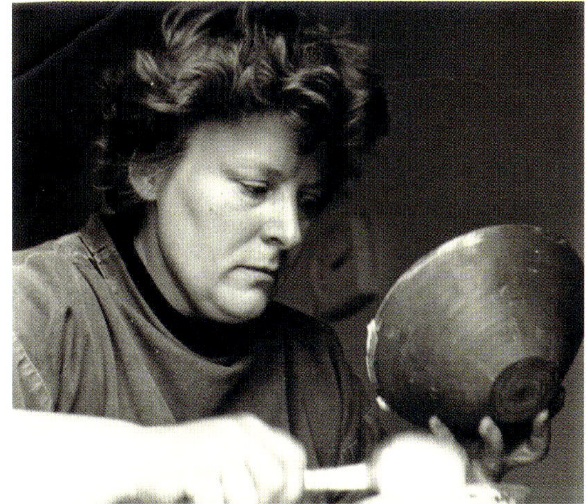

Boots Redgrave

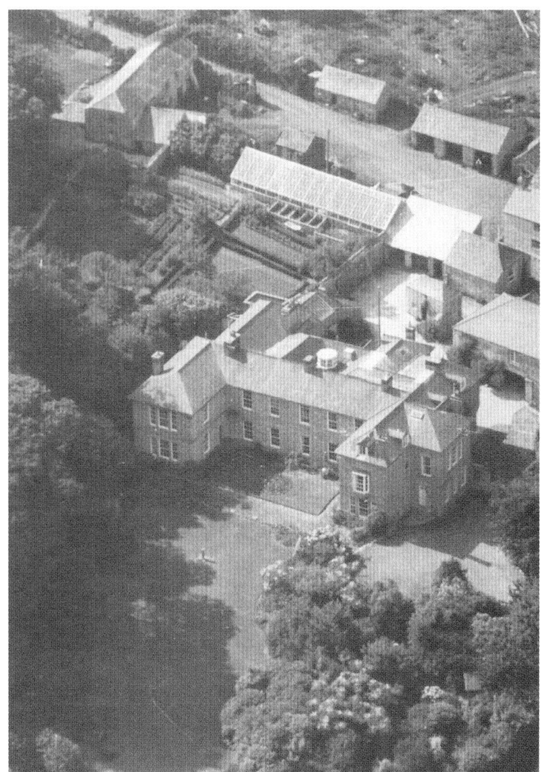

In 1962 she bought, with the potter Boots Redgrave, Trevaylor House, a large country house with grounds near Penzance. This was mainly eighteenth century but parts of it dated back to Elizabethan times. Nancy and Boots had various rooms and stables converted into studios. This was to prove a stimulating environment for artists and writers to work and exchange ideas. The poet Sydney Graham and his wife Nessie lived there (moving into the lodge on the other side of the road). Tony O'Malley moved in and found the natural setting and privacy highly conducive to his own development in non-figurative work, producing some of his finest paintings there. Another resident, the Canadian sculptor Bill Featherston, also found the amenities allowed his work to flourish. For a period Bryan Wynter availed himself of a studio, and the place became a magnet for other artists to stop by.

This worked fine for a couple of years, but the place gradually acquired a reputation for unruly parties (orgies, according to the righteous locals), as more and more hangers-on found their way there. However, the results speak for themselves, though all concerned may have played hard, they clearly worked hard as well.

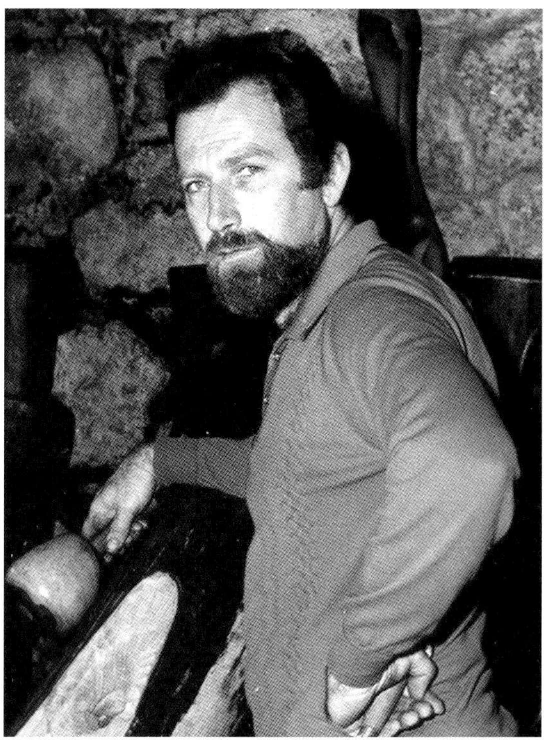

Bill Featherston

Nancy was particularly generous to the Grahams, later providing them with a rent-free house, thus allowing the impecunious Sydney to pursue his bardic calling with fervour, for the rest of his days.

She was especially devastated by the death of Lanyon (following a gliding accident in 1964), but the presence of the artist Conor Fallon, sixteen years her junior, provided Nancy with succour and solace and they married in 1966.

The marriage completely changed the dynamic at Trevaylor; there was also a souring of the friendship between Nancy and Boots and

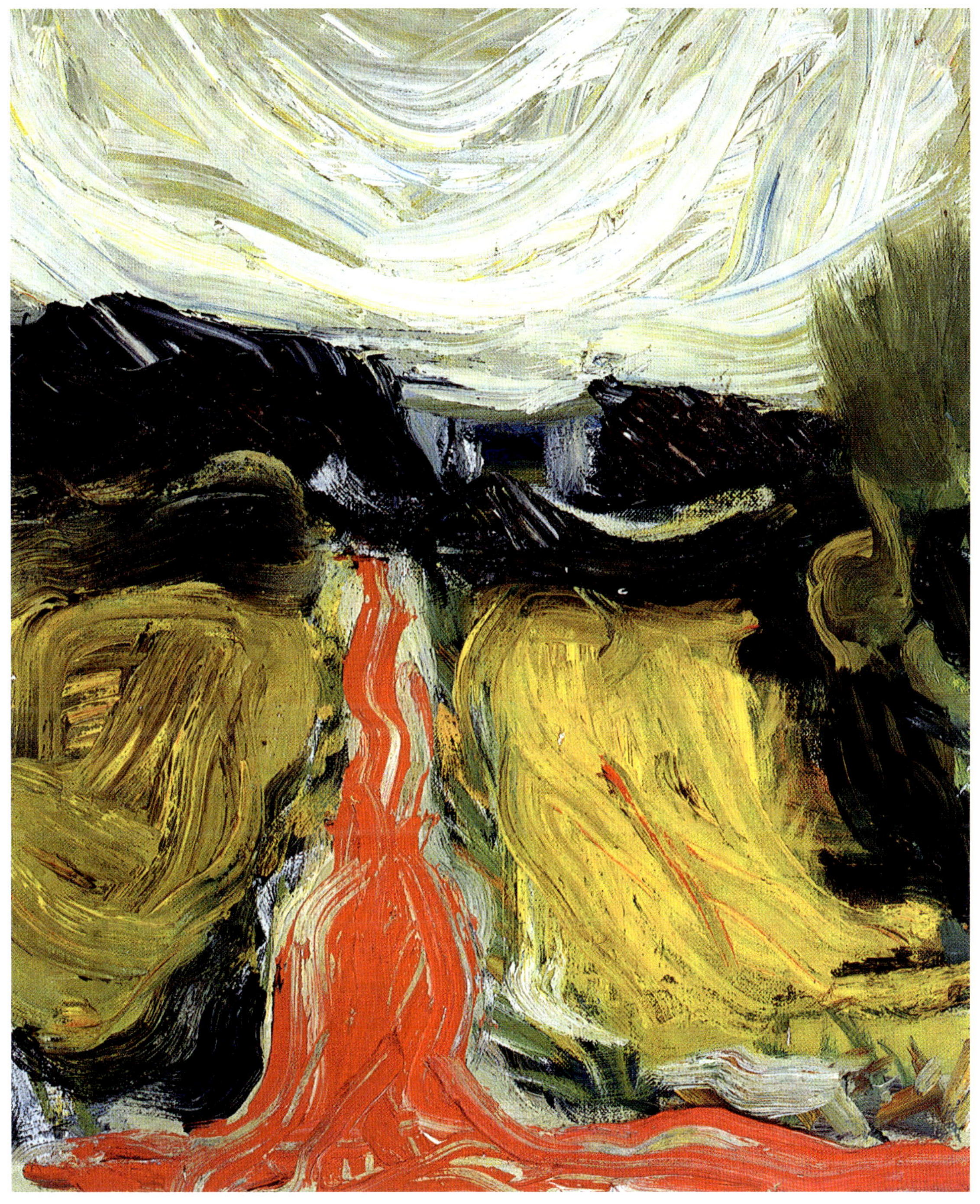

The Red Path 1966, oil on canvas, 56 x 46 cm

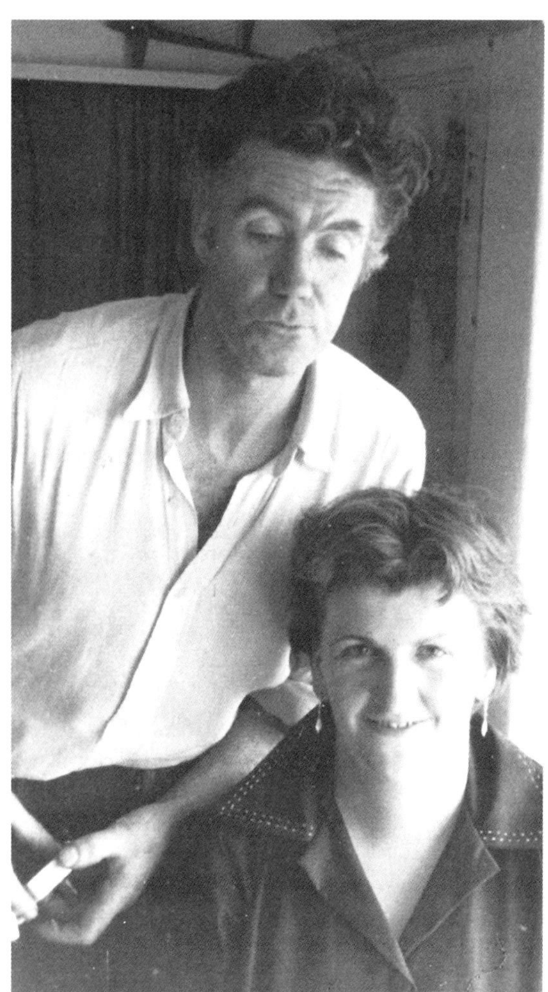

Nancy with Sydney Graham, *c.* 1958

the place was sold in 1972. Thereby bringing to an end a unique little art colony within the larger St Ives colony.

In 1970 Nancy and Conor adopted two young children – the siblings, John and Bridget – and the family now moved to Kinsale in County Cork. Nancy's work became more intimate with a period of still-life, while she also got back into composing. In 1987 the family settled in the more mountainous Rathdrum area in County Wicklow. She was now showing regularly, notably with the Taylor Galleries in Dublin and was elected an Honorary Member of the Royal Hibernian Academy.

For Nancy the discovery, in the 1990s, of the large bogs of County Mayo came as a revelation. It was her desire to possess and be possessed by this multi-textured landscape that galvanised her into a late flowering with a unique vision blending abstract and figuration to convey the total sensation of atmosphere.

Out on the big bog, the feeling of space is amazing. It feels like the beginning of the world, before man was thought of, both awe-inspiring and energising. The marks of old turf-cuttings articulate the bog, the air is filled with light bouncing back from the mountains, contradicting the big receding distance. The mountains are both near and far, the multi-coloured bog both solid and ephemeral.

I had to evolve a way of making something which could begin to convey the complexity of this huge, simple landscape. So I began to try to make my strokes and stabs and smudges of paint themselves fill the space between the mountains and my possessing eye. My categories of space – traditional, shallow – became irrelevant. Here I had to do something new.

Earthy and moist, their rich warm, subtle ochres and reds appealed to Seamus Heaney who referred to them as 'place and palette and spirit, all equal'. Four decades on from his death, the spirit of Peter Lanyon was still in active attendance, guiding the eye and hand of Wynne-Jones in the far west of Ireland.

She will also be remembered for her genuinely benevolent contribution to the St Ives creative community; without her its history would have been much the poorer.

Nancy Wynne-Jones died, aged 83, on November 9, 2006.

THE MILKING OF cows and the shaping of sleek modernist steel sculpture went hand in hand for one of Ireland's leading sculptors, Conor Fallon.

Fallon was born in Dublin on January 30 1939, the third of six sons to the renowned poet Padraic Fallon, from County Galway, and Dorothea 'Don' Maher, native of Dublin. The family soon moved to Wexford where they all shared in the running of a farm, while their father worked as an official for Customs and Excise. It was a highly cultivated milieu with the house regularly visited by writers, painters, musicians and various members of the Irish intelligentsia, including the poet Austin Clarke and the painter Tony O'Malley. The example of Padraic acted as a muse, while his writings remained a source of illumination for Conor throughout his life.

As a child Fallon was fascinated by the local wildlife, especially birds and often drew copies from an edition of Thorburn's *Book of Birds*. He recalled the importance of his older brother Brian (later the senior art and literary critic for *The Irish Times*) who introduced him to stories from Homer's *Odyssey*.

Fallon entered Trinity College to study natural science. But a perceptive professor advised him to leave and turn his attention to art, much to his father's consternation who declared his son's paintings 'dreadful'. As a pragmatic compromise Fallon worked as an accountant by day while learning his art by night. His early works were landscapes in acrylic and gouache clearly influenced by the imposing presence in Irish art of Jack Yeats.

In 1964 Fallon visited Cornwall to see Tony O'Malley, who had settled in St Ives four years previously. Following O'Malley's advice he hoped to learn from Peter Lanyon. Unfortunately on the very day of his arrival Lanyon had his gliding accident, dying suddenly a few days later. Fallon found a grieving community, deep in shock at the loss of a towering figure. (He maintained that Lanyon was the living dynamo that fuelled the art movement in the locality, and his death spelt the end of a unique period for British art.) However, this event led to his meeting one of Lanyon's pupils Nancy Wynne-Jones, who owned nearby Trevaylor House, where a highly talented group of writers and artists convened (Fallon's parents also lived there for a while). They developed an instant and deep rapport and in 1966 they married. Fallon now returned to his agricultural roots by buying, with a neighbour, a derelict farm at Zennor, which they converted into a successful dairy farm (there to this day).

Meanwhile, he had become disillusioned with his painting (he subsequently destroyed most of them). But the friendship of two of Barbara Hepworth's assistants, Breon O'Casey and Denis Mitchell would prove to be a potent turning point in discovering his true vocation. A tentative start at making a three-dimensional object drew this response:

> *I made this sculpture (of an owl) from scrap aluminium, cut and slotted, as I didn't know how to weld. Denis Mitchell saw it and told me that I would never paint again, that I was a born sculptor. I didn't believe this but he himself was a painter turned sculptor, and so spoke with some authority.*

Mitchell in particular took Fallon under his wing, teaching him a disciplined work ethic and insisting that the last one-hundredth of an inch was essential to the integrity of a piece. (To an extent there is a lineage here: Hepworth begat Mitchell who in turn begat Fallon who in

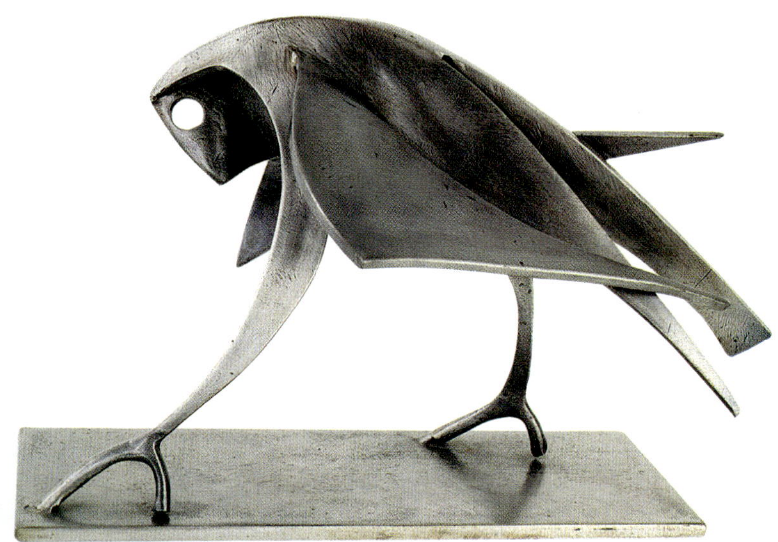

Hawk 1978, mild steel, 23 x 20 x 41 cm

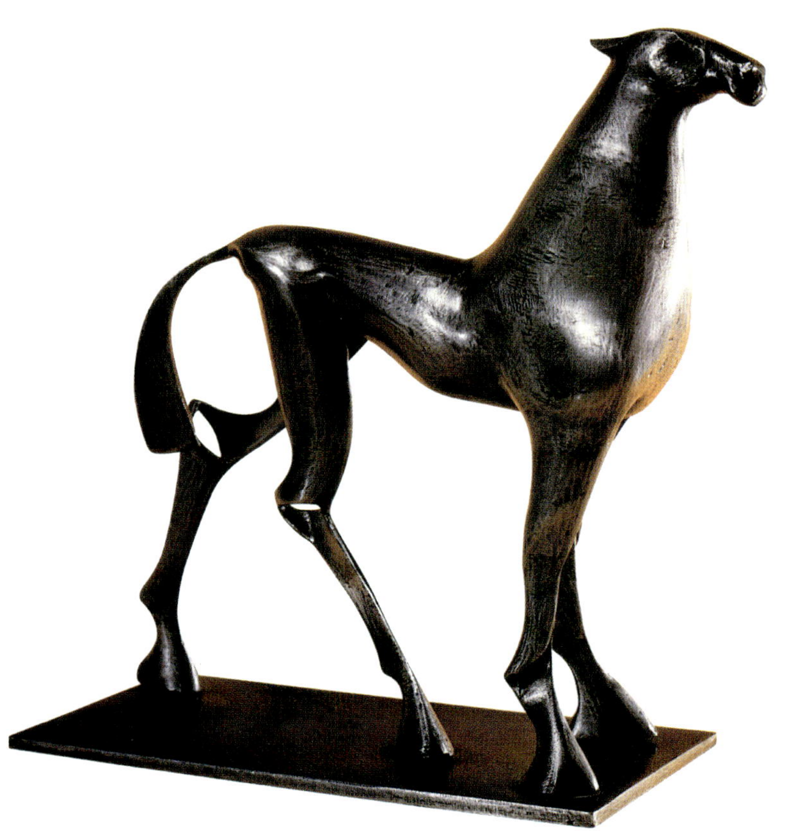

Greek Horse 1978, mild steel, 28 x 15 x 30 cm

turn influenced O'Casey.) Regular discussions
with John Wells in his Newlyn studio were also
important for Fallon's development.

In 1972 he and Nancy, with their recently
adopted children, the siblings John and Bridget,
moved to Kinsale in County Cork, where they
remained for 15 years before finally settling in
County Wicklow.

Fallon now threw himself full time
into sculpting, mainly in stainless steel and
occasionally bronze. Always acutely sensitive to
the natural world, his subjects were primarily
wildlife, particularly birds, hares, fish, as well
as horses (all part of the archetypal Celtic
tradition). He retained a passion for birds of
prey, their balance of taut energy in stillness
with rapid movement of attack perfect
examples for the clean aerodynamic lines
that gave his work its poetry in motion. In
contrast his crows were more solid earthbound
creatures.

*I think that all my work deals with myth, or
my very personal concept of what myth is.
And I feel that the artist must feel his own
life to have a mythic dimension – perhaps
many other people feel this too? – where the
events of his life have a dimension outside
himself. The awareness of that dimension
gives the sense of being part of that huge
adventure, the journey of man and, beyond
that, of the cosmos.*

In form and style he harked back to archaic
Egyptian and Greek statues, emphasising
equilibrium over repose; from modernism
he looked to Naum Gabo (a resident of St
Ives during the war) who demonstrated
the avoidance of mass in sculptural space.
Cubism, Brancusi, Giacometti, and Picasso's
often overlooked three-dimensional work, all
nourished his creativity.

*I found the idea of landscape as the subject
for sculpture enormously exciting, and still
do – that inference of space – but I try to
have it there indirectly and through other
things: for instance, the hawk gathering the
energies of the landscape into its core.*

*I think that a sculpture should be a kind of
nexus of energy. Brancusi made sculptures
which have this quality: everything
contained within, as dense as a black hole.
And I feel that energy is a dynamic which I
have to contain in the sculpture.*

Throughout the 1980s and 1990s various
high profile commissions followed quickly.
Large-scale works are familiar at many venues
throughout Ireland including Enniscorthy
Bridge, St Patrick's Hospital, Bank of Ireland
Centre, University College Dublin, University
College Cork and a landmark piece for
Independent Newspapers. He was awarded
the Oireachtas Gold Medal for Sculpture in
1980. Fallon also devoted a great deal of time
and energy to his role as secretary of the Royal
Hibernian Academy and board member of the
National Gallery of Ireland.

A perfectionist craftsman and highly
articulate, it was especially tragic for his family,
friends, and Irish art that he should die of
cancer, on October 3, 2007 aged only 68, within
a year of losing Nancy.

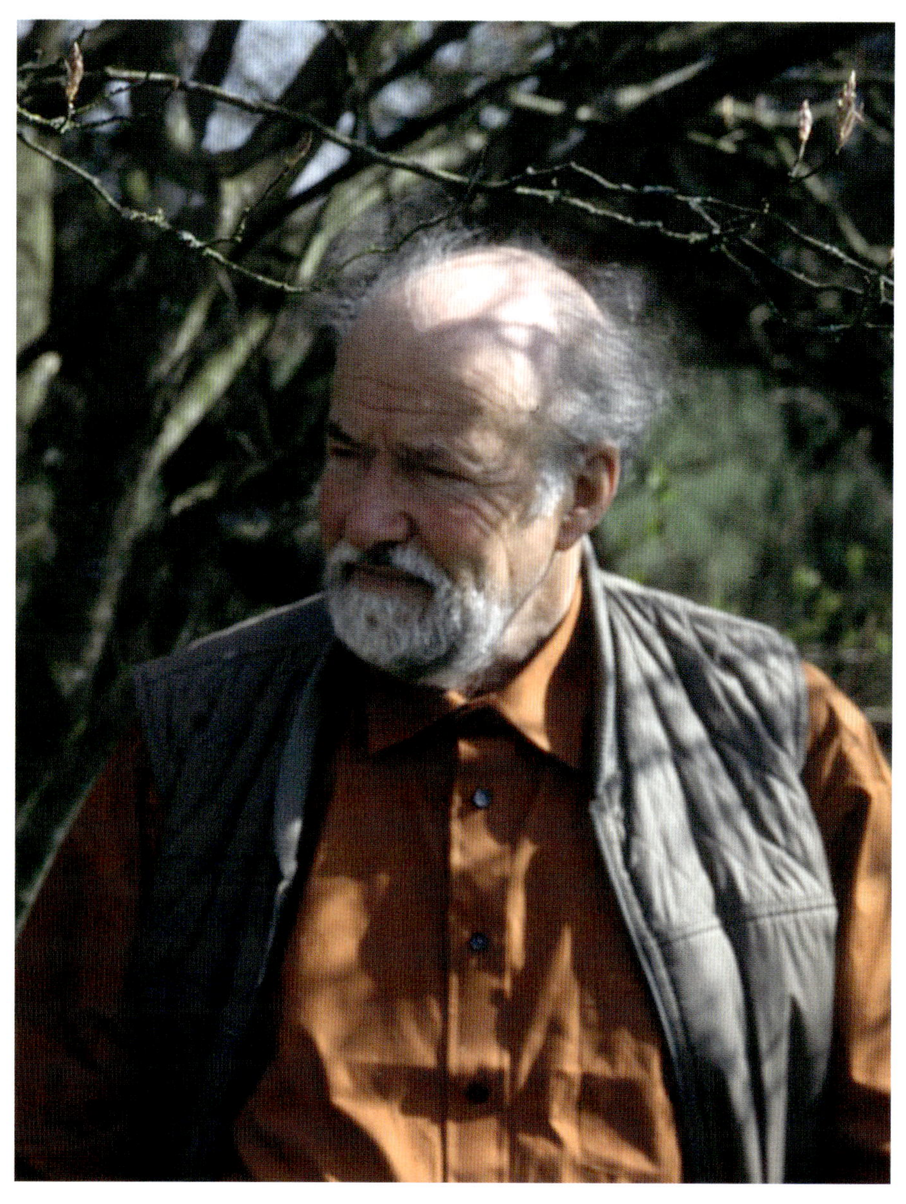

11

Michael Snow: But is it Finished?

PARTICLE PHYSICS, GEOLOGY, astronomy and music were among the essential elements that informed the art of Michael Seward Snow.

My own researches into post-war St Ives artists led me to Michael and his wife Margaret who I got to know quite well over the course of twelve years, during which they generously shared their wealth of knowledge with me.

Born in Manchester in 1930 (his father was a primary school headmaster), Michael was educated at Lawrence Sheriff School in Rugby. He then worked for a period as a librarian. His love of poetry prompted a fan letter to

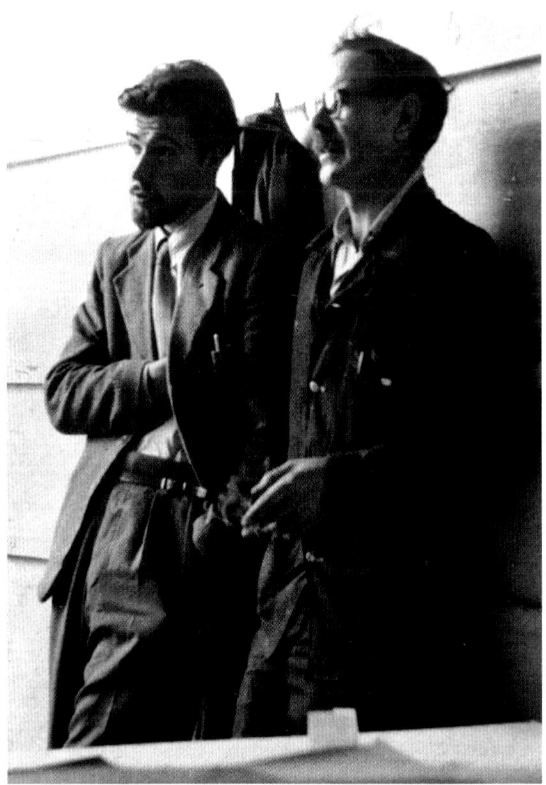

Michael (left) with Terry Frost, 1953

Dylan Thomas to which he received a reply. In 1950 he married Sylvia Jarrett. An exhibition in Liverpool of St Ives artists motivated his departure for Cornwall in 1951.

It is generally agreed that Cornwall at this time was a golden era for innovative British art and Michael quickly discovered his vocation as a non-figurative painter, becoming good friends with most of the important artists working there, including Ben Nicholson, Terry Frost, John Wells, Wilhelmina Barns-Graham and most significantly of all, perhaps, the poet Sydney Graham and his wife Nessie. Michael also kept in touch with Nicholson long after the latter moved to Switzerland and he remained a significant and generous mentor for the younger artist. On one occasion the Snows drove across Europe to his home in the Ticino, with an unusual weight testing the suspension of their camper van: a large ovoid granite boulder from a local Cornish beach, apparently requested by Nicholson.

Michael was a co-founder of The Peterloo Group (1957) with his friend the poet and literary critic Robin Skelton. The two men's relationship soon developed an unusual twist when they exchanged marital partners, Margaret Skelton and Sylvia Snow, reasonably amicably. They all continued on good terms for the rest of their lives.

Throughout the 1950s and '60s he was highly active as secretary to The Penwith Society of Arts, while he taught at Exeter School of Art and Design for twenty years. At the same time Margaret was an inspirational teacher of

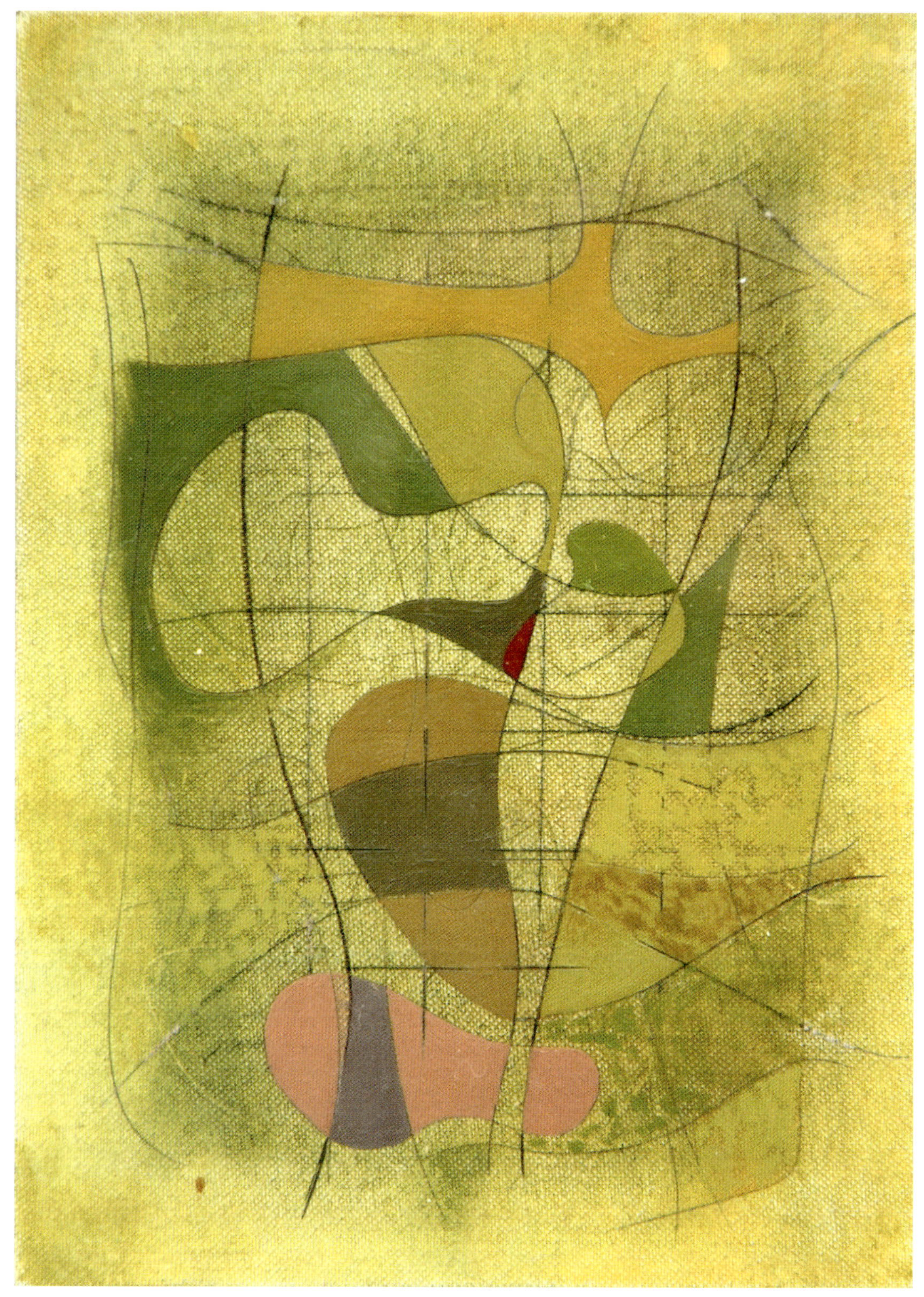

Penwith Forms 1974, oil on board, 18 x 12.5 cm

English at Penzance Grammar School. They had a son, Justin.

A self-taught artist, Michael was a decidedly cerebral painter and a perfectionist who would agonise over whether a painting was finished or not, in some cases for decades. His reticence meant that some excellent work was never allowed a public airing. I recall arguing with him about this and recalling Paul Valery's maxim that a work of art is never completed but is merely abandoned – this made him wince. Equally, my suggestion that perhaps the viewer played a role in completing the picture, as part of an aesthetic transaction, was met with a derisory snort. Michael's austere attitude led him to be hypercritical of other artists: for example, though he admired Peter Lanyon on one level for the great energy he put into his work, at the same time he felt that many of his paintings remained unresolved. And the very idea of preparing work on a regular basis for a selling exhibition was anathema to him. He once admitted the tension he put himself under in a letter to me, saying: 'I have to live on the edge of my criticism of my own work every day. It is not a comfortable place to be.' In 1964 he wrote:

> Any sort of painting matters if it is honest – a live experience as opposed to fashionable rhetoric or propaganda. The pursuit of a pure research imposes its own discipline, often puzzling to onlookers, but art is important to everybody, or should be, because it is not only a visual addition to our environment – it is the only way to see.

For Michael the notion of structure was the essence of all aesthetic craft, whether painting, sculpture, music or poetry. At first his work had strong Constructivist leanings but gradually loosened into more landscape style configurations. Some of his finest later paintings resembled the dance of subatomic particles, while his large metal constructions explored the interplay of three-dimensional form and space (these were erected on school sites in Manchester and Penzance). For one of his rare showings, in 1993, he prepared this statement:

> Looking back over my work today I notice two strong strands of thought and feeling within it. The first has to do with making new compositions. There is an intrinsic beauty which can be drawn from apparently simple forms, colours, and intervals. A sort of visual 'music'. The second is the product of my immersion in what, for lack of a better word, I call my landscape. These places and objects where I sense the clarity and power of deep structure, colour, and atmosphere generate a whole complex of perceptions and reflections. I do not stop at the surface only, I want the whole geology and weather of them, the feel and smell of the elemental earth, air, fire, and water.
>
> These two themes are in the work, they are not a programme for it but a sort of parallel poetry of form and experience.

The Snows were devoted to promoting the life and work of Graham, and in 1999 they brought out *The Nightfisherman: Selected Letters of W.S. Graham*. Publication was met with enthusiastic critical acclaim; Harold Pinter called it 'a brilliant collection'. It is, arguably, this book that will stand as Michael's major legacy rather than his own artwork. The last decade or so of their lives was largely preoccupied in dealing with the growing appreciation of Graham's work and they were tireless in assisting and encouraging the tide of researchers who made their way to 'Stonemark' on the edge of Dartmoor. It gave them immense satisfaction to see that, largely thanks to their efforts, Graham is now widely considered to be one of the great masters of twentieth-century poetry in English. They were also very friendly with the poet John Knight, who lived near Cot Valley, and they published his posthumous collection, *Edges of Fact*, in a limited edition in 1977.

I was fortunate enough to have stopped off on frequent occasions, en route to and from Cornwall for lunch and to have sampled not only their scholarly patience but also Margaret's great culinary gifts. She was an avid reader and writer of poetry but shared Michael's hesitance in releasing her work into the world.

The Snows always showed a keen interest in my various projects and offered to read through and offer constructive criticism on any writings I cared to send them. Given their extreme fastidiousness on such matters this could sometimes be a little daunting. I well recall a lengthy piece that I spent many months burnishing to the point where, as far as I was concerned, I felt there were no further improvements possible. I posted this to them a couple of weeks before a visit. Eventually, on arrival, the first thing Michael said to me was:

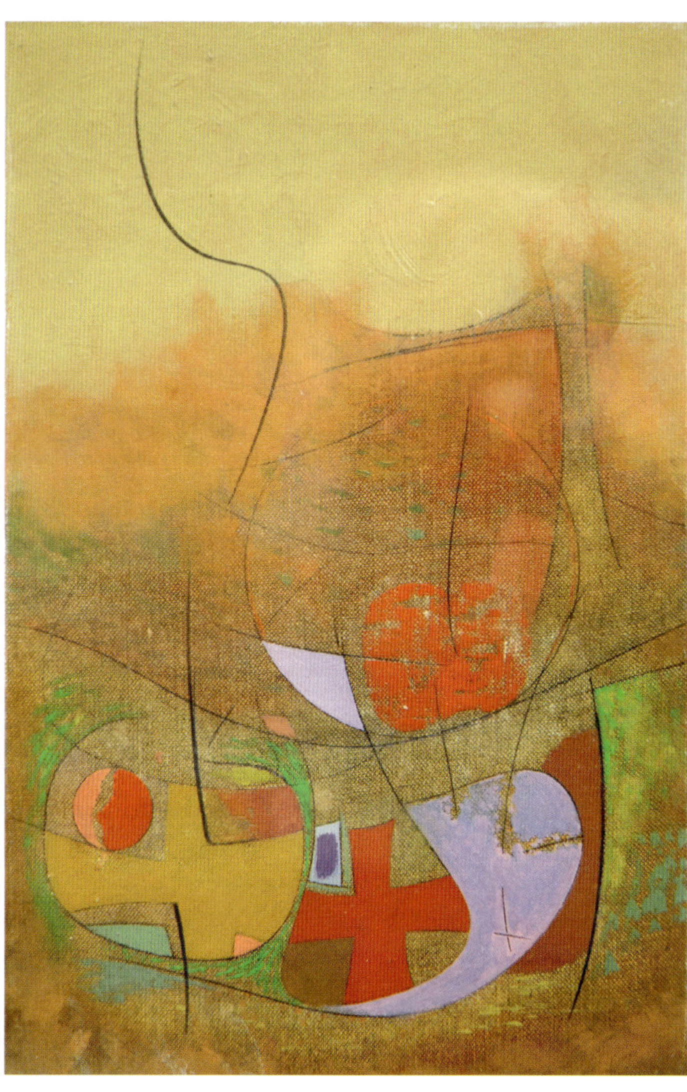

Apple Crosses 1989, oil on board, 23 x 15 cm

'This latest piece of writing is clearly a very early draft ...'

He also enjoyed a joke. When I published my books, I often sent out a letter in advance looking for subscribers to make a contribution to my printing costs, and in exchange their names would be immortalised in the book. On one occasion the Snows very kindly sent a cheque with this proviso attached:

We enclose our contribution on condition that you don't include us in any list of subscribers! It reminds me of:

> *A traveller dining at Crewe*
> *Found quite a large mouse in his stew.*
> *Said the waiter 'Don't shout & wave it about*
> *Or the rest will be wanting one too'.*

Margaret predeceased Michael in 2009. He died, aged 82, in his sleep on July 15, 2012.

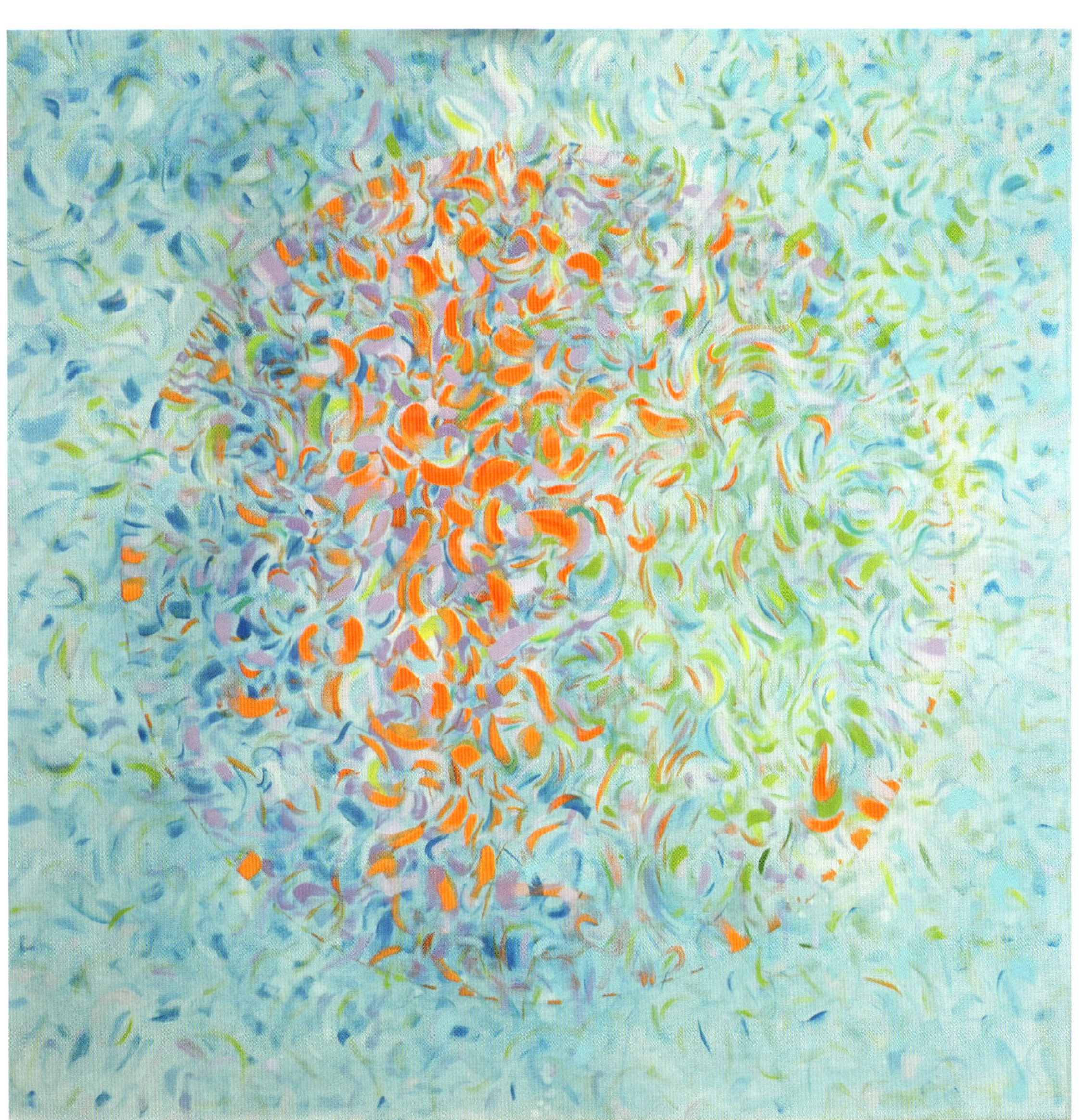

Leaflight 1989, oil on canvas, 91.5 x 91.5 cm

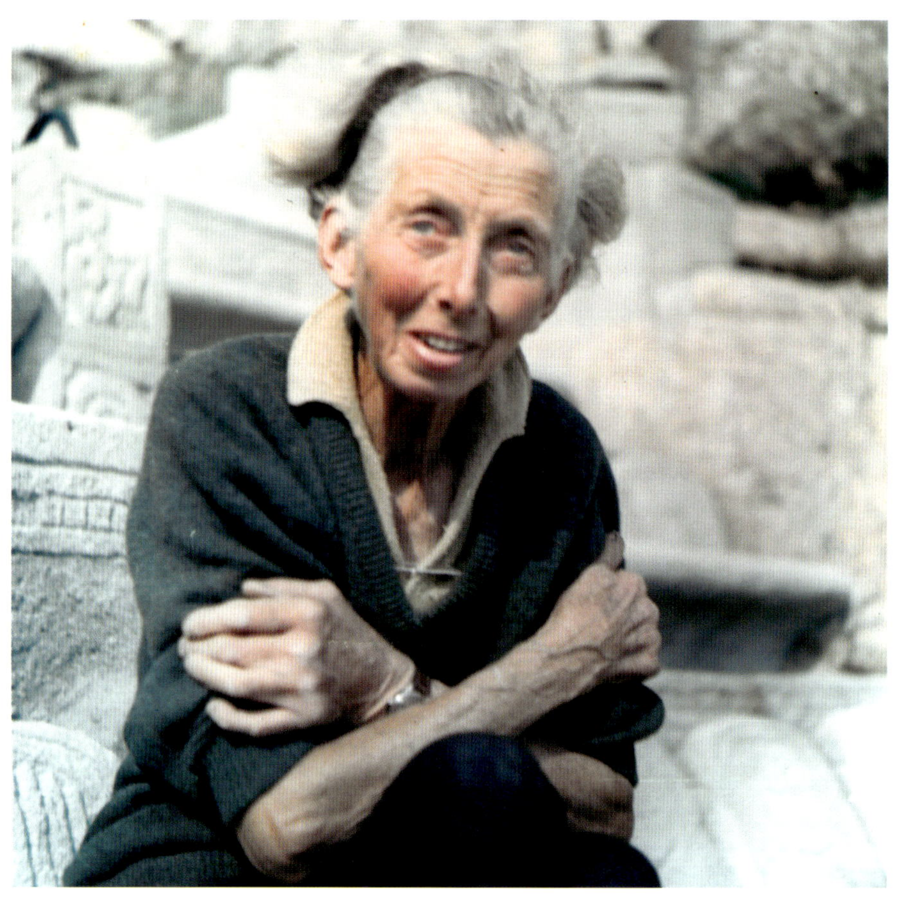

12

Rowena Cade
& the Minack Theatre

On my first visit to Cornwall, in September 1976, I had the following surprising encounter:

One day I took the bus to Porthcurno and went for an amble along the coastal path. What I stumbled across astonished me: a classical amphitheatre carved from the almost sheer cliff face! In outstanding condition, given the fact it must have been thousands of years old. Probably the Romans, I surmised. Having marvelled at their engineering prowess I continued on my way.

On the return loop I got lost. In the garden of a large house I noticed an elderly woman pruning a tree and stopped to ask directions. There was something most striking about her appearance, she blended in with the blasted trees and hedges of her surroundings with her lean sinewy limbs and weathered complexion. She had a charismatic elemental presence. I mentioned the 'ancient' theatre on the cliffs. She looked taken aback and said that she had built it herself! With the help of friends and volunteers, over several decades, she had hauled sack loads of sand from the beach far below (hence her elongated arms) to create the eighth wonder of the world: the Minack Theatre … We chatted about various things including her diet, which consisted mainly of honey. I left her, feeling I had met a remarkable human being. It was many years later before I discovered that I had met the legendary Rowena Cade. (Whittaker, 2003)

It is now over forty years since that chance meeting and it is extraordinary how fresh that 'elemental presence' still feels to me.

This amazing woman drew her first breath a long way from the Cornish coast in Spondon, Derbyshire, on August 2, 1893, to a prosperous family. (The painter Joseph Wright of Derby was a great-great-grandfather.) She was the second of four children. (She also had a distinguished sister, the feminist, dystopian author Katherine Burdekin.) At the age of eight she had her first taste of theatre when she played the title role in a family production of *Alice Through the Looking Glass*. The family moved to Cheltenham in 1906 where Rowena enjoyed a comfortable education. During the First World War she had a job breaking in horses who were shipped across for combat duty to the frontlines in Belgium and France. Soon after the war, with the death of her father, she and her mother moved to Cornwall, initially renting a house at Lamorna. On impulse, they made a purchase of the Minack headland, by Porthcurno, for £100 and built Minack House there from granite quarried at St Levan. (Apparently Miss Cade's pronunciation, in keeping with the locals, was 'Minnick'.)

An artistic bent and an interest in drama led to her designing costumes for a local production, in a nearby wood, of *A Midsummer Night's Dream* in 1929 (some film footage exists of this performance). This proved so popular that a production of *The Tempest* was mooted to take place in the large garden of Minack House, which led down to the cliff side (overlooking a

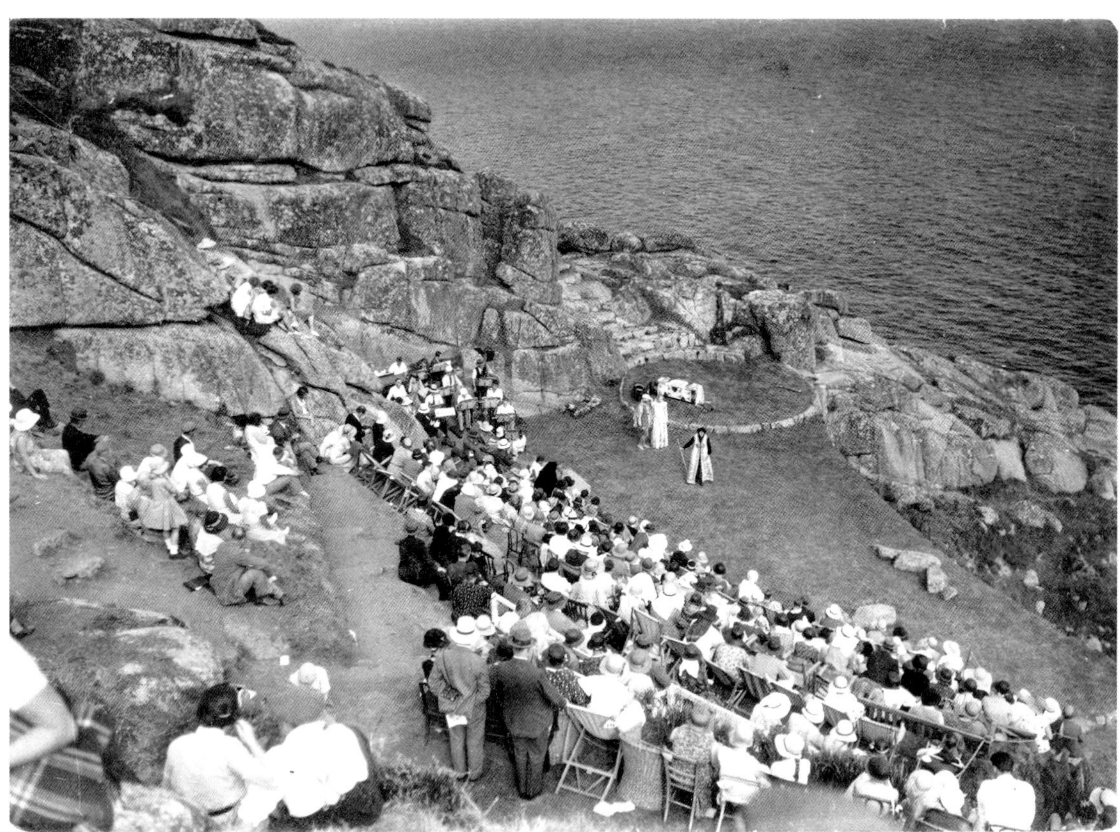

The Tempest, 1932

cavernous zawn), for the summer of 1932. But Miss Cade had a better idea. Here are extracts from some notes she published in 1957:

> So I proposed, during the winter and spring, to build a larger terrace across the steep slope above the zawn, where (with luck) we could also make an auditorium. The slope was covered with rough grass, bracken and gorse, and was not naturally concave, but jutted out in a pile of huge boulders, opposite where there is now the big chair. These boulders, my gardener Billy Rawlings, aided by another Cornishman, cut up by hand, much as the English cut butter. A few slices fell into the zawn as they split, followed by some good dialect expressions of regret; most were handled into position inch by inch with bars, on the slippery slope where a careless step would have meant a ninety foot fall into the churning sea. I filled in behind them with earth and small stones.

> Our first anxiety was that we should come to 'carn' – that is, solid rock – before we had achieved a roughly curved auditorium; and our second, that there would not be enough filling both for a long, narrow cleft (now part of the seating) and also to bring the stage-level high enough (about ten feet) to build an entrance over the narrow spine of granite between the theatre and the dressing terrace to the east.

> But everything worked out well; and we had the stage turf down in May, having started after Christmas: a good enough rough and ready job for what we thought would be a single week of playing.

A single week of playing! At the time of this writing we are 86 years on from that production and the playing goes on unabated, busier than ever. Miss Cade also expressed a few regrets as she gradually realised the scale of her work:

Had we known that the theatre would prove a lasting attraction, many things should have been done at the time of building; notably we should have cut a passage through that spine of carn to the east, so that players could get back to base without being seen; or, alternatively, climbing right to the top of the cliff to get round behind the audience. The seating should be safer, more comfortable, and should obviate having to have uncomfortable park chairs and benches, or having to lean against other people's legs.

We found we had to build a balustrade-edge to the stage for Twelfth Night *in 1933, as, when the stage had been lawn with no concrete at all, the audience for* The Tempest *had been nervous of the players going overboard.*

Rowena Cade turned thirty-nine the summer of that successful production of *The Tempest* (it even had a favourable review in *The Times*). She can hardly have dreamt that her destiny was now set in concrete, sand and granite for the half-century of life that lay ahead of her. This was the spark of an obsession, a gradually expanding vision of possibilities to transform this modest corner of wilderness into an unlikely phenomenon of cultural entertainment: the first and last theatre in England.

But, despite Miss Cade's fierce independence and self-reliance, she needed help with the gargantuan physical labour required in a somewhat hostile environment. Billy Rawlings was a local man who had the job of gardener at Minack House but whose role now also

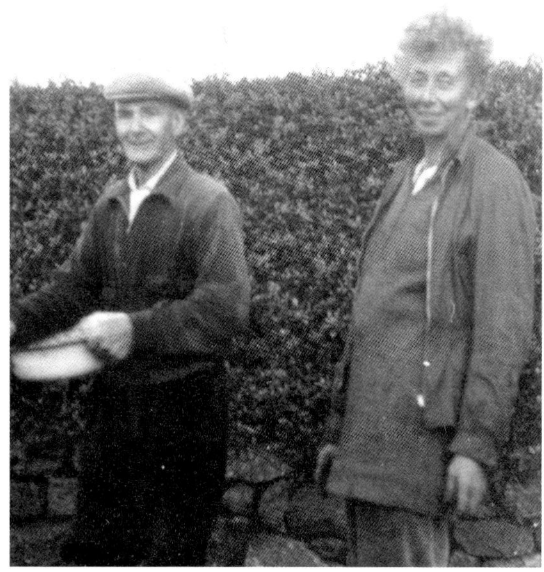

Miss Cade with Billy

developed in unforeseen ways. His list of jobs multiplied into heavier tasks as the project gradually took on a life of its own. He was a quick-tempered little man, dwarfed by his tall languid employer, and these two extremely different personalities sometimes clashed as Miss Cade's ambition and expectations increased. From time to time he would walk out in exasperation saying, 'I'm never coming back', to which Miss Cade replied, 'See you in the morning Billy'. And indeed she did, as he always returned, remaining her loyal helpmate until his death in 1966. He would be replaced by Tom Angrove and Frank Thomas, who also helped over the decades. The gentle, but determined, Miss Cade with her Minack vision induced this sense of devotion from many people, indeed her enthusiasm proved infectious.

The rest of the 1930s saw more plays most years, including *Twelfth Night, Anthony & Cleopatra* and John Masefield's *Tristan & Isolt* in 1939. By now the sound of war drums around Europe were heralding a more ominous drama as the world launched into a new conflagration for the second time in Miss

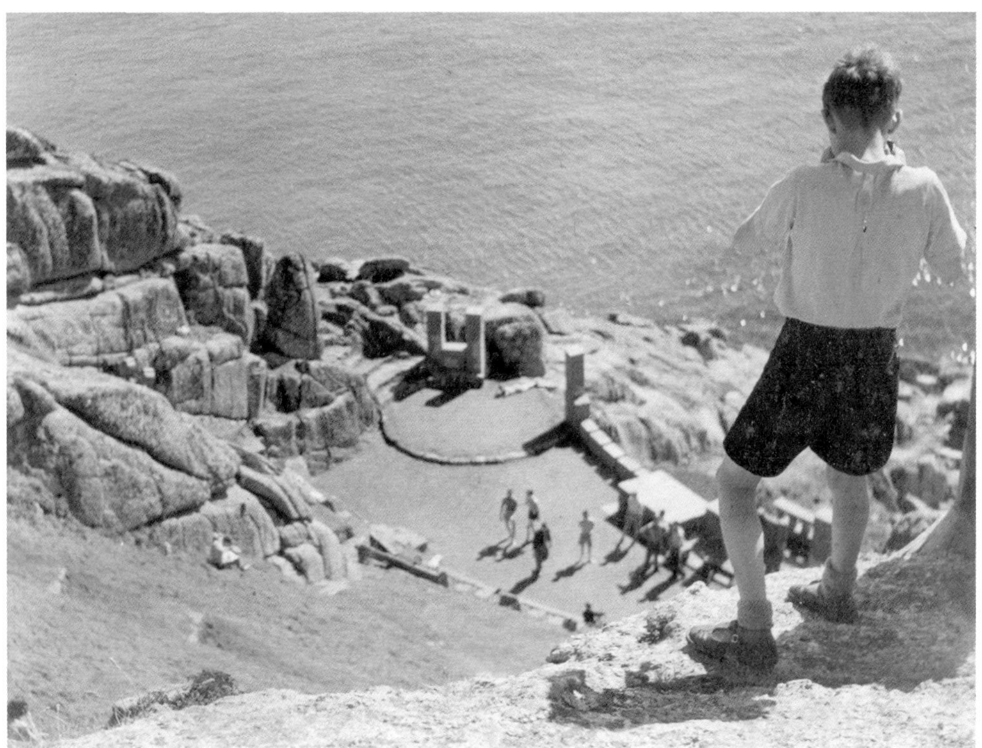

Bedford schoolboys rehearse *The Tempest*, 1952

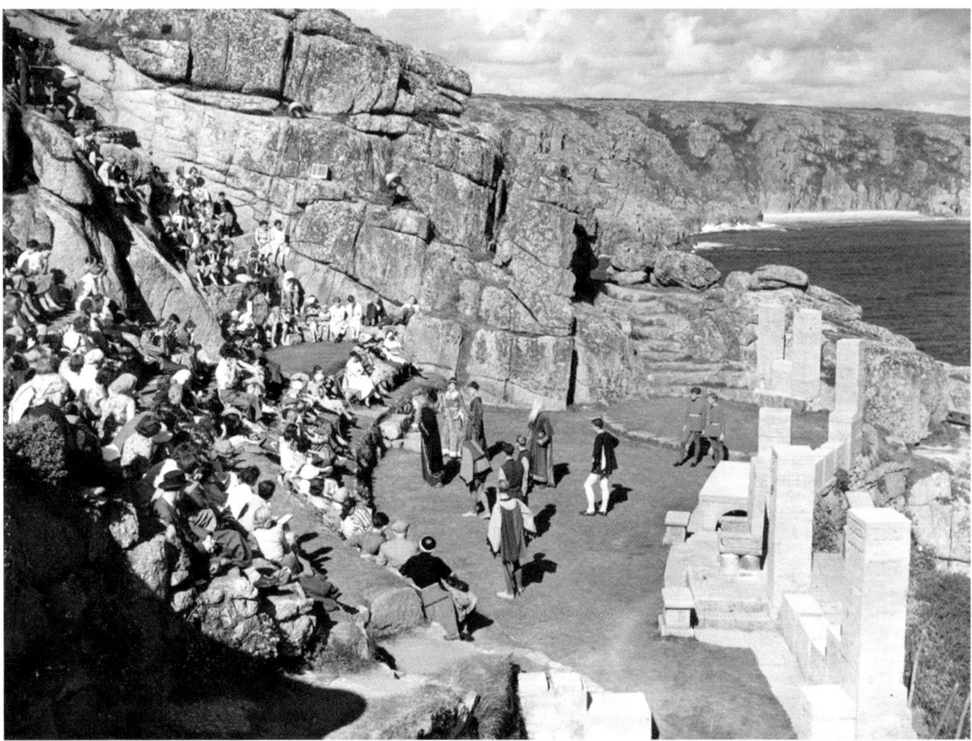

Ardingley College perform *King Lear*, 1953

Cade's life. Activities at the Minack ceased as the cliffs were entangled in barbed wire all the way to Land's End and an anti-aircraft pillbox built as part of the defences. (For a time Miss Cade acted as a billeting officer dealing with the needs of evacuee children fleeing the Blitz.) There was a brief interlude of light relief when Gainsborough Pictures Ltd used the theatre, with its exotic backdrop, as a location for filming *Love Story,* starring Margaret Lockwood and Stewart Grainger during September and October 1943. At the end of conflict it was time for the Minack to shed its hostile demeanour and, curiously enough, Italian PoWs were employed to remove the barbed wire, accidentally knocking part of the balustrade and a big chair into the sea; while Miss Cade's utilitarian gaze seized on the ugly pillbox and it was given the new peacetime role of ticket office. It took time and energy to get the place back up and running and on with the show! It was summer 1949 that the theatre reopened its 'doors' with a production of Euripides' *Trojan Women* performed by the Penzance County Grammar School for Girls. The Minack would now go from strength to strength with ever more elaborate productions of plays, opera, ballet and concerts up to the present day drawing an audience of an astonishing 80,000 people, in addition to a further 150,000 visitors a year.

The very idea of such a wildly enterprising and arduous project came with more than its share of challenges. For a start, the weather would always be an unpredictable and risky element for every production. Any company choosing to perform at the Minack had to arrive with a certain steely resolve that the show must go on regardless of what the weather gods threw at them (occasionally they can be very obliging and an early production of *King Lear* was remembered to have suitable thunder and lightning bang on cue for the storm scene). Likewise the audience, or at

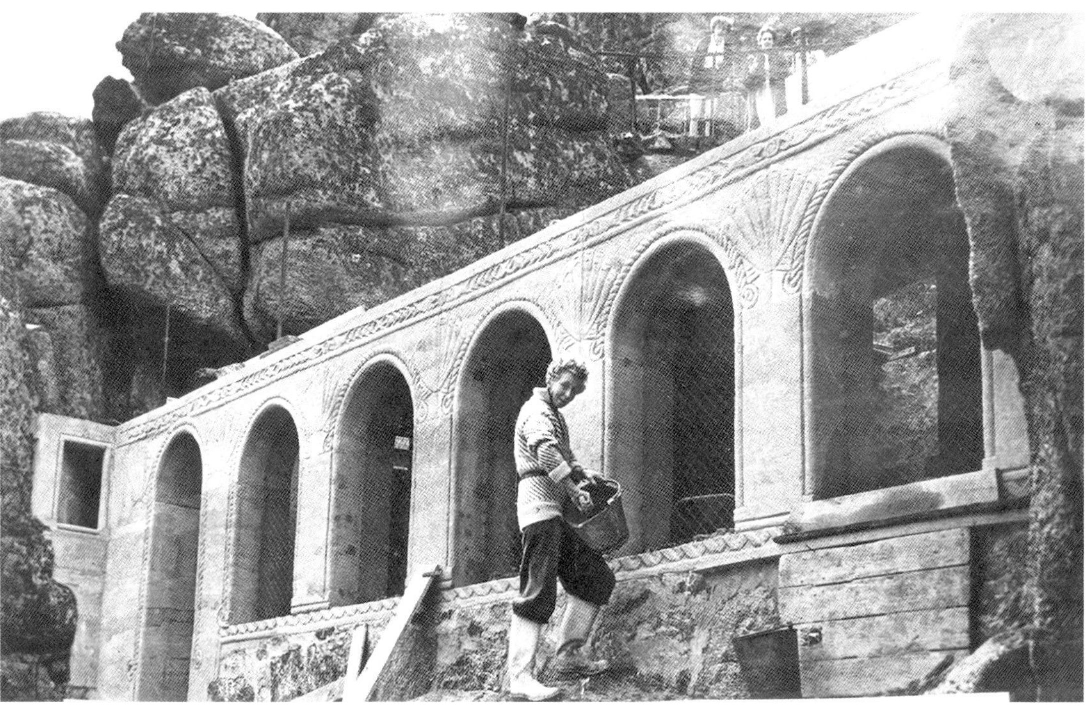

Building the dressing rooms, 1950s

least those in the know, arrive armed to the teeth with waterproofs, blankets, cushions, thermos flasks, sandwiches and torches. As it happens, it has been rare for a performance to be cancelled, though they have sometimes been delayed or interrupted. On certain occasions when precipitation has threatened a show the audience has been known to shout, 'You play, we stay!' All theatre requires some degree of suspension of disbelief, but the Minack takes this to another level altogether. For example, try imagining a Harold Pinter play set in a bedsit (but it has been done). Sharing such difficulties has usually led to a warm and good-natured bonding between the audience and performers. Though periodically the stunning setting can threaten to distract the audience from the play at hand, particularly on a glorious evening with the Logan Rock aglow in the sunset, perhaps testing this relationship. Also, incidents at sea

have been known to bring about a near divorce. There was one performance where a ship in serious trouble required a daring helicopter rescue, this real life drama totally engrossed the audience's attention and caused a near mutiny when the actors demanded they pay attention or they would down tools and leave. While a member of one company leaves us this bizarre account of an unrehearsed incident that took everyone by surprise:

Just before one performance was due to begin … a real Cornish fog descended, obliterating the surrounding cliffs and sea and considerably reducing visibility on the stage. Naturally the mist was too thick for us to be able to see the Atlantic waves some ninety feet below, but we were rather startled to hear the dickens of a noise from down there. We couldn't imagine what had possibly happened, but a little later on when

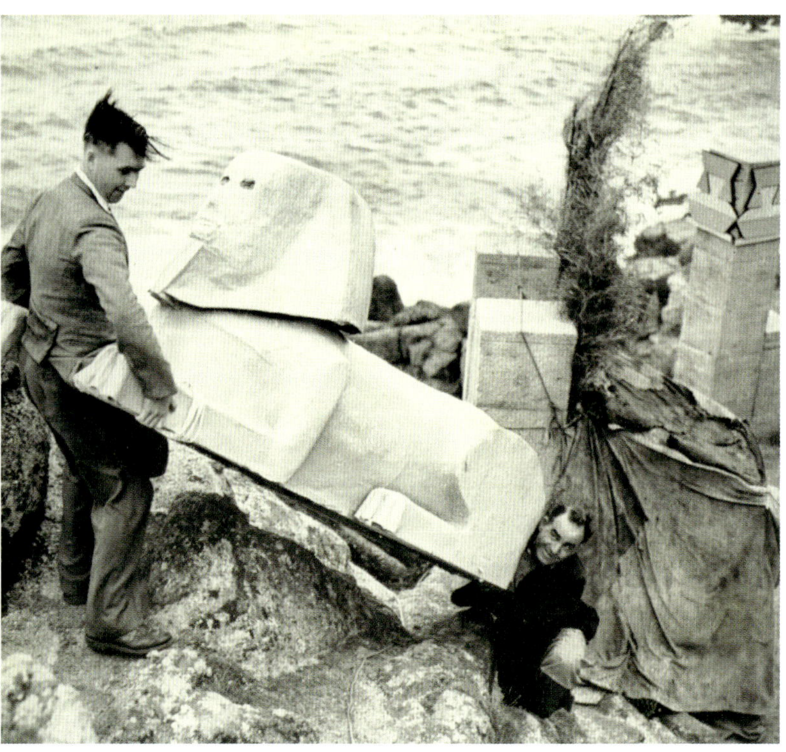

The hazards of being a stagehand at the Minack are fairly unique

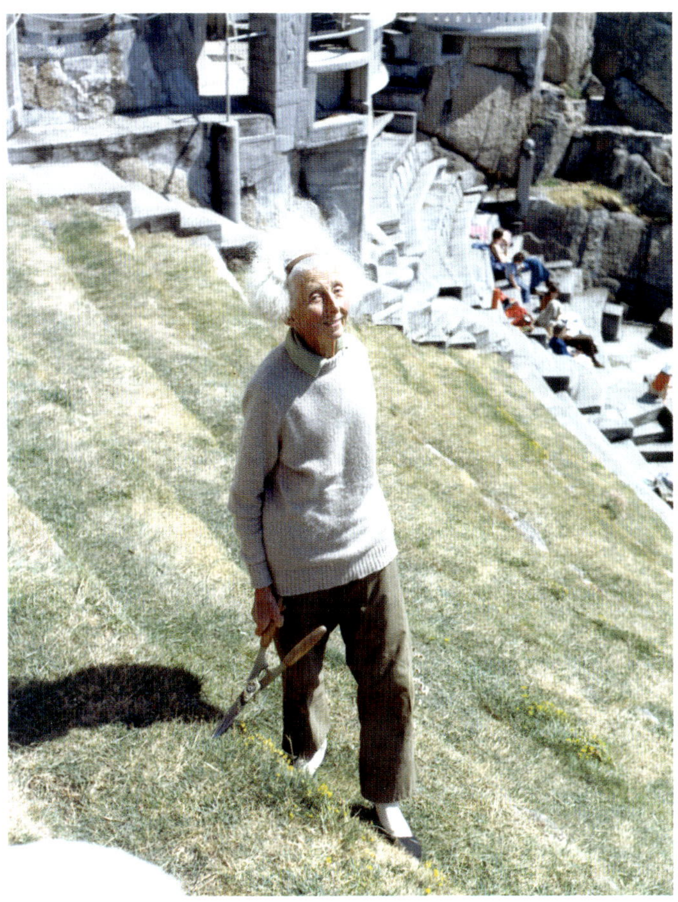

Even as early as 1932 the exceptional rough
and ready nature of the place prompted this
cautionary programme note:

Alas, this disclaimer excludes the poor old
performers. In a 1964 production of *Twelfth
Night* one of the actors skidded on loose gravel
and smashed his kneecap. Of course the show
went on with the producer stepping into the
role.

Not for the faint-hearted or vertiginously
challenged, one might even call it zero health
and safety gone mad.

After the war, with new hope in the air, the
Festival of Britain became a focus of artistic
endeavour and the Minack played its part, in
the summer of 1951, with the specially written
Tristan of Cornwall by Nora Ratcliff (who
went on to become something of a writer
in residence). From here on the theatre was
rapidly acquiring a reputation and becoming an
essential experience for tourists visiting Land's
End. Of course this created an urgent need to
develop various facilities, from car parks to
toilets to an access road plus a modest dressing
room for the cast. The place now needed extra

staffing to cope with the crowds. The National Council of Social Service took over the running and financing in 1952 for three years before pulling out after making a financial loss. Some bright spark came up with the idea of midnight matinées, not foreseeing the traffic chaos that ensued on the surrounding narrow roads as cars trying to get out after the evening show met up with those trying to arrive. Miss Cade also constructed ninety steps up from Porthcurno beach allowing access for the stout-hearted walker, while the stage area was gradually covered with hexagonal concrete panels.

At least these midnight performances sometimes benefitted from a magical full moon providing the atmospheric lighting. Artificial lighting is a very tricky business (in the early days worked from a small hut), with all the electrics in need of serious waterproofing. Sound is another trial for the production team and actors alike. The granite and concrete provide a certain natural acoustic resonance, but wind is often an unpredictable factor. An on-shore wind would seem to carry the actors' voices to the audience, but it also carries the sound of the crashing waves from below; while an off-shore wind can carry the actors' voices out to sea. But somehow, most of the time it works. It can't be stated enough: this theatre stretches the imagination of the audiences like no other, as well as stretching the skills of the performers and production crew. People go to the Minack not so much to see a play but for a unique *experience*.

The Minack Theatre Society was set up in 1959, with Dame Sybil Thorndike as Founder President, to help raise funds. It should be pointed out that Miss Cade never made any money from her exertions, in fact the opposite and she funded it herself for most of her life. In 1976 a Charitable Trust was established (the same year I met her). The creation of a

Visitor Centre with cafe (open all year), with a longer season of shows, at last started to make the enterprise pay. (An architect tells an affectionate story about some buildings he was hired to design and erect. Some time later he had a call from Miss Cade saying she no longer liked one of his huts and had arranged for some miners to arrive the following week and blow it up, so could he please be present to direct them in where to place the gunpowder!)

Looking back over those first five decades of the Minack Theatre we are left in awe at the daunting physical achievement of the tall, lean Miss Rowena Cade. Where on earth did she draw so much strength from? She set herself a punishing regime. Day in day out, battered by the elements, this two-legged nimble mountain goat was spotted slogging up the cliffside with sackfuls of sand on her back or large pieces of driftwood that might be incorporated into a structure. Shortly after a Spanish freighter was wrecked nearby, in 1953, she hauled twelve 15ft beams, found on the beach, up the ninety

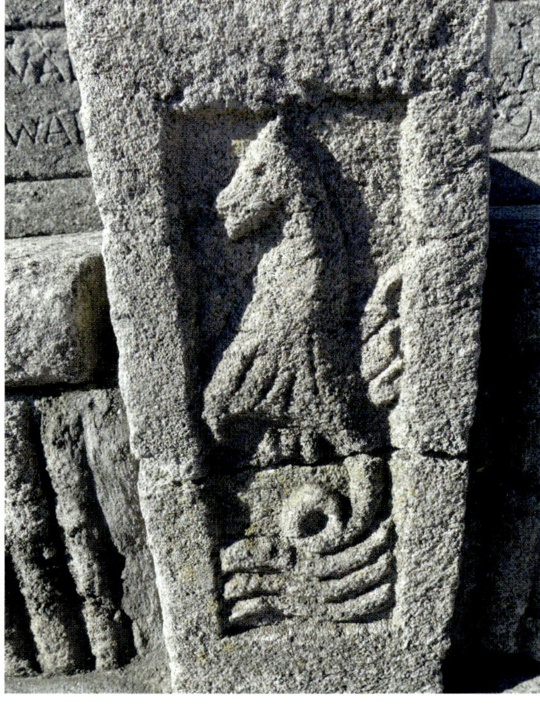

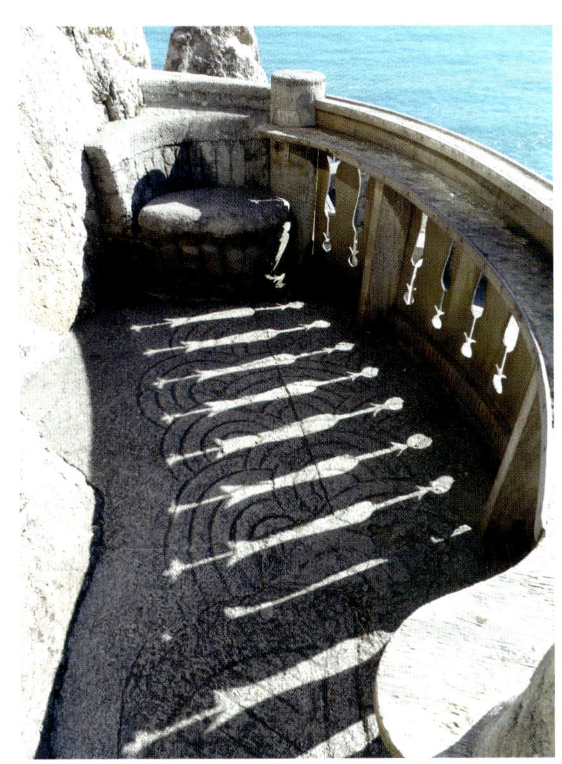

a most frugal existence, with only her dogs for company. A genuine eccentric, she had chosen a harsh life of solitude. Nevertheless, it was also a hugely fulfilled life. Ironically, her lonely labours contributed to a very social experience for countless people from all over the world, bringing them together in a most improbable venue to be entertained, charmed, saddened (and sometimes scorched or soaked) as they witnessed tragedies and comedies drawn from the whole gamut of the dramatic arts.

Rowena Cade breathed her last on March 26, 1983 aged 89. Only latterly was she too frail for scampering about the cliffs, nevertheless her mind retained its agility, allowing her to draw up elaborate plans for further developments. Her resolute spirit is evermore interwoven, like one of her Celtic knotworks, into the very fabric of the Minack headland, and who knows what future generations will make of her 'ancient ruins'.

steps all on her own. Getting into her seventies she started driving an old mini up and down the road well loaded down on its rusty springs with sand and anything else she found while beachcombing after her swim. The bleak winter months were the best time to get a lot of work done in advance of the summer season ahead. She and Billy gradually filled in the sloping terraces with tiers of earth and small boulders to make rudimentary seating and in time each seat got carved listing a production with its year. Miss Cade took great pride in her delicate carving of Celtic patterns (using an old screwdriver) all around the theatre, particularly on her columns. These were carefully constructed using rolls of lino tied together with string and she would then pour the cement in and leave to set. Billy, after a day of splitting open granite boulders by hand, would usually knock off at 5pm (uttering various oaths) but Miss Cade carried on until the last ray of light was gone. Privately at Minack House she lived

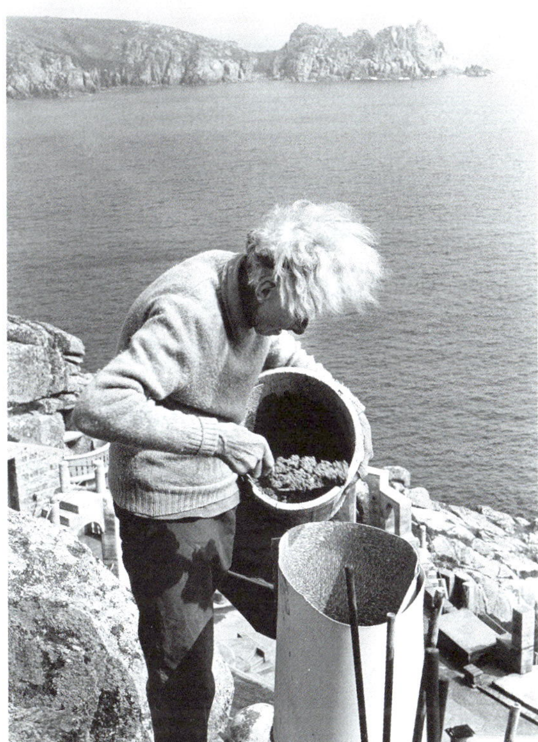

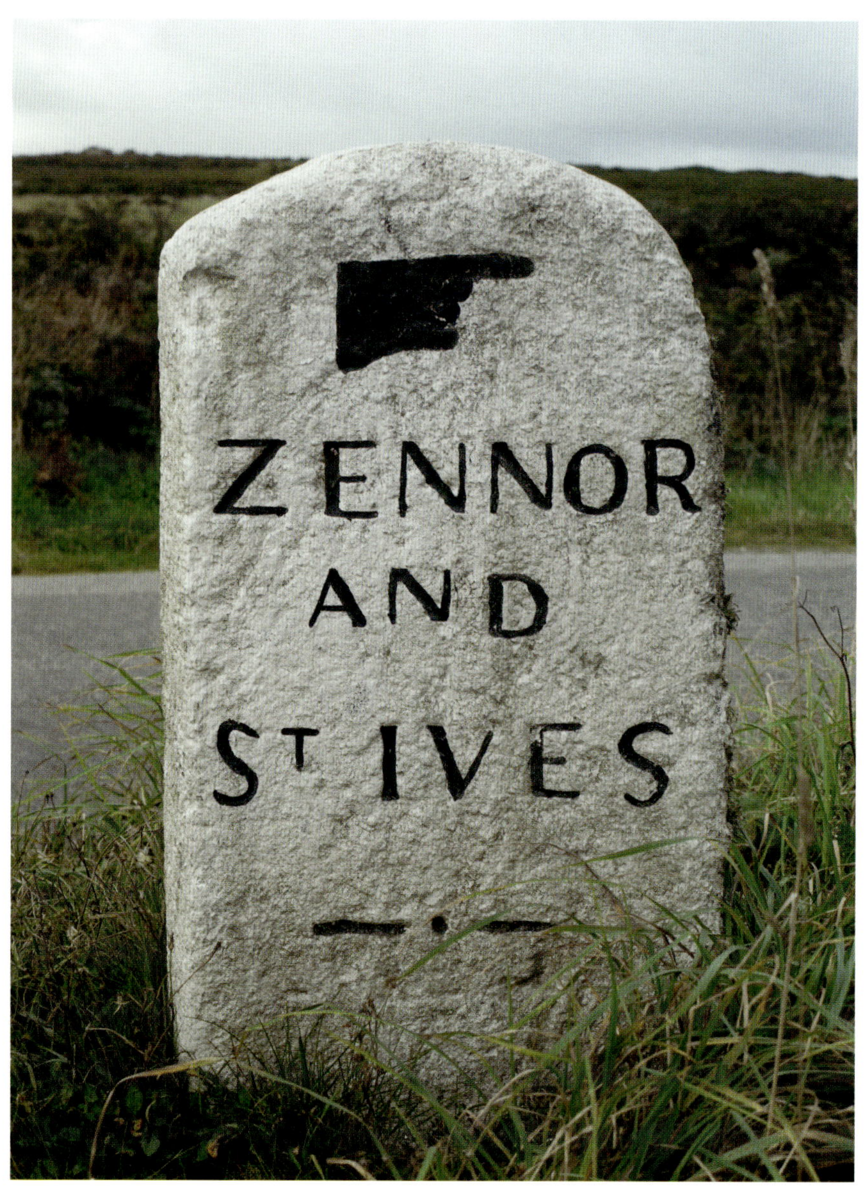

13

Selected Place-Names of West Penwith

This selection provides nothing more than a simplified and brief guide to the enormous complexities of Cornish place-name decipherment. The interested reader should look to the substantial studies by Padel, Pool and Weatherhill, who are by no means always in agreement (see *Further Reading*).

Having produced two earlier books, *Cotswold Place-Names* and *Oxfordshire Place-Names*, I'm well aware that a good deal of informed guesswork goes into interpreting the meanings of many of these names. The spellings we're accustomed to seeing today often bear little resemblance to the original spellings from many hundreds of years ago. Names have gradually mutated, with slight variations, or become corrupted ending up a long way from the true meaning. Alas, there isn't the space here to include all the earliest spellings. Debate is ongoing and it has to be admitted that there are certain intriguing place-names that will forever elude scholarly interpretation.

Further frustration is experienced where the personal names of individuals are linked to places, as no written record exists of who these people were. Saints' names also frequently occur with little or no information – perhaps just a scrap of legend – to provide any biographical context. With those caveats in mind it's worth remembering that 'possibly' and 'probably' need to be attached to many names on this list, usually indicated by (?).

I believe the sound of place-names adds a flavour to how we experience the feeling or atmosphere of a region, and the Cornish language has certainly contributed some wonderful names to the county that make the place feel quite foreign and strange. The following names have been subjectively selected with random precision.

Common place-name elements (with prominent corruptions & mutations)

Als cliff

Bal mine, tin workings (usually applied in a more general way than **Whel**)

Bod/Bos dwelling

Bounder lane, pasture

Bre hill

Carn tor, rock-pile, crag

Carreck rock

Chy/Ty house, cottage

Cos/Coose/Goose wood

Crows cross, crossroad, crossing

Crug/Creek/Creeg burial mound, barrow

Dowr river, stream

Dynas/Dennis/Dinnis castle

Eglos church (derived from Latin *ecclesia* & French *église*)

Enys/Ennis/Ninnis island, isolated place

Fenten/Venton natural well, spring

Forth/For road, path

Gun/Goon/Woon down, downland

Gwel/Gweal/Gul field

Gwedhen/Withen tree

Hal moor, marshland

Heyl tidal estuary

Kelly/Gilly/Gelly grove, copse

Ker enclosure (often of a fort)

Lan sacred enclosure, or religious settlement

Lyn pool, pond

Lys/Les stronghold

Marghas/Maraz market

Melyn/Vellan mill

Men/Meyn stone

Meneth/Menna hill

Mor sea

Nans/Nance/Nant valley

Park field

Pen/Pedn head, promontory

Pons/Pont bridge

Porth cove

Pol pool, pond

Res/Ris/Rice ford

Ros/Rose heath

Ton/Todden turf, grassland

Towan/Tewen dune

Tre farm, settlement (this is the most common prefix of all the place-names in the area and is usually combined with a forgotten or indecipherable personal name)

Treth/Treath/Dreath sand

Whel/Wheal/Huel mine works (usually attached to a specific mine name)

Zawn chasm or cleft (appears as a deep narrow fissure in the cliffs where the sea has eroded a softer mineral, usually tin, from the harder rock on either side)

Place-Names

Alsia slope

Amalveor great slope

Barnoon summit of the down

Bojewyan dwelling of Uyon

Bologgas dwelling of mice

Boscawen dwelling by an elder tree

Boscregan Zawn dwelling by the barrow chasm

Bosigran dwelling of Garan (?)

Bosullow dwelling by house of light (?)

Boswednack dwelling of Wednack

Botallack dwelling of Talek or dwelling on a steep brow (?)

Bowgyheere long cowshed

Brisons from French *brisant* 'reef' or 'breaker'

Carbis causeway

Carn Bargus buzzards' crag

Carn Euny after St Euny

Carn Galva lookout tor

Carn Gloose grey rock pile

Carnyorth roebucks' tor

Castle-an-Dinas castle at hill fort

Castle Horneck iron like-castle

Chun house on a down

Chyandour house by the stream

Chykembro Welshman's house

Chypraze house in a meadow

Chysauster house of Sylvester

Cockwells after Cockwell family

Cornawheely lapwings

Crankan fort of misery

Crowlas weir-ford or hovel-ford (?)

Crows-an-Wra cross of the witch

Deveral watery

Drift the farm (?)

Embla slopes

Ennis isolated place

Escalls thistle slope

Fuggoe cave

Gear fort or enclosed farm

Goonmenheer longstone down

Greeb Zawn reef chasm

Grumbla cromlech/dolmen

Gunwalloe after St Gunwalloe or Winwaloe

Gulval from a female St Gwelval (?)

Gurlyn high pool

Gurnard's Head from the resemblance to a gurnard fish

Gwavas winter dwelling

Gwythian after St Guidian

Halsetown settlement founded by James Halse (19th century)

Hayle estuary

Hellsvean old court

Hendra home farm

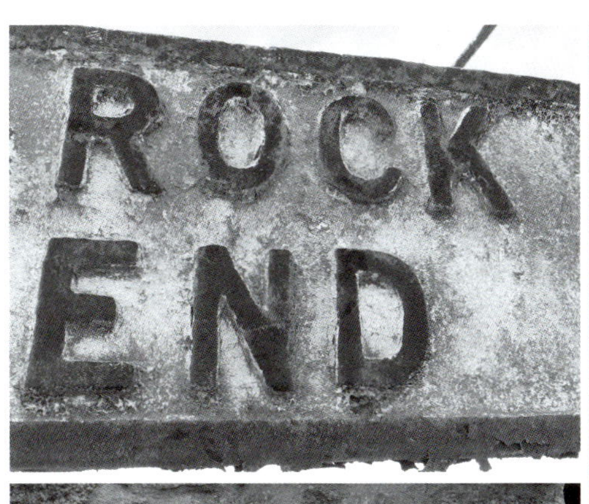

ROCK
END

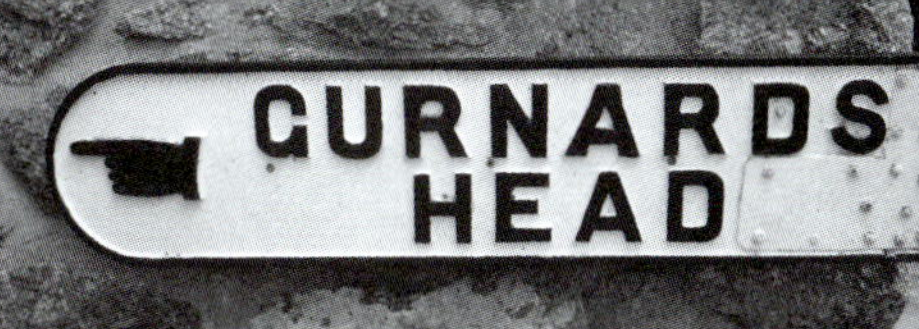

GURNARDS
HEAD

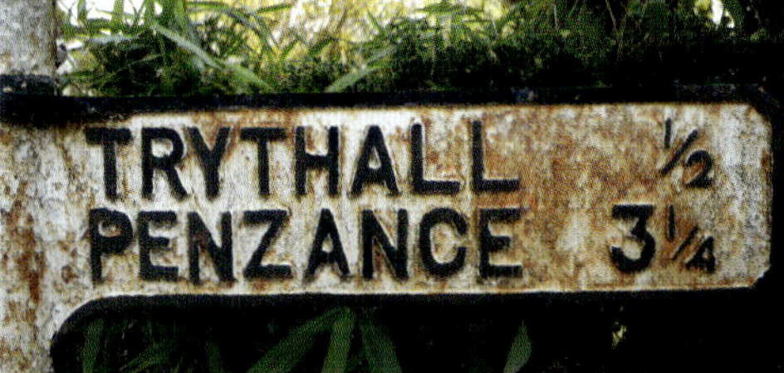

TRYTHALL   ½
PENZANCE   3¼

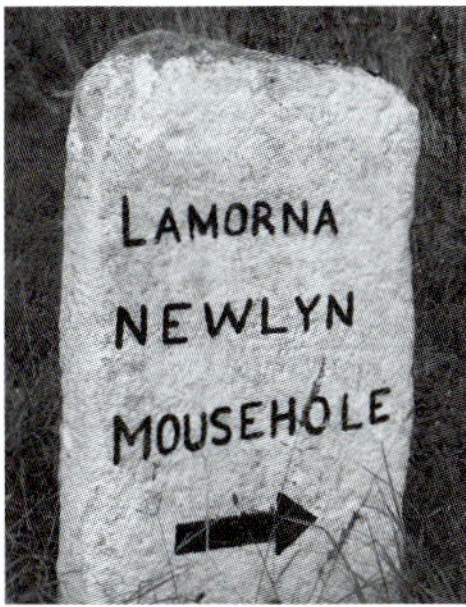

LAMORNA
NEWLYN
MOUSEHOLE

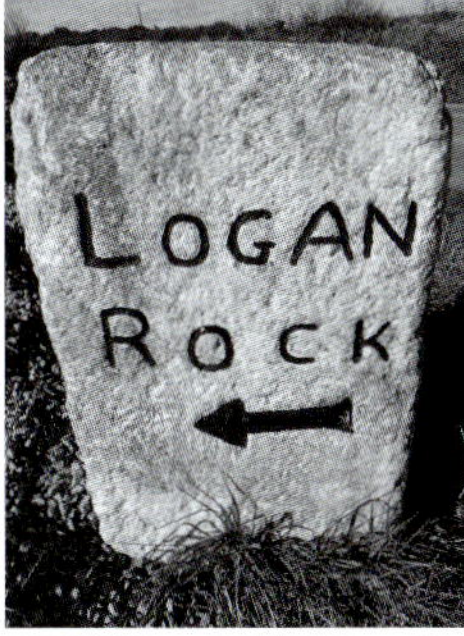

LOGAN
ROCK

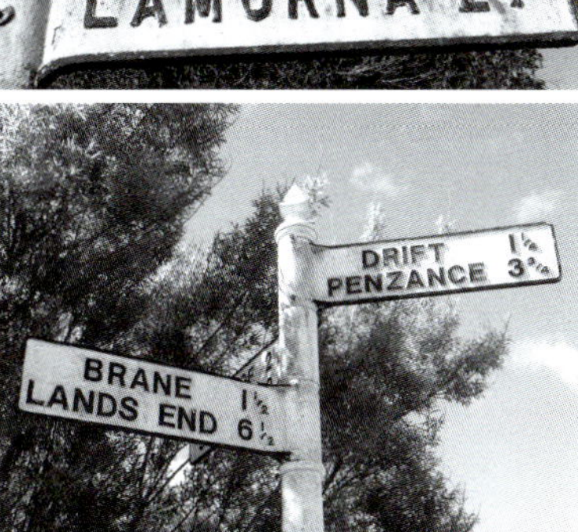

LAMORNA 2¾
DRIFT   1½
PENZANCE   3¾
BRANE   1½
LANDS END 6½

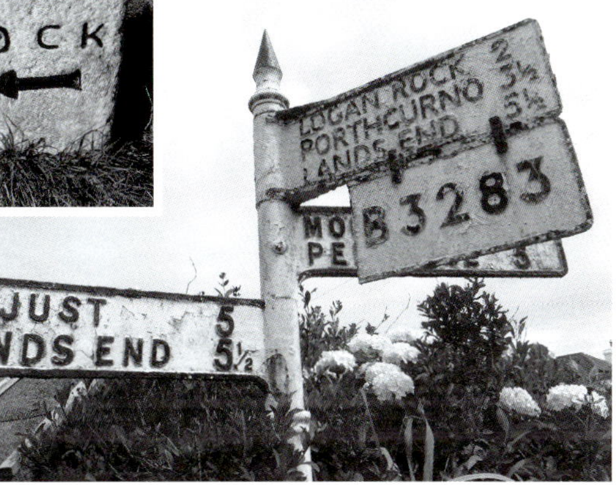

LOGAN ROCK   2½
PORTHCURNO   3½
LANDS END   5¼
B 3283
MOU
PE
ST JUST   5
LANDS END   5½

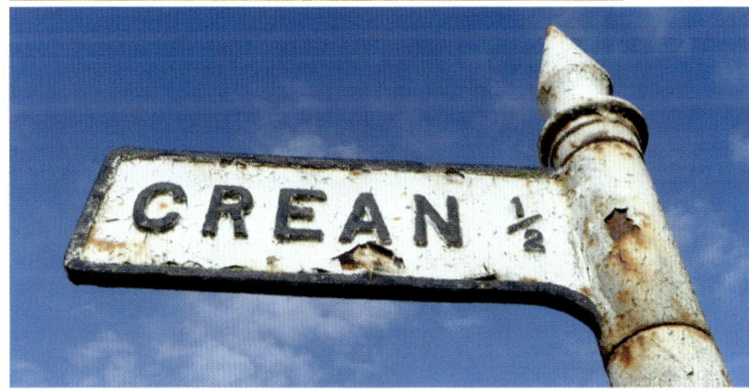

CREAN ½

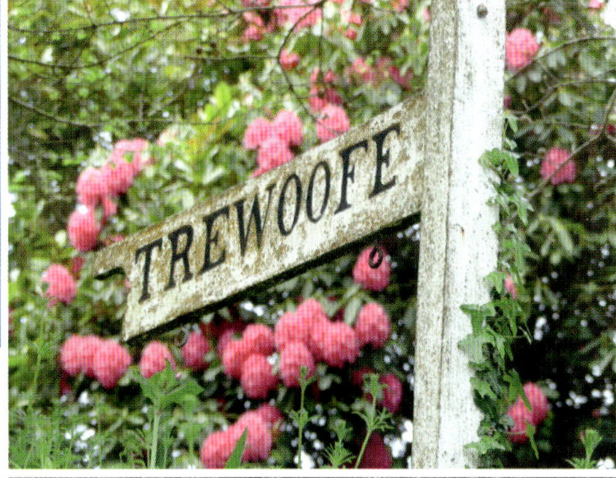

TREWOOFE

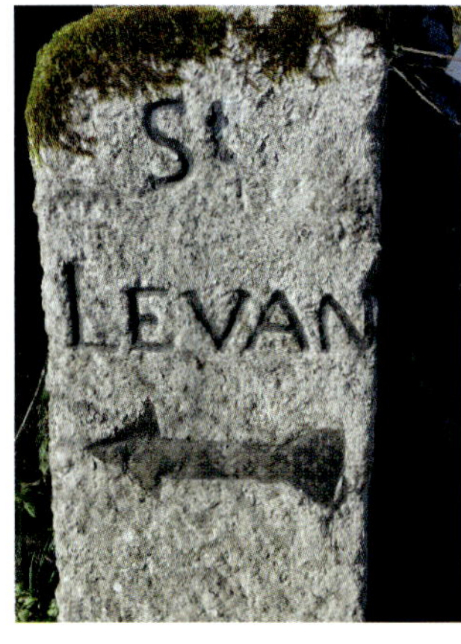

ST
LEVAN

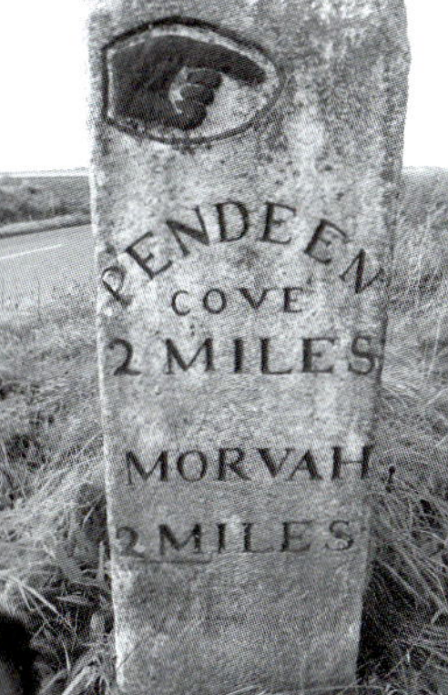

PENDEEN
COVE
2 MILES
MORVAH
2 MILES

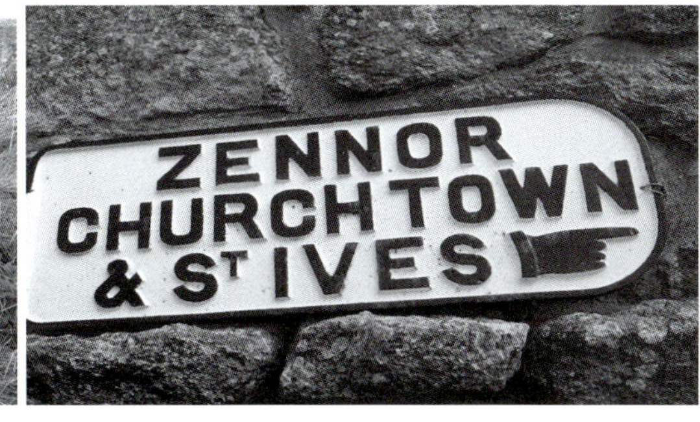

ZENNOR
CHURCHTOWN
& ST IVES

Joppa smithy/workshop (?)

Keigwen white hedge

Kelynack holly grove

Kenidjack fuel-gathering place

Kerrow forts

Lamorna valley of a stream called Mornow (?)

Lanyon cold pool

Lelant after St Anta

Lescudjack wooded valley

Logan Rock rocking stone

Ludgvan place of ashes

Luthergwearne slope of alders

Madron after St Madern

Marazion little market

Men-an-Tol stone of the hole

Men Scryfa writing stone

Minack stony one

Morrab seashore

Morvah after St Morvethe (?)

Mousehole mouse hole (!)

Mulfra bare hill

Nancherrow valley with an acre of cultivated land (?)

Nancledra valley of Clodri

Nanjulian elbow-shaped valley

Nanseglos church valley

Newlyn fleet pool

Ninnes isolated place

Paul after St Paul or Paulinus (Welsh saint)

Penberth foot of the river Breyth

Pednavounder end of the lane

Pendeen fort headland

Penolva lookout headland

Penzance holy headland

Penwith end-district

Plen-an-gwary playing place, amphitheatre

Polgigga hefers' pool

Polkinghorne Cynhoern's pool

Polostoc Zawn fox's chasm

Porthcurno cove of horns

Porthgwarra higher cove

Porthmeor great cove

Progo cove with a cave

Prussia Cove named after an 18th-century wrecker & smuggler, John Carter, nicknamed the 'King of Prussia'

Relubbus Lehoubed's ford

Rissick dry ford

Roseangrouse watercourse at the cross

Rosemergy heath of horse stables

Rosewall ford by a wall

Rosudgeon ox heath

Sancreed after St Sancred

St Buryan after St Beriana

St Erth after St Erc

St Ives after St Ia

St Just after St Justin or Yestin

St Levan after St Selevan

Sennen after St Senan

Skewjack sheltered

Skillywadden poor nooks (?)

Splattenridden bracken plot

Stennack tin-bearing ground

Tolcarne brow of a rock-pile

Towednack after St Winnoc

Treen farm by a fort

Tregenna Ceneu's farm

Tregerthen rowan-trees farm

Tremenheere standing stone farm

Trencrom farm by the curve

Trengwainton springtime farm (?)

Trereife king's farm

Trevescan sedge farm

Trewoofe winter farm

Trink Frenchman's farm

Trowan oxen farm

Trungle farm by a stone quarry

Truthwall Iudhael's farm

Trythall farm where root crops grow

Vellandreath beach mill

Vellandruchia tucking mill

Vellansagia sifting mill

Ventonleague slab well

Wheal Owles cliff mine

Wheal Reeth red mine
Wicca from Old English *wic* 'dairy farm'
Woon Gumpus level downs (?)
Zawn a Bal chasm by the mine
Zawn Brinny crows' chasm
Zawn Buzz & Gen chasm by giant's dwelling
Zawn Duel dark chasm

Zawn Gamper chasm where currents meet
Zawn Kellys hidden chasm
Zawn Peggy plural of 'pyg'
Zawn Pyg pointed beak chasm
Zawn Reeth red chasm
Zawn Wells grass chasm
Zennor after St Senara

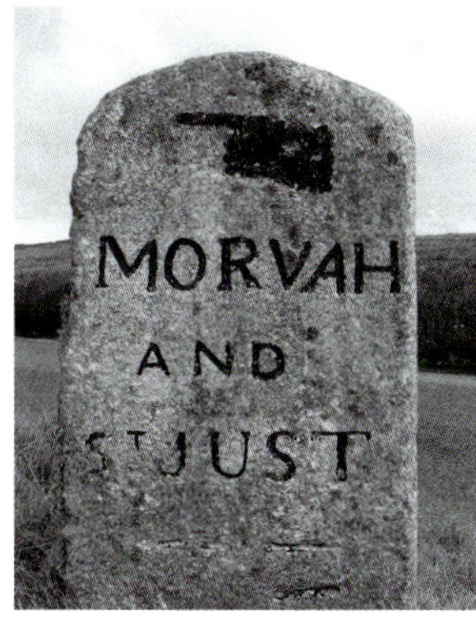

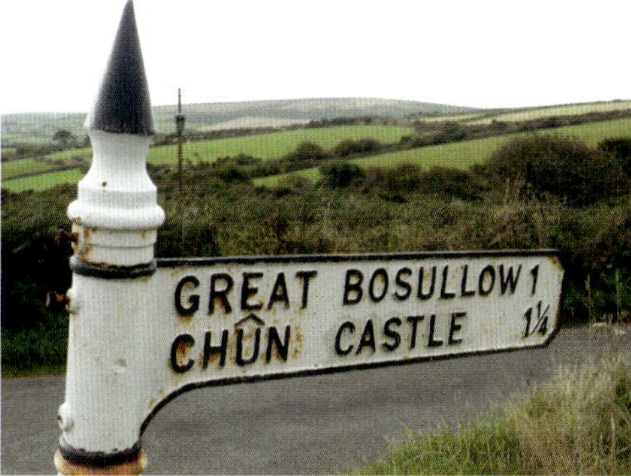

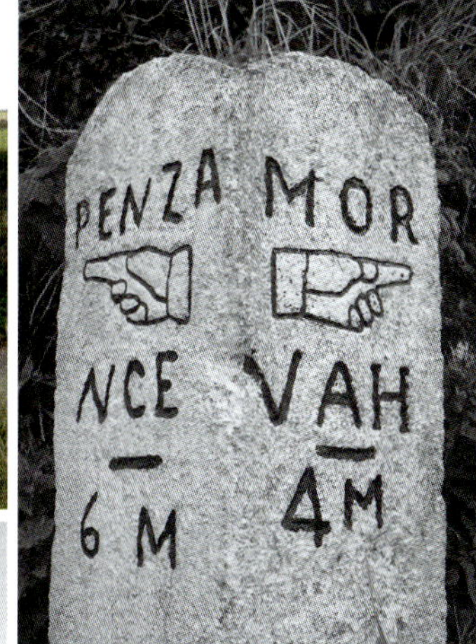

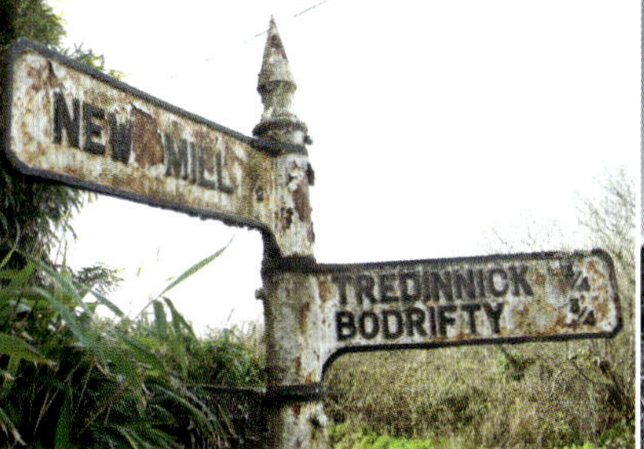

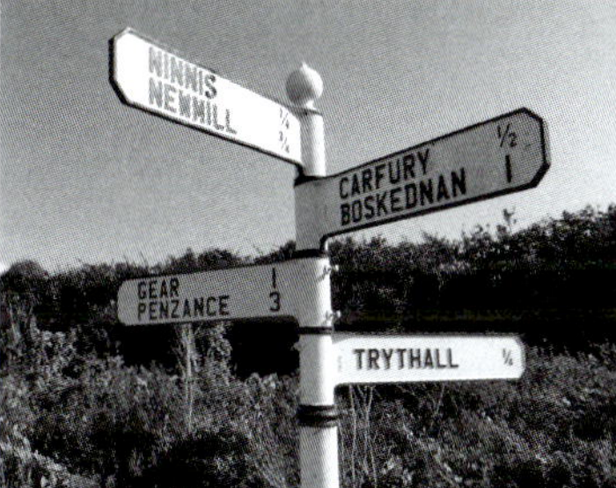

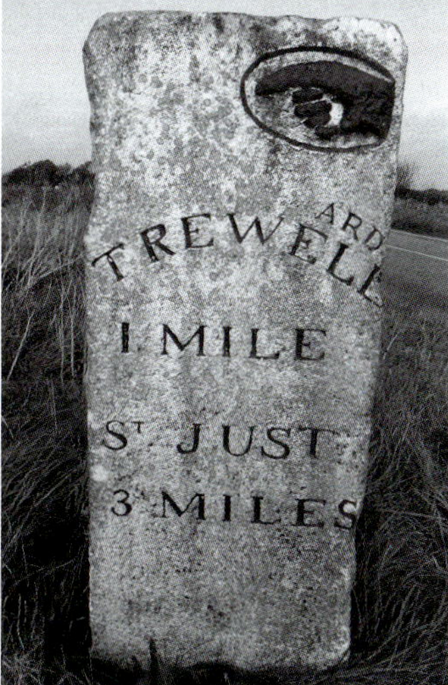

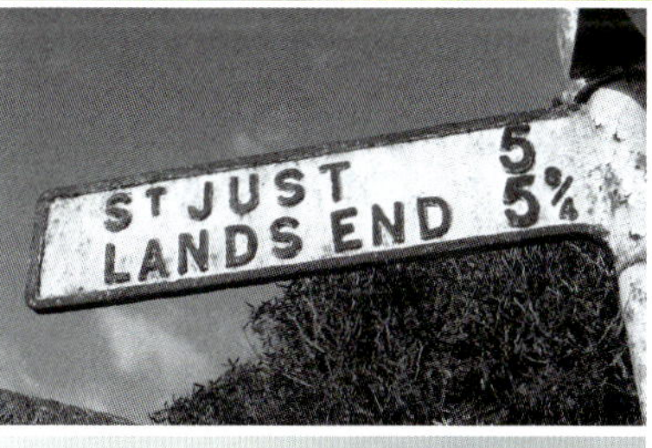

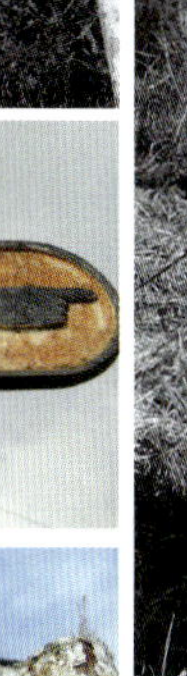

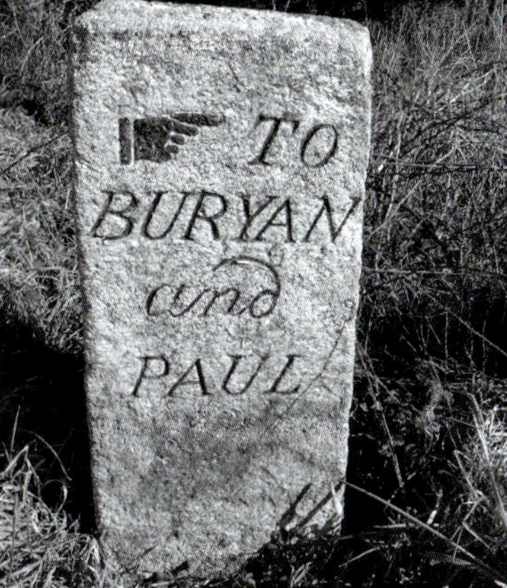

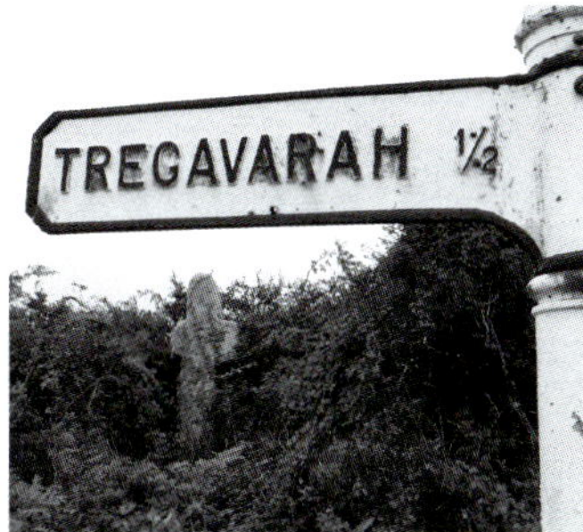

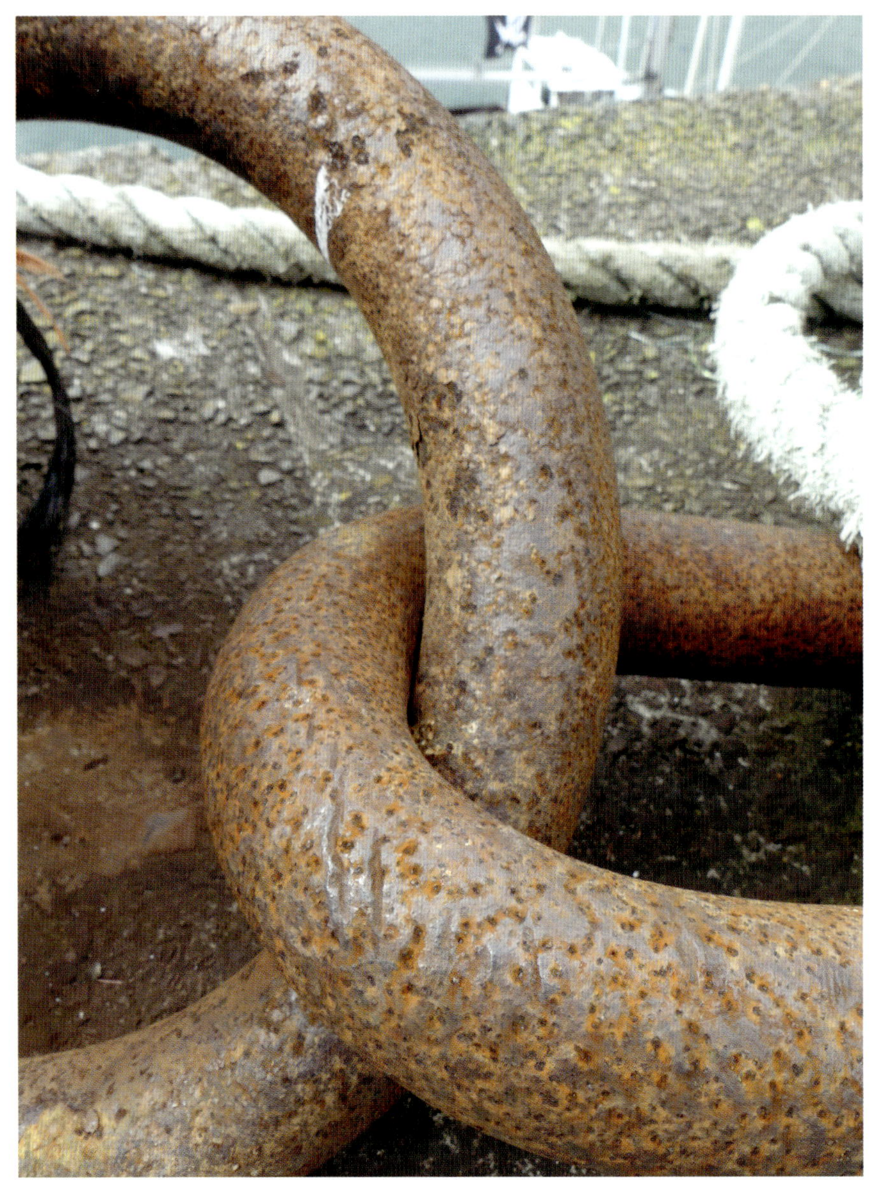

14

Rust, Rocks, Ruins & Wrecks
(a photo essay)

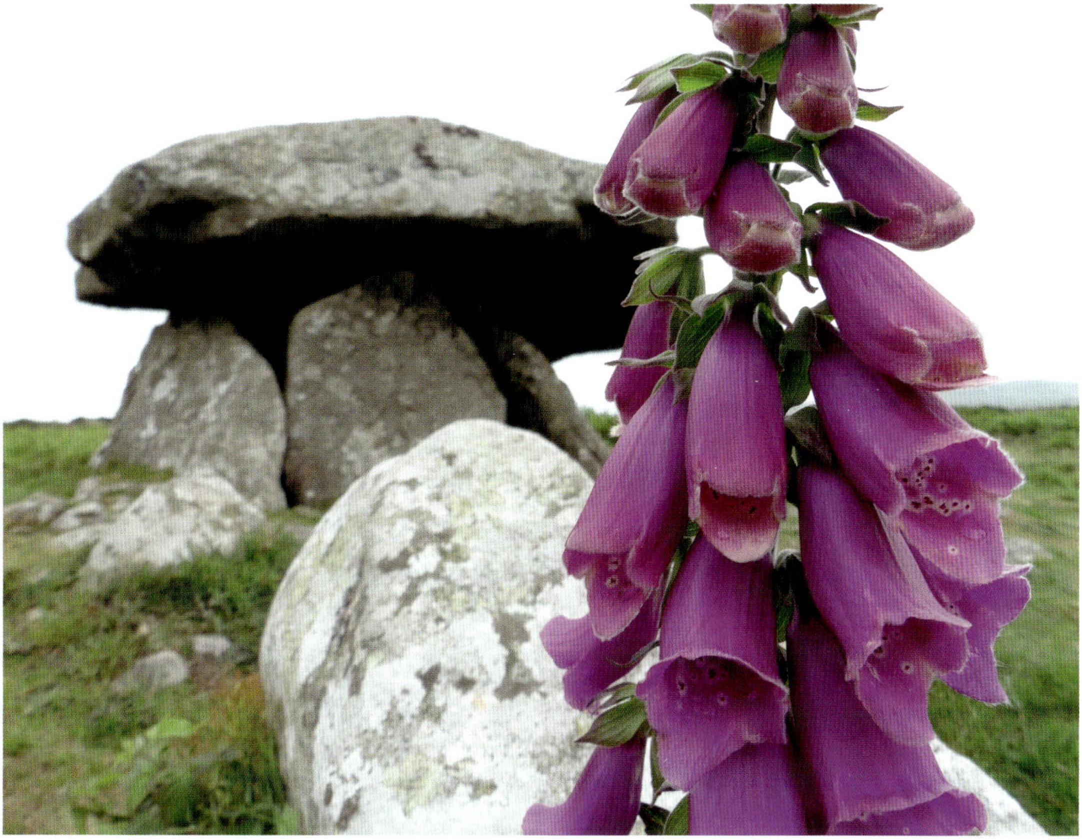

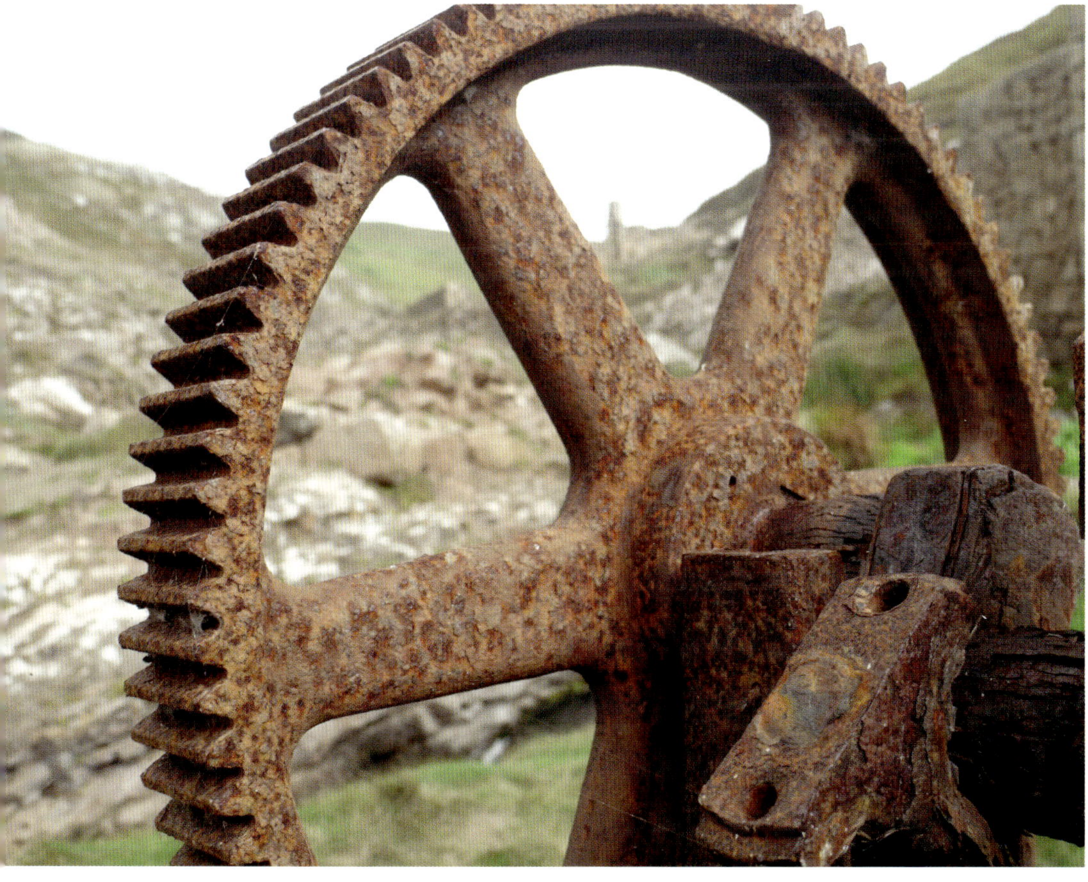

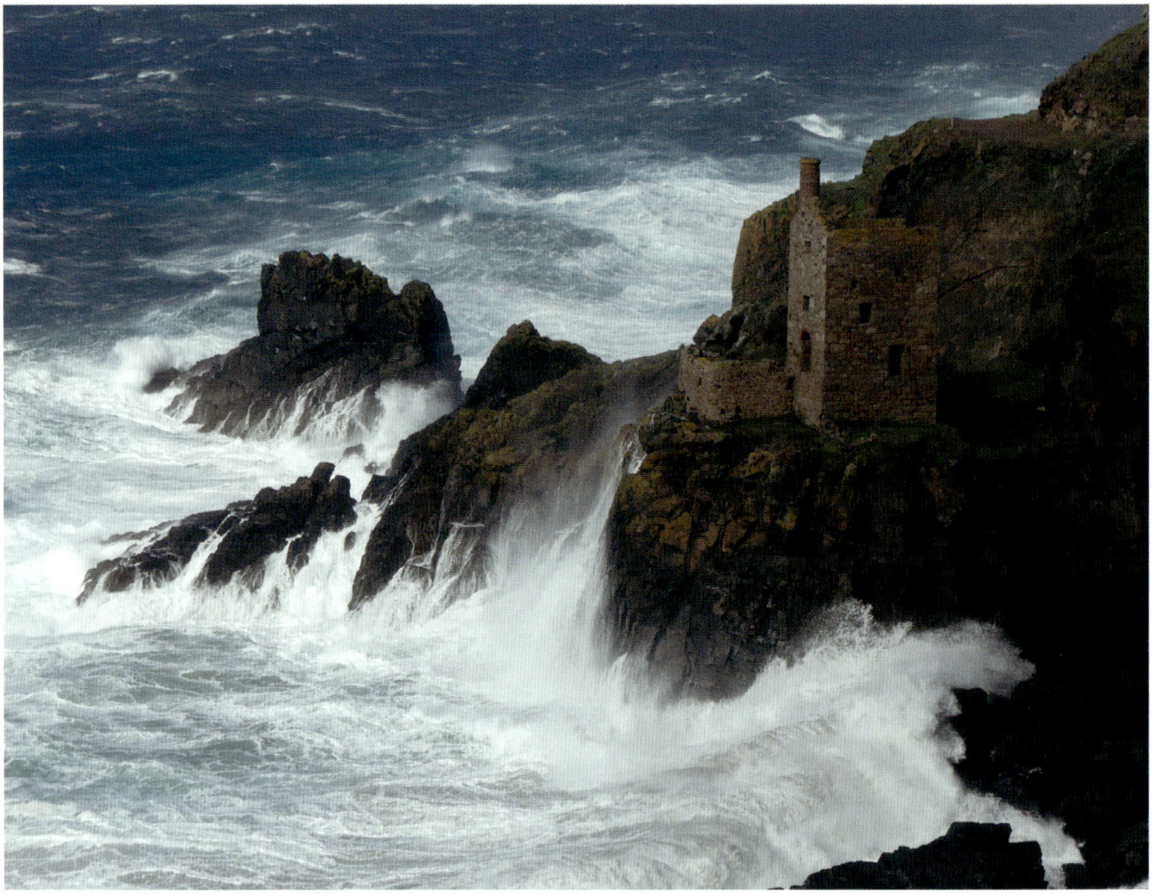

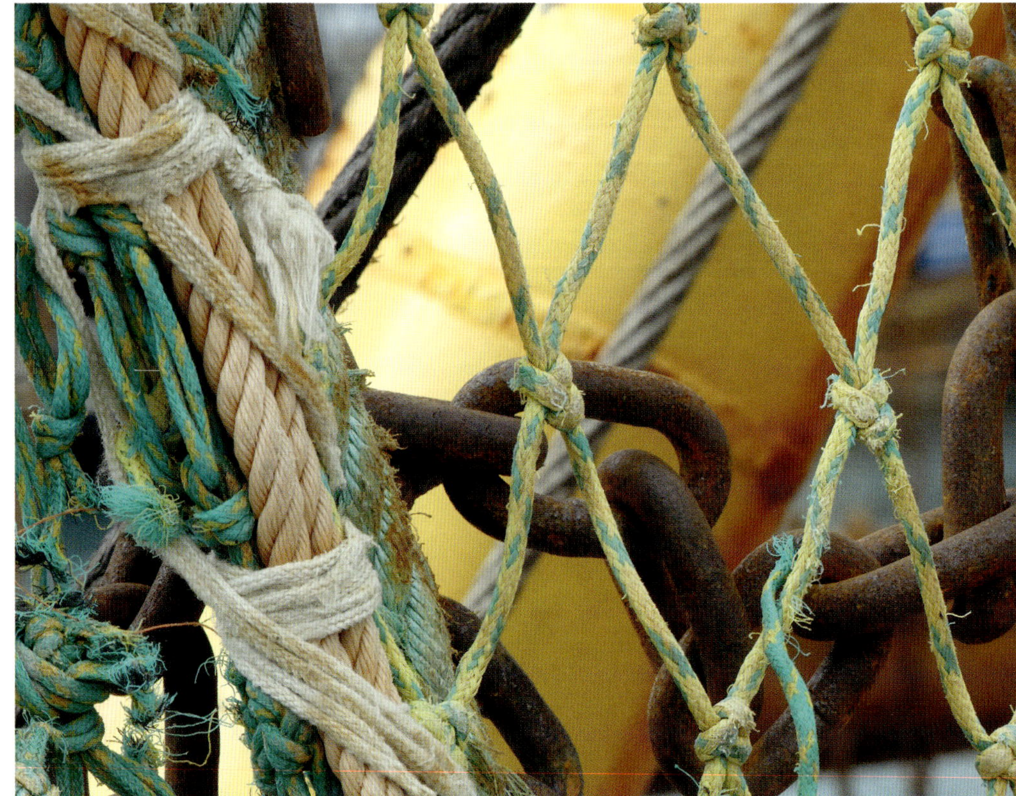

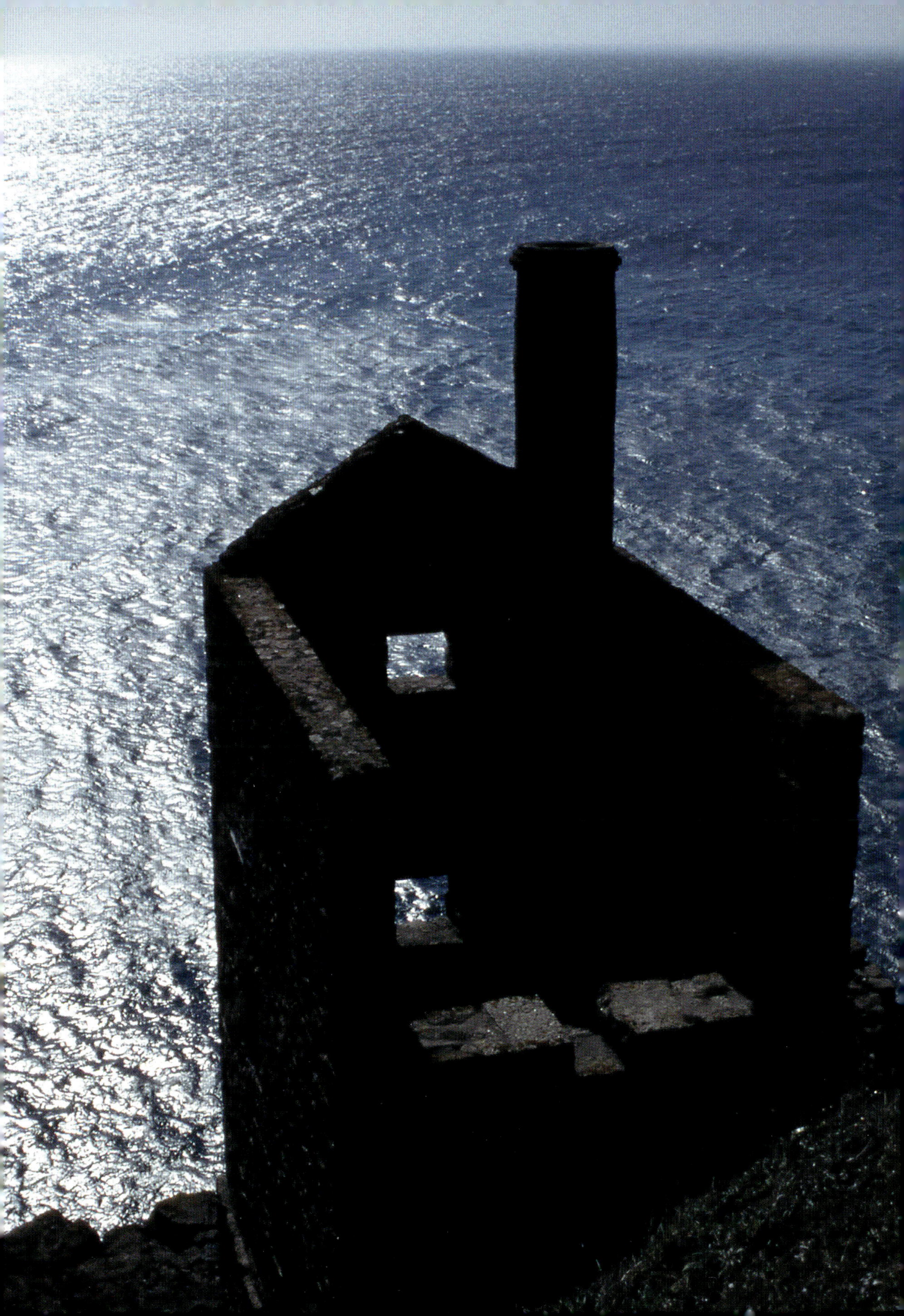

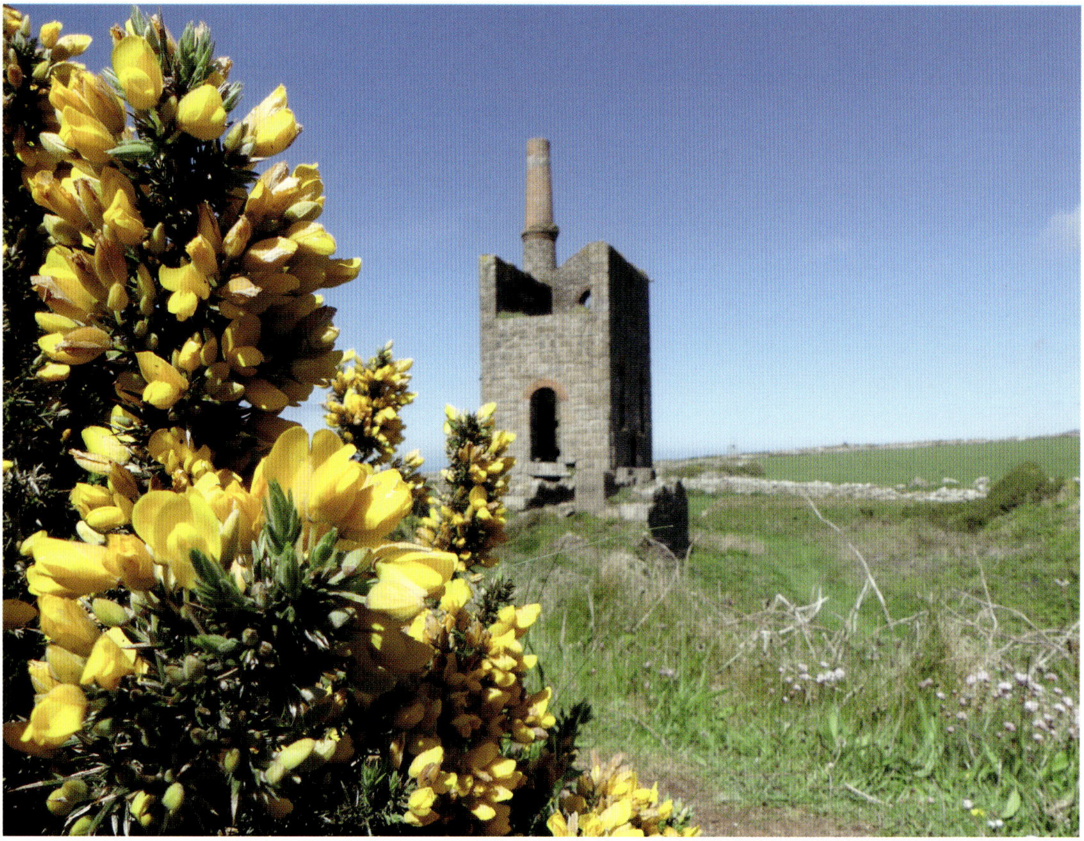

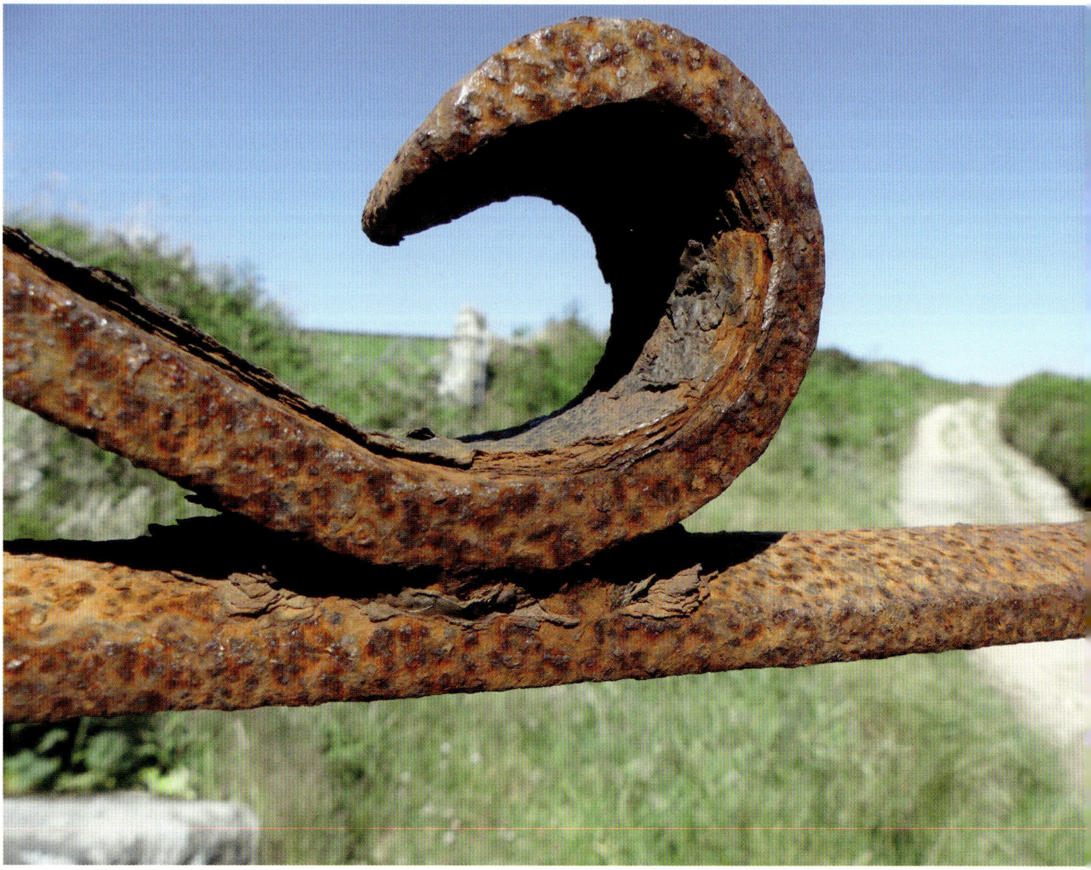

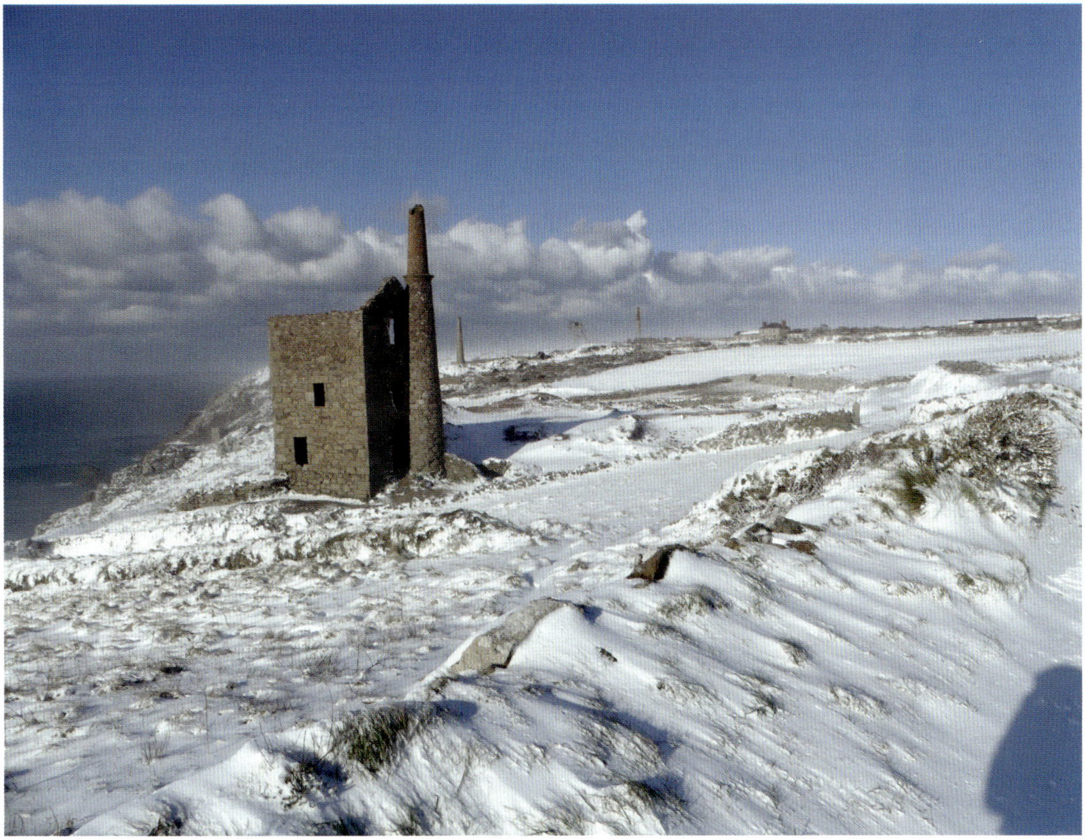

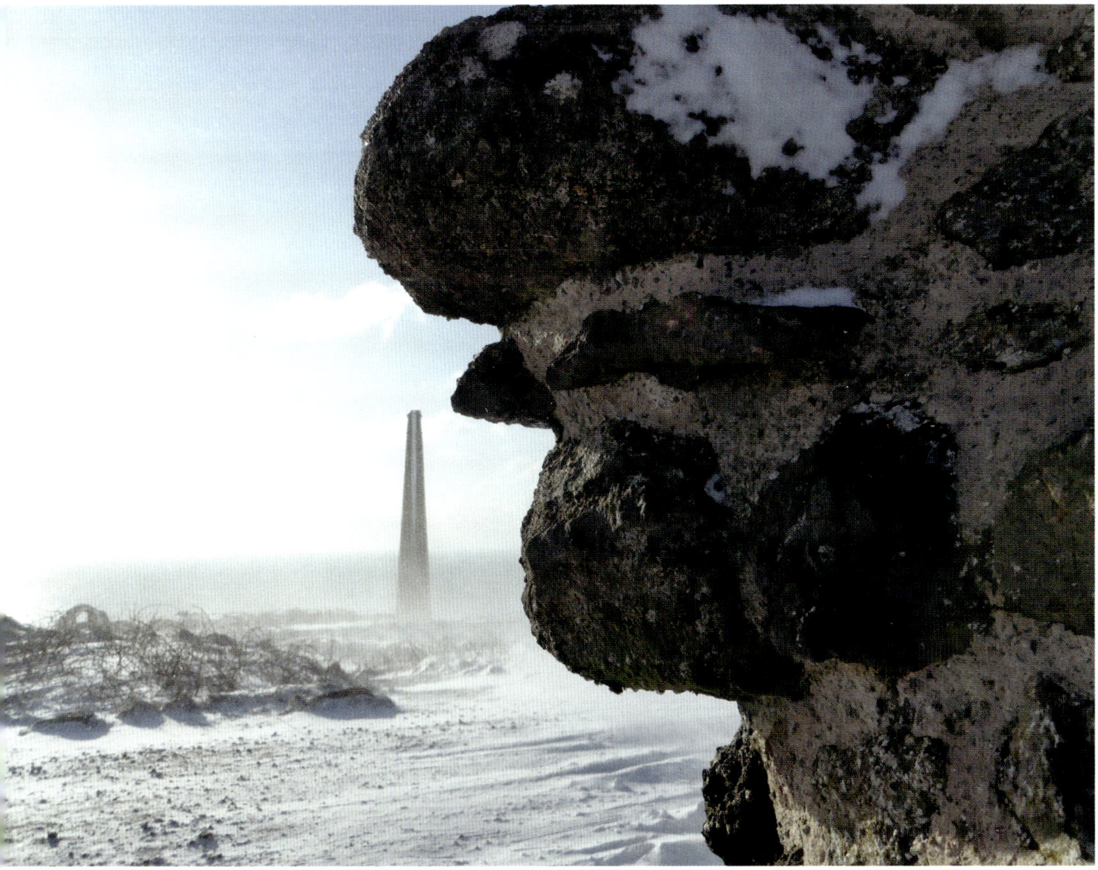

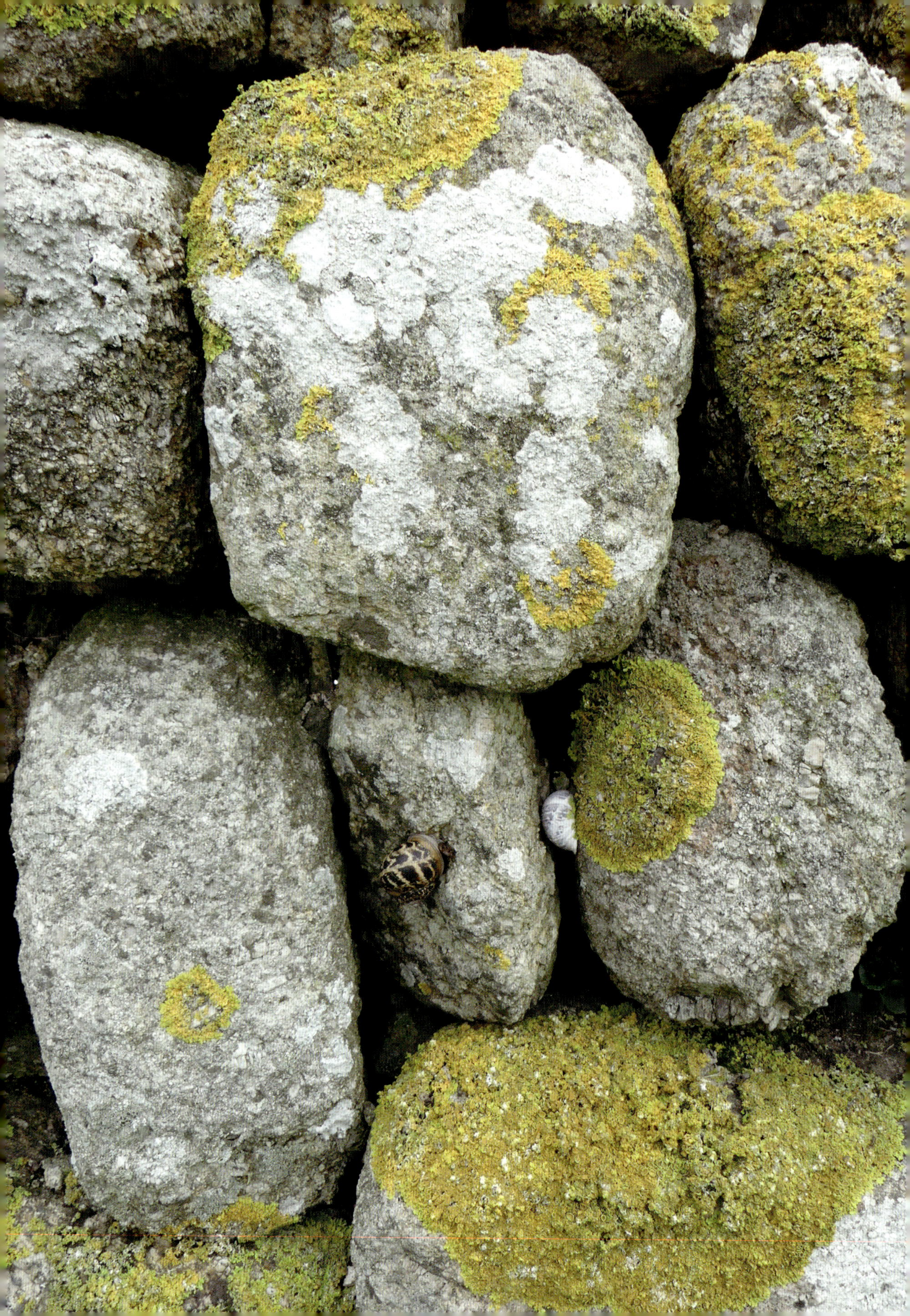

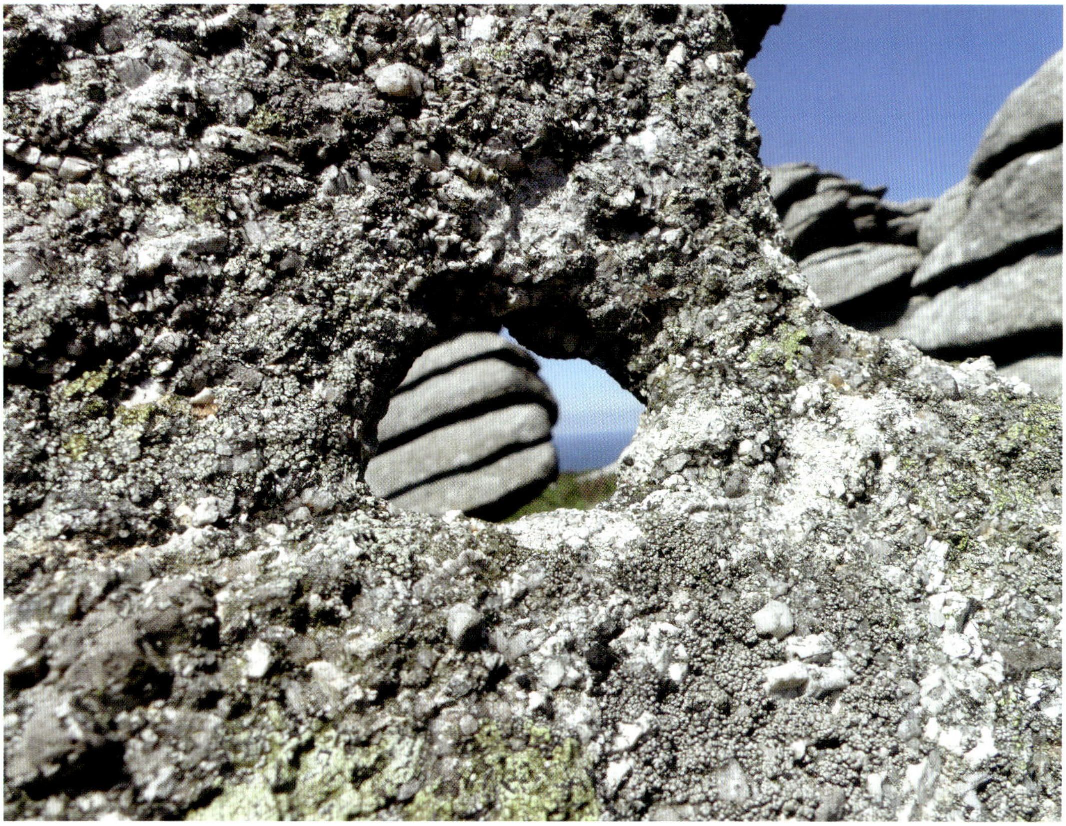

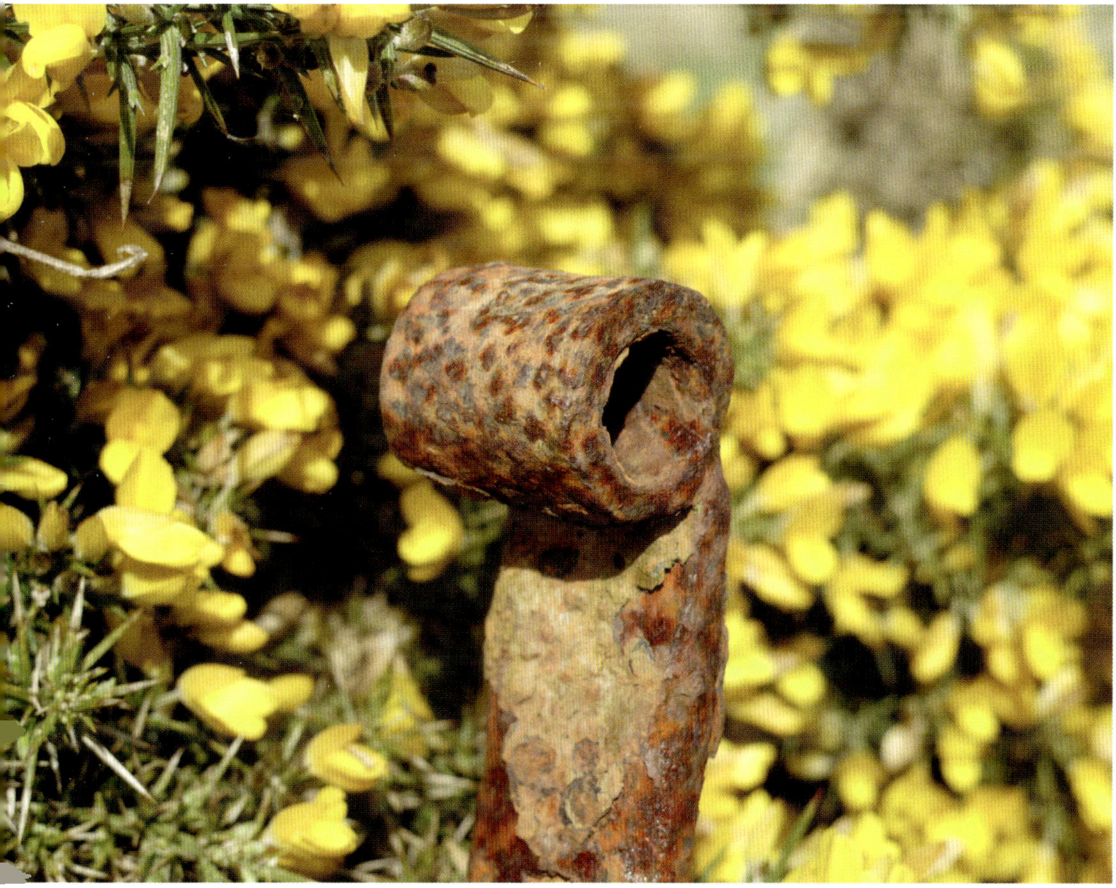

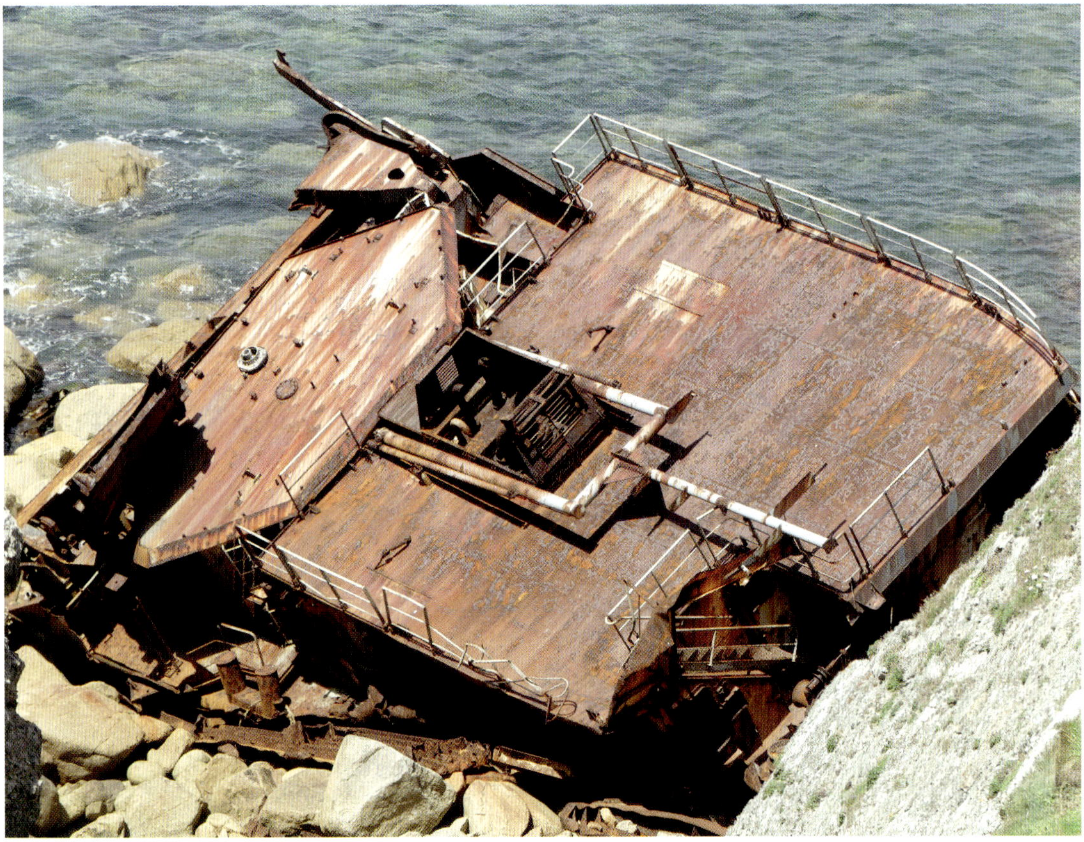

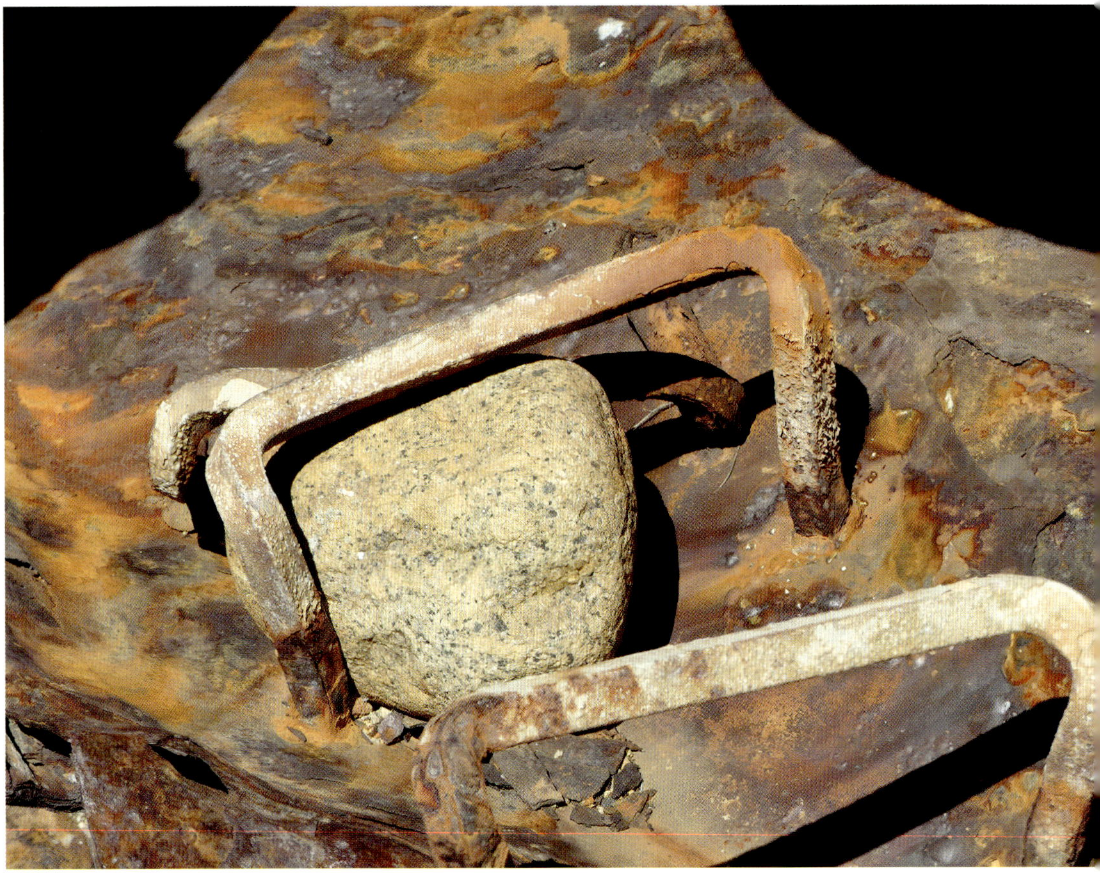

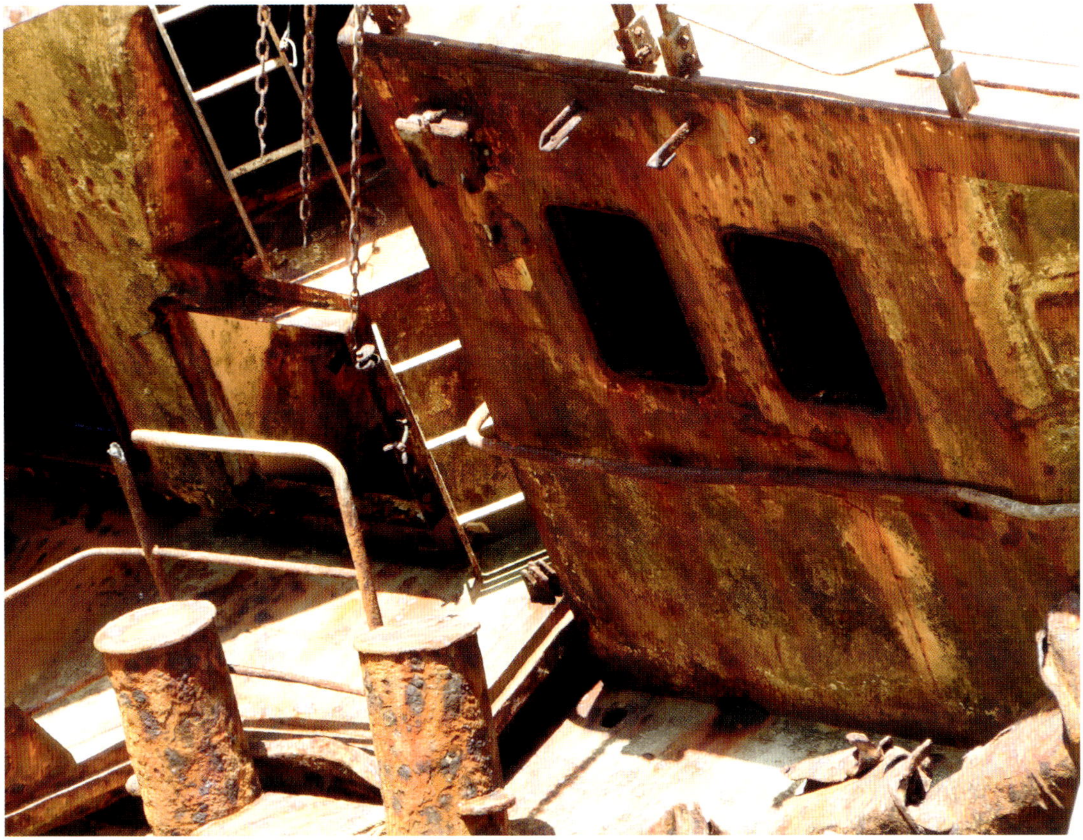

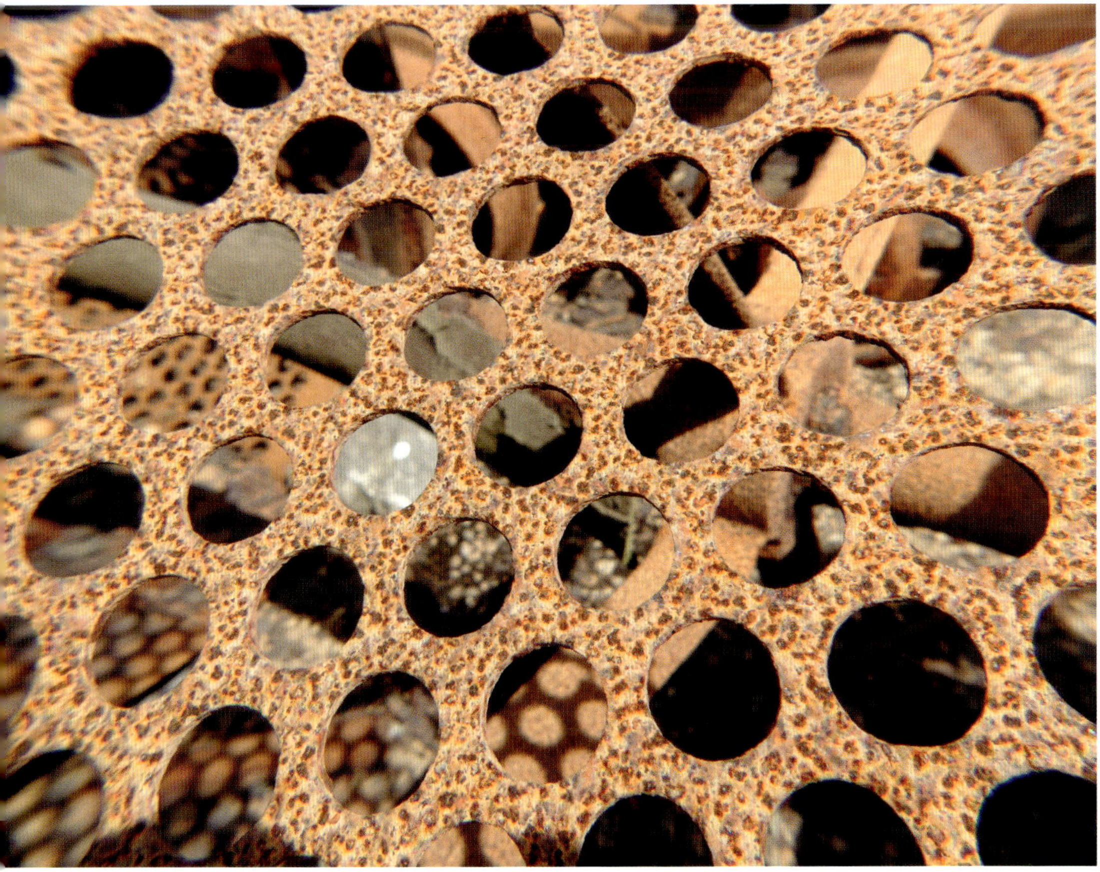

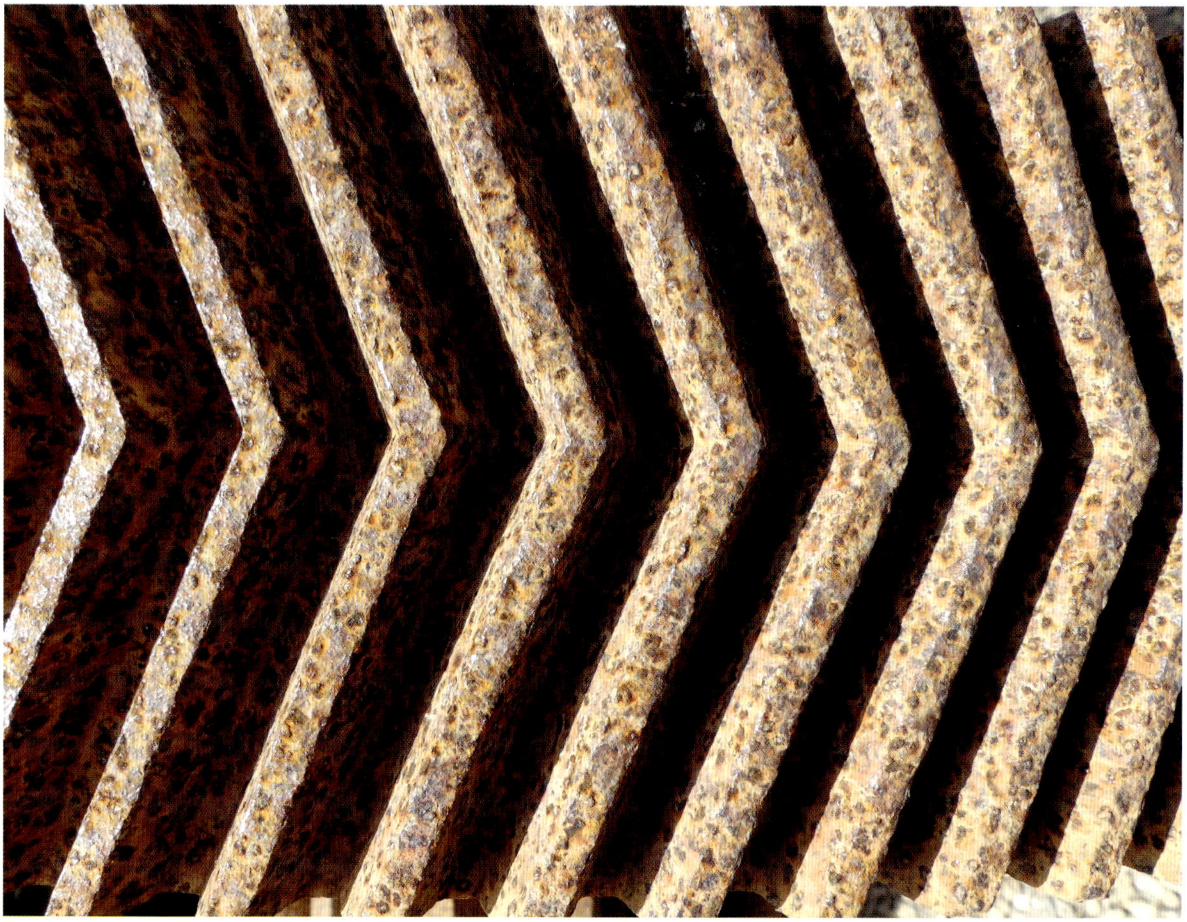

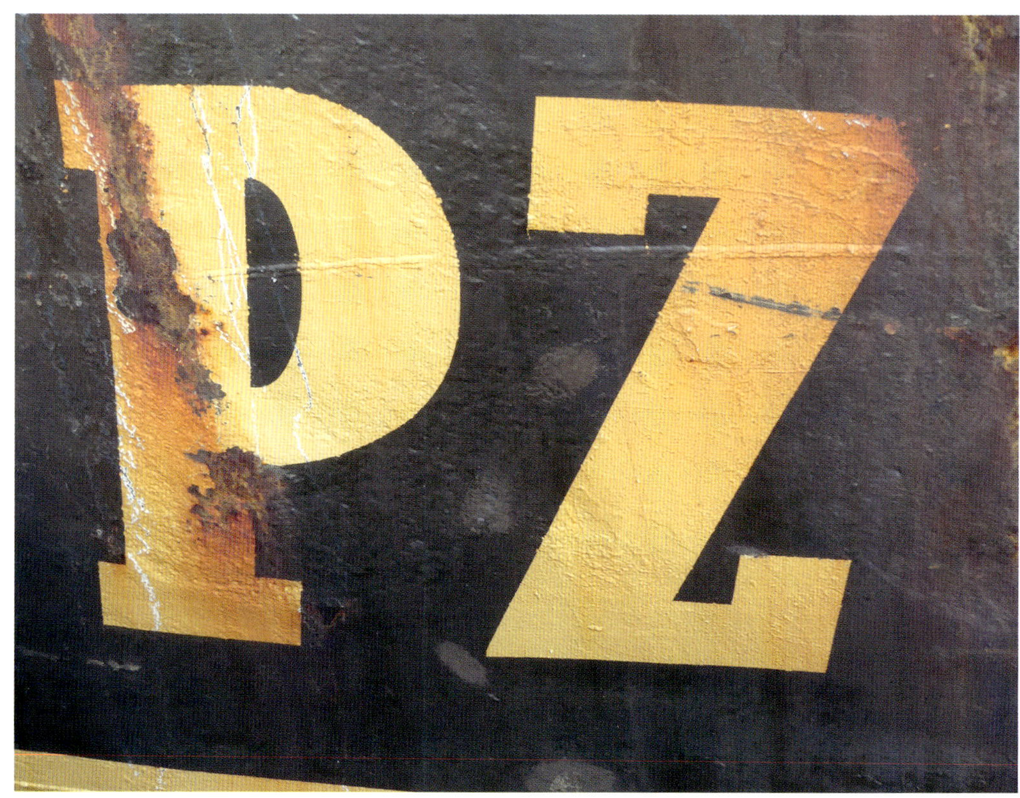

PZ

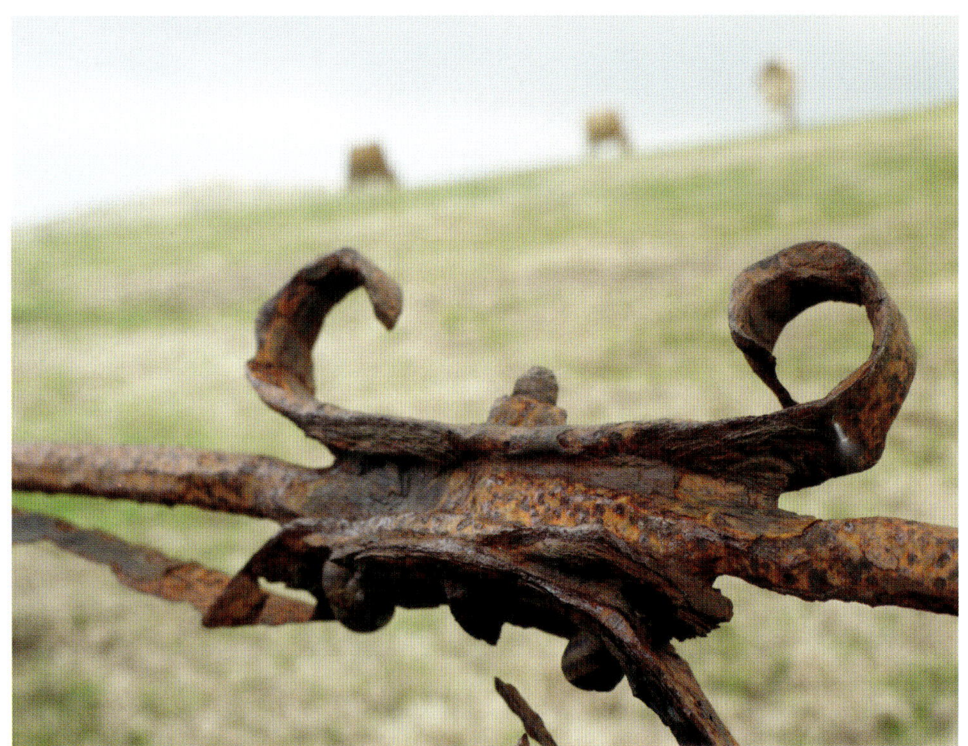

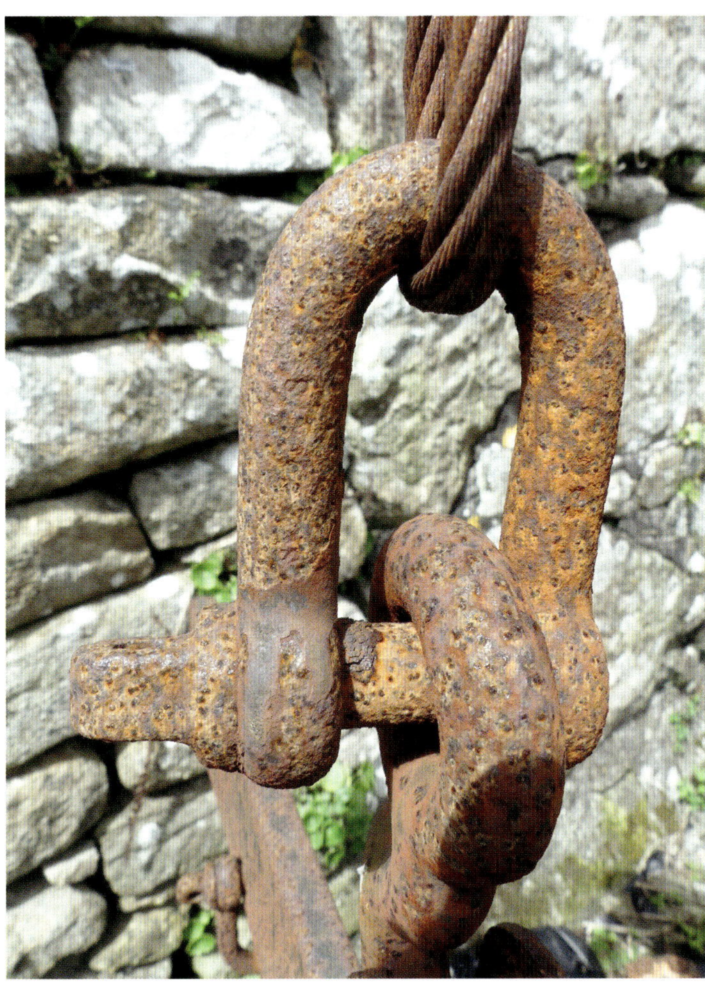

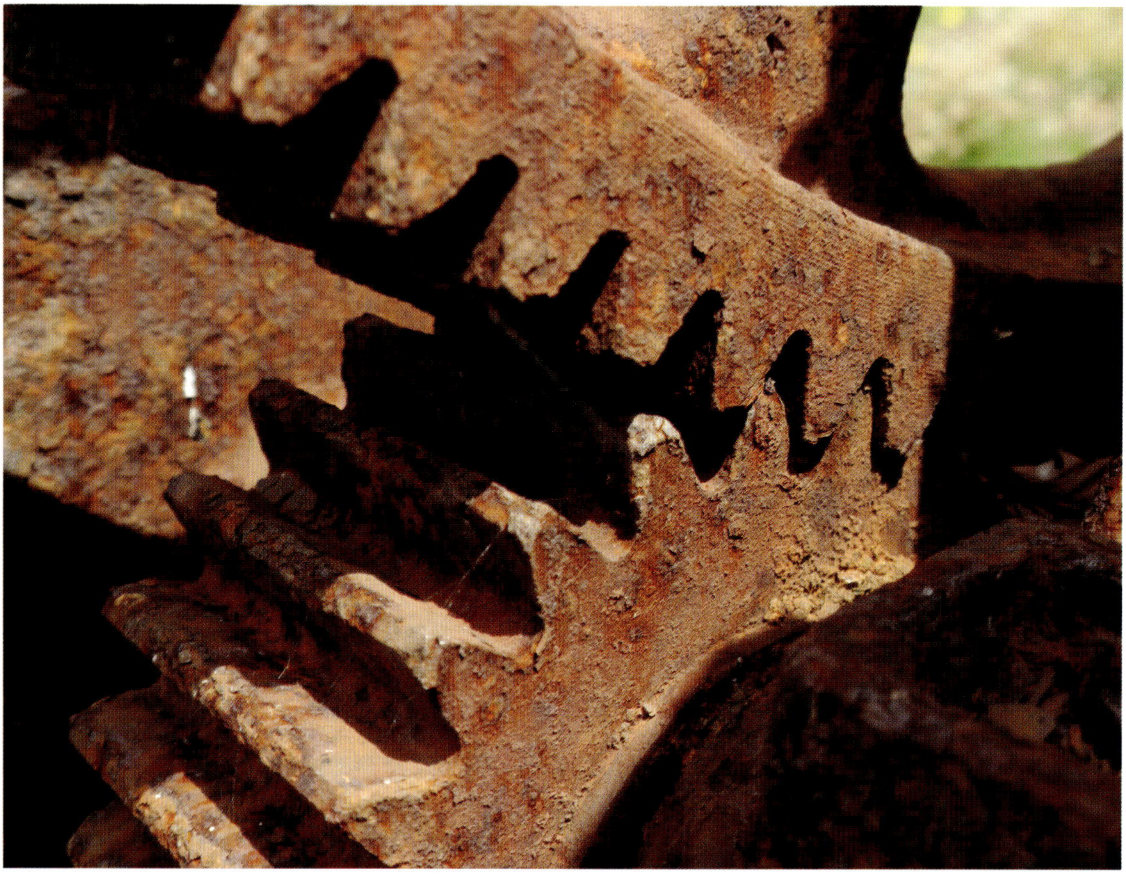

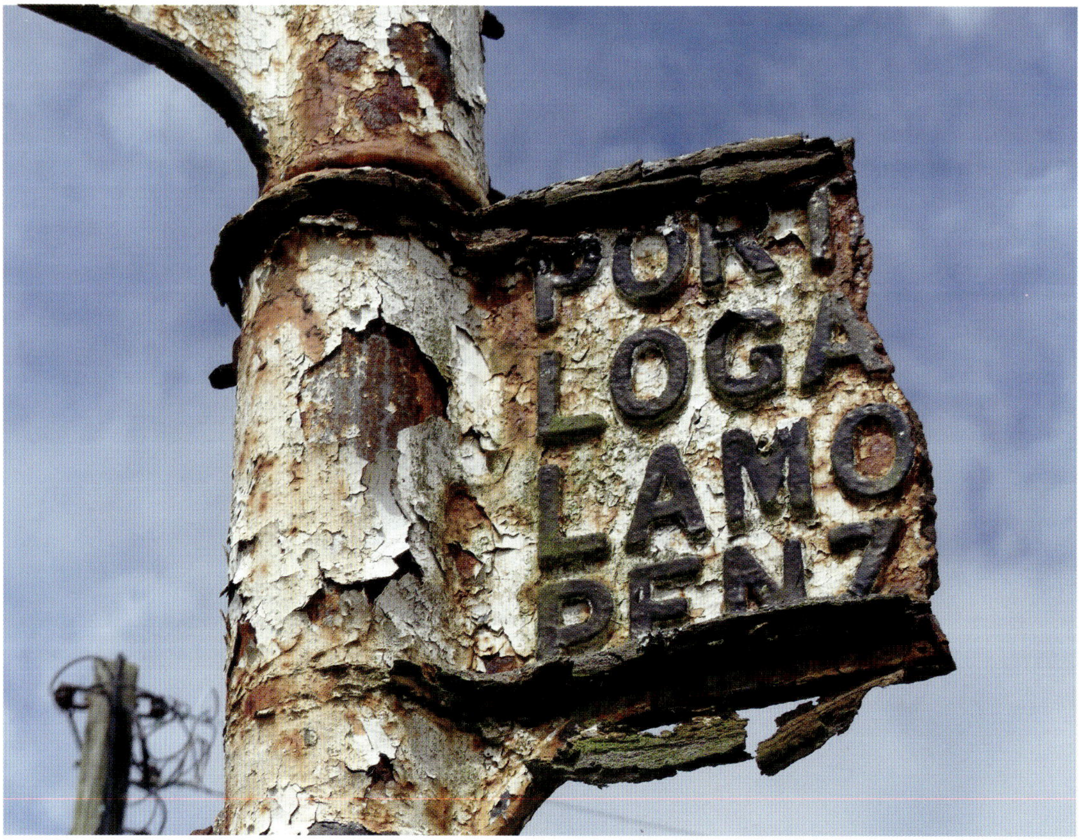

PORT
LOGA
LAMO
DEN 7

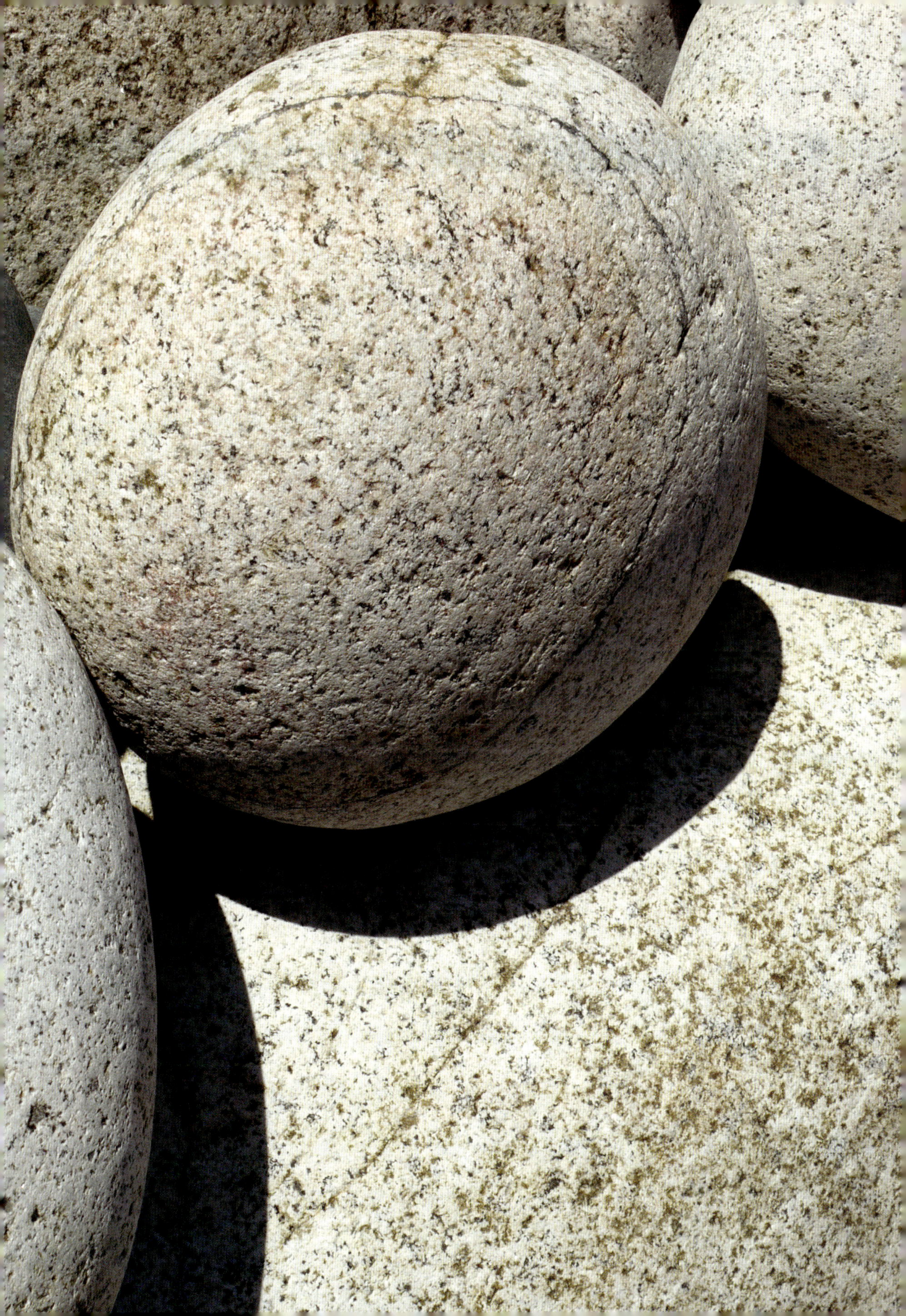

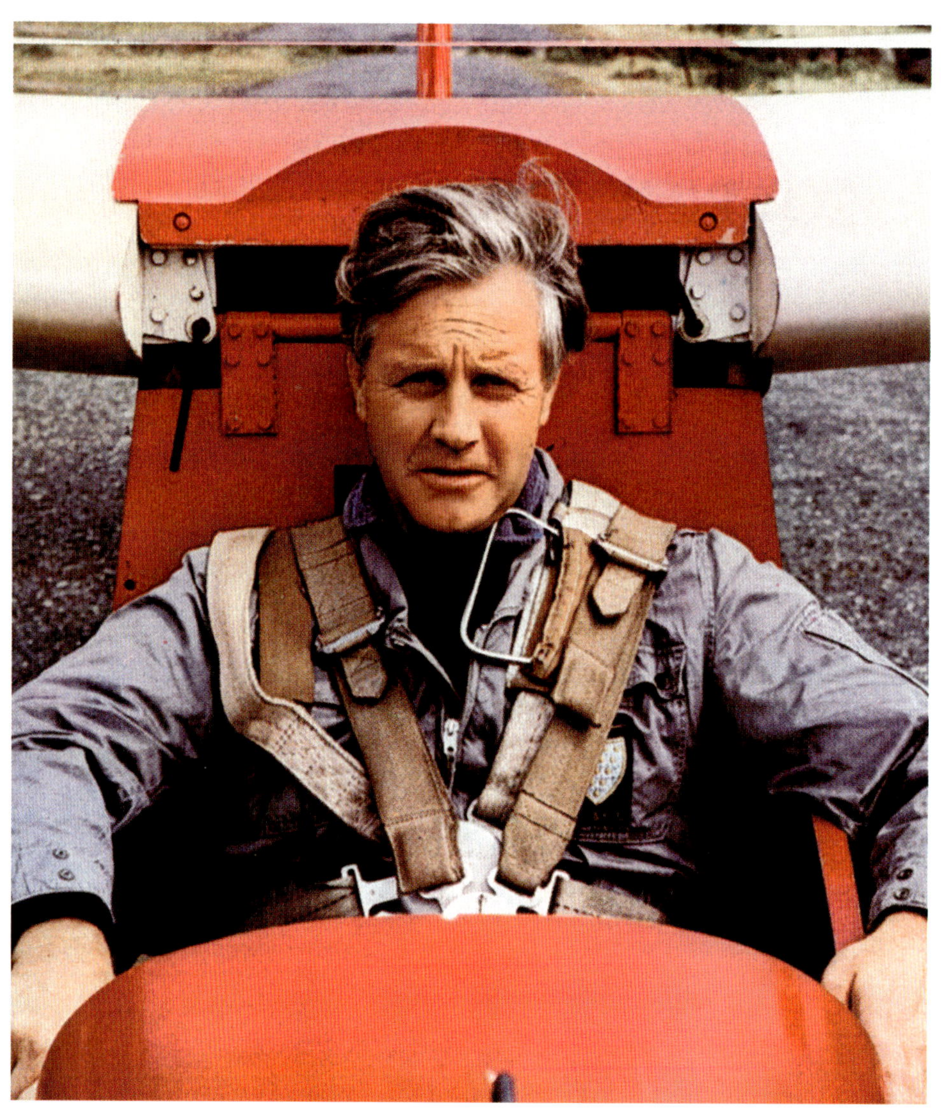

Appendix A

Peter Lanyon's Articulations
of Place

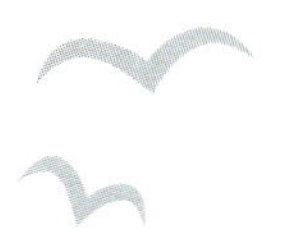

The Face of Penwith

The Cornishman is not double-faced, but multiple-faced, facets of character which add up to a sort of innocence. He is never still himself, except in death, but all the conflicts that lead to a game of hide and seek between native and so-called 'foreigner' are part of a process that constantly surfaces the most diverse and conflicting factors. The Cornishman is fond of private secrets. A solemn intercourse of native with native, often intimate, is mistaken for gossiping and vicious moralizing. The bush telegraph, which puts the GPO to shame, is a part of this intimate revelation from native to native. The part of this game that is revealed to the unfortunate 'foreigner' is that part which concerns him alone, the rest is none of his business. Prayer is a strong force, and in the greatest days of revivalist services, in Wesleyan chapels, a poetic resolution was achieved. The loss of such inspiring services is as sad for Cornwall as the closing of the mines.

There is a main force that is centrifugal and centripetal, a giving out and a taking in. In extremes this means a complete trust and desire to give absolutely everything and a converse withdrawal, a returning to a protective native envelope. The eye is prospecting and adventurous, it has also an inward look. Perhaps these qualities are most often found in insular people, and perhaps Cornwall itself has for centuries been almost an island. The intimate contacts of native with native, revealed in

Cornish Stories (understood and enjoyed for their peculiar flavour by natives only) remains. The Cornishman will change according to basic rhythms which are suggested here and will make a good job a 'fitty' job, as he says, not one just fit for purpose, but a fitness within a rightness which is determined by his whole history and the nature of his country.

The following sketches offer suggestions towards a revelator process. They are made from outside by a certain detachment which is the artists' method, but from within also, in the hope that processes of revelation, extension and creation (latent in familiar objects) may themselves be revealed and shown to have a relativity in time and space. This complication of a familiar and plain scene is made in the interests of an analysis of Cornish character. In the congregation of the Cornish cross, a circular theme, the symbol of this process stands erect, revealed and outward, in the landscape.

1 *Landscape*

From Wicca to Levant the coastline emerges out of carns and bracken and cultivated green land, revealing on its varied faces a sea history and a land history of men within and without and a commerce of man with the weather. Here, in a small stretch of headland, cove and Atlantic adventure, the most distant histories are near the surface as if the final convulsion of rock upheaval and cold incision, setting in a violent sandwich of strata, had directed the hide and seek of Celtic pattern. A motorboat in some solemn gaiety with insistent cough, searches out the exacted payment of ocean on land; the small rituals of business at the junction of rock and sea wall.

On carns of Zennor, Hannibal and Galva, where giants may have hurled their googlies in mild recreation, an outline of earthwork makes evidence for a primitive brotherhood of man, of the great and small in life and death, wherein animal joy and terror found resolution in the protective care of monolith and fort. Hereabouts, perhaps, the sun set westwards, shifting down the monolith to bury the light of primitive fire, and rose again in the hearts of men from the east. The saints were in Cornwall.

From Levant to Wicca, an easterly direction, chimneys are crowned by brick flourish and the towers are lichen-covered, castellated and pinnacled. They rise upward out of the horizontal ground, as if the thrust of stone had surfaced to the call of the native, given up its wealth to his endeavour, and been revealed by manufacture as an expression of inner intent. Invention, leading to extension of native culture, made present in time a process of ancient development. The craft and skill and meaning of the native journey are outward and revealed at the land surface.

2 Voyages of the Native

To bring the world within the hand and make immediate the farthest shore, seamen set sail for the mistress of the sea. From storm and shipwreck the homing seaman returns with cargo, unloading on granite quays a wealth of image. What stories he tells, and in his sea soul gives to the land, remain outwardly in his artefacts, are revealed to generations by the face of man and the character of his sea-born gear. This process has been a source of man's struggle to make himself as outward and revealed as this place of granite. Here sea and land answer the deep roots of man and present him with a face.

At Levant Mine, where tin and ocean meet, men fished for food after labour beneath the ocean bed. What is within the granite arms of harbour, sheltered from surface mood and ground sea, is concerned with an intimate bobbing, the playful game of boat with mooring, a small outward exchange reflective of deep, ocean movements. A happy commerce in granite embrace. But the centre and focus of lighthouse, port and parent are left alone as masts and sails, clumsy with their clawings, move out to their own aggressiveness. Man-engine and steam haulage pass contact to deep levels with man-baited rod and line. Where shifts go down and come up and ships in regular exchange remove themselves and return to parent, the resources of Cornwall are best displayed and landed. In every small and intimate departure or arrival a wholeness of living is revealed, and in commerce of man with granite and Atlantic the transitory is made immediate, each facet being related elementally to the next as aspect and image of a whole.

3 Journey of the Visitor

Running along Hayle estuary and round points to St Ives terminus a local train brings the man from pavement, office and city statue to a most complete revelation of history in the earth, to the open face of his country, the ultimate and prized beauty of the flower.

Richard Trevithick made a steam engine, a concoction of homely kettle and manufacture, a concept of extension whereby man's muscled arm is replaced by an idea made solid, of motion and power in simple movements. Steam expansion and piston, valve gear and con rod, cranked for transference to rotary motion; the divider and compass, straight line and circle, all set on the wheels of a horseless cart for the ride up Camborne Hill in glory.

The industrial revolution moved inward and

outward down and up the line: Par, Lostwithiel,
Truro, Redruth, Camborne, Truro, St. Austell
and Saltash. From within, the drawbridge fell
across the Tamar.

To the demands of extension the
Cornishman, evolving his time theme,
the centrifugal and the centripetal, makes
invention, making real the face of his own time,
making object and image from within.

(From The Cornish Review 4 – Spring 1950)

Letter to Paul Feiler

I paint places but always the Placeness of them.
In the Farms painting you saw at Corsham
there are many meanings of farmness – animals
are implied and not represented to a photo-
vision. My painting is the revelation, a turning
outward of experience – a making immediate
of a time process-in-space. Paint represents
experience and makes it *actual*. I do not start
with the idea, but with the experience. My
source is sensuous. Organisation composition in
depth as in surface is the outcome of experience
in the process of painting so that EG what was
painted six months ago underlies what is finally
painted today. Also plastic form is arrived at
not by modelling with chiaroscuro and fixed
perspective but by sensory paint manipulation.
The whole composition, meaning and colour
is arrived at by a constructive process of
experience. Arrangement is not made in a
detached manner but as an integral part of a
whole. No part exists without reference to the
whole. My art follows Constable – it is to be
found in the hedgerows but my heaven what
apprehension there is today even in a country
lane! And my aim as far as I can see it is to
make a face an 'actuality' or 'thingness' for
experience. To present for sensory experience a
face.

(c. 1952)

St Ives Carnival

Abstract painting has been the mainstay
of what is known today as the new St Ives
School. The paintings in this exhibition are
not abstract, nor are they landscape. They
use abstraction as a method and landscape
experience as a source. An artist who remains
where he was born cannot see his country
from the outside, he already knows it in his
bones. These paintings, done over a period of
25 years, are concerned with this feeling in the
bones, for a county which is both very old and
always fresh. They reflect what appears to be
an irreconcilable conflict; an abstract style
appropriate to the international scene with a
local source. This conflict is, however, due to
a false idea which has been maintained in St
Ives, that abstract art and figurative art are so
different as to be irreconcilable. The tradition
of St Ives art has been mostly landscape. These
paintings reject the conventions of landscape
but remain recognisable in the county. They
are concerned with environment rather than
view, and with air rather than sky. The artist
paints as if from the air, where horizons are not
fixed. The county is used to make something,
just as clay is used to make a pot. The observer
is encouraged to move and become a part of the
painting, as a dancer becomes part of the music.
If there is nothing but paint to see, then look
at this and let the rest look after itself. These
works, to the artist himself, are both strange
and familiar, a mixture which is another
quality of art, wherein opposites are sometimes
reconciled. They are work in progress, in which
the artist can claim only to have touched the
edges of these aims. If others can gain from
these attempts, then this exhibition will have
fulfilled its purpose.

(From The St Ives Carnival Programme – 1961)

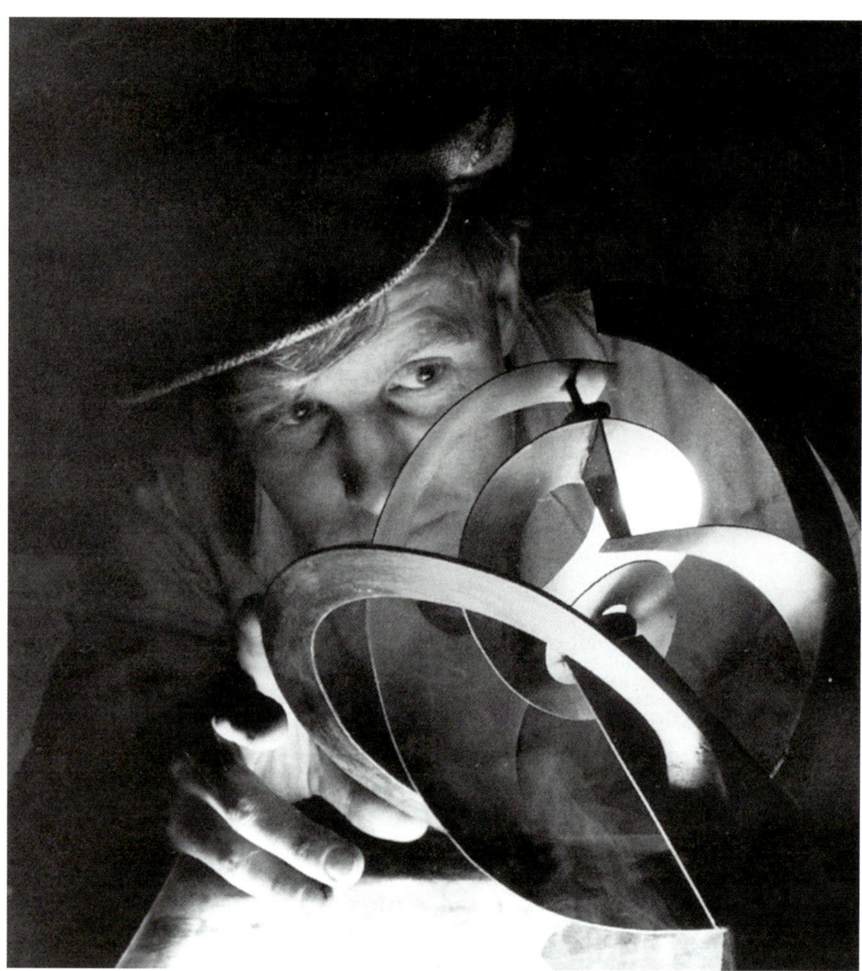

PL with his *Construction*, painted aluminium & plywood, *c.* 1947

Peter Lanyon Talking

A painter's business is to understand space – the ambient thing around us. I don't mean the old approach to landscape – sitting in one place and taking the view, as you get in traditional painting. What I'm concerned with is moving round in this space and trying to describe it. That's one reason I go in for fast motor racing, cliff climbing and gliding – gliding particularly: I like using actual air currents: I feel I'm getting to the root of the matter.

This problem seems peculiarly British because we are the only country in the world that has had a school of landscape painting. The Dutch did have one but it was not as strong as the British. The problem of landscape painting is to try and understand this vast thing in which we live and which is so much bigger than ourselves. You might say I'm trying to paint my environment both inside and out. Where some painters – Constable is a great example – have a particular affection for green grass and trees, my interest, I think, is very much in weather.

St Ives had, up to 1930 or so, a very strong landscape-painting school and it has a very distinctive landscape. If you're a cliff walker like me, you meet the problem of space all the time. The way the coast rises and dips, it's pretty silly just to stand there and paint the horizon the traditional way. It's even sillier if you're a glider. When you glide, the sea is likely to be all over the place, right, left, centre, above and below. You can't accept the conventions for painting space.

But I don't know what turned me into a painter – just idleness or something. Perhaps it was the war. I was in the Air Force in the Western Desert and Italy, and I had a little colour box with which I used to do a bit of painting whenever we were not fighting. Probably if I had not been going to be a painter, I would have done something else. I would still much rather drive fast motor cars than be a painter. Who wouldn't? I married after the war and settled in a studio my father had built in St Ives. He was one of those people thrown up in Victorian times who had a certain amount of money – his came out of mining in Cornwall – and who spent much of their life becoming not necessarily expert at any one thing but fairly knowledgeable about a lot of things. You can't do that today. Today you've got to be a specialist.

For a time I was an abstract artist. You may think I am still but I'm not. I would rather have the traditional label now of landscape painter. But if people don't understand what you're doing they call you an abstract painter today. I know that awful feeling of looking at something and fearing the painter is pulling your leg.

I'm beginning to like mural painting more and more. It suits landscape painting and modern architecture – the modern glass buildings. But it is easier to do this in the US: easier to get the commissions: and the majority of my work is there now, though I'm having a London exhibition in October. Part of the challenge of the mural is to understand something much bigger than yourself – one I'm doing for America is over thirty feet long – and we don't have the old kinds of walls any longer.

We have sides of glass: walls that have windows onto space: that enclose space. It's tremendously exciting to paint for them.

In a sense the person looking at the painting is in it – you are participating in it, in that space, walking through that landscape. I paint and draw the nude quite a lot because you have to paint the figure to understand the form. In a Turner a wiggle might be a dog in the distance, in a Constable there are marvelous little dots, but that sort of scale I don't use at all. In a sense the subject is the person who looks at the painting.

This is terribly difficult to get hold of. It's rather like good jazz. You can't help getting up and dancing to it. The painting gets you moving and then you get moving in the painting. I know there's an error in the argument, but most talk about painting is only approximate. I feel sometimes I'll go hook, line, and sinker for painting portraits. Perhaps as you mature you want to concentrate on people. I did a painting recently about a beach girl. It was really hilarious. Many people can't tell what is beach, girl, or bikini, but it may become more precise eventually. The viewer has to learn a language and I have to learn to be more precise. If they don't get the point, I always feel it's my fault: a failure in communication.

I think one fault of us modern painters is that we exhibit too many of our experiments. This can happen very often through living in a society which does not understand what you are trying to do. Your critical judgment is not shaped enough.

Artists generally have one or two reactions to a white canvas – they either feel they want to make a mark on it or it terrifies them – like going on the stage. I suffer from this kind of stage fright. It doesn't represent a nice flat white canvas to me, but the whole of space around me, the complex experience I get gliding or

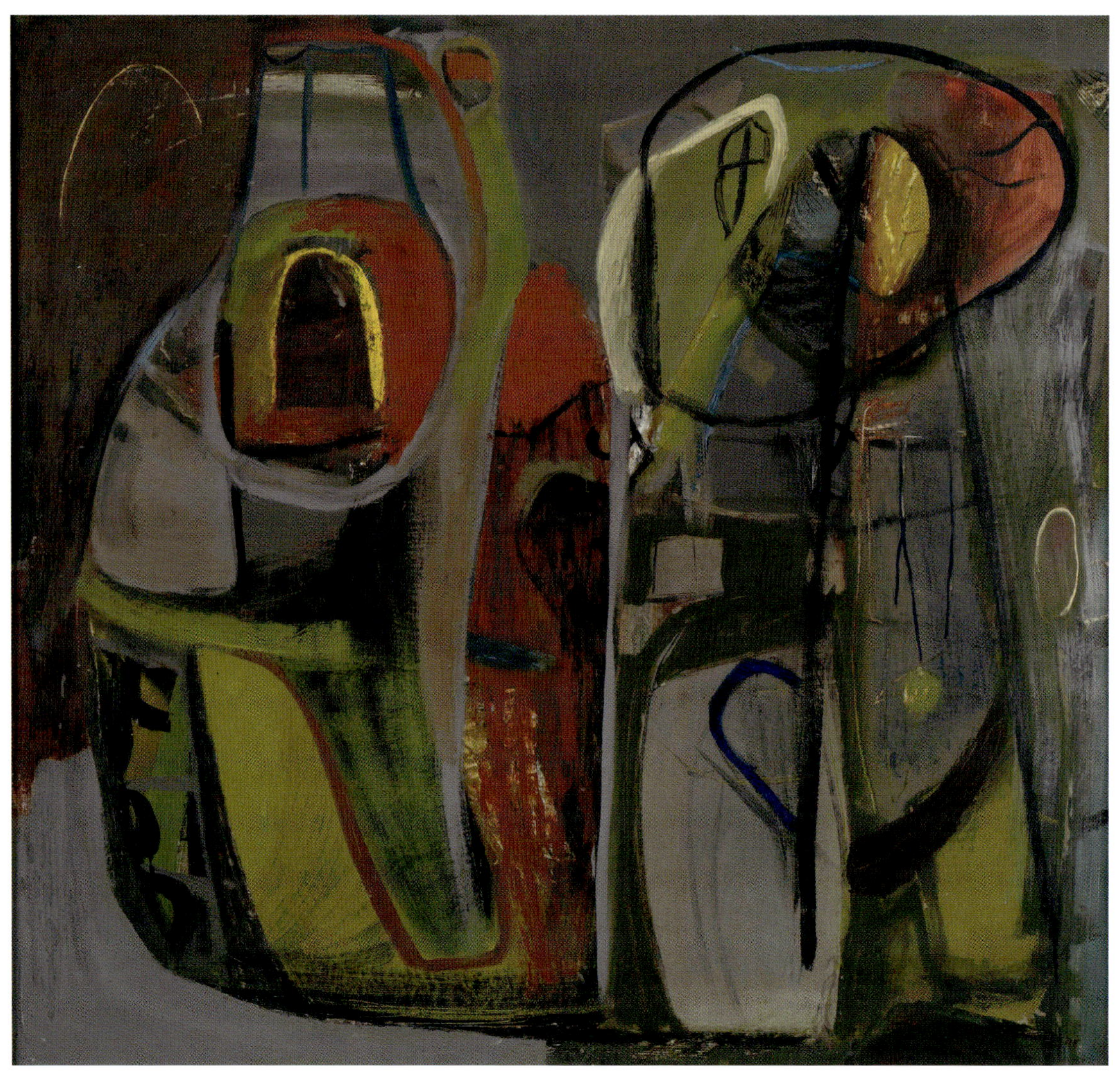

Levant Old Mine 1952, oil on masonite, 119.4 x 127 cm

walking along the cliffs. I have to construct a new space to represent the one I have felt, the one I have lived in. I have endless arguments about this and many people say it's a whole lot of nonsense. It just depends on your own experience and how you see it and try to convey it.

One effect of gliding, of experiencing more and more in space, has been to lighten my paintings. They tended to be rather heavy. Sitting in the air, you are sitting in all dimensions. You come down from 2,000 to 150 feet and then you suddenly go up again with one of those Atlantic gales coming in. I don't paint a purely visual experience. Gliding – the peace and quiet up there which makes you stay up even when you get hungry – or the cry of a gull – these things may crystallize something, and then I'm off. That construction over there and that painting are sketches that have been crystallizing while I've been in the States. I think they will work into something.

(Recorded by W. J. Weatherby for the Guardian,
May 17, 1962)

A Sense of Place

Notes on my painting in general

I think it is essential to know the process by which my paintings are made. (I hope that this process will become commonplace and perhaps it does not need clarifying.) I do not begin a painting until I know what I want. I do not always see the result but I am sufficiently conscious of a developing image to make drawings or objects which have a direct bearing on the resulting work. The final state of the developing image (which goes on developing through the process of making the painting) has invariably been a flat surface which is broken into, extended and vitalized by the style of realization. Its final state has a look about it which in some cases is very personal and in others remote, but mostly there is an awkwardness and incompleteness such as I find in all human events. An openness representing nakedness is what I aim for because in this way I think of revelation. A look on the surface. Today if I want an area of colour I make the colour and put it down without correction. I proceed with these wants until the painting answers me back. This simple statement is not all the truth because I am rarely capable of such a direct process, more usually there is a long period of struggle either in the painting or in myself to clarify the essential image. There is a species of failure which drives the artist to the inevitable and the only mark his desperation will permit. It is however only at this extreme point that I am able to make the certain mark into a positive want. Because of this desperation I am led to explore the region of vertigo and of all the possible edges where equilibrium is upset and I am made responsible by my own efforts for my own survival. Without this urgency of the cliff-face or of the air which I meet alone, I am impotent. I think this is why I paint the weather and high places and the places where solids and fluids meet. The junction of sea and cliff, wind and cliff, the human body and places all contribute to this concern. It is perhaps the very young and the adolescent in the old and scarred country of West Penwith that have concerned me, their contact is most poignant in wild places.

About construction

Art is often confused with imitation. A photograph is thought to be an accurate picture of reality. This attitude forgets that the camera was derived from a vision constructed by artists. No one for example had seen an angel until an artist painted one. Painting is concerned with the making of images, not with imitation. These images modify the idea of reality. The painting is primary. The painter constructs out of experience making an object which modifies and develops further experience. Without this process, experience is not communicated nor is it directed. A familiar construction of landscape is an horizon set low in the picture, dividing the canvas into a top and a bottom. This is now accepted as the correct view but it presupposes a fixed viewpoint upon which the theory of linear perspective is based. Perspective is a method adopted in the West and operates historically between the primitive and cubist traditions. Traditional painting today is cubist. The academic tradition is embedded in linear perspective. It is incapable of describing the new and many dimensioned experiences of today. (This does not deny the possibility of significant and valuable paintings being produced in an Academic idiom.) The form that any art takes does not depend on rules, but it also does not exist outside a tradition built by other artists. To go beyond this is to attempt the impossible. To deny the tradition of this century as much as that of others is to become parochial. This is very different from being local or rooted. A painting is a manufacture, it is a thing. It is nothing unless it is constructed out of experience and returns to experience.

My aim is to hold experience in time and suffer it through until it is fixed in space, until it is exhausted. I am therefore concerned with process. The process is one of precipitation. A specific site or occurrence may cause an apprehensive reaction, answers are expected. A continuous process is fed by sensation. This is 'informing'. It is the process of collecting and sifting information which is being fed to the artist. He trains himself to select information which is relevant. Provided this information is not attached specifically to objects but to their relations, to process itself, a formative action is set up. The artist proceeds to make marks in an apparently automatic fashion. Considerable training is required to precipitate marks which relate to information received. The artist must proceed beyond the inspired guess to certainty. The surest way to inhibit development of a painting is to remain at the guess. Here the mark itself becomes important (it is in fact the small change of aesthetics) and not that which is signified by the mark. The significance begins to show when the informing process or gathering is complete and the forming process begins.

To assist this changeover I make three-dimensional constructions. This is done as a therapeutic activity: hands making an object release meaning. These objects are essentially throwaway things and could be compared to scaffolding. They should not be confused with complete and determined work. They are not space constructions but they are indications of a constructive process. The final painting surfaces as a determined action fixed in space and time. References to content in the final work may not be obvious, they operate on the senses outside the painting. Therefore the content is manifest in the observer. The effect of this will be related to the integrity of the formative process which the artist has undergone.

Note about Porthleven

I was not content to play variations on a theme of areas and dynamic tensions. I discovered that when I began to construct a space I was invaded by images of a misty kind which became more insistent as I tried to suppress them in the interests of structure. I had to accept the fact against my will, that I functioned best when concerned with my immediate environment. I realized that it was essential to recognize the painting as a *thing* and that the brush mark and the paint itself were a part of this *thing* as

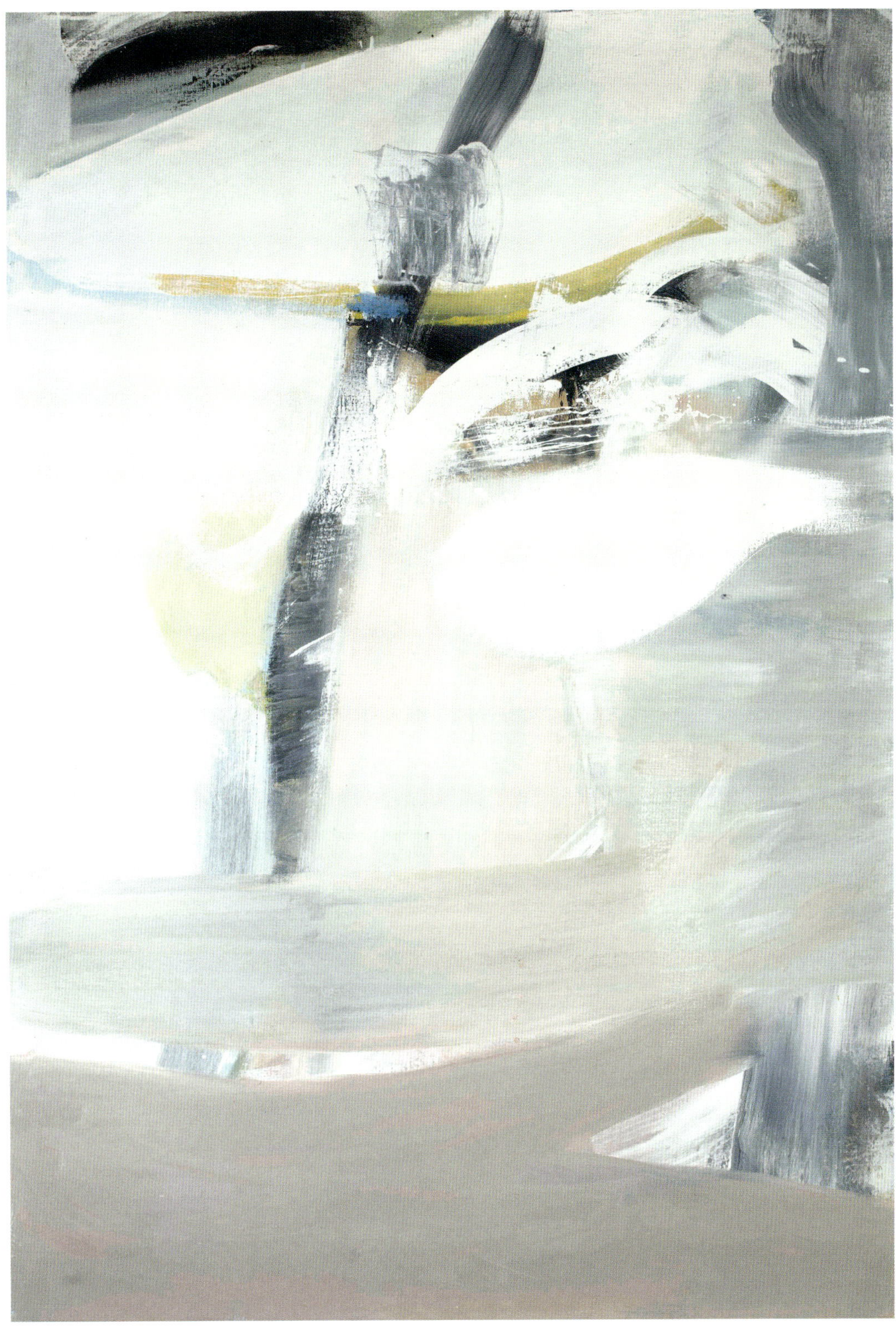

Drift 1961, oil on canvas, 152.5 x 106.5 cm

much as the division of the surface, and that all these things were illusions. I began to doubt the claim that some artists were constructing a concrete reality. The image that emerged can be traced back through drawings to a basic first conception. I had to learn how to take control of complex images and allow them to emerge at the end of my brush. To do this I had to accept another characteristic; that of an apparent provincialism, I became a *place* man.

(From Painter & Sculptor 5 – Autumn 1962)

Illustrated British Council Lecture

(*Photograph of Cornish Coast*) The south-western end of Britain juts out into the Atlantic. Waves fetching from the Gulf of Mexico, Newfoundland and Labrador break on these shores. The rocks are hard and old, worn down by the sea and the winds that sweep over the Cornish peninsula. The climate is both gentle and terrible like the Cornishman himself.

(*Cliff Wind*) Many of my pictures are paintings of weather. I like to paint places where solids and fluids come together, such as the meeting of sea and cliff, of wind and rock, of human body and water. Some of my earliest pictures are also of this image, but, when I began to paint, the cliff edge and winter storms put more pressure on me than I could absorb. My pictures became so wild, messy and dispersed that I was driven indoors and I settled for experiments in the technical problems of painting.

(*Cloud Base*) I wasn't satisfied with the tradition of painting landscape from one position only. I wanted to bring together all my feelings about the landscape, and this meant breaking away from the usual method of representing space in a landscape painting – receding like a cone to a vanishing point. I wanted to find another way of organizing the space in a picture. For me,

painting is not a flat surface. I've always believed that a painting gives an illusion of depth – things in it move backwards and forwards.

(*Photograph of St Just*) This is a photograph of St Just, which is the last town in England before you reach Land's End. It's an old mining town, with disused mine shafts all round it and structures like the telegraph poles in the photograph which interfere with the view from the hills around the town. I don't want to paint a view from a single place like this photograph but a picture about St Just – the complete place, with all its associations. If you walk about the place you might see the bits and pieces that I combine into a picture.

(*Boulder Coast*) This painting is called Boulder Coast, and it's about all these things – the weathered stones, the weight of the boulder, and the lichen that grows on the surface of the rock. Paintings make something permanent, they can have layers of meaning that a photograph lacks. While I work at a picture, I like to build up associations, and an image crystallizes during the painting.

(*Photograph of surf*) The photograph shows the movement of surf. When you are much closer to the water than this, the horizon disappears. The surf comes in and undermines the land at your feet. I am fascinated by this kind of unbalance, the feeling you have when you look over the edge of a cliff and turn your head to one side. In my pictures I often explore these sensations of vertigo.

(*Thermal*) *Thermal* is about the same sort of thing. Terrific turbulence – action going up on the left hand side, then slowing down completely into the deep blue below, which is almost static, like a threatening thunder cloud. A glider pilot needs a thermal to gain height. The rising warm air lifts him up in a great spiral, sometimes meeting the cold layers of air with an impact as sharp as being hit by a stone.

(*Loe Bar*) Loe Bar is a small bar, dividing the sea from an inland lake. Walking along this bar – this isn't a gliding picture – you find odd bits of old wrecks rusted and brilliantly coloured …

Beachcombing is a favourite activity of mine, and for me the painter is a kind of beachcomber. I live in a country which has been changed by man over many centuries of civilization. It's impossible for me to make a painting which has no reference to the very powerful environment in which I live. I have to refer back continually to what is under my feet, to what is over my back, and to what I see in front of me. I am not interested in standing still in one position and I would use anything – bicycles, cars or aeroplanes – to explore my relationship to my environment.

My paintings have been influenced by cubism and the constructivism of Naum Gabo and Ben Nicholson, and now like most paintings today they look abstract and expressionist. But I am only using these means as part of the process of making an image of my environment. My concern is not to produce pure shape or colour on a surface, but to charge and fill up every mark I make with information which comes directly from the world in which I live.

(From Illustrated British Council Lecture – 1963)

Fragments

I'm probably letting into myself, as it were, or feeding into my own consciousness a lot of information and a lot of varied information just as the weather is varied. I believe that this is what happens, the artist is like a sponge and he absorbs a lot of information; now his process of actually making this into a painting owes a lot today to the abstract painters,

because he has to turn it into shapes which, not only represent, say, specifically one apple in a very definite time and space or place; it has to represent not only an apple, but a bald head, or maybe a football: things which are closely related to an apple; but which will give overtones of meaning to the shape that anybody is looking at. It requires in fact from a spectator, that they should look at the picture and be prepared to invent for themselves information about what they're looking at. I have claimed before and I think it's so, that today the person who is looking at the picture is very much the subject. This may be a very difficult thing to understand that in fact the picture doesn't come to life until somebody looks at it. And this person who is looking at it, participates in it, just as we participate in jazz, or if we hear twist music we begin to move in a twist movement. A picture can set somebody going, not only physically moving, but in a poetic sense: an imaginative sense; and then they become, as it were, the person who is acting this picture out. The picture is a lot of things which are generating information, which anybody who is receptive can pick up, if they're prepared to do it.

(From a BBC West of England *Horizons* radio
discussion, May 22, 1963)

I believe that landscape, the outside world of things and events larger than ourselves is the proper place to find our deepest meanings. I do not in saying this wish to diminish the achievements of painters like Francis Bacon, whom I am proud to acclaim, or to place myself in any way near him in excellence. I want to make the point that landscape painting is not a provincial activity as it is thought to be by many in the US, but a true ambition like the mountaineer who cannot see a mountain without wishing to climb it or a glider pilot

who cannot see the clouds without feeling
the lift inside them. These things take us into
places where our trial with forces greater than
ourselves, where skill and training and courage
combine to make us transcend our ordinary
lives.

(From an illustrated lecture on modern British
painting – January 1964)

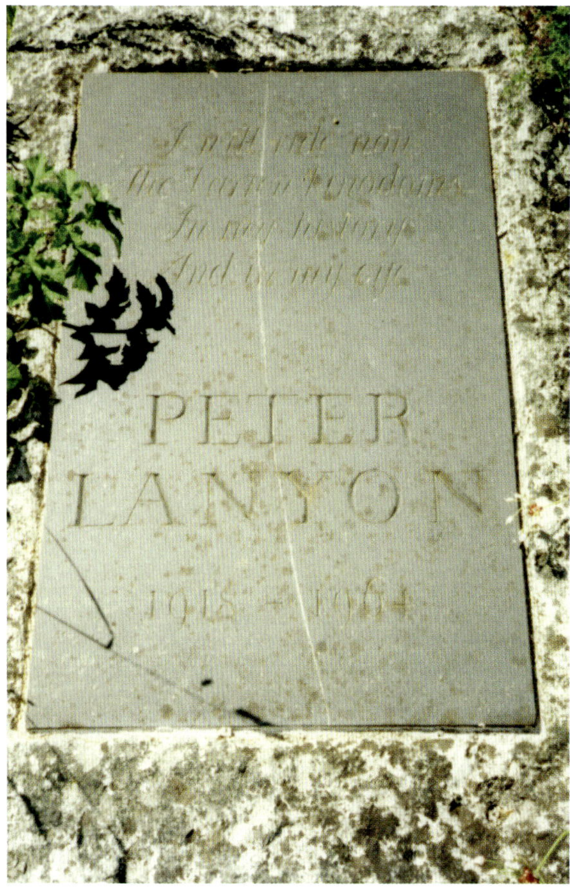

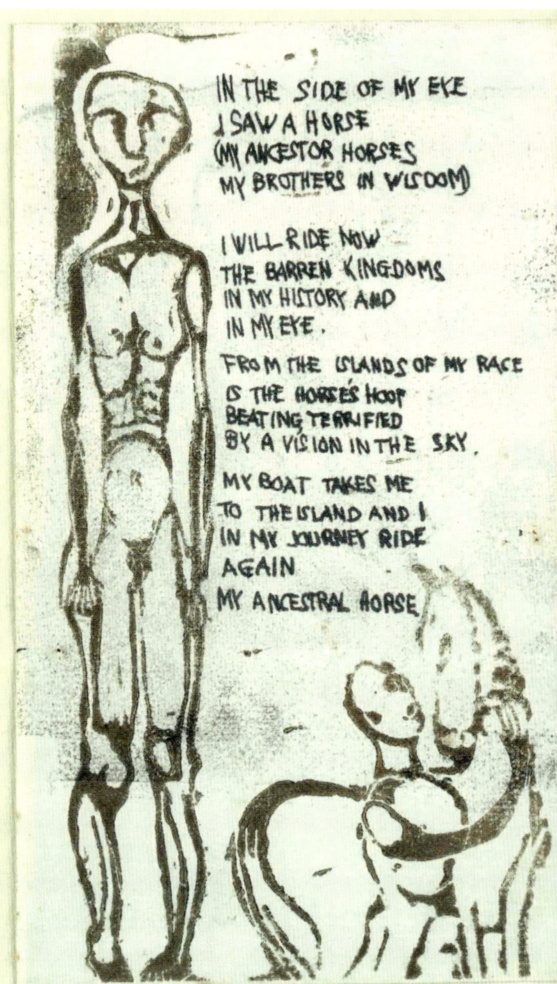

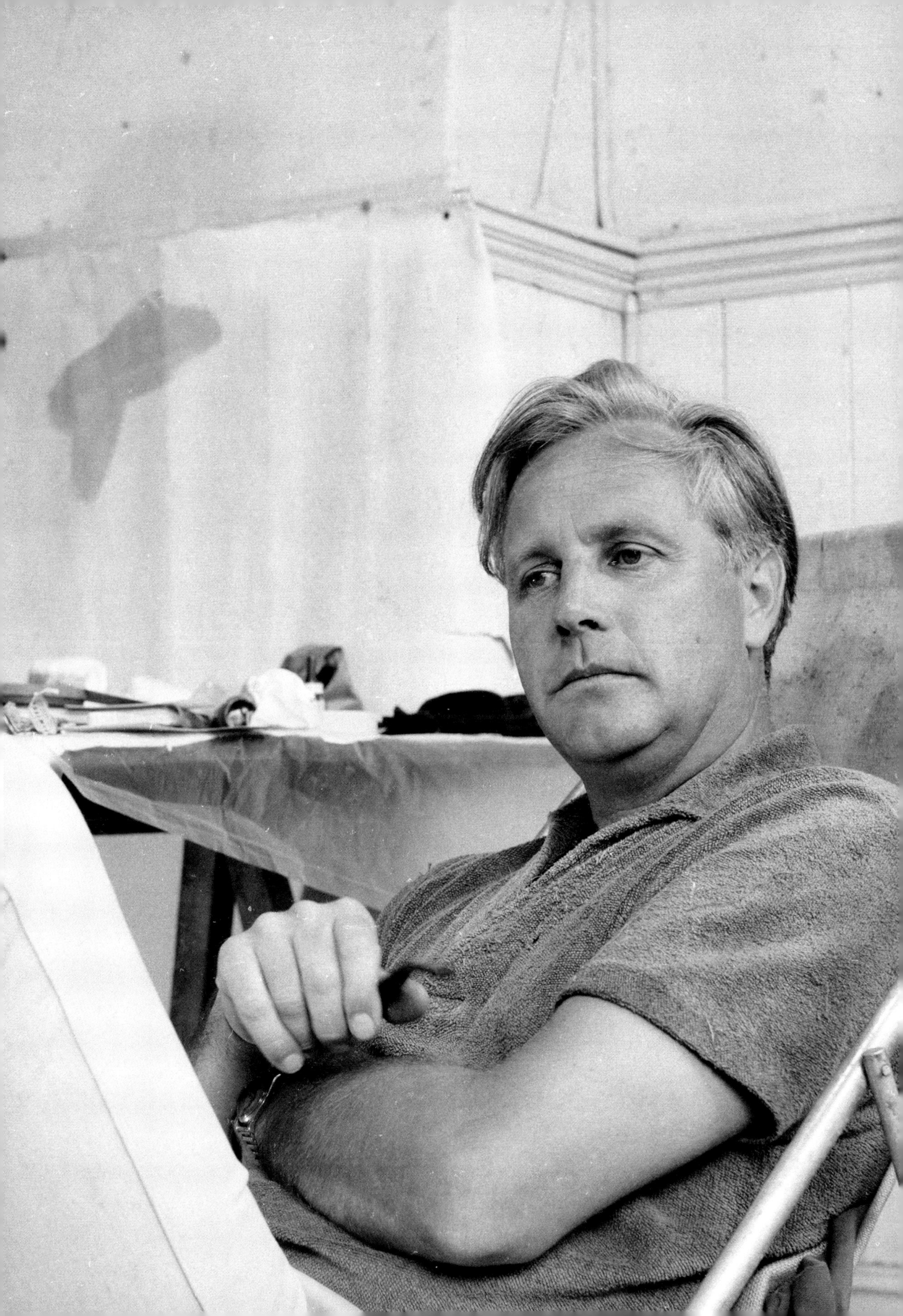

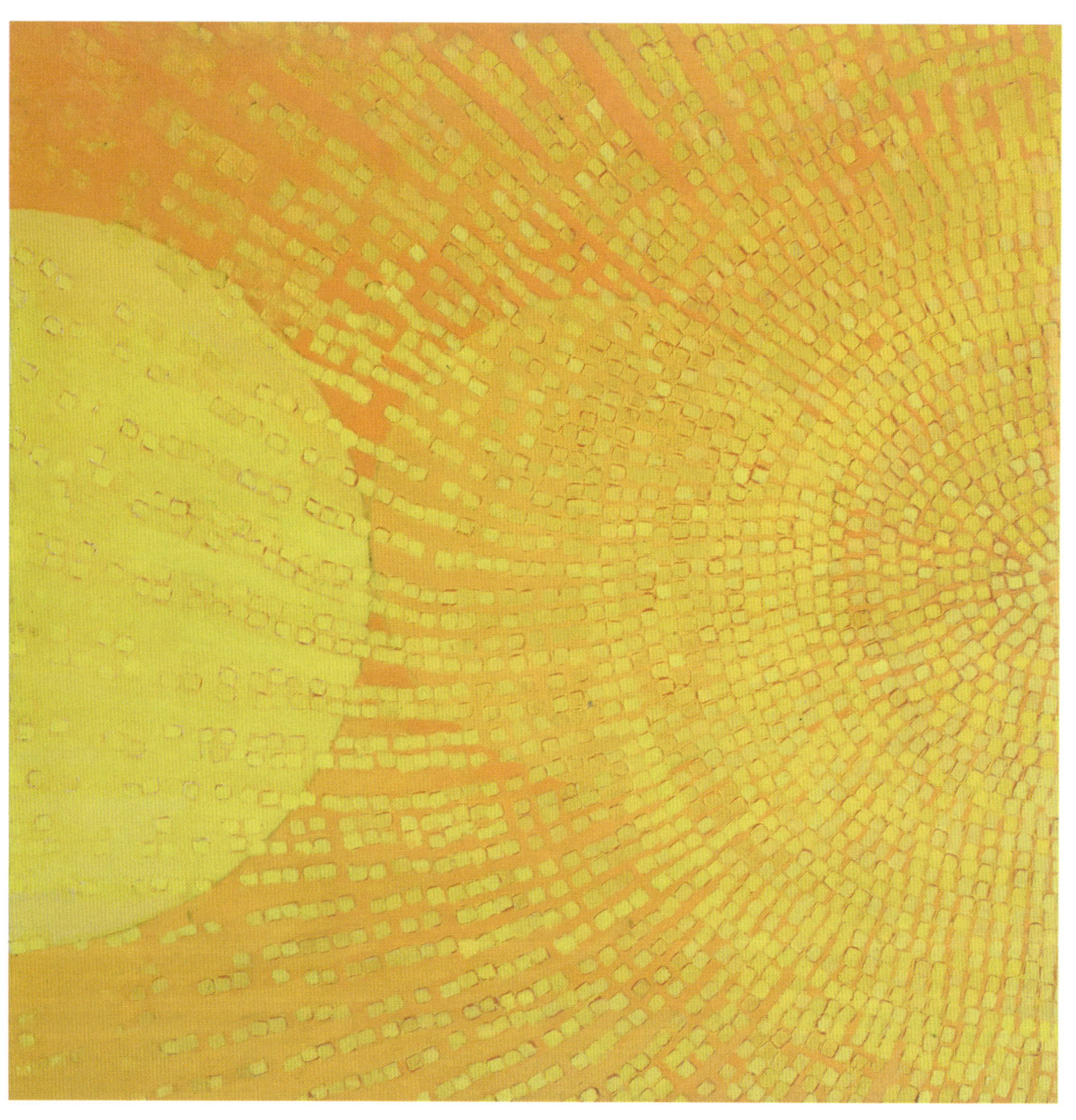

Appendix B

Artists on Artists & a Writer

Wilhelmina Barns-Graham: Collected Thoughts

I was eight years old when I knew I wanted to be an artist. Amongst my earliest memories are my pencil and crayon drawings, abstract irregular or rectangular shapes, usually outlined in blue and filled in with a single colour. These were very private, like secret rooms. I remember being embarrassed when, on a train with my parents, a member of staff of the Glasgow School of Art drew their attention to them. In later childhood, using a compass, I made many abstract pencil designs. In my teens I discovered Cezanne and have admired his well-structured 'architectural' painting ever since.

I moved to St Ives in March 1940. Within two weeks Borlase Smart had found a studio for me. I soon felt at home, as parts of the coast and the colours reminded me of the west of Scotland. I painted a series of paintings known as the 'Island' series. From 1940 to 1955 I kept some photographic records of my work, and later on transparencies, but due to financial difficulties I had to destroy some works by scraping out, sandpapering, or turning the canvas, so as to continue painting.

When I arrived in St Ives I was something of a lone wolf, as I was recovering from a recent illness. This changed with the friendship of Borlase Smart and Leonard Fuller, and then of Ben Nicholson, Barbara Hepworth and Bernard

Left: WBG – *Meditation East No. 4* 1968, oil, acrylic on board, 35.5 x 35.4 cm

Leach, who were visiting my studio; and later of David Lewis. There were continuous meetings in the town, and much visiting of studios in these early years, when discussions on art and work took place.

I have always been interested in drawing and have spent considerable time constructing my compositions. I sought to discover abstract shapes, for example the effect of the sun on glaciers, rain on clay country, wind on sand, the volcanic rocks near my mother's home where I spent years drawing these cylindrical forms; the volcanic rocks of Sicily, and very recently those of Lanzarote.

After sessions of drawing, I turn my back on the experience and return to painting in the abstract, where there is a meeting point of abstracted ideas. This swing between outward observation and inward perception, or vice versa, has always increased my awareness. I suppose I am what Winifred Nicholson called 'the looking in – looking out' kind of artist.

I tend to work in themes, some of them lasting me for years as I can return to a theme again and again; for instance the abstracted glaciers, rock forms, line motifs, abstract reliefs, squares and circles, and painted constructions. In my glacier paintings I aimed at bringing in all the angles at once, through and all round, as a bird flies, a total experience.

During the late 1940s and '50s, I experimented with the Golden Section, adapting an intersected grid on a board or canvas on which I placed one of my rock forms or glaciers or some other idea that suggested itself, sometimes using coloured chalk and pencil. In the early 1950s I restricted my palette to earth colours, expanding into more primary colours by the 1960s. After a visit to Spain in 1958 I painted a series of gouaches with fewer and larger shapes, as with oil paintings. Shapes were touching or leaving the edge of the canvas.

Sometimes a small shape balanced or was pushed by a larger. Forms hid behind one another, present or not present, making a colour note sing in space.

At the end of the '50s, partly due to the events in my life and my philosophical and theological ideas at this period, I became involved with formal relationships. 'Order and Disorder of Things of a Kind' was such a theme. I used also the progression of a single square to several, circles, egg-forms, oblongs, lines following each other in pen and ink, breaking the rhythm deliberately or by accident, simple wave movements, cell formations, bird flights, fish shoals, backs of fern leaves, dots inside foxgloves, rain drops, leaves in the wind, diamonds on water, human gatherings.

From 1975 to 1985 I had a sense of increasing freedom and strength coming into my work. I was again using oblongs in my abstractions, as in the 'Tribute' series. In the mid-70s I started a series of linear motifs (line drawings). In 1980 I painted a series of large canvases such as *Expanding Forms*, and the 'Touch Point' series. Later I painted the hard-edged *Windbreaks* and *Kites*. The experiment with small reliefs progressed into constructed painting, just before my visit to Orkney in 1982. Sometimes it is not easy to know which experience came first, as the discovery of the large slab formations on the coast of Orkney expanded a series already begun.

In 1988 I was invited by the Crawford Art Centre, St Andrews to make a statement for a catalogue regarding working as an abstract painter: 'the positive aspect of working in an abstract way, for me, is the freedom of choice of medium, space, texture, colour. The challenge of feeling out the truth of an idea, a process of inner perception and harmony of thought on a high level. Abstraction is a wide field and is not all necessarily abstract. Abstraction is a refinement and greater discipline to the idea; truth to the medium perfects the idea.'

In May, June, September and October of 1988 I worked with acrylic or gouache on paper, taking up again motifs of 1951-53 and 1958. Done with a large brush, these paintings are bolder, stronger in colour, simpler and more free, allowing things to happen! Frequently I abandoned the hard edge and severe construction, enjoying the medium and colour until that moment of excitement and held breath when the work appeared to speak and sing. This was the outcome, I believe, of the illness I had in January and February, the joy of living after an uphill struggle to regain my health. I now had a sense of urgency of purpose and could make decisions without restriction. While working on this series I visited the exhibition *Late Picasso* at the Tate Gallery. Did I recognise something of the same spirit of urgency, a desperation to 'say it now' as powerfully as possible, as death haunts?

I found at this time the words of Psalm 100: 'Come before His presence with a song'.

(From *W. Barns-Graham: Retrospective 1940-1989* – City Art Centre Edinburgh 1989)

Nancy Wynne-Jones on Peter Lanyon

In appearance Peter was very handsome, a big golden man in a black fisherman's jersey with large shapely hands and a charming smile. His physical presence was impressive and delightful, but what I remember best about Peter is his energy. He was a great natural force. To a young painter he communicated the feeling that one could do anything, that nothing was forbidden, and that the possibilities of art were endless. He used to say that if one experienced anything that excited one, one ought to celebrate it by making something about it – a painting, a drawing, a little sculpture of glass – anything at all as long as it was something to celebrate the event.

Each of his own pictures was profoundly experienced, and led up to by endless drawings, glass sculptures, and historical and physical explorations – experiences, in fact – of the place to be painted. He would drive the roads, and pointed out to me how the landscape appears to swing round you as you go round a corner; he would stand on a cliff top looking across the sea to the next headland – 'see how that seagull articulates the space' he said to me one time, 'without it one couldn't interpret the distance at all, the flight of the gull fixes it'. He climbed cliffs, too, although he had a bad head for heights, to experience, as he said, 'the thinness of the land'; he went down mines; he learnt to glide; he lay down in the summer grass and looked at the landscape through its unfocussed fuzz (the painting *Rosewall* was about this, he told me); he swam above and below the water; I remember him holding out a handful of sand to me at Portreath and telling me to look at all the colours in it – 'a handful of jewels' he said. He would do dozens of drawings of a place from all angles, and from this gradually would emerge an image, not like the place and yet somehow profoundly the place, with all the unexpected holes in space, and odd angularities, of reality.

He was artistically very cultured, especially basing his art on Cezanne and Cubism, and also on the spiral space of Naum Gabo – he told me once that Gabo perfected this theory walking on Porthmeor Beach in St Ives and watching the big Atlantic waves curve and turn. His other acknowledged masters were Ben Nicholson, Chagall, Alfred Wallis; but the technique that he evolved to convey his personal experience of landscape was so original as to be incomprehensible to many artists. I remember looking at a reproduction of one of Peter's paintings with Willie Barns-Graham, and she saying: 'I don't know what he is about, I just don't know what he is about'. And yet ordinary, unsophisticated people would react immediately to his work.

Peter was fun to be with. When I was his student he would take us down to the beach and draw a horse or a bull maybe a hundred yards long, too big to see all at once. He had us drawing with candles, only putting a wash over the invisible drawing when we got home, to see what we had. I think perhaps he was at his best with students and young people, who posed no threat to him. With his peers he could be awkward and uneasy, aggressive and competitive. Perhaps he unconsciously wanted them to acknowledge his greater genius, as a sort of panacea for the self-doubt that afflicts all artists.

He was a great man at a party, loving to dance and to joke. It was he who brought the Twist to St Ives, straight from New York, and how he enjoyed dancing it at the great parties thrown by John Berryman and Willie Craze in the stone barns at Tremedda, down the lane along which one walked by starlight. He and Roger Hilton used to have ritual fights at these parties. Roger would insult Peter, which he would ignore, and then insult Sheila, which he could not ignore. So Roger would take off his glasses and put them on a beam, they would go outside. Peter would hit Roger, who would fall over, and they would come in again.

He gave a party for Mark Rothko when the latter was staying with him. Rothko was one of the most impressive men I have ever met, and I was proud when he crossed the room to tell me

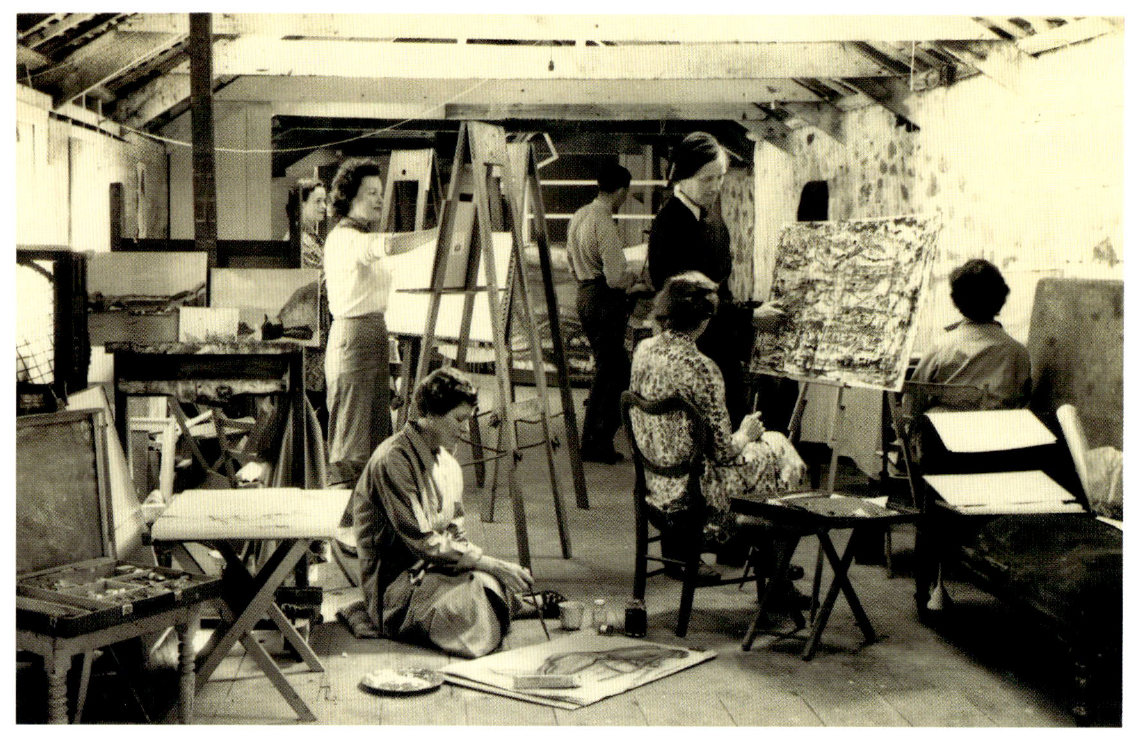

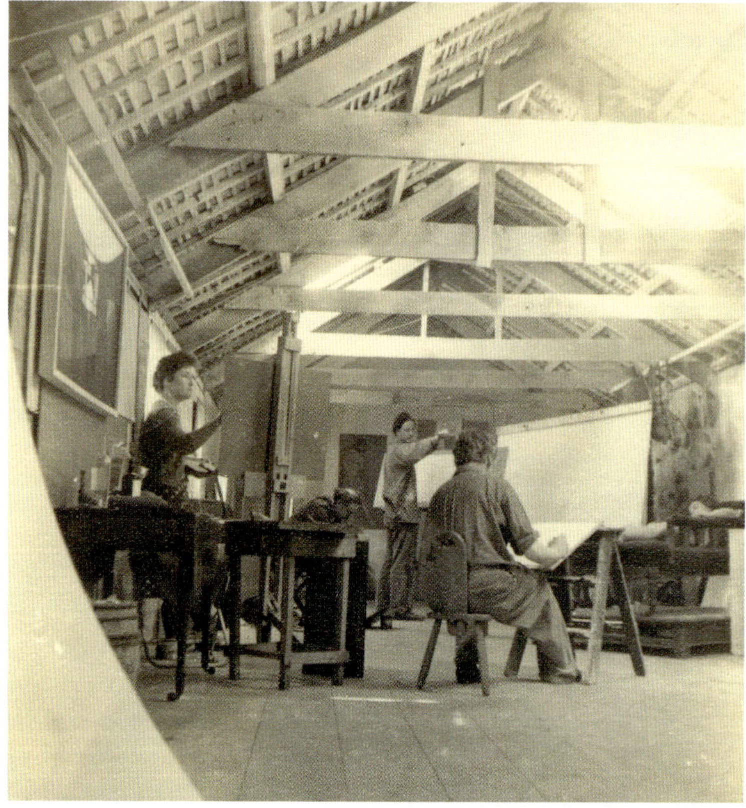

Peter Lanyon teaching at St Peter's Loft, St Ives, late 1950s

he had admired my painting which he had seen in Newlyn.

Peter had made a tape, a sort of diary of his day-to-day thoughts during the painting of a picture. Rothko wanted to hear it, so he and Peter scoured the country for me one evening, I being the only person around with a tape-recorder. They drove from St Ives to Gurnard's Head to the Tinners, and finally walked up to Bryan Wynter's house on the moor above Zennor, where I was and where a party had developed and everybody was dancing. Rothko joined in, and enjoyed it all enormously. The tape was played next day. David Brown has told me that this tape is now in the archives of the Tate.

Peter was kind, and helped many young painters with advice, materials, and lifts to London in his big van. He liked driving and drove well. Trips to London with him were fun, with stops for meals and drinks and much talk and laughter. He liked to drink – rum, or a pint of mild – but I never saw him drunk. He would come into The Sloop on Saturdays, rarely in the week and then only for half an hour after a day's work. On weekday evenings he would play dominoes in the Golden Lion for an hour or so after taking his children's nurse home. Always he worked and I think he thought about his paintings all the time. Technically he was very sound. He ground his own colours, at one time in stand oil, and later, when he found that stand oil always remained a little tacky, in sun bleached linseed oil. Hardboard he would size and then gesso. He taught his students – or at any rate he taught me – to do all these things. His paintings are as bright and fresh today as when they were painted over twenty-five years ago.

In trying to remember Peter's conversations about painting, I recall most clearly his insistence on honesty and the necessity of personal experience. He came back one time from a visit to Derbyshire, very pleased to have seen *white* stonewalls. 'Now I can put white lines in my paintings', he said. He pointed out to me once how conceptual is much of our seeing. The big seine nets were laid out on the green grass of the Island, and he remarked that although the nets were actually above the grass, visually they were dark holes in the green. This interest in what one actually sees, as apart from what one thinks one sees, and the characteristic penetration of the surface, was an important part of his own painting. He kept himself always open to sensation and discovery; if, say, a grin appeared in a painting he was working on, he allowed it to stay and even developed it. He walked always on the edge, risking everything. It must have taken incredible courage for a man as highly-strung as he, with a skin too few, like all artists, to have held himself so open, and I think it was this, over and above his great talent, which marked him as an artist of genius.

(From Andrew Lanyon's *Peter Lanyon*)

Michael Canney on Bryan Wynter

Bryan Wynter was, and still remains the most enigmatic figure in post-war Cornish art. On his own admission he painted works that avoided any conscious organisation, works that asked the viewer to approach them as the artist had done, without preconceptions. This is very much 'participation art', for the viewer has to find his or her own imagery in the work.

It always seemed that an apt simile for Wynter's paintings could be found in his immediate Cornish environment, in the tangle of gorse and undergrowth, and the barely discernible and rocky track that led up to his studio. Those who wished to view his work had to negotiate these obstacles and chart their own course. In the paintings the view found, not gorse, but a screen of coruscating and stabbing lights barring the way. It was only after a lengthy visual journey around the picture that one could enter the darker regions beyond.

Much has been made of Wynter's debt to Cubism, and it is true that his mark-making is closer to the flicker of small planes in Analytical-Cubist painting than to anything else. The half-moon brushstrokes threaded on verticals do indeed bring to mind the bottle-top and wine glass shapes of Cubist still lives, but the Cubist image is always centred, whereas Wynter's painting presents an overall field of marks. The pictures appear to be sections from a larger whole, fragments from a continuum which itself is emphasised by an underlying vertical structure reminiscent of Futurist 'lines of force', travelling from top to bottom or obliquely across the canvas. It is these striations that seem to discipline the characteristic flurry of small flicks and whorls of his brush that animate the surface.

There is however another aspect to the works, not often remarked upon, a dark and menacing quality that is only banished in the very last paintings. This seems to refer back to the Surrealist overtones of his early gouaches, in which a dark and sharp edginess is combined with the disturbing chance patterns of 'decalcomania' and other Surrealist techniques. The combination of such antipathetic and disparate movements as Surrealism and Cubism in his early development is evidence of the polarities in his own character, and may well have given his work not only its enigmatic quality, but also a certain strange poetry.

The Surrealist obsession with automatism and a variety of ingenious methods for generating a new and haunting imagery was almost scientific in its concern with the nature of mind and vision. It was something with which Wynter empathised. Intensely curious about his environment and his visual and mental self, he too was a great experimenter with materials and techniques, and he was, despite a penchant for isolation and self-sufficiency in an ancient landscape, very much a twentieth-century man. Indeed, his work with polarised light and his remarkable mobiles or 'IMOOS' (Images Moving Out Onto Space) are some of the most challenging kinetic works of the 1960s, and belong to the world of science and art at the same time.

If Wynter wished his paintings to resemble a kind of primordial vision before the associations established by experience, he appears to have succeeded. Whatever extraneous associations his works may promote, from the glint of light on water to Piranesi's dungeons, they remain in the mind first of all as works that appear to research the very nature of seeing and of vision.

Wynter believed that the elemental forces in the landscape around might seem at odds with his other scientific and questioning self. What makes him such an interesting artist is, however, that he would also have subscribed to that often quoted remark of Constable's, 'Painting is a science and should be pursued as an enquiry into the laws of nature. Why then may not landscape be considered a branch of natural philosophy, of which pictures are but experiments?'

Naum Gabo on Peter Lanyon

I knew Peter from the very beginning of the Second World War, 1939.

I remember him arriving at my studio with a portfolio in response to my invitation after I met him with friends in Carbis Bay. Looking through his sketches and paintings, the very first few attracted my attention so strongly that I did not really need, later, to look at the rest so attentively. I call them 'sketches' – but these were the kind of sketches which are, by the finality of their expression, saying more of the artist's world than the most elaborate paintings. The way the volumes, the surfaces and the lines, the inside world of objects, were treated in the sketches told me that before me was a young but already accomplished artist. Already in these sketches his vision was manifestly abstract in its approach to the world, though naturalistically rendered. He very soon found himself entirely at home in the abstract world, which he used in his painting only as a means to convey his vision of the naturalistic world.

It is unfortunate that very soon he, like many others of his generation, had to go to war. He stayed away long enough to mature both in life and in art, but he did not lose his artistic energy and the clarity of his vision.

On his return he threw himself into his work and never tired of investigating new paths, and he kept in his later work the high quality of his colours and the soundness of the composition in his painting. It must be deplored that accident should break up an artist's life in the very hey-day of his creative ability.

My attraction to Peter never terminated. During all the later years he was fast developing and remained devoted to the abstract ideas, remaining all the time himself and never falling into the trap of repeating what had already been done by others, but constantly going ahead. What he has done remains, and to me it is obvious that it will serve as an excellent example of both the achievements and the tribulations of the young generation of artists of our time.

(Introduction to Causey's Peter Lanyon)

Michael Canney on Peter Lanyon

I am writing about Peter Lanyon from California, a state that I think he would have enjoyed, not only because Cornishmen came here once as miners, but because there are still Cornish communities here preserving many of their original customs and traditions. You may judge, therefore, that anything, even remotely related to Cornwall and the Cornish people, interested Peter Lanyon, not only as a Cornishman but also as an artist.

To understand Cornwall and to have a feeling for its landscape is useful if one wishes to understand his art fully, but the experience that finally clarified his painting for me was not Cornwall at all, but America. This is not altogether surprising. He had made many visits here, teaching American students, enjoying the vitality of American life, being stimulated by the landscape and the cities, and also by the artists that he met. But in spite of his obvious excitement over America, he always came back to Cornwall again, with a sense of relief. He was a person who believed in having firm roots somewhere, and somewhere for him meant specifically West Penwith and St Ives.

His art was one that was primarily concerned with landscape, and most people would have called it abstract, but he did not accept this he would insist that it reflected a particular region of England, and with wry humour would add that he was likely to 'end up painting sheep like the old Victorians'. But if his painting was abstract in appearance, with figurative overtones, one could define it more exactly from the middle fifties onwards, as having the general 'look' of American Abstract Expressionism. It seems to me therefore that he will ultimately be judged, not only within the context of English art as a whole, but also in relationship to what was going on in America during the post-war years.

I have recently had to ask myself, as distance gives me perhaps a more detached view of an artist with whom I was intimately concerned, whether he actually succeeded in establishing the new approach to landscape that he believed was necessary to English art. Did he really manage to assimilate and to metamorphose the brave new gestures of American Abstract Expressionism? Did he indeed lay the foundations for a new English art of landscape painting, that could not be accused as English art had been so often in the past, of incomplete absorption or imitation of foreign idioms? In the case of Peter Lanyon, I feel sure of one thing, that in spite of his debt to Abstract Expressionism, he remained at heart a very English artist, part of an indigenous tradition, with all those qualities of lyrical elegance and craftsmanship that give to our art much of its character and charm. But the major stumbling block that prevents anyone from making a final assessment of his contribution to the art of our time is that the movements and currents of art, in which he was a major and lively participant, are still in full spate, and attempts to view them in perspective at this time are out of the question.

It is therefore more profitable and more interesting to speculate why he was drawn, as were others in Britain, towards Abstract Expressionism in the first place – a movement that was so peculiarly a product of the American contemporary scene and situation. To say that it was because the Americans were the most exciting artists, and that the School of Paris was in decline, is true, but it is not saying enough. Could it perhaps have been the heroic nature of the movement? Despite a respect for the giants of European painting and sculpture, there had been in America a desperate need to find a way out of the impasse of an imagery imposed by European tradition and art. The artists had discovered this way of 'prolonging the European past into the future' without becoming in any way subservient to it, and at the same time had enjoyed the fruits of self-discovery by creating the first American art to receive world-wide recognition. But they were only able to achieve this because they had behind them an historical development that included memories of the Depression, the WPA projects, the new artistic milieu created by distinguished European émigrés, such as the Surrealists, hard-hitting discussions at 'The Club', and the underlying violence and vitality of American life and of New York, of which their art often seems to be a reflection.

What had the drama of this situation to do with an artist far away in the quiet seclusion of the South-West of England? Part of the answer lies in the fact that Abstract Expressionism was basically Romantic, and Peter Lanyon was an artist with an exceptional quality of poetic vision and a romantic temperament. His agile and sensitive mind was always open to new experiences. There is no doubt that he was instinctively attracted by the appearance of the new American painting, by the work of artists such as Franz Kline, who had Cornish connections anyway, by De Kooning, Motherwell, and Rothko. Also, I think that in some curious way, he was able to sense similarities between their situation and his own. When Lanyon was maturing as an artist, England had just emerged from her wartime isolation. The interests of the English artists after that war were more outward than inward-looking, and there was a sense of disillusionment in the parochial nature of the home product. Certainly, Lanyon was quick to realise that although he existed within a tradition, traditional 'artists by the sea' in Cornwall had nothing to offer him any longer. He lived in an area of landscape, and in a country of landscapes – but there had to be a new attitude to landscape painting if it was to survive. Robert Motherwell has compared Abstract Expressionism to 'an intimate journal'. This American sense of commitment and desperation suited Lanyon well, and it was a welcome antidote to the dangerously lethargic and complacent life of the far West of England. The rawness of technique in many of the paintings was the antithesis of Ben Nicholson's immaculate panels, or of Barbara Hepworth's smooth-surfaced carvings. Lanyon was reacting, as was natural, against these two powerful personalities. In the American paintings he could see personality vividly expressed through active paint on a grand scale that the spectator could hardly ignore. For a young artist the scale of these pictures was exciting.

I think that Peter Lanyon had always been conscious of the importance of individual responsibility in art, but it is interesting that he also welcomed the spirit of renunciation and aesthetic asceticism in American painting, which was akin to the severity of religious Nonconformism in his own native county. It might be objected that an artist such as De Kooning was sensuous rather than ascetic, but there is a stern discipline and 'suffering-through' in a creative act such as the one that he celebrates. In the vigorous gestures of Lanyon's paintings we find this same determination to push the picture past the point of no return and into the realms of total commitment. The danger of this position for the artist and his work is very real. He is often stalked by the spectre of abject failure in bringing the work to a successful conclusion. The reward for success is a haunting imagery. The images in De Kooning, for example, play visual hide-and-seek, like half-seen aspects of reality flitting across the field of vision. In Lanyon's work there are these same transient images, distorted, elongated, mysterious, which he attributed to movement through a landscape. The Americans at one period placed great emphasis upon the need to create a new and personal mythology for themselves, but here Lanyon had the whole history and mythology of Cornwall in his

blood. How often the Celtic cross appears in his work, in one form or another; or long shapes, reminiscent of the Cornish peninsula. In this Cornish mythology lies the magic of his art, as personal as that angular line, his own handwriting, which dances an awkward jig around the paintings and drawings. There are his constructions, too, splendid and inspired improvisations, which I have always regarded as being as Cornish in tradition as the old tin-streams, with their inventive wooden gullies and machinery. Personal, too, are his thin scraped pictures, such as *Porthleven* in rich browns, creamy whites, terra vertes and sensitive greys, in which colours spring to life at the hint of a pale blue sea or sky. And the heavy, disturbed, monumental hardboard panels, with their boulder shapes – some of his best work, I think – in which a pervasive mood communicates, and the glorious mess of paint, structured by dark knifed lines, lingers in the mind's eye long after the encounter. These pictures are all bracken, gorse, lichened granite, fields and hedges, tin mines, headlands and bays. This is the record of a Cornwall that barely exists anymore, an amalgam of the first excited post-war years and pre-war boyhood memories, when one could bicycle or walk a country lane all day, it seemed, in safety and in peace. But these heavy pictures, evoking the moods of West Penwith, were not merely romantic effusions. Behind them lay a Cubist structure, acquired from Ben Nicholson, coupled with a sound professional discipline. From a profound contact with Naum Gabo, Lanyon had fashioned a personal aesthetic, thinking deeply about constructivism and the relationship of time and space. From the paintings of Piero della Francesca had come a feeling for the tautness and geometry of form and contour. From his own experience and determination emerged a sense of the weight and density of the landscape. From his abiding love for Cornwall was distilled that delicate and sensuous perception of the moods and feelings of place, so that one could walk a cliff path or climb a carn, or, in the case of *Porthleven* explore a harbour, with a joyous sense of recognition through his art. This is what he did for all of us who felt for his kind of painting, and for Cornwall.

Perhaps his aestheticism was so complex, so all-embracing, that any question of integrating these multiple aspects of life and art into one comprehensive form was a superhuman task. There were some who felt, and may still feel (although I think that they are wrong), that the ideas that he adumbrated were even better than his paintings. From a shifting and elusive pattern of discussions I can recollect but a few. The physical immediacy of the landscape or of the figure was important to him. He seemed to have a strongly empathetic talent, a tactile sense that is obvious in his feeling for the quality of paint, which he prepared himself so as to achieve total involvement. Like Michelangelo's slaves, figures slumber in his rocks, or in the smooth hillsides, and more originally, he would remark upon the way an object 'looked out' at one from such a setting. He had a profound feeling for the male and female elements in nature and in art, in the beautiful contrast of a girl in the midst of a very old landscape or place. His need to identify with places was such that he would even make constructions on the spot with objects that were lying around – which became a consecration of locality and event.

At one time he talked much of the all-enveloping picture, of placing the spectator in the picture by way of the large canvas, but this was, of course, of current concern in America, too. More individual was his insistence, that after a deep involvement in the act of painting, he was able to step back and discover an image that could subsequently be traced to a specific landscape form, subconsciously absorbed. It was here that he parted company with some of his fellow artists in his conviction that all imagery had its origin in nature, and that it was up to the artist to recognise the derivation of his own images.

With his questing mind, he was interested in certain aspects of seeing, including peripheral vision. Alfred Wallis naively showed the way in which a sky can be painted down the side of a picture. Lanyon not only used and developed this device, but was also able to rationalise it, by referring it to the sensation of the sky falling on either side when climbing a hill, or of the displacement of sky when the spectator adopts positions other than the vertical. For him, the sky's position was dictated by both structure and feeling. But its displacement was one of the prime factors that enabled him to take liberties with landscape forms that would have been impossible with normal orientation. Of major importance, too, is that unique combination of fragmentary experiences in his work which he welded into one compelling image. His collection of significant aspects of reality and their reconstitution on the picture surface has been compared to the art of Kurt Schwitters. In his constructions, 'found objects' are combined with a rare sensibility, although the intention was to use them as spatial 'work-outs', to understand by 'doing', what he was subsequently going to arrive at intuitively, in the spatial organisation of his paintings. Latterly, his new constructions had also become exciting and colourful objects in their own right, perceptively related to his experiences as a glider pilot.

I suppose that Peter Lanyon was the first artist to really understand the artistic possibilities inherent in flying. Paul Nash had transcribed in a more literal manner the pattern of vapour trails or the shark's nose of a bomber in flight during the war, but Lanyon actually flew the plane himself, partly because he enjoyed it and its extension of his world, but also because he wished to accept the striking images of movement across and above the landscape, of movement up and down, in turbulence or in smooth soaring flight. The spiral which climbed to the heavens carried him, moving freely and silently in space itself. He came close to the weather, to physical involvement in its very nature. That English preoccupation, the weather! How right that an English artist should again, like Turner lashed to the mast, become physically involved with our favourite topic of conversation! Peter Lanyon's ability to deduce the universal from the particular experience, to deduce principle and concept from, perhaps, underwater swimming, from flying or merely driving around West Penwith, was the quality that endowed his work with more than a regional interest.

Here in America, many critics assert that all our artists' achievements are 'too little and too late!' There may be a grain of truth in this. We seem to produce few revolutionaries who can exert an international influence on others. We can, however, hazard a guess that Lanyon had qualities that single him out from the majority of his contemporaries, and in his chosen field of landscape painting, he was certainly unique.

A handful of artists before the war endeavoured to bring painting and sculpture in England into line with avant-garde developments abroad. Lanyon belonged to that post-war generation who continued the fight to prove that, as a nation, we had something to offer the world. If the young English artists today find that they are able to command a respect in America and elsewhere that has seen no parallel since the days of Turner and Constable, this is due, I believe, to the struggle and achievements of artists such as Peter Lanyon. He was one of those who created the new standards, the new professionalism, and the new public for English art and English artists in our own age.

(From The Cornish Review 1 – Spring 1966)

Michael Snow on W. S. Graham

I had moved to west Cornwall and began to paint there in 1951 not really expecting, as a beginner, to meet other artists whose work I admired. However, David Lewis introduced me to Denis Mitchell, Terry Frost, Ben Nicholson and Wilhelmina Barns-Graham. In 1956 Denis Mitchell (knowing that I was interested in poetry) urged me to seek out Graham. 'He will be pleased to see you, he likes someone to talk to about poetry.'

When Graham originally settled in Cornwall in 1943 it was for very practical reasons – he had been offered free accommodation, a caravan on the south coast in which he could live very cheaply. After 1948 he made two lengthy visits to give readings in North America, and at other times stayed with friends in Italy, France, London, and in other parts of England. Now in 1956 he and his wife Nessie returned to live in one of the Old Coastguard Houses at Gurnard's Head near Zennor. Their home was very close to the sea. It had no electricity and was half a mile down a very rough track.

When I walked there Graham ('You may call me Sydney') welcomed me warmly into the clean white room containing his table and chair, typewriter, an improvised couch for visitors and a very small paraffin stove. Beyond a pile of books and manuscripts I saw a rather beautiful old paraffin lamp and on the end wall were propped the sheets of cardboard torn from old cartons upon which Sydney pinned his strips of typed or hand-written verses in various stages of their revision. A few utensils and some old cutlery in the kitchen shared the space with Sydney's drawings of female faces, some of which were painted on large fragments of broken mirror glass. There was no sign of food or drink. Few artists and writers in the Cornish countryside had more than a minimal income in those days, and that often came from sources other than their own work. It was no surprise to find him living in such formidably bare surroundings in his wild sea landscape, his own liveliness and invention amply filled the airy room with activity.

Nessie was away doing seasonal work in a St Ives hotel, Sydney seemed very friendly and alert. Born in Greenock he spoke particularly clearly and confidently, his Scottish accent being apparent but not obtrusive. When he used the broad Scots it was for effect, almost like a quotation. There was little formality, we appeared to get straight down to the poetry. At least, I thought that was what we were going to do, there were various topics about which I wanted to know his views. Somehow I found it impossible to steer the conversation in any straight line. My polite questions were either unanswered or served simply to remind him of something more interesting. Fierce enquiry: 'Did you bring anything with you of the visual nature? No matter! You realise I could paint you into a corner any day of the week!' Then with a disarming smile, 'My dear, you realise I think I can do everything, I must be daft.'

The conversation became increasingly one-sided, it changed into a sort of public performance for one-man audience. In this imaginative drama he became, in quick succession, a Red Indian chief, an explorer trudging through the snow, or Livingstone lost in the jungle. Enlisted as a fellow-companion (and becoming rather lost in the language jungle myself) I began to realise that it was not going to be at all easy to get simple answers to what I had originally thought were relatively simple questions. Naturally my name attracted his atrocious puns, always followed by elaborately charming apologies. At intervals he would burst into song, Scottish ballads or snatches of operatic arias, sung with great voice and considerable feeling. The words were so convincing that it took a few minutes to realise that he was making them up as he went along (he never learned any foreign language). Exhorted to sing myself I joined in rather nervously, unsettled by his accompanying variations and some entirely unprovoked mock challenges. 'Will you come outside – I could flatten you. Away and boil yer heid!' He appeared to be introducing himself in an unusually informal way ('Do you not know I am a hard man, as hard as iron?') whilst, all the time explaining his own language – 'My dear Michael – you must not think because I call you my dear it is anything to do with some sort of homosaxon. It is not that. It is a Scottish phrase. PAY NO ATTENTION!'

I was asked to read out his poetry. I gave this my full attention and must have managed at least two or three verses before he said 'OK, OK' and proceeded to read them so much better that I understood it had not been 'OK' at all. It also became clear that he was absolutely sober and that the preceding half hour must have been some sort of test. The rest of that first afternoon was rather more peaceful but, no less strenuous. I had taken with me T. S. Eliot's *Four Quartets*, some Robert Frost, and e e cummings. We read aloud and talked about James Joyce and my correspondence with Dylan Thomas about Joyce's work. Sydney's critical attention to the language we used was so needle sharp that it raised my own by several notches. In later years I understood that with Eliot, Joyce, and

Thomas I had unwittingly chosen work close to his own interests.

Characteristically, he never said anything at the time about his own much more extensive conversations with Thomas and several others with T. S. Eliot. Neither did he mention his article 'Notes On A Poetry Of Release', a classic statement of his ideas about poetry and one particularly useful to anyone struggling with the dense textures of his early work. To Mary Harris he described these poems as 'an architecture of associations'.

Sydney was usually very discreet about his friends and offered very little information about his own past career. It was not until 1993 when my wife and I researched his correspondence and biography that we discovered how many artists he had known. Amongst them were Jankel Adler, the Roberts Colquhoun and MacBryde, Bet Low, John Minton, Ben Nicholson, Sven Berlin, Bryan Wynter, Terry Frost, and Peter Lanyon.

I have described my first visit in some detail because it was so intriguing. He asked me to return and we met fairly frequently until his death in 1986. The preliminary 'soundings out' became less necessary but there was never any lessening of his attention to language and to poetry. Sydney and Nessie were always welcoming. With barely enough food to live on they kept up morale and appearances with a certain Scottish dignity. Sydney would often refuse an invitation to a meal with 'My dear, we are trying not to eat'. Drink of course was a different matter; with the minimal amounts of alcohol that either of us could then afford Sydney would still be excellent company but his letters apologising for bad behaviour show how deterioration occurred when ample drink was available. He and Roger Hilton once called at my cottage when I was absent so they just climbed through a window and drank my home-made wine. I was not particularly pleased with the invasion but I did feel rather relieved not to have witnessed the consequences.

When T. S. Eliot wrote to Sydney in March 1954 accepting *The Nightfishing* for publication he commended him for keeping to the salt water, 'his proper element'. He also commented on Sydney's ability to keep the flavour of Scottish speech in his work despite writing in the English language. Some of the place-names in *The Nightfishing* may have had a Scottish, Cornish or even Irish origin, just as in his later poem 'I Leave This At Your Ear' he mentioned the 'naked-woman tree' near Trevaylor, Cornwall, but also spoke of 'the Kyle farm', a purely Scottish term. The 'place' of a poem was a re-created, imagined, space unrestricted by particular geography. The fact that he was also a master of brilliantly observed detail made his newly imagined world sharply 'real' and available to everyone. Modelling and carving his language until it achieved maximum expressive tension was a way of making a new reality.

Small wonder then that some of the more creative and experimental of the St Ives artists recognised not only his dedication to his craft of poetry but the resemblance which his method, that of constructing a new reality by radical reorganisation of the materials of the craft, bore to their own endeavours. The St Ives community of artists as a whole appeared to me to be composed of clusters of individualists rather than a group sharing a collective ethos. A relatively small proportion of the total could be described as at all 'experimental' and many artists were only aware of Sydney Graham as a rather over convivial and anarchic drinker. The fine elegies which Sydney wrote after the deaths of his friends Peter Lanyon, Bryan Wynter and Roger Hilton are amongst his best-known works and his own slow rise to fame has begun to give rise to a mythology which places him at the heart of the painting community.

Perhaps it would be more accurate to say that he was close to the hearts of a group of friends, some of whom were artists. One remembers that he was a mature poet, very sure of his own methods and values and only indirectly concerned with other arts. It would be difficult to establish any direct influence which he might have exerted upon the style or content of the work which his artist friends produced. I think that they would have done their work whoever had been writing in the vicinity. What Sydney provided for them was companionship, an example of perseverance and some excellent poetry. What he gained was a group of friends with whom he could talk about poetry and art with some expectation of being understood, sharing those problems common to practitioners of any of the arts in a relatively philistine world. Amongst such friends were painters such as Patrick Dolan, Terry Frost, Karl Weschke, Bryan Wynter, and writers Frank Baker, Arthur Caddick and Norman Levine lived in Cornwall, and several other writers such as Ilse Barker, George Barker, David Wright and John Heath-Stubbs worked there for shorter periods.

During those first few meetings at Gurnard's Head I wrote out some of Sydney's unpublished poems and sent them off to my friends. It was an excellent way of getting to know the work better and I was only one of several well-wishers trying to mobilise practical help for him. I shared Sydney's love and respect for the sea, the sea had affected the evolution of my own painting. He talked about going fishing with his father and his work on the fishing boats when he lived at Mevagissey. At Gurnard's Head he had occasional employment as a temporary coastguard keeping bad weather watch in the lookout post there. He once took part in the rescue of a drowning man. For food he fished and collected shellfish. I remember lending him an old pike rod which was lost when he was washed off the rocks. Luckily subsequent waves re-deposited him in almost the same spot.

When Sydney and Nessie found Gurnard's Head impossibly harsh during the winters they were invited to stay at Trevaylor House in 1962, moving to its lodge in 1963. My visits became less frequent for a while. In the small colony of artists Sydney's drinking became tedious, though it had its bizarre moments. I have preserved the hatchet with which, so I was told, Roger Hilton inefficiently aimed blows at Sydney while awkwardly pursuing him round the room. Fortunately Sydney was just sober enough to avoid them. On another occasion Sydney's great friend Bryan Wynter (who had a mischievous sense of humour) tied his Land Rover to a column of the small portico, convincing Nessie that he would demolish it when he drove home.

I saw much more of Sydney and Nessie after 1967 when Nancy Wynne-Jones gave them a little cottage and they moved to Madron, just to the north of Penzance. Some of their friends were still relatively nearby, Albert Strick, Don Brown, the poet John Knight (whose work Sydney respected), Monica Wynter, Tony O'Malley, Robert Brennan. Others came long distances to see them, Ronnie Duncan, Ruth Hilton, Sylvia Thompson, Ruth Rosen, Harold Pinter, Anthony Astbury, and Geoffrey Godbert. There were many other visitors too. The house began to reflect its occupants more, though it was later to reflect their sad decline in health. During periods of illness or depression the front door remained closed, knocks unanswered, for weeks at a time while the Grahams remained hidden upstairs. Supplied with food and drink by Hilda Strick.

In more normal times visitors were treated to Sydney reading his latest work-in-progress, affectionately hugged and politely questioned as to their sanity. He gave, as well as received, much encouragement …

In later life Sydney Graham sometimes expressed a desire to return to Scotland. His childhood experiences there echo throughout much of his poetry, memories of both the land and its language affected him profoundly. However he was not, to my knowledge, a Nationalist of any sort. An 'Internationalist' perhaps. He criticised what he saw as the unnecessary parochialism of efforts to recreate a specifically pure Scottish language for a new nationalist literature. Although proud of his Scottish background and very knowledgeable about Scottish poetry he had a deep suspicion of all politicians, English or Scottish, and of academic institutions.

With the publication of *Malcolm Mooney's Land* in 1970, *Implements in Their Places* in 1977 and *Collected Poems* in 1979 Sydney's fame grew and he was much in demand for readings. These performances so strongly established his own interpretation of the work that they made a great impression upon his listeners. Alcohol made increasing inroads on his health and two major projects remained unfinished, the poems about his time in Crete and those about his journey to read in Calgary and Victoria, Canada, in 1973.

If I ask myself what I may have gained by my encounters with Sydney Graham, by knowing the poet in addition to knowing the poetry, one answer must be that I had the opportunity to hear him read it so often, that was a major gift, an insight and a delight.

I also enjoyed the privilege of reading so many of the intermediate drafts of his poems. These were often discarded later but they gave me an opportunity to study how he worked, the building bricks by which his architecture of associations was slowly achieved. Just as in painting, his 'objects' eventually reached a state of autonomy such that they stood outside their maker. This could not have been achieved simply by his taking thought. As he wrote to John Knight: 'Remember the poem is not the thought/feelings behind the poem, what you went through when you wrote it. It is those words on the page left for other different strange people which maybe we do not understand (I mean the people do not understand) … The lovely thing about making poetry is reordering the dictionary.'

I witnessed many stages in the execution of his grand 'symphonic' poems such as 'Malcolm Mooney's Land' and 'Clusters Travelling Out', as well as the equally powerful but smaller scale meditations on the nature of language and existence, the epistemological chamber music of 'The Beast In The Space', 'The Constructed Space', 'Approaches To How They Behave'. Poetry was the way in which Sydney Graham encountered his world and himself. I never had any doubts that, as he modestly put it, 'A value is there lurking somewhere.'

(From 'When Who We Think We Are' – *Aquarius* 25/26, 2002)

Ruth Hilton: The Influence of Music on W. S. Graham

In the thirty years that I (a professional musician) knew him, music – the listening to it, the talking about it, the discussions on technical methods of performance, the backstage stories about musicians – always formed a part of our talks together. But it is only now through Nessie, that I learn that the precentor of the church choir in which he sang as a boy, had actually suggested to Sydney's parents that he should have his voice trained. Moreover, the precentor even offered to pay for the initial lessons; so there is no doubt that he must have had a marked talent in that direction. He certainly had a voice! – (sometimes abused) – and would occasionally talk (nostalgically) about how he would play this or that operatic role. But, if I ever asked him whether he had seriously considered a professional singer's career, he would simply answer 'My dear – NO. I do not think so.' And he was right of course. Many very talented musical people fail to survive in the profession because their temperament proves unsuitable for such a volatile, show biz life.

Growing up in Greenock, though, he availed himself of every opportunity to go up to Glasgow to hear singers such as Heddle Nash, Walter Widdop, and Joseph Locke (famous tenors of their day); and the well-known Glasgow Orpheus Choir, conducted by Hugh Robertson. And there were records (also in Nessie's family home) of such international stars as Gigli, Caruso, di Stefano, Chaliapin, Isobel Baillie, and others. Along with these enthusiasms, he was, of course, saturated with the traditional melodies of Scotland and Ireland – his mother came from Galway. I do not know if his father sang, but he was much in demand as a pianist and violinist, and was also a leading amateur actor in the district. So I think it likely that Sydney would have learned these songs from very early childhood. Certainly *Moore's Melodies* – the popular nineteenth-century collection – was well known to him. But it was not just that he had an inbred and romantic enthusiasm for music, which might have been surmised from his impromptu performances at parties or in pubs: we had some of the most interesting discussions I have ever known about technical aspects of performance. To take just a very few examples: he was thrilled to hear, and to see me demonstrate, the direct correspondence between a string-player's

bowing arm and a singer's breath; to be told that a string-quartet player must be able to hear the other three parts while playing their own; that, for a singer or a player, the stance, freeing the torso for breathing, or the arms for playing, was of the utmost importance. I sent him a book by the eighteenth-century flautist Johann Joachim Quantz, *On Playing the Flute*, which I had just read with much interest, because it was full of just such practical information, and I thought he would love it – he did!

Once, when he was staying in London (*c.* 1958), I took him to a rehearsal for a concert performance of Wagner's *Meistersinger* – not without trepidation – as I knew he rather fancied himself as an interpreter of the 'Prize Song' – and I needed the job! But he sat quietly at the back of the hall – (only once or twice did I notice his chair was empty: and it was a three-hour rehearsal) – and afterwards it touched me to see how very much it had meant to him to be present.

For Sydney was undoubtedly a very 'musical' man – one to whom music spoke directly as a familiar language exploring every nuance of feeling and thought. In many years of teaching, mostly children, I know the signs, and can recognize such a person – quite different from one for whom music is just a pleasant change from silence. Sydney's peremptory use of the word 'listen' (in more than one poem, I think) is the usage of a musician, waiting to 'disturb the silence' with his own language.

(From The Constructed Space – ed. by Duncan & Davidson)

Patrick Heron on Tony O'Malley

The timing of this major exhibition of the paintings of Tony O'Malley is most fortunate for two distinct – but related – reasons. Firstly, O'Malley has been working during the past five years with a consistently rising pressure in terms not only of inventiveness and expressive profundity, but also of sheer prolific output. And, secondly, the entire pictorial climate, internationally speaking, is now far more sympathetic than it was, even a mere couple of years ago, to painting which betrays in every square millimetre of the picture surface, evidence of its having been *made by hand*, and proof that that hand is indeed the personal and unique instrument of expression of a sensibility which, again, is itself evidence of one man's visual reactions to the stimuli with which mere physical vision (or sight) unendingly supply him. Tony O'Malley, unlike, for instance, the conceptualists, and unlike too many of the internationally identifiable Op or Pop or hard-edge painters who have had things very much their own way for so long, actually goes around with his eyes open. He *looks* at objects – of any or every description; he looks at light; he cannot help all the time consciously absorbing the actual visual nature of whatever reality or scene, or environment he finds himself placed in at any given moment. Hence the thousands (literally) of very small drawings, colour notes, texture-statements, which he makes at practically any hour of the day – any day, every day. Hence, too, the lightening fact that his notebooks switch, from hour to hour, from page to page, from a great variety of purely abstract linear and colour statements to a host of exceedingly accurate and evocative notations of the actual *appearance* of, for instance, a couple of window panes or half a face; of three isolated waves of the sea or the ripples in wet sand; of a table top conventionally cluttered with bric-a-brac or of a plain lopsided walled field on a hillside; of an entire mountain on Clare

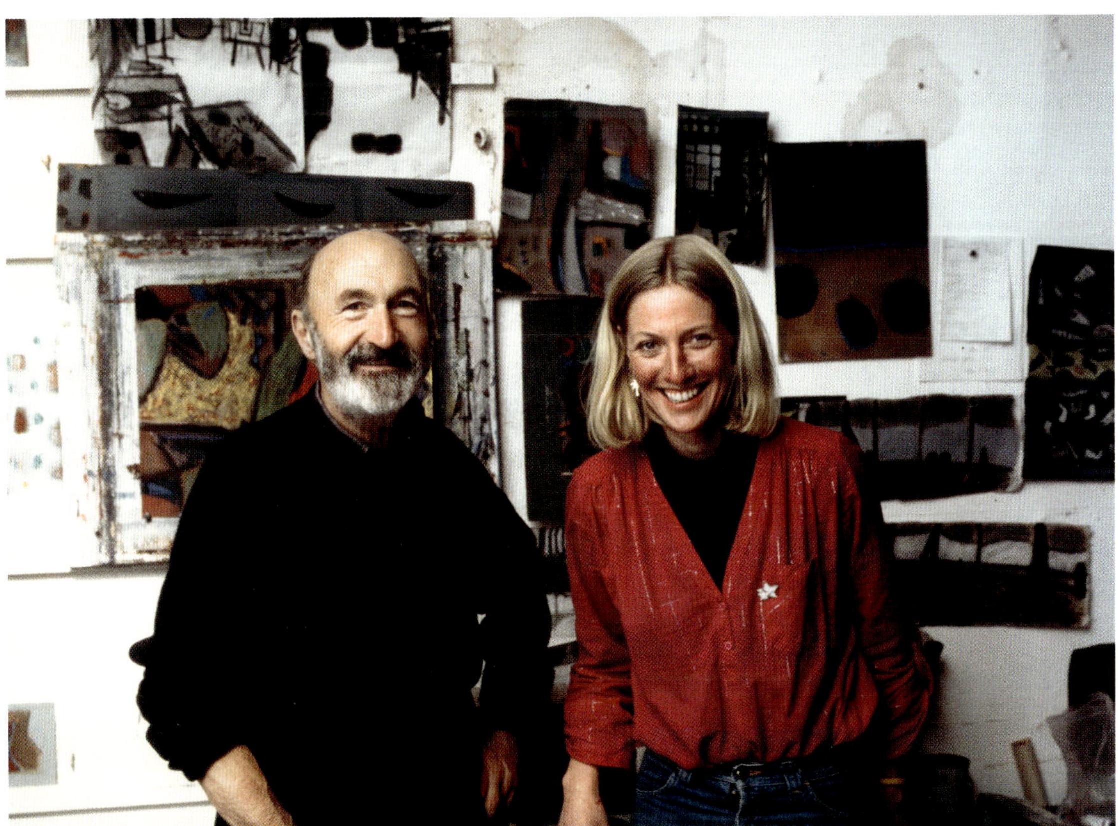

Jane & Tony O'Malley in their St Ives studio, 1980

Island or of three blackbirds thrashing around in the empty space of the sky over his head; of the curiously Baroque panels in the front of a wardrobe in a Swiss bedroom, or of a nude girl lying in the grasses and flowers in a remote meadow. The list is endless. His visual curiosity is, one might say, like his own particular sensitivity, practically without limitation – at least in the sense that that sensitivity has never confined his work to a consistency of style or idiom which would restrict its basic configuration to a limited formal range. The formal range of O'Malley's nonfigurative work is in fact, extremely wide – far wider perhaps, than is always apparent to those who are seeing it for the first time.

O'Malley has a rare and remarkable talent. He is certainly one of the most profoundly gifted painters ever to have come from Ireland. As I have already begun to suggest, although long at odds with many characteristics of the dominant nonfigurative painting of the past fifteen years, O'Malley's extremely personal qualities (of surface, of image and of colour) suddenly appear to be qualities of special relevance to us, at a moment when international painting has begun to turn away from a condition in which it had been over-saturated with bland, mechanically produced, often immaculately smooth surfaces – the surfaces after all, of academic abstract idioms which were more conceptual in origin than sensory or intuitive. Despite its low key, chromatically speaking, and despite its almost granular textures, the surface of an oil painting or a gouache by O'Malley *invariably* glows. Most colourists today in fact deploy paint as a continuous, unbroken, unmodulated skin, to cover the canvas. It is rare at the moment, to find any painter who is concerned to elicit that vibration which is colour, as it were from the depths of the pigment instead of from its

surface merely. I am not arguing against the use of the surface of the paint as a conveyor of the colour vibration (frequently I do this myself); but merely pointing to the fact of O'Malley's instinctive use of the alternative mode whereby we feel that the colour is glowing at us from *inside* the actual pigment and this gift of producing controlled luminosity in his pigment is something which, in O'Malley's case, extends to the handling of those dull colours – the dingy khakis or grey or near-black he so much loves. His darkest or most muted schemes are invariably alive with the vibrancy of the born colourist. His paintings do not, however, achieve their luminosity by merely importing *atmospheric* qualities – although his surfaces are indeed not flat and hard in the sense we all understand since Mondrian. Where O'Malley's paint is misty and transparent (as opposed to the hard opacity of the academic moderns) he still nevertheless maintains that shallow-space unity of pictorial image which gives his works their consistency and frontal power.

This exhibition properly concerns itself almost exclusively with O'Malley's nonfigurative painting, and not with his small, often tiny, figurative drawings and watercolours, although these are nearly always powerful and exquisite and in the same instance both informative and decorative. Like Nicholson, Lanyon or Hilton, he has always preserved two idioms – figurative and non-figurative – side by side as parallel activities. And although there is an absolute unity of feeling informing *all* his works in either idiom the images which O'Malley has nurtured, developed, perfected and made most his own are the strong economic images which are in fact totally abstract. But, as always with important painting, we do unconsciously *project* a totally autonomous abstraction – made known to us in the painting – back on to the natural scene, so that we often have the illusion that these abstract forms exist out there, independently in the natural scene. But this is not the case.

This note cannot adequately introduce a painter as subtle, varied and prolific as O'Malley. But I hope it will at least indicate the natural terrain which his unassertive yet extremely original talent is exploring. There is a round-cornered, blunt-angled rhythm in the drawing of his images and designs that is intensely personal and so natural. Seeming as to appear almost artless at times. But in this very quality lies his strength – the strength of the truly gifted wielder of both a brush and pen or pencil.

(From Arts Council travelling exhibition catalogue, 1975)

Michael Canney on John Tunnard

The new forms which science presents to us are absorbed by the artist, and they sink into the subconscious alongside the apple and the nude, until they finally emerge upon the canvas, when the proper and significant relationship between them has been found, and a new image has crystallized.

An artist whose work in this connection has been of great interest is John Tunnard, and his paintings have commended themselves in particular to scientists and engineers during the last thirty years. An examination of his work might incline the spectator to think that his interests ranged over the strange 'Wellsian' machines and structures which litter the contemporary landscape, and can be found in the factory or the laboratory. But this artist has in fact devoted his life, when not painting, to the study of natural science – from the collection of small insects to the study of the habits of wild fowl and the creatures of the countryside and seashore. He has discovered

that there are many similarities between these things and modern machinery; it is not entirely fortuitous that the tail of an invertebrate such as the dragonfly should be similar in construction to the fuselage of an aircraft, and one can find many other parallels between nature and engineering.

John Tunnard has always insisted that he has no interest in modern technology and that it is a closed book to him; in fact, he lives in a remote part of Cornwall in order to avoid seeing the disfigurement of the landscape by power stations and modern industry. Yet, quite intuitively, many structures that have now become familiar to us, such as the radio telescope and radar antennae, have appeared in his pictures, sometimes before their erection or invention. In one particular case, a scientist, with some surprise, recognised in one of Tunnard's paintings the general atmosphere of a problem on which he had been working. In another case, a television engineer was moved to remark that one of Tunnard's paintings seemed to sum up everything that he knew, and it was difficult to convince him that the artist was not also obsessed with television and radio circuits and the cathode ray tube. Perhaps an explanation lies in the fact that every age seems to have shapes which belong to it and which therefore appear in its art. The very words rococo and baroque carry with them images of certain forms and shapes, and the resemblances between the early biplanes and Cubist paintings of the same period are quite remarkable. Is it coincidental that the shapes seen in much of modern sculpture are similar to those found in the jet plane of today, or is the artist in this case following in the wake of the aircraft designer? Both are concerned with producing a perfect form, in one case functional and in the other aesthetic, and yet how often the purely functional form is aesthetically satisfying as well. In the case of John Tunnard his shapes are eminently contemporary and this explains the appeal of his pictures to the scientist, engineer, and architect.

(From 'Science & the Artist' – Discovery, December 1959)

Bryan Wynter – A Memoir

Nine years have rolled round since my brother Bryan died, leaving us the poorer. His original thinking, his understanding of the country and his relish in communication had been bringers of freedom.

He was born during the 1914-18 war and spent his first years in Highgate, where he became Mother's lifelong hero and founded a lifelong antagonism to Father, who was serving in the army in North Africa as a private. After that war the family moved to Potters Bar, Father was in the laundry business in London, and I was born. We were there living comfortably in semi-detachment until Bryan was about twelve. He was already making cartoon-like-drawings for the entertainment of younger children, and showing signs of resisting convention. In about 1928 we moved further north to Hertford, where Father had bought a small farm and built a mock-Elizabethan house called Windyridge. Bryan was sent as a boarder to prep school at Seafield Park near Lee-on-Solent, and then to Haylebury, a fiercely conventional public school centred on church and army, where he learned to sharpen his independence and became a fine gymnast.

During the thirties under Father's guidance we would go to remote places for our family holidays – including Scotland, Pembroke, North Wales and Cornwall. This was when the Land's End peninsula first gripped Bryan.

From Haylebury he went into the family business with some reluctance but under pressure from his seniors who saw in it a life of security in a world of slump. He made something of it, and spent an enjoyable part of his training in Zurich, but it wasn't the life for him and after some years his love of art won. He left the laundries for the Slade in 1938.

War was brewing again. We had both become pacifists after long discussion over Aldous Huxley's book *Ends and Means*, and when war was declared Bryan registered as a C.O. He spent the war years in various manual jobs – land-drainage, monkey house keeping for Solly Zuckerman's experimental animals in Oxford, market garden work and farmwork. He had his first paintings reproduced in the Oxford magazine *Counterpoint*. These showed strong influence by Surrealists, especially Dali and Ernst.

The war years quietly frustrated him because he was having to do unskilled jobs to the side of his mainstream commitments in painting. There was a good deal of savagery in his elaborate and bizarre practical jokes, which curiously endeared him to the people he worked with. They respected his integrity, perhaps envied it and they loved his humour. But the 'shorthaired mad executives' disliked him, for his satire put their fortresses at risk.

As soon as the war ended Bryan went down to Cornwall and rented Carn, a primitive, wet, granite-built miner's cottage on Zennor Moor 800 feet above the sea and accessible only by a rock and peat bog track from the coast road. At Carn in his thirtieth year he found release to work as he wanted, though very short of cash, and for some years he turned out small paintings and drawings of the raw high land of rocks, gulls, villages and sea. These brought him recognition through exhibitions at the Redfern Gallery. His body of friends grew (picked, someone said, for their eccentricity). Patrick Heron, his nearest neighbour, Edward Walton, and the poet W. S. Graham were among the closest. He also befriended wild animals, climbed the great Cornish cliffs, skin-dived, drank in St Ives pubs and mooched around the moors, coming to know their communities of wildlife as an appreciative observer without wishing to take a scientific interest in them. He teased the animals and ate the plants. In his head he carried a library of appalling stories, some of them true, most just possible: they were used to make points in discussion, which he enjoyed. He would talk about inventions, people, jazz, poetry, about underwater, about discoveries on walks, but he rarely, though glad to show his work, talked about the processes through which his paintings came into being. Looking back I think he preserved a deliberate silence on them, perhaps in order to prevent

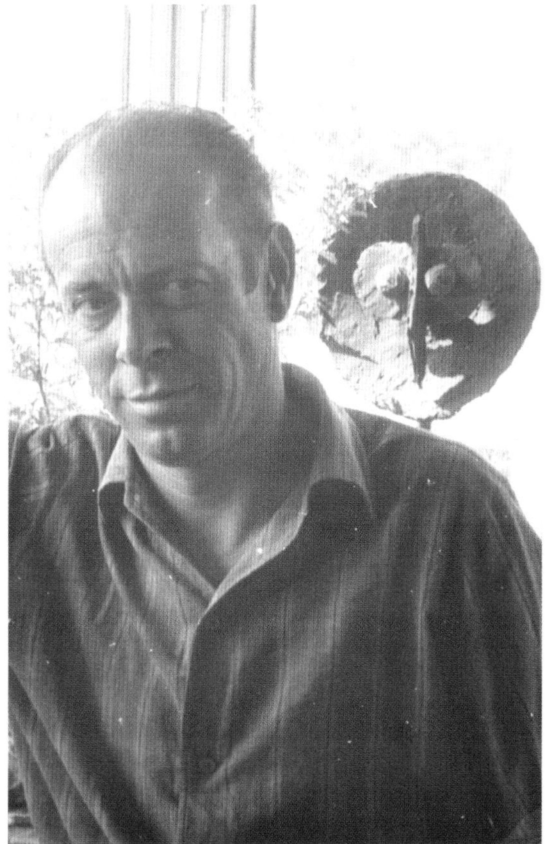

his verbal processes from swamping them. He didn't talk much about art at all.

He married Susan Lethbridge in Cornwall. They had two children.

In the early fifties Bryan went to teach at Bath Academy of Art in Corsham, partly to make ends meet. During that time he did little work of his own. Returning to Zennor in 1956 he began to work again, but the work now moved away from recognisable landscape into a kind of abstraction lit up by dimensions underwater. He spent much time exploring below the surface of rock pools.

In 1959 came his second marriage, to Monica Harman, and they also had two children. In 1961 he suffered a serious heart attack, and was then told to stop energetic pursuits such as climbing and diving. The family moved house to St Buryan, on the milder south coast. He took up canoeing by Kayak, gently at first, and soon became absorbed in the narrative character of rivers. White water in small streams excited him. At the same time his painting changed its focus (to put it crudely) from watery interiors to the surface motion of rivers in relation to their beds. There emerged the theme of 'Meanders', which threaded nearly all his work from then on.

A few days before Bryan died, in February 1975, I went to St Buryan on a visit. I hadn't seen him look so well and full of ideas for a long time. He had embarked on a series of small paintings in acrylic, had turned out some cartoons of preposterous dogs, and bought a very heavy cast iron bath which had to be unloaded and trundled down to the brook below the house. Was this load the last straw?

(Eric Wynter – 1984)

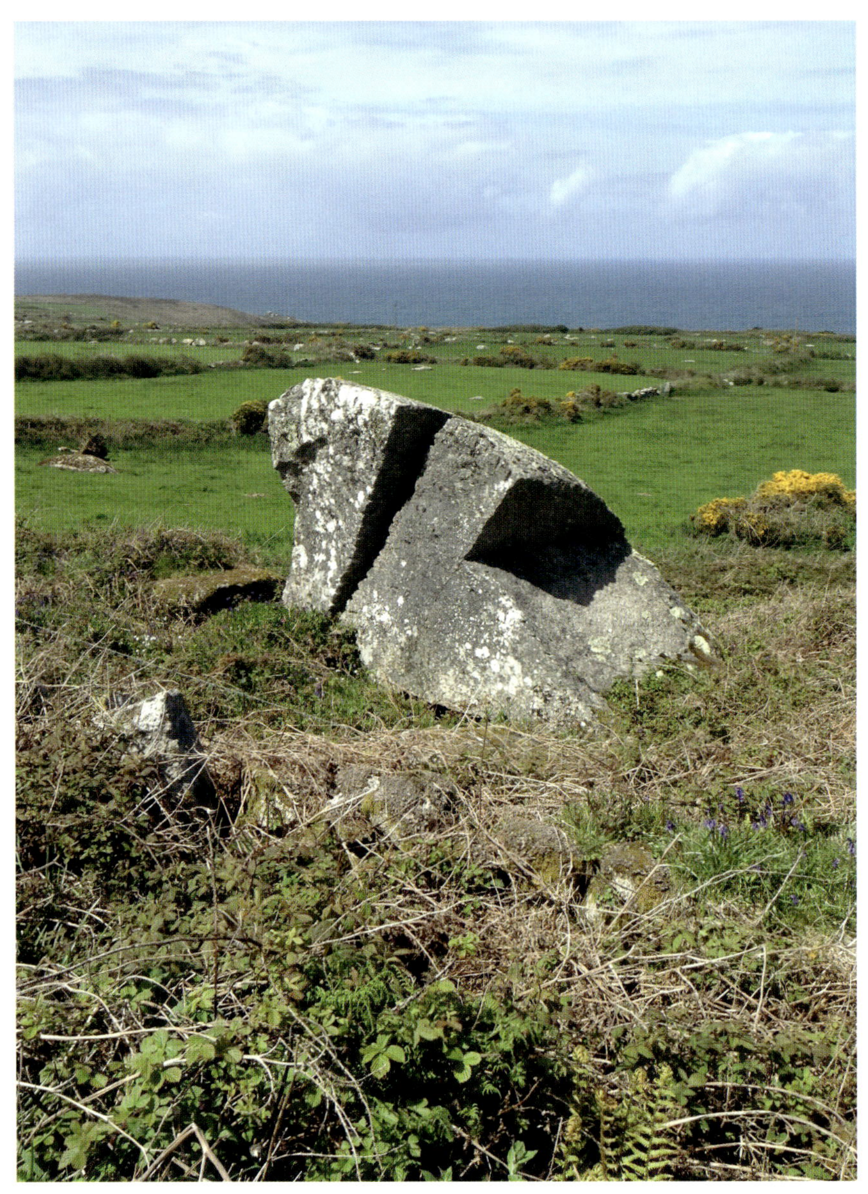

Appendix C

Setting the Seen
(& the Unseen)

On your first visit to Cornwall, which came first, art or place?

That's a fairly straightforward question, but the answer is a little more complex. While working in a bookshop in central London in 1976, I felt in need of a holiday away from the hurly-burly of city life. I was gasping for a sea breeze, as it had just been the hottest summer on record. So in September I took a coach, with my rucksack and tent, to St Ives.

I was aware of the work of Barbara Hepworth, which I admired enough to have the little Thames & Hudson *World of Art* book about her, and I was alarmed the previous year to hear of her death in a fire at her studio. But I somehow knew that her gardens had just opened to the public and this is what got me heading to that far flung place. So I can honestly say that Hepworth was responsible for my discovery of Cornwall. But this was my sole awareness of the Cornish art scene.

On arrival, I pitched my tent at Hellesveor campsite on the edge of town. I promptly visited the Hepworth gardens and thought it a wonderful place. I wandered around the various little galleries in the town and was struck by the diversity of unusual paintings, sculpture and pottery. I'd never seen anything like it. But I was not very knowledgeable about British art at this time.

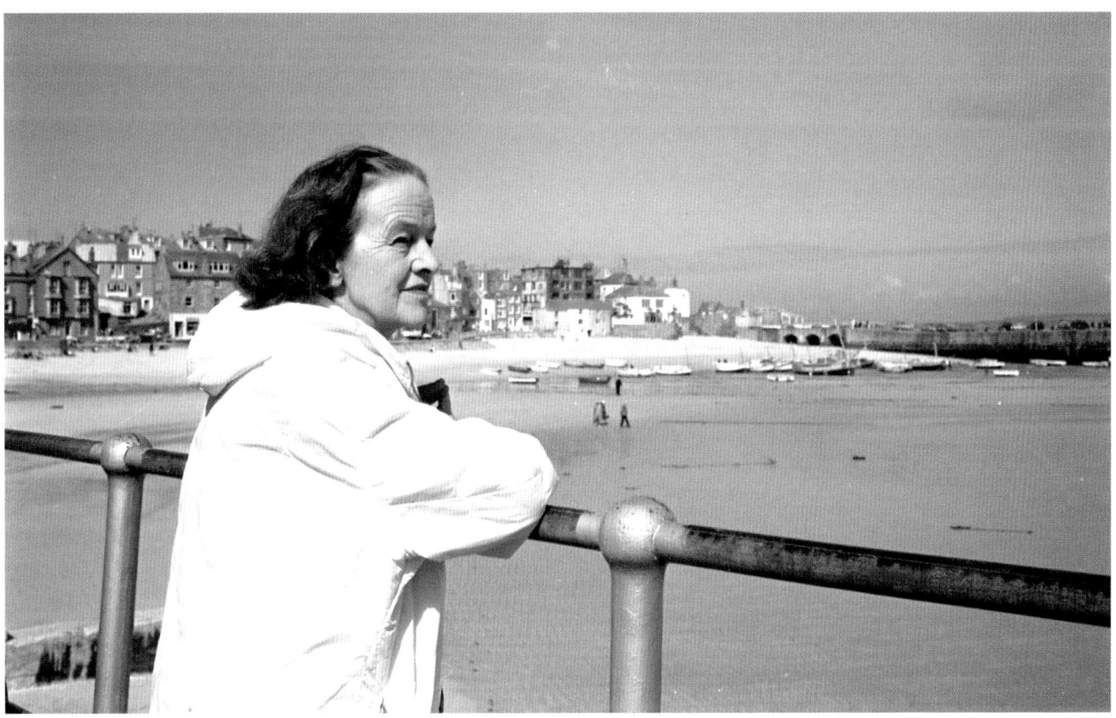

Barbara Hepworth, St Ives, 1964

As I began to explore, on foot and by bus, I was totally bowled over; in fact it was love at first sight. I walked along the road to Zennor on a hot, sunny day. It felt like I was on another planet. I remember it was a Sunday afternoon and the Tinner's Arms was shut. I was desperate for a drink and the man in the Wayside Museum gave me a glass of water. He also advised me to walk back across the fields over the stiles. On another day I took a bus out to Porthcurno and while walking the cliffs stumbled on the Minack Theatre and also happened to meet Rowena Cade, without knowing who she was.

You were lucky to meet her. It's curious to think that many of the characters you subsequently researched were alive and well at the time of this visit.

I often wonder who I must have passed in the street or sat in the same bar with. Wynter and Hilton had died the previous year, but many of the other big names were certainly around then, and I did spend my evenings mooching around the bars. I came away from the area feeling invigorated and vowed to return.

And did you?

Just over a year later I came to Cornwall again. This time I stayed with the writer Colin Wilson at his home in Gorran Haven, near St Austell. I was seriously thinking of moving to Cornwall at this point. But when I returned to London a whole new life opened up when I started dealing in books at Camden Passage market, in Islington, alongside the writer and psychogeographer Iain Sinclair. I learned a lot from him about the book trade.

But you became more aware of Cornish art?

The Tate in London had a big St Ives show in the mid-1980s and I came across the superb and informative catalogue one day at

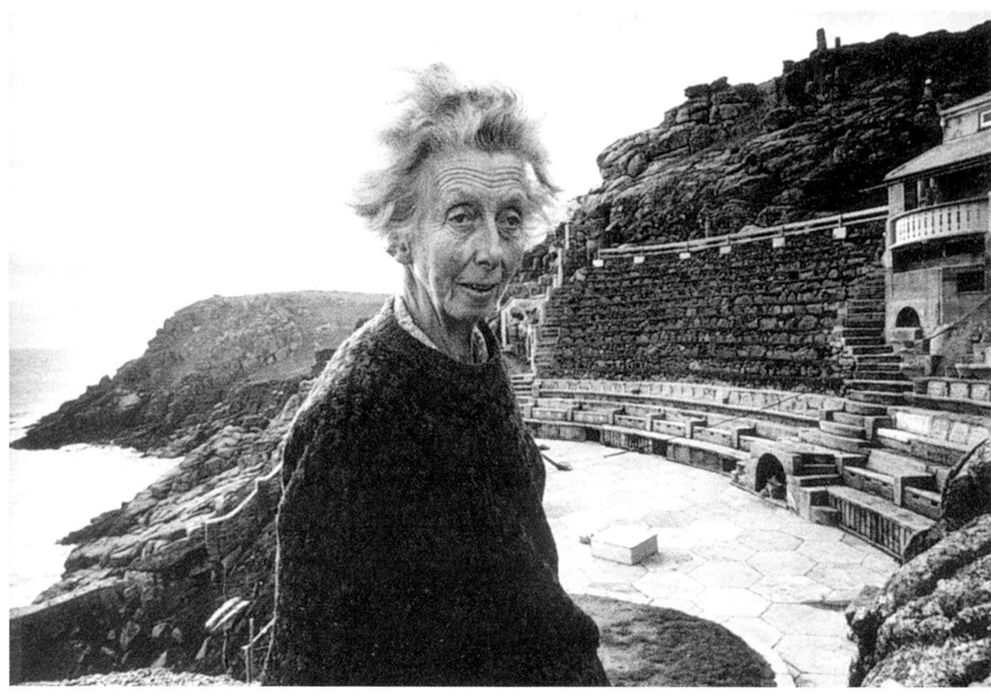

Rowena Cade with her creation

the book market. Soon after this I became a frequent visitor to West Penwith, with my family, walking and exploring the cliffs and moors, using a wonderful walking book by Des Hannigan. The opening of Tate St Ives in 1993 was very important for me, as I could then start to see so much of this art in the flesh, as it were, and I began to research the art and artists more. Though they all had a different take on the place, much of this diversity of art seemed to resonate with the landscape in subtle ways. I was fascinated by a famous letter from John Wells to Sven Berlin (from 1945), where he made this lyrical statement:

> So all around the moving air and the sea's blue light, with points of diamond, and the gorse incandescent beyond dark trees – countless rocks ragged or round and of every colour – birds resting or flying, and the sense of a multitude of creatures living out their minute lives … All this is just part of one's life, and I want desperately to express it – not just what I see but what I feel about it and beyond it. If I paint what I see the result is deplorable. But how can one paint the warmth of the sun, the sound of the sea or the journey of a beetle across a rock or thoughts of one's own whence and whither?

This really caught my imagination, and I now had the curious experience of the art starting to inform and shape how I saw and engaged with the place.

Can you give us some examples?

Many of these artists were experimenting in shifting away from the tyranny of the eye looking out at a static landscape, to getting under the skin of the place by including the shifting sensations of movement and feelings and moods, through the different seasons. Peter

Lanyon in particular was a strong influence in getting me out and about over rough terrain in all weathers. I would walk all day visiting the places featured in his paintings, including Levant Mine, Bojewyan Farm, Wheal Owles, Botallack and so on. He once said: 'Walking, the feet are informed.' It was the physicality of his approach, an embodiment of place I suppose, that got me clambering about in the most unlikely places and I felt exhilarated in my quiet explorations. I became conscious of his dynamic multi-perspectival approach to knowing a place. He made me appreciate that perception involves all of the senses, plus imagination (which includes memory). Lanyon also makes you aware of the history of the mining industry in the region, and he was particularly sensitive to the tragedies and hardships endured by the Cornish people over the centuries. I've also spent a good deal of time on the boulder strewn moors around Bryan Wynter's house above Zennor. I love that place. His old studio that he built was still standing when I first used to visit. I found him a particularly appealing figure and I was fascinated by the way he incorporated natural processes, like the movement of streams and rivers, or the patterns left on the sand by the tides, into his art. Wynter was attempting to 'see' behind appearances. He was also very influenced by Zen.

You take your time on these trips?

The four Ss are paramount: solitude, silence, stillness and slowness. I hasten to add I also need companionship sometimes! Especially my family. But those four qualities are essential to my well-being and nowhere quite does it like Penwith. Paying attention is the key, contemplating the varying moods of weather, light, cloud formations, seasonal flora, the elegant ballet of the gulls riding the spiralling thermals, and of course the amazingly diffuse wave formations crashing onto, or gently caressing, the cliffs. To the casual visitor the place looks like a wilderness, but in fact it's teeming with evidence of human activity going back many thousands of years from Neolithic antiquities to Iron Age and Bronze Age stone walled fields – 'hedges' (this tesserae or labyrinth of fields is particularly apparent around Zennor), up to the haunting vestiges of toil from the industrial revolution. Penwith is a place where the past lies ahead of us, time is stretched out as space. We tend to see and traverse a place horizontally, but here you become aware that there are also vertical riches beneath the soil. You need to let the place sink into your consciousness. There's a German word I like the sound of, *stimmung*, it refers to tuning or harmonizing. It makes me think of tuning into the frequency of a place.

But why Cornwall in particular?

I think it has something to do with being in self-exile from Ireland. I grew up there in the 1960s when the Catholic schooling was quite brutal, and I got the hell out when I was 18 and headed for London. I feel Cornwall is perhaps my Celtic substitute for Ireland. I'm not sure if I've adopted Cornwall or Cornwall has adopted me! But my psyche feels totally in tune with the *genius loci* of this far end of the land.

Is this how you picked up on O'Malley?

I remember being terribly excited, in the mid-1990s to discover a fellow Irishman had spent so much time here. I was determined to meet him, even though he had retired back to Ireland by then. And meet him I did, alas it was only a few months before he died. But I feel a particularly strong empathy with him and hugely admire what he did with his life. He also had a deep engagement with Japanese ideas.

That leads me to ask about your photography. What is it about rust, rocks, ruins and wrecks?

It was when I escaped school I felt my education began. Dealing in books was my university, and very early on I discovered Zen Buddhism and Taoism. These doctrines have remained of crucial importance to how I understand and deal with the world. They emphasise the impermanence of all existence, an acceptance of transience. Everything is in a state of flux or metamorphosis. In Japan a whole aesthetic developed in the arts and literature celebrating this evanescence. The Japanese have words for all manner of subtle and delicate qualities of nature that we have difficulty even recognising.

Any examples?

An obvious one is *wabi-sabi*. In fact there are two concepts here that over the centuries fused into one. In a nutshell, *wabi* refers to a condition of material poverty or rusticity, and the opportunity this offers for immaterial wealth. While *sabi* emphasises the melancholic tranquillity to be found in quietly surrendering to a mood of loneliness. Basically, it is an approach that sees beauty and dignity in the patina of ageing, a perfectly natural process. When I point my camera at an old bit of rusting gatepost I'm acknowledging its solitary uniqueness and bringing it to awareness, no two objects decay in exactly the same way. By the way, the kind of paintings I'm drawn to also display some degree of this roughness and I like to detect a mysterious sense of place which draws me in, without a necessary referent to the outside world.

Stones, pebbles and mountains are also significant in China and Japan, look at Japanese rock gardens for example. Of course Cornwall is rich in geology and Penwith has wonderful varieties of stone formations to keep me busy with my camera. Some of these rocks are my best friends, I'm always delighted to come back and find them still there! Cot Valley is a favourite venue. Everyday is like a constantly changing sculpture show, you can see where Hepworth got many of her shapes from. I find it deeply rewarding to reflect upon their distillations of silence echoing down the aeons. I never cease to be awed by the fact that no two pebbles are exactly alike.

Just by the way, this Japanese ethos is not entirely foreign to St Ives. Bernard Leach acted as a significant cultural bridge between East and West for decades. Many Japanese potters were lured here because of this and shared their ideas with local people. In fact the great Zen scholar D. T. Suzuki came to visit Leach in the late 1950s and met up with some of the artists in the town.

Why do you mainly concentrate on the artists from the 1950s and '60s?

Because they were the innovators. Several of these artists came down at the outbreak of war, including Hepworth, Nicholson, Gabo and Barns-Graham but many more came after the war. Some were disillusioned with the state of civilization and looked for a fresh, remote start on the edge of society. Cornwall was then very cheap and accommodating. As time went on a kind of critical mass led to artists attracting more artists and so on. But being in this place led many of them to experiment and try and break new ground. It was a safe place to do this without fear of being mocked or suffering a conservative backlash. It's generally felt that the collective energy for all this started to dissipate after the death of Lanyon in 1964.

Why are they nearly all outsiders?

Lanyon was clearly the main local boy and he was rather irked by all these 'blow-ins' elbowing into his territory! But it says a lot for West Penwith. First of all it lured people here from all different backgrounds. Then when they arrived, the novel and invigorating potential of the place demanded of them that they raise their game to a new, unpredictable level of creativity. Whereas when you grow up in a place it's easy to become inured to its idiosyncrasies. It's the incredible spontaneity of that earlier period, in a specific time and place that continues to fascinate, it was a remarkable, unique phenomenon and can never be replicated. Subsequent generations have been weighed down by the cultural baggage of what went before. It's tough now to be original. That's not to say there aren't still good artists around!

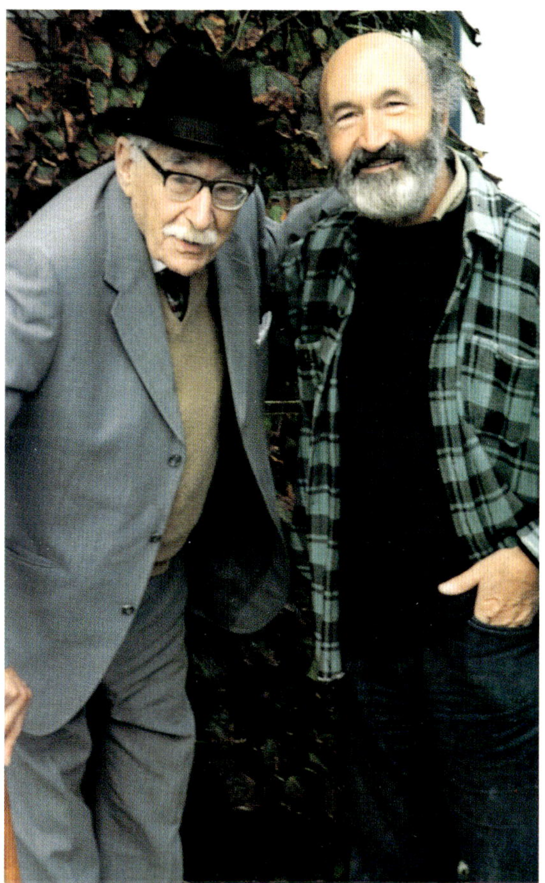

Bernard Leach and Tony O'Malley, 1975

I believe we tend to be too anthropocentric in how we understand place, as if it's a blank slate that we humans impose meaning on. But this is rather hubristic and reductionist. Most places are buzzing with non-human life, and this vast, dynamic array of flora and fauna also shapes a place. Nor is the land simply an inert mass, its mineral accretions, and the mood they bestow, should not be underestimated.

Our own bodies are teeming with tens of trillions of microbes, in fact we're each a walking ecosystem. They're all going about their business totally unaware they're contributing to someone's sense of distinct identity. Maybe it's the same for all of us on a different scale. We're busily going about our affairs unaware we're contributing to a larger body of existence, or consciousness, beyond our comprehension.

Places are not all the same. Places are like people and vary enormously in characteristics, some are more alive (and lovable) than others. Being respectful of certain locations, and paying selfless attention, can trigger a response from that place. Hopkins said: 'When you look hard at a thing it seems to look hard at you.' But a place isn't a thing, it's a transaction. There is a subtle, reciprocal loop between the observer and the observed. And it's not merely looking, but a multi-sensual immersion in an atmosphere.

For me, it's via the ambiguities of certain suggestive poetry, art and music that I catch a glimpse or a fleeting insight into an ineffable, elevated dimension of existence. There's much more to be said on this topic, but this isn't the time or the place …

I'll wind up with a quote from the Mexican writer Octavio Paz: 'Perhaps the real name of creation is *recognition*.'

It's been a pleasure talking to you.

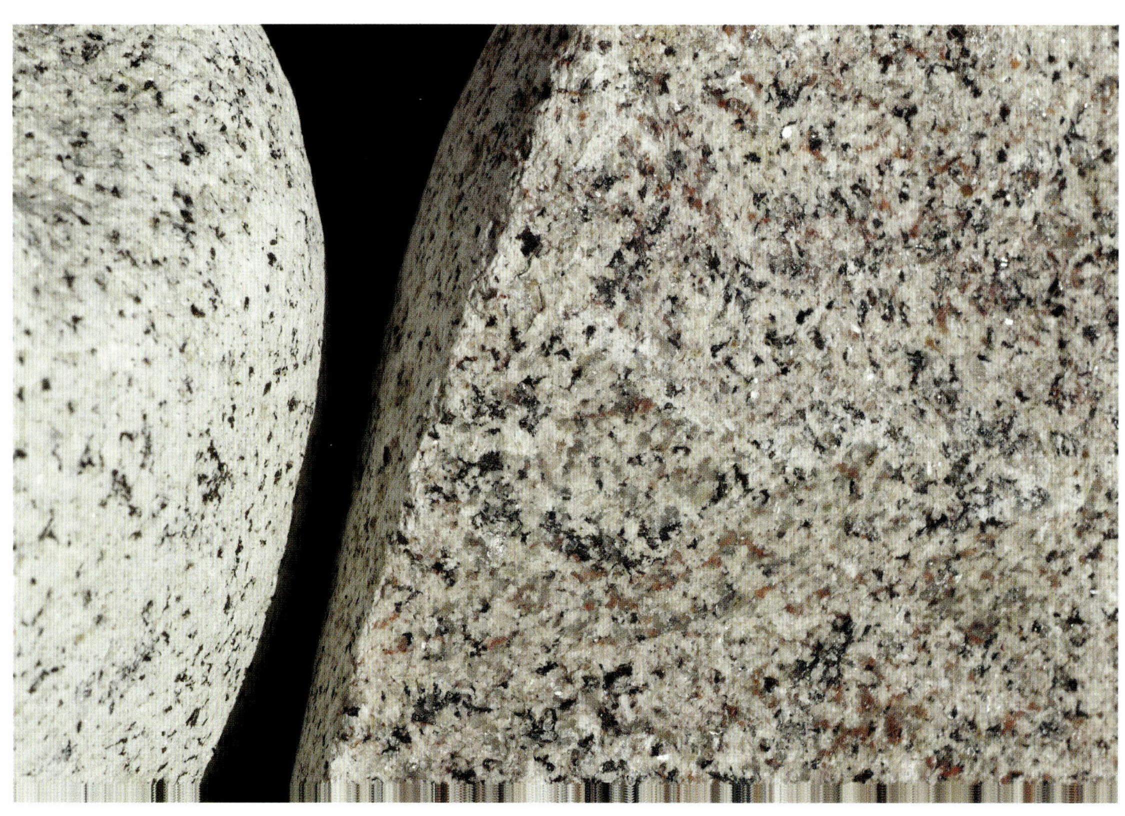

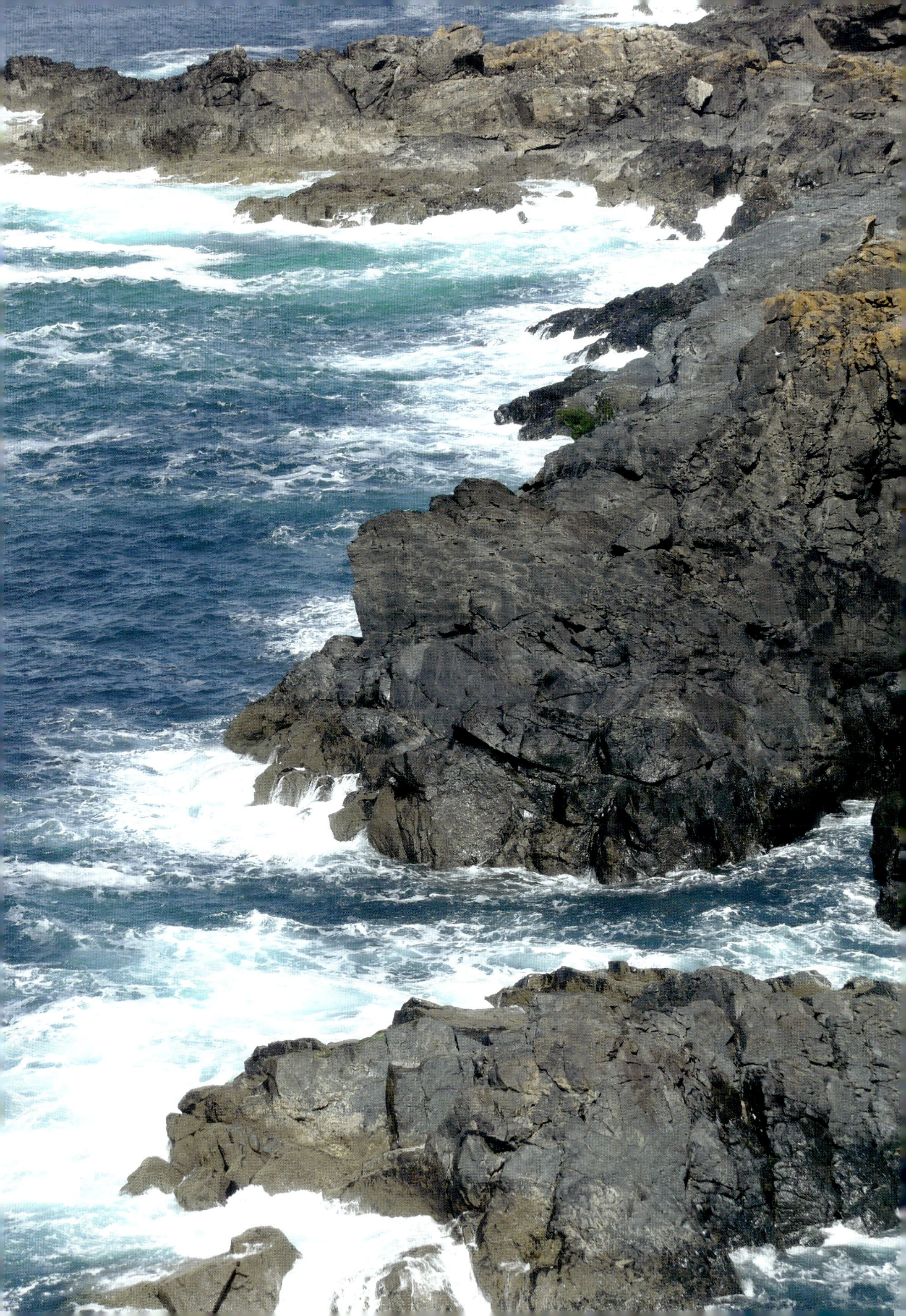

Further Reading

Bryan Wynter & the Carn

Bird, M. *Bryan Wynter*. Lund Humphries 2010

Bowness, A. *Bryan Wynter 1915-1975*. Hayward Gallery 1976

Stephens, C. *Bryan Wynter*. Tate 1999

Tea with Miss Barns-Graham

Green, L. *W. Barns-Graham: A Studio Life*. Lund Humphries revised ed. 2011

Gunn, A. V. *The Prints of Wilhelmina Barns-Graham: A Complete Catalogue*. Lund Humphries 2007

W. S. Graham & the Artists

Boast, R. *et al.* (ed.) *The Caught Habits of Language: An Entertainment for W. S. Graham for Him Having Reached One Hundred*. Donut Press 2018

Duncan, R. & Davidson, J. (ed.) *The Constructed Space: A Celebration of W. S. Graham*. Jackson's Arm 1994

Graham, W.S. *New Collected Poems*. Faber 2004

Snow, M. & M. (ed.) *The Nightfisherman: Selected Letters of W. S. Graham*. Carcanet 1999

Stephens, C. *The Constructed Space*. Bradford Art Galleries & Museums 1994

Whittaker, D. *Give me Your Painting Hand: W. S. Graham & Cornwall*. Wavestone Press 2015

Tony O'Malley: The Watching Windhover

Fallon, B. *Tony O'Malley: Painter in Exile*. Irish Arts Council 1984

Lynch, B. (ed.) *Tony O'Malley*. New Island Books 2004

Whittaker, D. *Tony O'Malley: An Irish Artist in Cornwall*. Wavestone Press 2005

Whybrow, M. *Free Spirits: Jane & Tony O'Malley*. St Ives Printing & Publishing Company 2014

The Healing Art of Dr Roger Slack

Whittaker, D. 'Doctor Roger Slack: An Appreciation' in *Under a Western Sky: The Art of Newlyn & St Ives*. Bonhams 2008

Seize the Day: Jeremy Le Grice

Le Grice, J. *At Seventy*. Royal Cornwall Museum 2006

Michael Canney & Newlyn Art Gallery

Davies, P. *Michael Canney: Paintings, Constructions, Reliefs*. Katharine House Gallery 2005

Hardie, M. *100 years in Newlyn: Diary of a Gallery*. Patten Press/Newlyn Art Gallery 1995

Miller, R. *Michael Canney: Oils, Alkyds, Reliefs*. Fine Art Society 2007

Lamorna Trio: Marlow Moss, Ithell Colquhoun, John Tunnard

Colquhoun, I. *The Living Stones: Cornwall*. Peter Owen 1957

Dijkstra, F. *Marlow Moss: Constructivist + the Reconstruction Project*. Patten Press 1995
Glazebrook, M. *et al.* *John Tunnard*. Arts Council 1977
Martin, S. (ed.) *John Tunnard: Inner Space to Outer Space*. Pallant House Gallery 2010
Peat, A. & Whitton, B.A. *John Tunnard: His Life & Work*.
Ratcliffe, E. *Ithell Colquhoun: Pioneer Surrealist Artist, Occultist, Writer, & Poet*. Mandrake 2007
Read, H. 'Rediscovery: The World of John Tunnard' in *The Saturday Book 25*. Hutchinson 1965
Schaschl, S. *et al.* *Marlow Moss: A Forgotten Maverick*. Hatje Cantz 2017
Shillitoe, R. *Ithell Colquhoun: Magician Born of Nature*. Lulu 2010

Timeless Art: Breon O'Casey

Coulson, S. & Bowness, S. (ed.) *Breon O'Casey: An Anthology of his Writings*. Yorkshire Sculpture
  Park 2005
Fallon, B. *Breon O'Casey*. Scolar Press 1999
O'Sullivan, J. *A Celtic Artist: Breon O'Casey*. Lund Humphries 2003

A Celtic Item: Nancy Wynne-Jones & Conor Fallon

Fallon, B. *Nancy Wynne-Jones*. Gandon editions 2002
Fallon, C. *Thoughts on Sculpture*. Gandon Editions 2012
O'Regan, J. *Conor Fallon*. Gandon Editions 1996

Michael Snow: But is it Finished?

Davies, P. *Michael Snow*. Belgrave St Ives 2014

Rowena Cade & the Minack Theatre

Demuth, A. (ed.) *The Minack Open-Air Theatre*. David & Charles 1968
Val Baker, D. *The Minack Theatre*. George Ronald 1960

Selected Place-Names of West Penwith

Padel, O.J. *Cornish Place-Name Elements*. English Place-Name Society 1985
Pool, P. *The Place-Names of West Penwith*. Peter Pool 1985
Weatherhill, C. *The Place-Names of the Land's End Peninsula*. Penwith Press 2017

Peter Lanyon's Articulations of Place

Causey, A. *Peter Lanyon: His Painting*. Aidan Ellis 1971
Causey, A. *Peter Lanyon: Modernism & the Land*. Reaktion Books 2006
Garlake, M. *Peter Lanyon*. Tate 1998
Lanyon, A. *Peter Lanyon 1918-1964*. Andrew Lanyon 1990
Stephens, C. *Peter Lanyon: At the Edge of Landscape*. 21 Publishing 2000
Stephens, C. (ed.) *Peter Lanyon*. Tate 2010
Treves, T. & Wright, B. (ed.) *Soaring Flight: Peter Lanyon's Gliding Paintings*. Courtauld Gallery/
  Paul Holberton 2015
Treves, T. *Peter Lanyon: Catalogue Raisonné of the Oil Paintings & Three-dimensional Works*. Modern
  Art Press 2018

General

Baker, F. *The Call of Cornwall*. Robert Hale 1976

Berlin, S. *The Coat of many Colours*. Redcliffe Press 1994

Bird, M. *The St Ives Artists: A Biography of Place & Time*. Lund Humphries revised ed. 2016

Bowness, S. (ed.) *Barbara Hepworth: Writings & Conversations*. Tate 2015

Bowness, S. *Barbara Hepworth: The Sculptor in the Studio*. Tate 2017

Brown, D. & Lewis, D. (ed.) *St Ives: 1939-64*. Tate revised ed. 1996

Button, V. *St Ives Artists: A Companion*. Tate 2009

Cross, T. *Painting the Warmth of the Sun: St Ives Artists 1939-1975*. Westcountry Books/Lutterworth Press 1995

Davies, P. *St Ives Revisited: Innovators & Followers*. Old Bakehouse 1994

Gooding, M. (ed.) *Painter as Critic: Patrick Heron – Selected Writings*. Tate 2001

Hannigan, D. *Wildlife Walkabouts: Land's End Peninsula*. Wayside Books 1986

Noall, C. *Botallack*. Bradford Barton 1972

Oldham, A. *Everyone Was Working: Writers & Artists in Postwar St Ives*. Tate 2002

Priestland, G. & S. *West of Hayle River*. Wildwood House 1980

Stephens, C. et al. *Modern Art & St Ives: International Exchanges 1915-1965*. Tate 2014

Stone, J. H. *England's Riviera*. Kegan Paul 1912

Val Baker, D. *Britain's Art Colony by the Sea*. Sansom & Co. 2000

Whittaker, D. *Zawn Lens: Words & Images from West Cornwall*. Wavestone Press 2003

Whittaker, D. *Stonelight: Words in Place, Images of Time*. Wavestone Press 2007

Whybrow, M. *St Ives 1883-1993*. Antique Collectors Club 1994

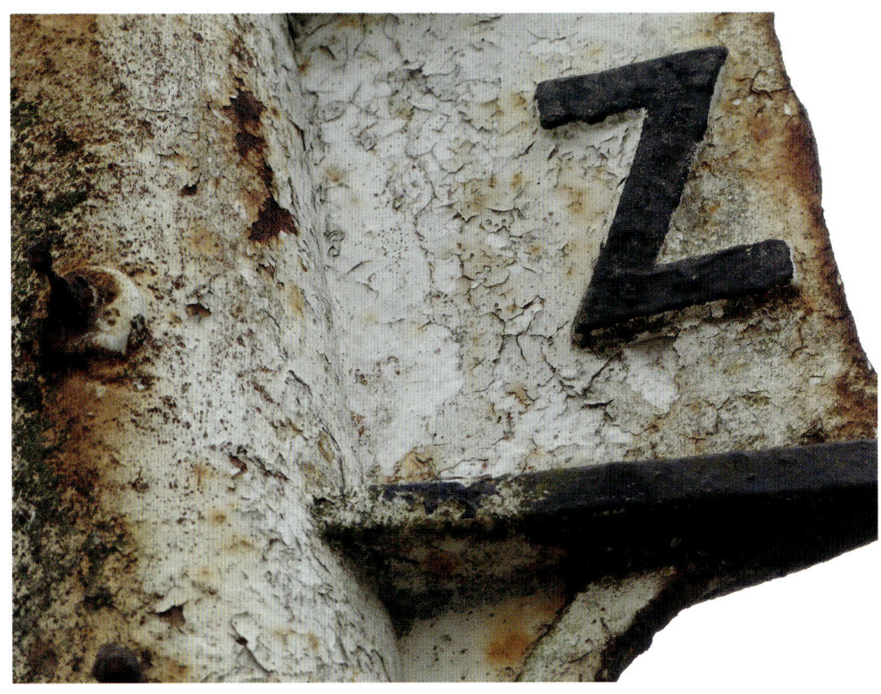

Picture Credits

All reasonable attempts have been made to locate copyright holders of the various images on show. Unfortunately, in several instances I have been defeated and I apologise to those I have inadvertently overlooked (wherever you are). With old photographs in particular, coming from many scattered sources, proving frustratingly difficult to detect who took them and when.

Photos: Page 10, 13, 16, 19, 37, 179 courtesy of Bryan Wynter Estate; 21, 23, 27 courtesy of Wilhelmina Barns-Graham Trust; 28 unknown; 30 unknown, courtesy of St Ives Archive; 31, unknown; 32 unknown, courtesy of Brian Wall; 33, 36 unknown; 38 unknown, courtesy of Luke Weschke; 39 unknown; 40, 53, 54, 55, 56, 175 © Roger Slack Estate, courtesy of Pippa Stillwell; 42 unknown; 66 unknown; 70 unknown, courtesy of Simon Canney; 74 unknown; 81 unknown, 83 Stephan Nijhoff, both courtesy of Florette Dijkstra; 84 unknown; 87, 90 unknown; 94 courtesy of Ursula & Toby Cornish; 95, 96 courtesy of New Craftsman Gallery; 98 unknown; 101 unknown, courtesy St Ives Archive; 102 (top) unknown; 102 unknown, courtesy of Gail Featherston; 104 © Michael Snow Estate, courtesy of Justin Snow; 106 unknown; 109 unknown; 114, 116, 117, 118, 119, 120, 121, 123 (bottom), 182 courtesy of Minack Theatre; 144 Kerry Dundas courtesy of Modern Art Press; 148 unknown; 157 © Jorge Lewinski Archive at Chatsworth/Bridgeman Images; 162 unknown, both courtesy of St Ives Archive; 181 Lee Sheldrake © St Ives Archive; 185 © Jane O'Malley; back cover, courtesy of Penny Thewlis

Art: Cover, 24 (City Art Centre, City of Edinburgh Museums & Galleries), 26, 158 © Wilhelmina Barns-Graham Trust; 18 © Bryan Wynter Estate/Bradford Museums & Galleries/Bridgeman Art Library; 35 © Rose Hilton; 34, 43, 45, 47, 48, 49 © Tony O'Malley Estate; 59 © Roger Slack Estate; 62, 64, 67, 68, 69 © Jeremy Le Grice Estate; 75, 76, 79 © Michael Canney Estate; 82 © Marlow Moss Estate; 85 © National Trust; 89 © John Tunnard Estate courtesy of British Council; 95, 96 courtesy of New Craftsman Gallery; 100, 103, 106 © Bridget Fallon; 110, 112, 113 © Michael Snow Estate courtesy of Belgrave Gallery; 150, 153 (courtesy of Alan Bowness) © Estate of Peter Lanyon. All Rights Reserved, DACS 2018; 156 © Estate of Peter Lanyon, courtesy of Modern Art Press

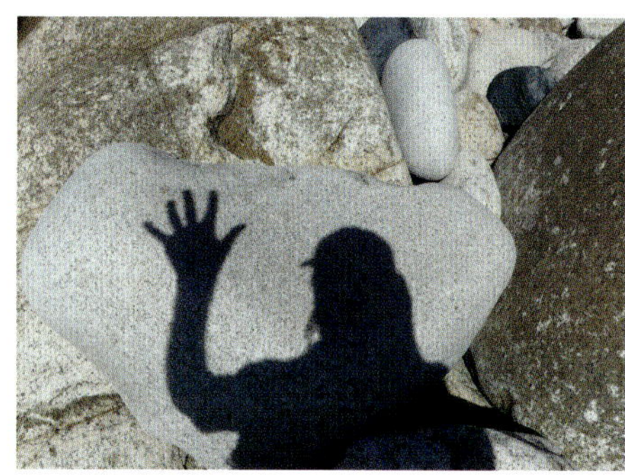

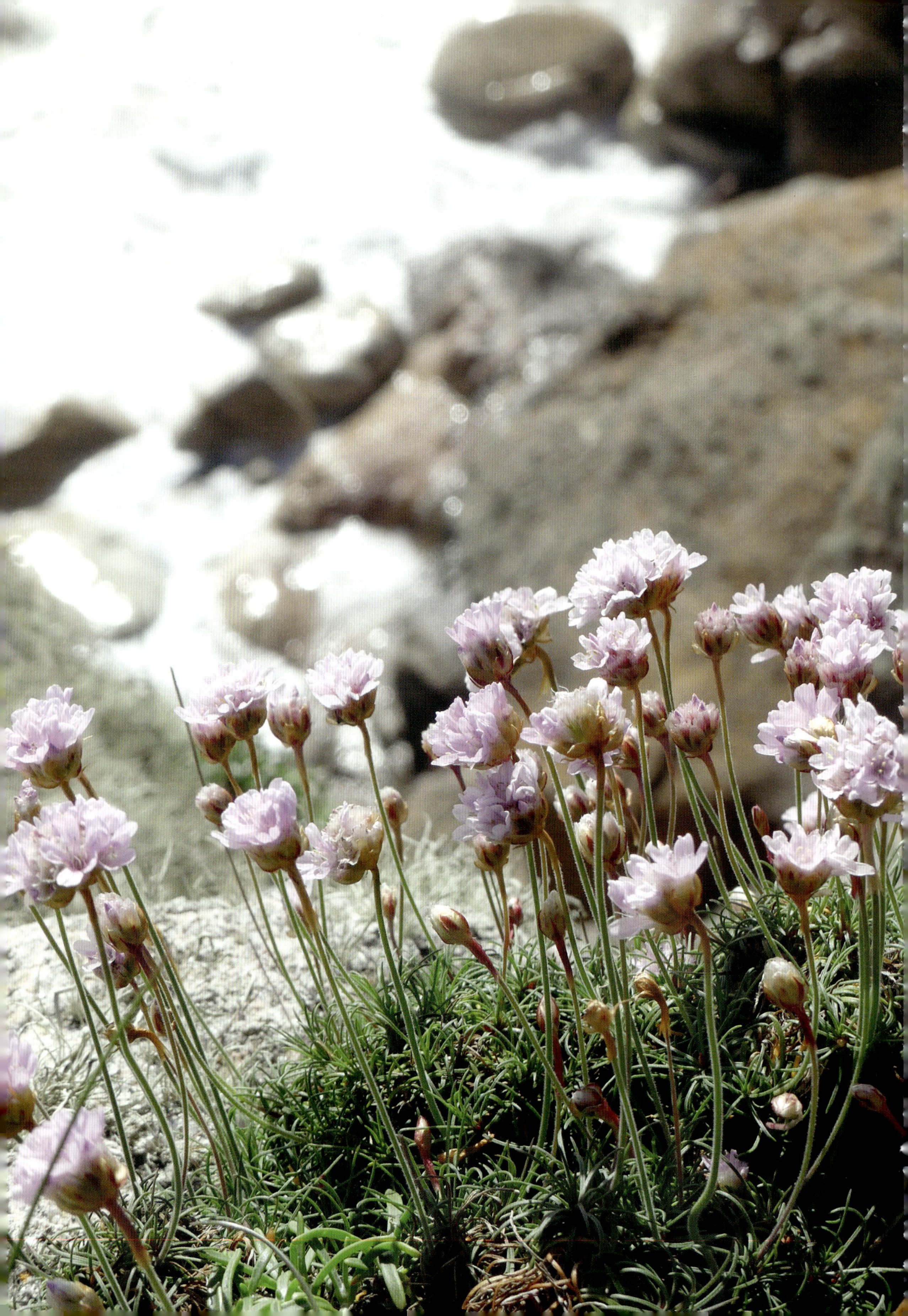